TIME FOR A CHANGE

Time for a Change
Reconfiguring Religion, State and Society

Paul Weller

T & T CLARK INTERNATIONAL
A Continuum imprint
LONDON • NEW YORK

Copyright © 2005 T&T Clark International
A Continuum imprint

Published by T&T Clark International
The Tower Building, 11 York Road, London SE1 7NX
15 East 26th Street, Suite 1703, New York, NY 10010

www.tandtclark.com

British Library Cataloguing-in-Publication Data
A catalogue record for this book is available from the British Library

ISBN 0567084876 (paperback)

Typeset by Fakenham Photosetting Limited Fakenham Norfolk
Printed on acid-free paper in Great Britain by MPG Books Ltd, Bodmin, Cornwall

This book is dedicated to Regent's Park College, Oxford, the Baptist Permanent Private Hall of the University of Oxford, where I first studied theology, 1974–77.

CONTENTS

Acknowledgements

1. *Copyright Permissions*

a. *Reworked and Further Developed Material*

This book pulls together many themes that have formed a part of my personal, religious and academic engagements over the past quarter of a century. In the process it seeks to develop them in a way that is integrated with the book's over-arching concern with the arrival of what, it argues, is theologically, socially and politically a 'time for change' with regard to the establishment of the Church of England. In doing so, in addition to much completely new material, the present book draws upon and reworks some already published writing while developing the arguments in a more comprehensive way. Therefore, as follows, the permission of relevant publishers and copyright holders to draw upon relevant previously published work is gratefully acknowledged.

The use, through reworking and further development of previously published material, includes the directory, *Religions in the UK: Directory, 2001–3* of which I was editor.[1] This directory is the product of the Multi-Faith Directory Research Project[2] that has been conducted jointly[3] between, and published by, © the Multi-Faith Centre at the University of Derby in association with the Inter Faith Network for the United Kingdom. In particular, in Chapter 3, materials from the directory's introductions to various religious traditions in the UK, as well as from its chapters on 'The Religious Landscape of the UK'[4] and 'Inter Faith Activity in the UK',[5] are drawn upon, reworked, updated and added to.

Chapter 3's coverage of Hindus and Jews also draws upon materials in my chapter on 'Hindus and Sikhs: Community Development and Religious Discrimination in England and Wales' and published by © Brill in K. Jacobsen and P. Kumar (eds.), *South Asians in the Diaspora: Histories and Religious Traditions.*[6] Much of the text in Chapter 3 is *descriptive* of the religious situation in the UK. Where that chapter – and indeed the book as a whole – also contains *interpretation* and *argument*, the views expressed are mine. They should therefore not be attributed to the Inter Faith Network for the UK nor to the Multi-Faith Centre, nor to any other of the authors or publishers whose work is cited.

In Chapter 4, materials are drawn upon from both reports produced by the Home Office-commissioned Religious Discrimination in England and Wales Research Project, of which I was Project Director (1999–2001) and where I was co-author. This includes a reworking of materials that were originally published by the University of Derby in *Religious Discrimination in England and Wales: An Interim Report. January 2000*[7] as well as of materials from the project's final report, *Religious Discrimination in England and Wales,*[8] published by the Home

Office. Materials from both these reports are © Crown Copyright and are used by kind permission, as also by permission of the principal named co-authors of the original reports, Alice Feldman and Kingsley Purdam.[9] However, once again, the *views* expressed in Chapter 3, as well as those in the book as a whole, are those of the author. They are therefore not necessarily those of the authors of the project reports, or of the Home Office, nor do they reflect Government policy.

The discussion of the definition of religion found in the Introduction to this book and the analysis of different kinds of religious discrimination developed in Chapter 4 draw upon a chapter authored by myself on 'The Dimensions and Dynamics of Religious Discrimination: Findings and Analysis in the UK'. This was published by © Martinus Nijhoff in N. Ghanea (ed.), *The Challenge of Religious Discrimination at the Dawn of the New Millenium*.[10] In Chapter 2 and, in a more limited way in Chapter 6, materials from a two-part article on 'Freedom and Witness in a Multi-Religious Society: A Baptist Perspective'[11] that was first published in the journal the *Baptist Quarterly*, published by © the Baptist Historical Society, are drawn upon and reworked. Chapter 6 refers to propositions and principles[12] that were first published in two parts in an article on 'Insiders or Outsiders?: Religions(s), State(s) and Societies: Propositions for Europe' that were first published also in the the *Baptist Quarterly*.[13]

Some of the themes that form a part of the overall argument of the book were previously developed in briefer book chapter form as 'Equity, Inclusivity and Participation in a Plural Society: Challenging the Establishment of the Church of England'. This was published by © Ashgate in P. Edge and G. Harvey (eds.), *Law and Religion in Contemporary Societies: Communities, Individualism and the State*.[14] These themes also formed a part of my unpublished Master of Philosophy dissertation on 'The Theology and Practice of Inter-Religious Dialogue: A Baptist Contribution to Ecumenical Debate in England'[15] and my unpublished doctoral dissertation on 'The Salman Rushdie Controversy, Religious Plurality and Established Religion in England'.[16]

b. *Other Copyright Material*
In addition to the materials authored or edited by myself which are drawn upon and reworked, the following additional copyright permissions are acknowledged. In Chapter 3, numerical data on religious affiliation taken from the results of the 2001 decennial Census and sourced from National Statistics (www.statistics.gov.uk) is used. Such data is presented in absolute numbers in tabular form, and is used as a basis for related percentage calculations and textual discussion developed by myself as author, the responsibility for which remains with myself. The chapter also uses data from Census Table M275: Religion (Most Detailed Categories). In both instances, the original Census data is © Crown copyright. Crown copyright material is reproduced with the permission of the Controller of HMSO.[17]

In Chapter 3, estimates of 'Church community membership', 'Church membership' and 'Church attendance' are quoted from P. Brierley (ed.), *UK Christian Handbook: Religious Trends 4, 2003/2004*[18] and published by © Christian Research. This information is (as with the Census data) presented in absolute numbers in tabular form, but is then used as a basis for related percentage calculations and textual discussion developed by myself as author, the responsibility for which again remains with myself. Permission to quote at length in Chapter 4 from an extract of Humayan Ansari's report on *Muslims in Britain*,[19] published by © the Minority Rights Group International, is gratefully acknowledged.

Every attempt has been made to identify and contact the owner(s) of any copyright material appearing in this book. In the event of any appearing without due acknowledgement, such oversight will gladly be corrected in any reprints or future editions.

2. *Personal and Professional Thanks*

Since the book draws so much on my personal, religious, academic and professional journey, I would also like to acknowledge the life and work of people of different religious traditions and none, who have been a significant part of the development of my life, work and thinking towards this publication. It is, of course, almost always invidious to single out specific individuals. But, in order to pay proper respect to all, I will need to take the risk of naming some. Acknowledgement of them does not, of course, imply that they would necessarily agree with the arguments that I set out in this book.

Such acknowledgements are, in the first place, due to my parents, Revd Dennis and Mrs Rhoda Weller, for bringing me up within the Baptist tradition of Christianity and for embodying a living religious faith within that tradition which enabled me to learn from their personal examples. Thanks are also due to the Baptist churches at Mount Pleasant, Ponciau; Golcar, Huddersfield; and Kingsland and Swaythling, Southampton, where I was brought up as a child. Then there is the Baptist church at Cecil Square, Margate, where I was baptized on profession of faith. Also, there are the congregations of the Tameside Fellowship of Churches (including the Baptist churches at Welbeck Street, Ashton-under-Lyne; Oxford Road, Dukinfield; Ridge Hill Estate, Stalybridge; Mersey Street Tabernacle, Higher Openshaw, Manchester; and the Union Street, Hyde, Baptist/United Reformed Church congregation) in which I served as an ordained minister, and the Baptist church in Didsbury, Manchester, where I served part-time within the ministry team. Finally, there are the Baptist/United Reformed Church congregations in Chorlton-cum-Hardy, Manchester, and Trinity, North Finchley, London, where I have been a member; as well as the Baptist church at Broadway, Derby, where I am currently both a member and an elected deacon.

Acknowledgements are also due to Regent's Park College, a Baptist Permanent Private Hall of the University of Oxford, where I first studied Christian theology, and to which this volume is dedicated. Special thanks are due to the specialist Angus Library of Baptist materials there, and to the librarian, Sue Mills, for use of relevant books, documents and articles in the research for this book. Acknowledgements are also due to the Universities of Manchester and of Leeds, where I completed my master's and doctoral research degrees, both of which feed into the present book, and to my supervisors for these theses, respectively, Professor Anthony Dyson and Professor Kim Knott.

Thanks are due to former colleagues in the Religious Discrimination in

England and Wales research project team, as also to colleagues and students in the University of Derby Religious and Philosophical Studies subject area, the closure of which at the end of 2001–2 was a great professional and personal sadness. Thanks are also due to colleagues in the Multi-Faith Centre at the University of Derby. As the realization of a dream that was first conceived over a decade ago, the Centre is now carrying forward some of the inheritance of what the Religious and Philosophical Studies subject area tried to achieve, as well as making its own distinctive contribution to inter-religious relations. Acknowledgements are due especially to the Centre Director, Eileen Fry, who, together with Professor Jonathan Powers, has translated the Multi-Faith Centre vision into a reality, and whose previous work as a researcher on the *Religions in the UK* directory, together with that of Michele Wolfe, was essential to that project.

My final thanks go to my wife, Margaret Preisler-Weller, for the encouragement that she gave to me, during a time of professional difficulty and disappointment, to make the effort to sit down and write this volume. Thanks are also due to her for having, since then, been prepared to live with the consequences of that encouragement which has entailed ongoing support to, and patience with, what turned into a rather larger and longer writing project than had originally been anticipated.

And then there are my children – David, Lisa and Katrina. They have patiently borne with the aspirations, the projects and the struggles of my academic career that I can sometimes get out of proportion with other things that matter in life, and of which they, together with Greta and my parents, are the best and most important reminders.

Paul Weller
School of Education, Health and Sciences
University of Derby

Notes

1 P. Weller (ed.), *Religions in the UK: Directory, 2001–3* (Derby: Multi-Faith Centre at the University of Derby in association with the Inter Faith Network for the United Kingdom, 2001).

2 See P. Weller, 'Religions in the UK: A Dialogical Enterprise', in *The Shap Working Party on World Religions in Education 2002–3. Religion: The Problem or the Answer* (London: Shap Working Party on World Religions in Education, 2002).

3 As part of this joint project, it should be noted that, together with the staff (particularly Brian Pearce and Harriet Crabtree) and Executive Committee members of the Inter Faith Network for the UK, a large number of academic experts and community representatives contributed to the processes that produced this directory. This was by means of making consultative comment on (and, in some cases, by originating) draft materials that were then editorially finalized. Those consulted are listed in full in P. Weller (ed.), *Religions in the UK*, pp. 643–50.

4 P. Weller (ed.), *Religions in the UK*, pp. 23–62.

5 P. Weller (ed.), *Religions in the UK*, pp. 79–90.

6 P. Weller, 'Hindus and Sikhs: Community Development and Religious Discrimination in England and Wales', in K. Jacobsen and P. Kumar (eds.), *South Asians in the Diaspora: Histories and Religious Traditions* (Leiden: Brill, 2004), pp. 454–97.

7 P. Weller, K. Purdam *et al.*, *Religious Discrimination in England and Wales: An Interim Report, January 2000* (Derby: University of Derby, 2000).

8 P. Weller, A. Feldman, K. Purdam, *et al.*, *Religious Discrimination in England and Wales* (Home Office Research Study, 220; London: Research Development and Statistics Directorate, Home Office, 2001).

9 The other members of the project team included Marie Parker-Jenkins (Associate Director), Kingsley Purdam (Research Officer), Alice Feldman (Field Officer) and Ahmed Andrews, Anna Doswell, John Hinnells, Sima Parmar and Michele Wolfe, together with (at various stages in the project) Karen Rowlingson, Martin O'Brien and Lynne Kinnerley. Contributions to the project final report were also made by Ahmed Andrews, Anna Doswell, John Hinnells, Marie Parker-Jenkins, Sima Parmar and Michele Wolfe.

10 P. Weller, 'The Dimensions and Dynamics of Religious Discrimination: Findings and Analysis from the UK', in N. Ghanea (ed.), *The Challenge of Religious Discrimination at the Dawn of the New Millenium* (Leiden: Martinus Nijhoff, 2003), pp. 57–81.

11 P. Weller, 'Freedom and Witness in a Multi-Religious Society: A Baptist Perspective. Part I', *BQ* 33/6 (1990), pp. 252–64; and P. Weller, 'Freedom and Witness in a Multi-Religious Society: A Baptist Perspective. Part II', *BQ* 33/7 (1990), pp. 302–15.

12 Earlier forms of the propositions that form the basis for the original and later publication of slightly variant versions of these principles were originally developed in brief conference presentations. The first was on 'Jews and Muslims in Europe: Some Propositions and Questions for European States, Societies and Religions' that was presented to a conference on 'From Xenophobia to Tolerance: Jews and Muslims in Europe'. This was organized by Academic Response to Anti-Semitism and Racism in Europe and the Simon Wiesenthal Centre, Europe, and was held at France-Amerique, Paris, 28–30 October 1995. A more generalized form of this presentation, entitled, 'Religion(s), State and Society: Theses and Propositions for Europe', was prepared for the Council of Europe Seminar on 'Religion and the Integration of Migrants' held at the Palais de l'Europe, Strasbourg, 24–26 November 1998. In almost their current form, they were presented at the author's Inaugural Lecture as Professor of Inter-Religious Relations at the University of Derby, on 'Insiders or Outsiders?: Religion(s), State(s) and Society: Propositions for Europe', given at the University of Derby on 8 November 2000.

13 P. Weller, 'Insiders or Outsiders?: Religions(s), State(s) and Societies: Propositions for Europe. Part I', *BQ* 39/5 (2002), pp. 211–22, and 'Insiders or Outsiders?: Religions(s), State(s) and Societies: Propositions for Europe. Part II', *BQ* 39/6 (2002), pp. 276–86. An abridged version of this original publication also appeared in P. Weller, 'Insiders or Outsiders?: Propositions for European Religions, States and Societies', in A. Race and I. Shafer (eds.), *Religions in Dialogue: From Theocracy to Democracy* (Aldershot: Ashgate, 2002), pp. 193–208.

14 P. Weller, 'Equity, Inclusivity and Participation in a Plural Society: Challenging the Establishment of the Church of England', in P. Edge and G. Harvey (eds.), *Law and Religion in Contemporary Societies: Communities, Individualism and the State* (Aldershot: Ashgate, 2000), pp. 53–67.

15 P. Weller, 'The Theology and Practice of Inter-Religious Dialogue: A Baptist Contribution to Ecumenical Debate in England' (unpublished master's dissertation, University of Manchester, 1988).

16 P. Weller, 'The Salman Rushdie Controversy, Religious Plurality and Established Religion in England' (unpublished doctoral dissertation, University of Leeds, 1996).

17 Source: National Statistics. www.statistics.gov.uk and Table M275: Religion (Most Detailed Categories). Crown copyright, 2004. Crown copyright material is reproduced with the permission of the Controller of HMSO.

18 P. Brierley (ed.), *UK Christian Handbook: Religious Trends, 2003/2004* (London: Christian Research, 2004).

19 H. Ansari, *Muslims in Britain* (London: Minority Rights Group International, 2002).

Journal Abbreviations

ABQ	*American Baptist Quarterly*
BQ	*Baptist Quarterly*
DCJIRE	*Discernment: A Christian Journal for Inter-Religious Encounter*
JCR	*Journal of Contemporary Religion*
MQR	*Mennonite Quarterly Review*
MC	*The Modern Churchman*
NC	*New Community*
RevExp	*The Review and Expositor*
WFE	*World Faiths Encounter*

INTRODUCTION

1. *The Key Arguments*

a. *Canterbury Change and The Census Results*

The enthronement of Rowan Williams as the Archbishop of Canterbury[1] and the publication[2] of the results of the 2001 Census questions on religious affiliation, both of which occurred in 2003, created new openings for debate concerning the continuation of the establishment of the Church of England.

The Times On-Line of 3.12.2002 reported that Rowan Williams had asked the Constitutional Unit at London University to examine disestablishment. The draft report was quoted as saying, 'Until recently, disestablishment was a non-starter. The Church of England did not want it, the State (in the shape of Tony Blair) did not want it, neither Buckingham Palace nor St. James' Palace wanted it. But now we have an Archbishop of Canterbury who comes from a disestablished Church.'

It is the argument of this book that the appointment of Rowan Williams as Archbishop, together with the socio-religious profile shown in the Census, signal that the relationships between religion, state and society embodied in the establishment of the Church of England have arrived at a 'time for change'. In other words, that the *circum*stances signalled by these developments call for a new *stance* to be taken in relation to the establishment.

While there are inevitably limitations with regard to the nature and interpretation of Census data,[3] for the first time these results provide at least some comparable information on the changes that have taken place in the *circum*stances of the religious landscape of the UK. With regard to *stances* relating to the establishment, Rowan Williams is an Anglican theologian of considerable stature[4] who, at least on occasion in the past, has raised questions relating to the appropriateness of establishment.[5]

Some degree of questioning of the establishment by leading figures of the Church of England is not new. At the same time, the representative character of the role of Archbishop of Canterbury inevitably shapes the public positions and freedom of action of all its incumbents. Among recent Archbishops of Canterbury, William Temple, Michael Ramsey and Robert Runcie all hinted at the possibility of a coming disestablishment. However, during their periods of office, none of them initiated significant moves in its direction.

Whatever is the case concerning Rowan Williams' current stance on the question of establishment (and some evidence of a change in this is noted at the conclusion of Chapter 1), he brings to his role episcopal experience[6] from a part of the Anglican communion that has been disestablished since 1920. Thus, together with his widely recognized theological reflexivity, Williams has come into this leading position in the Church of England and the worldwide Anglican communion as a bishop with considerable *practical* understanding of a different way of being an Anglican Church, without establishment, but still in an Anglican way.

Rowan Williams' appointment is therefore a reminder that alternatives to established religion are possible and that they do not necessarily entail some of the potential consequences feared by those who support the continuation of the establishment. Thus, the coincidence of Williams' appointment with a range of social, political and religious trends that in recent decades have been gathering pace, indicates that conditions now exist in which a reconfiguration of current relationships between religion, state and society in England and the UK is more thinkable and possible.

b. Deciding and Acting

Historically, there have been quite a number of commentators on establishment who have taken up what Theo Hobson, in his recent Anglican polemic against establishment, calls the position of 'Stoic' (as contrasted with 'Defiant') defenders of the establishment.[7] Robert Runcie exemplified such a stance in his book *Windows Onto God* when he argued that:

> We (as a nation) have not made up our minds whether or not to dissolve the Church/State partnership entirely and to admit that England has ceased to have a fundamentally Christian, homogenous culture or purpose and has become a geographical expression. I would not wish to hurry people into a decision one way or another: a neutral state or a Christian establishment. There is a sense in our suspicion of the doctrinaire: the attempt to impose a theoretical pattern on a confusing and diverse jigsaw of ancient institutions and modern attitudes.[8]

There are, of course, many complex issues involved in the debate about establishment and even more in relation to what might appropriately replace it. But in the end, as Hobson's polemic sharply points up, there is a *choice* that needs to be made – *for* or *against* establishment. The apparent alternative position of not *actively* choosing is, in itself, a position that by *default* lends *passive support* to the continuation of establishment. Indeed, it is generally the case that change is only initiated when *active* steps are taken to bring it about. In the case of establishment, such steps could be internal to the Church of England, external to it, or a combination of both. Not *actively* choosing could result in the future of establishment being shaped only or mainly by the direction in which the historical currents of circumstance happen to be moving.

Socially and politically the time is now becoming opportune for considering a change to the inherited pattern of relationships between religion(s), state and society embodied in establishment. But it is also the argument of this book that the present *circumstance*, in its conjoining of context ('circum') and choice ('stance') needs to be understood theologically in terms of the Christian concept of a *kairos*. That is to say, it needs to be seen as a moment in time that calls not just for consideration, but also for a *decision* and for *action*, in ways that are informed by theological and ecclesiological perspectives. In the *New International Dictionary of New Testament Theology*, it is explained that:

> The presence of two etymological groups, associated respectively with chronos and kairos for the concept of time, suggests that the Greeks distinguished individual periods of points of time which can be affected by human decision (kairos) from the stream of time, whose progress is independent of any possible human influence (chronos).[9]

The meaning of *kairos* is something that 'characterises a critical situation, one which demands a decision … Positively it implies opportunity … or advantage; negatively, danger.'[10] At such a *kairos* it is no longer adequate simply to move forward into the future on the basis of assuming the continued appropriateness of what has previously been in place. Rather, a clear decision is called for as to whether the inherited configuration of the relationships between religion(s), state and society should continue as previously, or should instead be *reconfigured* for the future. Specifically, the central argument of this book is that theologically, socially and politically it is 'time for a change' to the establishment of the Church of England.

To make this argument, the inheritance of establishment in social, religious, cultural, legal and political history is explored, as are some of the challenges that have emerged to it. Establishment is not something that is fixed. Aspects of its configuration have changed and evolved. But, despite these changes, it is shown that established religion still forms a 'constitutional nexus' which remains of much more contemporary significance than is usually allowed for by many, including many both among its supporters and its opponents. As was common in both the religious and political discourse of the nineteenth century, it is argued that the time has once again come to challenge the existence and the continuation of the establishment, albeit now in a different way.

In summary, it is the argument of the book that the perpetuation of establishment – whether through active or passive support – is something that is theologically and politically inadequate to the changed religious, social and political landscape of the twenty-first century. Furthermore, it is argued that a reluctance *actively* to consider alternatives is symptomatic of a lack of theological and ecclesiological confidence that needs to be overcome. Socially and politically speaking, too, for a society composed of people of many religions and none, but which aspires to be inclusive, the continuation of the establishment embodies an inequitable arrangement that needs to be changed.

The majority of those who support the continuation of the establishment – whether by conviction or default, whether Christians, people of other faiths, or none – do so while at the same time explaining that the current arrangements would not be something they would advocate as a principled starting point. However, since it exists, it is argued that it is wise to make the best of it. Therefore, among the main arguments that have been deployed against disestablishment has been a concern about what the consequences of disestablishment might be and an anxiety about what might replace it.

c. *Alternative Visions and Practical Implementation*

It is often the case that to argue negative positions is easier than to propose positive alternatives. The former requires only the identification of problems associated with what currently exists. The latter – and especially when the arguments relate not just to intellectual debating points but to options that entail actual historical choices – requires positive and constructive thinking, a willingness to assume responsibility, and a readiness to take risks. As the former Archbishop, Michael Ramsey, pointed out, 'Disestablishment is itself a negative formula. It says what should be discarded. It would be better to ask quo tendimus?'[11]

As an abstract position, disestablishment raises the spectre at least of considerable uncertainty about the future and, at worst, the possibility of less desirable alternatives. Therefore *only* to argue for disestablishment can be seen as taking an unjustified risk with an inheritance that – for all the undoubted discrimination and exclusion associated with its history – has also, in recent times, arguably provided an institutionalized reminder of the provisionality of all human power structures. Connected with this is a concern that disestablishment might either reinforce a view of religion as being a kind of private members' club activity for those who are 'inclined that way', or else might result in religion in the public sphere collapsing into a fiercely conflictual arena for sectarian groups.

These are significant and important concerns. Even such a sharp critic of establishment as Theo Hobson acknowledges that what he values in the Church of England – namely its being 'rich in tolerance, humour, moral equivocation' – would be 'endangered' by disestablishment.[12] In advocating a reconfiguration of the inherited relationships between religion(s), state and society in England and the UK there are, as in all *kairos* moments, dangers as well as opportunities. It is important to take account of both.

While the present arrangements should not be allowed to continue by default, theological and political courage are needed to move out of the security of a known and inherited present and into an unknown future. In addition, if historical change is *actually* to occur, *practical imagination* and at least a degree of *pragmatism* are also needed. It is therefore incumbent upon anyone who argues for change also to try to present both an alternative *vision*, as well as at least a sketched *outline*, of what might be realistic and practical ways forward for embodying a new configuration between religion(s), state and society.

The actual development of an alternative set of practical arrangements cannot be the product of a single person's proposals. In the end, it can only be an outcome of active engagement with the issues involved by all relevant 'stakeholders', including the Church of England, other Christian churches, other religious traditions and groups, the government, and the wider civil society. Thus there is no attempt here to present a systematically developed alternative. However, in trying to see how, in practical terms, it might be possible to move beyond the present position to a possible reconfiguration, this book argues that alternative (though in ecumenical Christian discussion often neglected) *theological* and *ecclesiological* traditions and perspectives exist that can assist in this. Together with contributing to an evolution of Christian thinking, it is suggested that when such resources are 'translated' into principles that could be more widely accessible they might have something to offer to wider social and political debate about religion(s), state and society relationships in England and the UK.

These alternative traditions and perspectives have, historically speaking, been associated with the nonconformist and Free Church traditions of Christianity.

In arguing for their present importance, this book in particular appeals to two key 'notes' of the Baptist Christian tradition's refraction of the Christian vision. These are its theologically founded commitment to religious freedom and a form of ecclesiology that is often described as 'voluntarist'[13] but perhaps could also be described as 'covenantal'[14] or, in the terminology adopted in this book, as 'covenantal voluntarism'. Through engagement with an empirically rooted exploration of changes that have occurred in contemporary socio-religious reality and reported experiences of religious discrimination and disadvantage, it is argued that the theological, social and political impulses that derive from these 'notes' of Baptist tradition can be of particularly creative importance for the future.

In the light of this, three basic options are examined for the future configuration of relationships between religion(s), state and society – those of a secularizing disestablishment; an 'extended' establishment; and the formation of something along the lines of a National Religious Council. Each of these alternatives is evaluated for its adequacy to the present context by utilizing various aspects of 'negotiation theory'.[15] This theory, taken from the wider world of organizational negotiation and change theory, provides a basis for exploring how, and under what conditions, transitions and changes that are recognized as being *necessary* can also become capable of *practical implementation*.

d. *Routes to Change*

Having examined the strengths and weaknesses of each of these options, the book concludes by setting out the 'headlines' of its own alternative approach on the basis of a number of key 'principles for a change'. Four key developments are identified and explored in relation to possibility of the creation, through dialogue, of a new 'socio-religious contract'. These are, first, the adoption of an ecumenically modified form of voluntarism; rooted in a mutual commitment to religious freedom and equity, as the basis for corporate religious identity and organisation. Then there is the encouragement of dialogical initiatives and structures between religions, as well as between religions and the wider society. There is also the evolution of a more adequately inclusive constitutional framework for the relationship between religion(s), state and society. Finally, there is the development of more equitable legal instruments relating to religious identity and practice.

These developments combine 'emergent' and 'bottom-up' processes internal to religions (voluntarism among religions, and the development of dialogical initiatives) with more 'managerial' and 'top-down' and external factors (constitutional and social policy developments and legal provisions). Taken together, it is argued that they could facilitate the coming into being of a new form of 'socio-religious contract' that could draw upon the developing experience of initiatives that provide real, albeit imperfect and fragile, 'worked alternatives' to that of establishment.

The recent experience in practice of the disestablishment of the Lutheran Church of Sweden[16] has shown that such a process need not be as protracted as many defenders of the establishment often argue. However, accepting that the establishment of the Church of England cannot simply end from one day to another, such parallel 'worked alternatives' could be developed in an *evolutionary* way alongside a dismantling of the establishment. Such a process will not be tidy, and may not guarantee particular outcomes. But it could enable the point to be reached where new structures to replace the establishment become possible to implement on a consensual basis. It will also begin developments that could be drawn upon should, in the meantime, any constitutional or other crisis for estab-lishment (as, for example, in connection with the succession to the Monarchy) force the pace of developments from outside the Church of England itself.

The historic nineteenth-century debates about establishment and disestablishment were cast primarily in terms of an inheritance of intra-Christian and Christian–secular concerns, debates and perspectives. These elements remain significant today, and need to be addressed as part of any rounded consideration of establishment and its altern-atives. Therefore part of the register in which this book is written is expressed in terms of Christian theology, ecclesiology and missiology. This is because it is unlikely that change – especially if it is to be on a positive and consensual basis – will come about without an Anglican Christian re-evaluation of the issues involved. In a Christian ecumenical age, this should naturally also involve Anglican engagement with the history and theological insights of other than Anglican Christian traditions in England and the UK, including those of the Free Churches.

But, given the religiously plural and secular context of contemporary society, it is also unlikely that debates conducted purely in terms of Christian theology and ecclesiology can, on their own, provide sufficient impetus for change. If change is to occur, such intra-Christian debates will need to be brought into conjunction with a wider re-evaluation of the issues involved. In this, people of all religions and none will need to be engaged. Therefore the book proceeds in terms of soci-ological and political analysis as well as theologically. It does so by taking into account the concurrent and complex patterns of ethnic, religious and value plural-ization and secularization in the contemporary socio-religious context, including the new processes and structures within England and the UK that are related to national devolution, regionalization, European integration and globalization.

e. *Context for Change*
The contours of religious belonging and affirmation in England and the UK have changed due to the impact of the twin processes of migration and secularization. In Chapter 3 it is argued that the most adequate way of describing the current religious landscape of England and the UK is as 'Christian, secular and religiously plural'. In other words, it is argued that the contemporary socio-religious reality is no longer the 'one-dimensional' religio-social unity of Christendom that has been the classical ideal of establishment thinking. It has also evolved beyond being a 'two-dimensional' modification in which the 'secular dimension' supplemented and, in some ways, supplanted the original 'Christian dimension'. The particu-larly new element that alters the previous terms of the debate from the historical alternatives of an established religion or a secularizing disestablishment is the significance of the UK's, and especially of England's, development as society that has *religiously plural*, as well as secular and Christian characteristics.

In relation to this religious plurality, in the latter part of the twentieth century claims began to emerge (and especially among Muslims)[17] that the experience of discrimination on the ground of religion is just as real and as important to take account of as discrimination based on gender, ethnicity, disability or sexuality. The reported experiences of such discrimination are explored in some detail in Chapter 4. The extended religious plurality of contemporary England and the UK, and the renewed salience of issues of religious discrimination, mean that, in addition to Christian theology and practice, secular politics and statecraft, the arguments developed here need to engage with the existence and perceptions of other than Christian religious traditions. Finally, in view of the development of a range of explicitly inter-religious bodies, initiatives and activities, it is also important to try to understand the dynamics and dimensions of these emergent dialogical structures, including those within which government is seeking to engage with religions in a more religiously inclusive way.

The book therefore proceeds in a variety of registers: Christian, sociological, political and inter-faith. But before proceeding to develop the main arguments, in order for there to be some transparency about the ways in which various key terms and concepts are used, it is first of all necessary to clear some of the terminological ground. The following section therefore seeks to set out some 'working definitions' that might help to inform an understanding of the arguments as they are later developed.

2. *Clearing Some Terminological Ground*

a. *Key Words and Working Definitions*

'Establishment', 'religion', 'state', 'nation', 'culture', 'ethnicity' and 'society' are all key terms used in this book. Each of them is used popularly and often with assumed meanings, but all of them are used in a variety of different ways and with meanings that are at the very least contested. It is therefore important to explain the particular ways in which these terms are used here.

b. *Establishment and Its Variants*

The predominant use of the word 'establishment' in this book is to be distinguished from a wider, and more popular, usage of the term 'the establishment'. The latter term refers to a group or layer within society that is perceived as having considerable power and influence, and which is characterized by a pattern of social, political and economic interconnections. There is, of course, a sense in which established religion can also be a part of 'the establishment' in this wider meaning. This is especially the case when establishment is considered in historical terms, but it is also to some degree still characteristic of the contemporary position when, for example, factors such as the social, class and educational profile of Church of England bishops are examined. However, in this book, the term 'establishment' is used primarily in the specific sense of indicating the kind of formal relationship that currently exists between the state and the Church of England. According to Jørgen Nielsen, 'establishment' in this sense should be understood as entailing either forms of special 'recognition' of particular religions by the state, or various forms of 'incorporation' in the state.[18] Such a relationship can include, but goes beyond, the notion of a 'national Church'.

Part of the distinctiveness of the Church of England is that it has played a significant historical and contemporary role in the life of English society in ways that are often described by the terminology of a 'national Church'. Such a description is also often used of the Presbyterian Church of Scotland that is also in some sense the 'Church by law established' in the specific context of Scotland. However, the Church of Scotland is not embedded in the structures of the UK state as a whole in the same way that the Church of England is through, for example, the position of its bishops in the House of Lords. In addition, whereas in ways that will be more fully explored in Chapter 5, the state retains ultimate powers in relation to the Church of England's liturgical life and the appointment of its leaders, this is not the case with regard to the Church of Scotland.

Because of the particular form of its established status, the Church of England retains a range of privileges relative to other religious traditions which contribute to what this book argues is a continuing nexus of real and problematic significance within the current pattern of relationships between religion(s), state and society. Its role within the multinational state of the United Kingdom of Great Britain and Northern Ireland is the key feature that sets it apart from the Church of Scotland or from other Churches that can more properly be described as 'national Churches'. Such Churches, despite having a strong and organic connection with their societies, do not have an analogous role within the state. At the same time, the Church of England's establishment is also different to the position of Roman Catholicism in the countries of the Catholic Concordat, the historic position of the Lutheran Church in Scandinavian countries, and the more 'mixed economy' position of the Protestant and Catholic Churches in Germany.

In the countries of the Catholic Concordat, legal agreements have been reached with a range of religious bodies including the numerically dominant Roman Catholic Church. Such agreements with the Roman Catholic Church have also often partaken of international and inter-state dimensions due to the diplomatic status of the Vatican as itself a state party as well as being a global focus of leadership in the international Catholic Christian community.

In the Scandinavian countries, Lutheran Churches have historically been departments of state and their ministers have had the status of civil servants. Such Churches have therefore more properly been understood and described as 'state Churches' than is the case when this description has sometimes been used as a shorthand description of the establishment of the Church of England.

In Germany, although 'state Churches' do not exist in the Scandinavian sense, the Evangelical and Roman Catholic Churches and their associated social service organizations have been an integral part of the post-war corporatist state of the Federal Republic. In this role they are financially supported by *Kirchensteuer* money received through the general taxation system, and from which individuals who do not wish to participate need to decide to contract out.

Thus, although the establishment of the Church of England shares some features with other forms of European arrangements in which there is a close connection between a particular religious tradition or traditions and the state, it also has distinctive elements. Therefore arguments about the desirability or otherwise of the continuance of the establishment of the Church of England need to take account of these elements as well as of more general issues in the relationship between religion(s), state and society.

c. *Religion, Culture and Ethnicity*

Although central to this book, the concept of 'religion' is, of course, itself far from being straightforward. It has many contested definitions and it is important to acknowledge these. Both in popular usage, and in some legal usage in connection with charity law, religion has often been considered to be something to do with belief in a God or divine being. Such an understanding is problematic, though, since it does not take account of the stances of the world religions of Buddhism or Jainism, which are 'a-theistic', let alone the beliefs of newer movements such as Scientology. In addition, such definitions locate the significance of belief more centrally than would be the case in some traditions. The sociologist of religion Grace Davie has argued for the recognition of a phenomenon of 'believing without belonging'[19] which means that some form of identification with a religion is likely to be considerably wider than active involvement in any particular religious tradition or community. But with regard to some traditions,[20] there is also the contrasting phenomenon of what I have elsewhere called 'belonging without believing', in which identification with the community can be as significant as the particular beliefs which may or may not be held by individuals.

Furthermore, in addition to the explicit forms of organized religious traditions and communities, scholars in the study of religion have also pointed out that there is a range of other at least potentially related phenomena. Thus the historian John Wolffe identifies four distinct categories, namely: 'conventional religion', 'civil religion', 'common religion' and 'invisible religion'.[21] By 'conventional religion' he refers to occasional participation in the festivals and life cycle rituals found in organized, particular religions. By 'common religion' he refers to generalized beliefs in the supernatural, to folk traditions and to popular astrology. By 'invisible religion' he refers to what is sometimes also called 'surrogate religion' or 'implicit religion' – in other words, those things which, though devoid of supernatural referents, give people meaning in life and which can range from following a football team to a commitment to ideological forms of nationalism. By 'civil religion' he refers to religious forms and language used in public life and which, especially in the UK, are ceremonially connected with the monarchy.

Wolffe underlines that 'these categories should not be understood as separating out definable groups of people, but rather as exploring a variety of ways in which a single individual not regularly involved in a religious organisation could nevertheless be "religious"'.[22] What all these concepts have in common is that issues that have some relationship with religion can still be of significance even where individuals do not have a very strong connection with a specific religious tradition.

In the academic study of religion the best that exists are a range of 'working definitions' of religion that tend to reflect the various disciplinary traditions within which the definitions are made. Etymologically, the English word 'religion' derives from the Latin word *religio* which has a root meaning related to the idea of a 'binding' together and which contains the sense of an organized culture. Clearly 'religion', 'culture' and 'ethnicity' are connected by what are at least related and interdependent realities even if they are, in principle, distinguishable. However, the nature of their relationship is evaluated differently both among and between the different religious traditions and within varied approaches to the study of religions. The patterns of overlap are not straightforward and most religious communities are ethnically diverse. For example, just as one religious tradition may embrace many ethnicities, so one country or region of origin can be shared by people from within several religions.

The sociologist Emile Durkheim's definition of religion is that of 'a unified system of beliefs and practices relative to sacred things'.[23] Clifford Geertz's anthropological definition sees religion as, 'a (1) system of symbols which acts to (2) establish powerful, pervasive and long-lasting moods and motivations in men [*sic*] by (3) formulating conceptions of a general order of existence and (4) clothing these conceptions with such an aura of factuality that (5) the moods and motivations seem uniquely realistic'.[24]

Within the social sciences the dominant tradition has tended to see religion as a dependent variable of ethnicity and/or culture. In this tradition, to varying degrees, religion has been seen as certainly a functional, and sometimes an almost instrumental, reinforcement of the primary category of ethnicity. Others have argued that religion and ethnicity are to be seen as much more clearly distinct, or in a reciprocal relationship. Some, such as Robin Gill, have argued for the importance of understanding that religion itself can also be seen as a 'social determinate'.[25]

The theologian and historian of religion Wilfred Cantwell Smith has critiqued the usefulness of the very idea of 'religion' itself. Instead, he has argued that what are today described as distinct 'religions' are, in fact, historical constructions superimposed upon what are actually the very diverse experiences of people of 'personal faith' who live within what Cantwell Smith prefers to call 'cumulative traditions'.[26] Within the non-confessional study of religion, scholars such as Timothy Fitzgerald have gone even further with this line of argument.[27] Thus Fitzgerald has held that the category of religion is a construct that need not be used, that there is no need to think of religion as a specific field of study, and that the notion of culture can generally cover what has traditionally been described by the word 'religion'.

In actual populations, religion, ethnicity and culture are often closely linked as a consequence of the history of when and where the religious traditions developed. For example, among religious minorities in the UK, 'culture' and 'religion' are sometimes used interchangeably. Thus, in a context in which members of a majority community might have used the word 'religion' rather than 'culture', people from within some of the minority communities can be heard to offer the explanation that, 'We do such and such a thing because it is our culture.' Hindus, in particular, often use the words 'religion' and 'culture' interchangeably regardless of whether they are living in a majority or a minority context – one's culture is one's religion and vice versa. Or, perhaps more accurately given the more corporate, societal nature of the Hindu tradition and way of life, the culture of one's people is the religion of one's people and vice versa.

Sometimes, positions in favour of the establishment of the Church of England are couched in terms of what is argued to be a particular and distinctive relationship between Englishness and the Church of England. Thus the former Archbishop of York John Habgood, in his book, *Church and Nation in a Secular Age*, speaks of 'large numbers of people whose residual allegiance to the C of E is bound up with the perception that in some obscure way it represents "England" '.[28] Historically, understandings such as these have been expressed in the assumption which could still be encountered until relatively recent times that, on admission to hospital, if one failed to indicate specific Roman Catholic, Free Church or other than Christian religious identity, then one would be recorded as 'C of E'.

In Protestant Christian theology, although it is acknowledged that in particular groups and contexts, 'religion' and 'culture' may be closely related, 'religion' is generally argued to be ultimately distinguishable from 'culture'. Those adopting this stance believe that culture modifies or, in more extreme cases, corrupts a purer or more original core of religion often seen as being characterized by a special revelational knowledge. In connection with this, the influential neo-orthodox theologian Karl Barth and those who have taken their theological cue from his basic approach, have seen Christ as standing in judgement on culture. They have therefore drawn a sharp distinction between the Christian message and the culturally shaped Christian religion. However, within Christianity there are more positive evaluations of the relationship between religion and culture. Indeed, in the Two-Thirds World a whole Christian theological movement has developed known as 'inculturation',[29] which seeks positively to find ways of giving expression to Christianity in terms of specific and appropriate cultural forms rather than to try and detach it from culture in a supposedly 'pure' form.

In this highly problematic and controversial area, an understanding of the term 'religion' that relates primarily to the self-definition of individuals and/or groups perhaps represents the most practical way forward. It is one that, for all its problems, at least connects with 'where people are at'. Therefore in this book, religion is basically understood according to a 'working definition' that the author has previously developed, which is that it is:

> a way of living in which some form of 'identification' (either in a weaker and more general sense, or in a stronger and more specific sense of alignment with particular movements, communities and/or organisational forms) is often (though not always or necessarily) to be found in conjunction with different forms of 'believing' (in various combinations of certain values, ideals and/or doctrines) and can be expressed through 'practice' (that is related to shared symbols, rituals, observances and ethical orientations).[30]

d. *Nation and State*

In an essay on 'Ethno-national Versus other Forms of Group Identity, the Problem of Terminology', the political scientist Walker Connor discussed other key terms used in this book. He points out that, 'It would be difficult to name four words more essential to global politics than are state, nation, nation-state and nationalism. But despite their centrality, all four terms are shrouded in ambiguity due to their imprecise, inconsistent, and often totally erroneous usage.'[31]

Etymologically, the word 'nation' derives from the Latin verb *nasci*, 'to be born', and the Latin noun *natio*, that connotes 'breed' or 'race'. Connor points out that 'One of the most common manifestations of terminological license is the interutilisation of the words state and nation.'[32] Such usage can frequently be found in popular political and media discourse in England and the UK, where politicians often invoke 'the nation' when they are actually intending to address the whole population of the UK, including its various constituent national groupings.

According to Connor, the concept of the 'state' is 'more easily definable as a political unit' while that of the nation is 'a psychological bond'. In the light of this, Connor argues that a 'nation-state' is a 'territorial-political unit (a state) whose borders coincided or nearly coincided with the territorial distribution of a national group'.[33] The state of the United Kingdom of Great Britain and Northern Ireland contains four – English, Welsh, Scottish and Irish – historic national groups within a single social, economic and political unit or society. This has, historically, been subject to an English dominance, albeit one that has been contested by various forms of Welsh, Scottish and Irish nationalism.

The one key term used in this book that Connor does not discuss, is that of 'society'. In contrast to Connor's 'psychological bond' of 'nation' and the 'political unit' of the state, 'society' relates to a form of more 'networked' belonging. This is characterized not so much by national or ethnic commonality, or by political participation and constraints, but by social belonging related to shared economic conditions and/or participation of the group in 'civil society'.

There are, of course, other possible 'working definitions' for all these key terms than those that are outlined above. But these are offered in order that the reader can, with some transparency, understand some of the issues and presuppositions that underlie this book's particular use of these concepts and the themes that are associated with them, and can take these into account in evaluating the arguments that are presented. But in addition to clarification of the key terminology used, it is also important to make transparent something of the underlying stances that inform the arguments of this book.

3. *Biography and Argument*

a. *Scientific, Confessional and Political Perspectives*

When the surface of theology and politics is scratched, it becomes clear that they are, at the very least, informed by biography. Thus, while this book does try to proceed in terms of arguments that it believes can be supported by empirical evidence and may correlate with the perceptions and experience of others, it is important to acknowledge where the argument is 'coming from'. Such an acknowledgement makes these factors explicit rather than leaving them to be guessed at. In this way it is possible for readers to take such factors properly into account when making their own evaluation of the cogency and persuasiveness or otherwise of the case that is presented.

I write primarily as an academic in the study of religion who generally operates professionally within the non-confessional mode of studying religion known as Religious Studies while, on occasion, also writing in more theological mode.

In this book, aspects of both these modes of approach to the study of religion are brought together. As an individual, I identify with the community of faith of Jesus of Nazareth and acknowledge a debt to the heritage of the Baptist tradition of Christianity. I have (1978–87) served within this tradition as an ordained minister. I also continue to identify with it as a church member and, currently, as an elected deacon of a local Baptist congregation (while also now, through marriage, having a connection with the Roman Catholic tradition and a local Catholic parish).

The Baptist tradition of Christianity is one that, since its origins in the sixteenth and seventeenth centuries, has been committed to bearing witness to the distinctive claims of a Christian vision of the world. At the same time, it has sought to combine this with a commitment to upholding a religious liberty for all that is rooted in a theologically informed anthropology. This, in turn, is expressed by advocating the importance of the separation between church and state, expressed in a voluntarist/covenantal ecclesiology. Such an ecclesiology is a corollary of the tradition's view of religious identity needing to be a free and chosen commitment, rather than something that is merely inherited, assumed or imposed.

Therefore, the biographical roots of the arguments developed in this book are found in reflection upon the contemporary relevance to debates about establishment of the inheritance of the Free Church and, more specifically, Baptist refraction of the Christian vision. This inheritance has been the sometimes explicit, but always implicit, root of most of the things with which, over the years, I have become engaged. Furthermore, during my academic career, I have always endeavoured to be what might be called an 'engaged academic' or a 'public intellectual'.

The role of the academic as a 'public intellectual' is one that is perhaps much more widely known, practised and welcomed in a number of other European countries than is the case in the UK where the predominant public ethos of pragmatism can very easily slip over into anti-intellectualism. In this context, a polarity can all too easily be reinforced between, on the one hand, a decontextualised academicism that is disconnected from the concrete issues and choices facing societies and individuals, and on the other hand, a subservient instrumentalism to short-term policy goals and mechanisms. But it is at least arguable that these polarities impoverish both society and the academy and that there might be something of value to contribute from the specific perspective of the 'researcher-practitioner'.

Thus my own attempts at research and scholarship have always, in one way or another, connected with the things that have been my engaged concerns over the past quarter of a century. These concerns have encompassed, first of all, issues of justice connected with religious and ethnic plurality that have included a political commitment to a multi-cultural polity. Second, they have concerned the relationships between justice and peace. Third, they have been related to the theology and practice, dynamics and challenges of inter-religious dialogue. Finally, they have been involved in the delineation of the contours of the religious landscape and the implications of this for equitable policy and practice in a society characterized by increasing religious plurality.

Therefore, underlying the argument of the present book is a personal and professional history of engagement with the religious and political implications of religious plurality, both for religions themselves, and for the societies and states of which they are a part. As a theologically reflective Christian engaged professionally and ecumenically with issues of racial justice and inter-faith relations, it has always seemed to me that traditional Baptist positions on religious liberty and equity might have something distinctive and important to contribute to a contemporary ecumenical theology and practice of inter-religious dialogue. Therefore during 1985–88, I undertook research that delved into the Baptist tradition, and sought to identify its distinctive 'notes', and then to bring those 'notes' into conjunction with the contemporary ecumenical theological and ecclesiological debates concerning the appropriate shape for, and content of, Christian witness in a religiously plural society.

This resulted in the previously mentioned Master of Philosophy dissertation on 'The Theology and Practice of Inter-Religious Dialogue: A Baptist Contribution to Ecumenical Debate in England'. In predominantly theological mode, this thesis explored questions concerning the relationship between theological stances and social and historical circumstances in determining the appropriate shape of Christian witness within a religiously plural society. It did so on the basis, among other key 'notes' of the tradition, of exploring its affirmation of religious liberty for all and the theological and ecclesiological principle of the Christian Church being understood as a fellowship of believers.[34]

The research demonstrated that the Baptist tradition of Christianity has always been concerned for religious freedom not simply among the variety of Christians alone, but as a principle relevant to people of all religions and to those confessing none. It also argued that this concern is rooted in a theological conviction about the nature of religious believing, belonging and witnessing, rather than being simply a politically expedient position of mere religious toleration. Simultaneously, it was argued that such a Baptist contribution can offer much to the emerging ecumenical Christian theology and practice of inter-religious dialogue as well as offering creative impulses to wider social and political debates concerning the best possible means for peaceable governance in a plural society.

The book also draws on research (1990–6) which resulted in a second thesis that, this time, proceeded in the mode of Religious Studies rather than theologically. The origin of this research was at the end of the 1980s in the early rumblings of the *Satanic Verses* controversy, when it became clear the controversy was likely to become indicative of critical and ongoing issues concerning the nature and implications of an ethnically and religiously plural society.[35] As developed into the doctoral dissertation on 'The Salman Rushdie Controversy, Religious Plurality and Established Religion in England', it was argued that the controversy acted as both a lightning rod and a catalyst for a range of theoretical and practical issues relating to the future of a plural society.[36]

In addition, it was argued that the issues thrown up by the controversy were unlikely to be resolved in a piecemeal way and that the controversy therefore focused an increasingly urgent need for reconsideration of the current configuration in the relationships between religion(s), the UK state, and English society. In the case of the thesis, the Rushdie controversy was examined as a kind of 'case study' of the wider issues facing religion, state and society in the contemporary, religiously plural context. In this book, the evidence and the arguments are developed in a more generalized way, although readers are referred to the thesis for a detailed discussion of how that particular case study supports the wider argument made here.

b. *Argument, Polemic and Positions*

In conclusion, if the tradition of the 'public intellectual' has something valuable to offer it is important, at least on occasion, for academics to come off the fence of descriptive analysis and to enter the currents of history, taking up committed positions on contemporary issues of religion and public life. At the same time, the serious attempt at objectivity, honesty and integrity is a vital part of the academic enterprise. Freedom, honesty, integrity and the striving for truthfulness are centrally important characteristics of academic life and authentic religious living. I am therefore indebted to the traditions of disinterested research in philology, textual studies, history and other such scholarly work upon which this book depends.

The arguments of this book aim to be informed by empirical historical and sociological data, as well as by an engagement with a breadth of ecumenical Christian tradition beyond that in which the author is most immediately located. It is thus not the intention of the book to be polemical. Polemics are an important genre for the way in which they insist on a clear differentiation of positions. But they are, perhaps, most appropriately undertaken from *within* the traditions with which they seek to engage. From a position outside of direct and personal involvement in the Church of England, it seems to me that the ethics of ecumenical courtesy require one to proceed with more restraint than may be appropriate when engaging in polemical work from the 'inside'.

At the same time, the ecumenical enterprise opens up all Christian traditions to mutual engagement, critique and modification of theology, ecclesiology and practice. The ecumenical enterprise is also one in which the historic *differences* as well as the commonalities between Christian traditions are important for the future of the whole Christian Church. Therefore, this book *does* take up a critical position with regard to establishment and argues that it *is* 'time for a change'. It is therefore not a work of detached observation, nor does it pretend to be a systematic, detailed, balanced and objective summary of the issues with which it is concerned.

In the final analysis, if the *conscious claims* of the Church of England that result from its established status mean anything at all then, together with their perhaps even stronger but often *unconscious implications,* they do have an *effect upon all the rest of us* as well as upon Anglicans. There is therefore a need for a debate to take place concerning the establishment in which it is important that ecumenical Christian, inter-religious, political and civil society contributions are made and for specific stances to be taken up within this debate. In this, it is important also that the Church of England *itself* again examines its own position, bearing in mind that it is now well over a quarter of a century since the report of its last commission on church–state relations.[37]

Overall, this is an *interpretative* work. Due to its conviction that a *kairos* has arrived in which debate needs to take place and *decisions of fundamental direction need to be made*, it takes up *positions* and it creates *arguments*. It does this with the intention both of stimulating *debate* and also of contributing to the possibility of *actual change* in the current configuration for the relationships between religion(s), state and society in England and the UK. It argues that *now* is a '*time for a change*'.

Notes

1   Rowan Williams was elected Archbishop of Canterbury on 23 July 2002. He was legally confirmed as the 104th Archbishop of Canterbury on 2 December 2002 in a ceremony at St Paul's Cathedral and he was enthroned in Canterbury Cathedral on 27 February 2003. For further background on Williams' life and work see R. Shortt, *Rowan Williams: An Introduction* (London: Darton, Longman & Todd, 2003).

2   The basic results relating to religion were published in February 2003 and are available through the National Statistics website at www.statistics.gov.uk.

3   See L. Francis, 'Religion and Social Capital: The Flaw in the 2001 Census in England and Wales', in P. Avis (ed.), *Public Faith? The State of Religious Belief and Practice in Britain* (London: SPCK, 2003), pp. 45–64.

4   See, for example, R. Williams, *The Wound of Knowledge* (Darton, Longman & Todd, 1979); *Resurrection: Interpreting the Easter Gospel* (London: Darton, Longman & Todd, 1982); *On Christian Theology* (Oxford: Blackwell, 2000) and *Writing in the Dust* (London: Hodder & Stoughton, 2002).

5   Williams has been reported (*The Sunday Times*, 27.1.2002) as having, in a question and answer session at the Greenbelt Christian festival in summer 2000, said that establishment as it currently existed was a 'relic' and was 'not good for the Church'.

6   Rowan Williams was elected Bishop of Monmouth on 5 December 1991 and enthroned in St Woolas Cathedral, Newport, on 14 May 1992. He was elected Archbishop of Wales in December 1999, and enthroned at St Woolas Cathedral on 26 February 2000.

7   See T. Hobson, *Against Establishment: An Anglican Polemic* (London: Darton, Longman & Todd, 2003).

8   R. Runcie, *Windows Onto God* (London: SPCK, 1983), p. 65.

9   C. Brown (ed.), *The New International Dictionary of New Testament Theology*, vol. 3, *Pri–Z*, p. 834.

10   C. Brown (ed.), *The New International Dictionary of New Testament Theology*, vol. 3: *Pri–Z*, p. 833.

11   M. Ramsey, *Canterbury Pilgrim* (London: SPCK, 1974), p. 176.

12   T. Hobson, *Against Establishment*, p. iv.

13   See W. Brackney, *Voluntarism: The Dynamic Principle of the Free Church* (Wolfville: Acadia University, 1992); *Christian Voluntarism: Theology and Praxis* (Grand Rapids: Eerdmans, 1997).

14   See P. Fiddes, *Tracks and Traces: Baptist Identity in Church and Theology* (Studies in Baptist History and Thought, 13; Cumbria: Paternoster Press, 2003) for a discussion of this. As Fiddes notes, 'The mutual and conditional nature of covenant has often been underlined in Baptist history by comparing it with various contracts in society which required free consent, and the covenanted community has often been declared a "voluntary" society' (p. 40). However, as Fiddes also points out, 'An intentional community like this is not just a "voluntary" society which people choose to join or not' (p. 77). As he further explains, 'the early Baptists spoke of the Church as a "gathered community", a phrase with a double meaning. Its members certainly agree to gather; there is "inward conviction" involved here. But they are also *gathered by* God' (pp. 77–8).

15   See R. Kramer and D. Messick (eds.), *Negotiation as Social Process* (London: Sage, 1995).

16   G. Gustafsson, 'Church–State Separation: Swedish Style', in J. Madeley and Z. Enyedi (eds.), *Church and State in Contemporary Europe: The Chimera of Neutrality* (London: Frank Cass, 2003), pp. 51–72.

17   See UK Action Committee on Islamic Affairs, *Muslims and the Law in Multi-Faith Britain: The Need for Reform* (London: UK Action Committee on Islamic Affairs, 1993).

18   J. Nielsen, 'State, Religion and Laïcité: The Western European Experience', in T. Mitri (ed.), *Religion, Law and Society: A Christian–Muslim Discussion* (Geneva: World Council of Churches, 1995), pp. 100–10 (106).

19   G. Davie, 'Believing Without Belonging: Is This the Future of Religion in Britain?', *Social Compass* 37 (1990), pp. 455–69.

20   As, for example, can be found among Jews, where belonging to the community can, from some Jewish perspectives, rank above adherence to particular forms of Jewish belief and/or practice.

21   J. Wolffe, 'The Religions of the Silent Majority', in G. Parsons (ed.), *The Growth of Religious Diversity: Britain From 1945* vol. 1: *Traditions* (London: Routledge, 1993), pp. 305–46 (309).

22   J. Wolffe, 'The Religions of the Silent Majority', p. 310.

23   E. Durkheim, *The Elementary Forms of the Religious Life* (New York: Free Press, 1947), p. 47.

24   C. Geertz, 'Religion as a Cultural System', in M. Bainton (ed.), *Anthropological Approaches to the Study of Religion* (London: Tavistock, 1990) pp. 1–46 (4).

25   See R. Gill, *Social Context of Theology: A Methodological Enquiry* (London: Blackwell, 1975).

26   See W. Cantwell Smith, *The Meaning and End of Religion* (London: SPCK, 1978).

27   See T. Fitzgerald, *The Ideology of Religious Studies* (Oxford: Oxford University Press, 2000).

28   J. Habgood, *Church and Nation in a Secular Age* (London: SPCK, 1983), p. 109.

29   See, for example, A. Shorter, *Towards a Theology of Inculturation* (London: Cassell, 1988).

30   This definition was first offered by the author in P. Weller, 'The Dimensions and Dynamics of Religious Discrimination', p. 66.

31   W. Connor, 'Ethno-national Versus other Forms of Group Identity: The Problem of Terminology', in N. Rhoodie (ed.), *Intergroup Accommodation in Plural Societies: A Selection of Conference Papers with Special Reference to the Republic of South Africa* (London: Macmillan, 1978), pp. 44–83 (54–55).

32   W. Connor, 'Ethno-national Versus other Forms of Group Identity', p. 55.

33   W. Connor, 'Ethno-national Versus other Forms of Group Identity', p. 59.

34   See also P. Weller, 'Freedom and Witness in a Multi-Religious Society. Part I'; P. Weller, 'Freedom and Witness in a Multi-Religious Society. Part II'; and P. Weller, 'Baptist Principles as They Relate to the Four Principles of Dialogue', *DCJIRE* 5/3 (1992), pp. 53–68.

35   S. Rushdie, *The Satanic Verses* (London: Viking Penguin, 1998).

36   See also P. Weller, 'Literature Update on the Rushdie Affair', *DCJIRE* 4/2 (1990), pp. 35–41; P. Weller, 'The Rushdie Affair, Plurality of Values and the Ideal of a Multi-Cultural Society', *National Association for Values in Education and Training Working Papers* 2 (1990), pp. 1–9; and P. Weller, 'The Rushdie Controversy and Inter-Faith Relations', in D. Cohn-Sherbok (ed.), *The Salman Rushdie Controversy in Inter-Religious Perspective* (Lampeter: Edwin Mellen, 1990), pp. 37–57.

37   The Chadwick Commission, *Church and State* (London: Central Information Office, 1970).

Part I

ESTABLISHED RELIGION: ITS INHERITANCE AND ALTERNATIVES

Chapter 1

THE HISTORICAL INHERITANCE OF ESTABLISHED RELIGION

1. *The Roots of Establishment*

a. *The Emergence of Christendom*

In order to understand the *kairos* that this book argues exists in relation to the contemporary establishment of Anglican Christianity in England and the UK it is necessary first of all to trace the key aspects of its historical inheritance. What is presented here is not a detailed historical survey, but an overview of the *key phases* in the development of the establishment as well as some of the historical challenges to it that emerged.

In its origins Christianity, of course, came from the Middle East, rather than from Europe. In this sense, Christianity is not an indigenous religion of these islands, although it has played a major part in their emergence and development as socio-cultural communities. In the first instance, Christianity was a minority religion of the Roman Empire having initially emerged as a grouping within the Jewish people, to which Gentile believers were then admitted. Only following the destruction of Jerusalem in 70 CE did it take shape as a religion in its own right within which its Gentile members came to outnumber the Jewish ones. To begin with, though, Christianity remained one religion among many in the Roman Empire. Often dismissed by the powerful as a religion associated primarily with slaves, the poor and the unsophisticated, and sometimes actively persecuted, it eventually became adopted by all strata of society, gathering adherents of varied backgrounds throughout the Roman Empire.

The fundamental change in the relationship between church and state occurred when the Roman Emperor Constantine adopted Christianity.[1] Through the Edict of Milan of 313 CE, Christianity became a tolerated religion instead of a previously marginalized and sometimes persecuted one. By 392 CE, when the Emperor Theodosius forbade all public and private pagan worship under threat of death, Christianity was well on the road to becoming the only tolerated religion in the Empire, with other religions often being subject to increasing restrictions and, sometimes, also to active persecution.

As Christianity expanded into Europe, it began to take bi-polar shape in what eventually came to be known as its 'Western Catholic' and 'Eastern Orthodox' forms. As well as leading to tension and conflict with aspects of the local cultures with which it came into contact, this expansion of Christianity brought about a significant degree of continental integration and the emergence of what was at least an idea of the politico-religious unity of European Christendom. In the West of the continent this took shape in the Holy Roman Empire, and in the East, that of Byzantium. The church historian Adrian Hastings suggested that the relationship between Empire and Church was characterized historically either by 'monism' (as in the developing Caesaro-Papism of Eastern Christendom) or 'dualism' (as in the struggles between the Holy Roman Emperor and the Popes over their overlapping spheres of influence in Western Christendom).[2]

In the West, from the eighth century onwards, monarchs were anointed and priestly vestments began to be used as the symbol of sovereignty. At the same time, the Popes wore a tiara symbolizing secular power. With the collapse of the Carolingian Empire, Pope Gregory VII claimed precedence as senior 'vicar' or representative of Christ over the Emperor, who was identified as the junior 'vicar'. However, a struggle for supremacy continued and underlying tensions remained between these two arms of power in Christendom.

b. *The Reformation and Phases of Establishment*

The Reformation prised open the historic Christendom vision (which, of course, was in any case as much an ideology as fully developed social reality) of a religio-political unity through the emergence of new configurations between dynasty, territory and religion. In England, King Henry VIII's eventual break with Papal jurisdiction over dynastic issues related to marriage and the royal succession changed this relationship in a distinctive way as compared with the religious and political upheavals that erupted in other parts of Europe and are collectively known as the Reformation.

While influences upon England from emergent continental Lutheranism and Calvinism did exist, the upheaval that took place in England was determined particularly by Henry's dynastic concerns. These were rooted in the inability, as he saw it, of his wife to provide him with a male heir to secure the stability of his dynastic line and his consequent need for an annulment of his marriage in order to secure, through another wife and mother, a legitimate heir.

Since the Henrician watershed, the particular form for the relationship between religion(s), state and society taken by the *Ecclesia Anglicana* has developed through a variety of phases. As the historian John Wolffe notes:

> It is widely perceived that the relations between church and state are one of the most unchanging and traditional features of English life. In reality, however, during the four and a half centuries since the Reformation, the constitutional situation of the Church of England, like that of the monarchy, has altered profoundly.[3]

In his polemical work on the establishment of the Church of England, the Anglican bishop and critic of the establishment Colin Buchanan identifies what he calls five 'phases of Establishment'.[4] Buchanan's particular schematization of these periods is, of course, only one among a number that are possible. His particular characterization of these phases is also, of course, at least partially indicative of Buchanan's particular evaluation of the significance of establishment. However, even if one disagrees with Buchanan's evaluations, his division of history into these periods is arguably a useful starting point for framing the establishment's changing historical contours.

2. *The Nationalization of Religion*

a. *Pendulum Swings: Henry, Edward and Mary*

Buchanan's first 'phase' of establishment, which he characterizes as that of 'the nationalised monopoly',[5] consists of the years between King Henry VIII's break with the Papacy and events generally known in British history as 'the Glorious Revolution' (1534–1689). In this, the inheritance of the Christendom approach to Christianity continued as before the Reformation, but now within specific territorial boundaries. The Church of England thus became what Stuart Murray called a 'mini-Christendom', in relation to the nature of which he comments that, 'The relative independence of a transnational Church from political control was lost: in the new mini-Christendoms church and state were more closely knit than ever.'[6]

The start of this phase was marked by the 1534 Act of Supremacy, in which King Henry and his successors were described as 'the only head in earth of the Church of England, called *Ecclesia Anglicana*'. Henry was, in fact, in many ways a religiously conservative man and it was because of this that he was previously given the title by the Pope of '*Fidei Defensor*' (Defender of Faith). But, as explained above, Henry was determined that the Pope should not constrain his dynastic concerns, and his break with Rome was initiated in order to secure these.

During Henry's reign, both 'Catholic' and 'Protestant' parties[7] vied for ascendancy within the English Church. Following Henry's death, during the reign of King Edward VI, the imposition of royal rule over the English Church carried through a more thoroughgoing 'Protestantization' of the English Church in which iconoclasm played a major role. During this period, in 1549, the first English Prayer Book became the legally adopted and required form for public Christian worship.

Following the death of Edward, and the accession to the throne of the Catholic Queen Mary, the religious tide in the Church of England once again flowed in the opposite direction. Mary set about restoring links with the Papacy, and around three hundred persons who would not accept this were burned at the stake as heretics, including one of the chief architects of the Henrician Reformation, Thomas Cranmer, Archbishop of Canterbury. Many more were fined, or imprisoned, or had their goods confiscated. The cumulative effect of this period was, as Leslie Paul put it, that 'Roman Catholicism killed its own cause by the savagery to which it had recourse.'[8] As Monica Furlong comments, the period 'did incalculable harm to the way in which Roman Catholicism was henceforth to be viewed in England'.[9]

b. *Elizabethan Erastianism*

In the subsequent reign of Queen Elizabeth I, a form of Church government developed that later became known as 'Erastianism', within which the church–state relationship became seen primarily in pragmatic terms in which the Church was effectively subordinate to the interests of the state. The notion of royal supremacy was once again reinforced by a new (1559) Act of Supremacy, although under Elizabeth the Henrician title of 'Head' of the Church was modified with it being claimed instead that, 'the queen's highness is the only supreme governor of this realm ... as well in all spiritual or ecclesiastical things or causes, as temporal'.

Against the background of the religious extremes of the reigns of Edward and of Mary, and reinforced by concerns about external political and military threats from France and Spain, Elizabeth sought to establish a 'middle way' between the 'Catholic' and 'Protestant' parties of the Church of England. In this context, loyalty to the Church of England came gradually to be identified with Englishness and loyalty to the Crown. Thus, in Book 8 of his *Laws of Ecclesiastical Polity*, the Anglican theologian Roger Hooker gave a classical expression to this when he claimed that, 'We hold that seeing there is not any man of the Church of England but the same is also a member of the Commonwealth; nor any member of the Commonwealth which is not also of the Church of England.'[10]

In such a context, Catholics still loyal to the Papacy were suspected of being potentially, if not actually, disloyal to monarch and country. At the same time, Puritans who wished to build on the inheritance of Edward's reign to complete what they saw as the unfinished business of the Reformation were seen as endangering the unity of the Church. Typical of this approach was the position taken by Edwin Sandys, Archbishop of York under Elizabeth I, who argued that religious plurality would inevitably be dangerous to the body politic:

> This liberty, that men may openly profess diversity of religion must needs be dangerous to the Commonwealth. What stirs diversity of religion hath raised in nations and kingdoms the histories are so many and plain, and in our times insuch sort have told you, that with further proof I need not trouble your ears. One God, one King, one profession, is fit for one monarchy and commonwealth. Let conformity and unity in religion be provided for; and it shall be as a wall of defence unto this realm.[11]

In 1593, the Elizabethan Act of Uniformity was passed, which was directed against 'seditious and disloyal persons'. Under this Act, absence from established worship for one month, or presence at what was characterized as a 'conventicle', brought with it liability to imprisonment. Non-submission within three months could result in banishment from the realm.

c. *Puritanism, Separatism and Anabaptism*

The end of the Elizabethan period and the beginning of the reign of King James I saw a growing 'Puritan' opposition to Erastianism. This opposition was concerned with trying to recover a form of ecclesial life that was thought to be modelled more closely on that of the early Christian communities and the teachings of the New Testament.

From this, some on this Puritan wing of the Church gradually developed a more 'Separatist' position that eventually led to the emergence of 'Independent' and 'Congregational' movements. The early precursors of this were the so-called 'Brownist' congregations, formed in 1580 or 1581 under the influence of the Puritan cleric Robert Browne. But after spending some time with the Dutch Anabaptists, Browne reverted to the established Church and during the last four decades of his life was an incumbent in Northamptonshire, while his colleagues John Greenwood and Henry Barrow were hanged at Tyburn in 1593.

Some parts of the Separatist movement developed in the direction of a Presbyterian ecclesiology and, in so doing, during the reign of James I came into conflict with a King who upheld episcopacy as the correct form of Church government with his appeal to the dictum, 'no bishop, no King'. Others became more influenced by the continental Anabaptist movement and moved towards Independency, Congregationalism and the beginnings of the Baptist movement. The exact relationship (which will be explored in greater detail in Chapter 2) between continental Anabaptists and the emergence of the Baptist movement in England has been the subject of some historical dispute,[12] although it is clear that some influence took place. Anabaptism was a diverse movement of the Radical Reformation[13] that originated in sixteenth-century Switzerland, Austria, Germany and the Low Countries. It took either more 'quietist' or 'activist' forms, but was generally seen both by other Protestants and by Catholics as threatening to the fabric of church and state, especially after the Münster uprising.

Anabaptism brought with it a particularly significant ecclesiological challenge to the inherited relationships between church and state. This was because Anabaptists argued not only that the Catholic Church was corrupt, but also that Churches ruled by Protestant princes were also *ipso facto* corrupt since they entailed alliance with the world, force and social ranking.[14] All of these the majority of Anabaptists eschewed, while advocating unrestricted religious liberty.

3. *Revolutionary Challenge and Restoration*

a. *Regicide, Radicalism and Upheaval*

The first of the 'five phases' of establishment identified by Buchanan encompasses the period from the 'nationalization' of religion, through the Revolution and the Presbyterian settlement, to the Restoration of the Monarchy and of the Church of England as an episcopally governed Church. However, within this period, the outbreak of the English Civil War that culminated in the 1649 execution of King Charles I, actually marked a very radical disjuncture in the previous pattern of relationships between religion(s), state and society. Both for the establishment of the Church of England, but also for the more general idea of the 'Divine Right' by which monarchs ruled, the execution of the King brought about a shocking break with the previous inheritance. Summarizing the impact of these events, the Baptist church historian of the seventeenth century Barrie White argued that:

> The Revolution made uncertain the simple age-old situation where Church and State were linked by one unquestioned partnership in which the Church supplied the cement of a common faith and the divine validation of the accustomed forms of society. This was gone by 1646, gone never to return.[15]

The years following the execution of Charles I were a time during which all kinds of new religious movements began to emerge and, in the context of heightened millenarian expectations, exploded into the formation of religiously and socially radical groups such as the Quakers, the Fifth Monarchists and the Levellers. Oliver Cromwell, as the new power in the land, in principle believed in the liberty of individual conscience in matters of religion. But as a matter of *realpolitik* as Lord Protector he decided that, due to the impact upon the state of the turbulent conflicts between different religious groups, he could not in practice allow unrestricted liberty. In one important respect, though, the period of the Protectorate saw the extension of religious plurality allowed in England: in 1652 the Jews, who had been expelled from England during the reign of Edward I, were allowed to re-settle in London.

The 1643 Solemn League and Covenant had committed England to a Presbyterian church settlement. Clergy of Presbyterian or Independent views, or those who could at least find accommodation with such views, were brought into the parishes to replace Episcopalians. However, all parish clergy continued to receive the traditional tithes. Therefore, while the connection between state and episcopate had been broken, a strong linkage remained between state and religion, albeit that the form of church governance now supported by the state was a Presbyterian rather than an Episcopalian one.

This did not, however, end the religious turmoil. A flavour of the times can be gleaned from Christopher Hill's classic historical study, *The World Turned Upside Down*, the title of which reflects a widespread contemporary perception of the period.[16] Thus, for example, groups such as the Fifth Monarchists tried to build temporal government based upon the rule of the saints as interpreted through the apocalyptic prophecies of the biblical book of Daniel, chapter 2. In the 1649 Agreement of the People, the Levellers demanded a limited freedom of conscience, but also tempered this by a political pragmatism that excluded Anglicans and Catholics as potentially seditious.

b. *Seeking Stability and Pressurizing Diversity*

Oliver Cromwell died in 1658, and in 1659 his son Richard Cromwell withdrew into private life. Following the decades of revolutionary turmoil in both governance and religion, a new Royalist Parliament met on 25 April 1660 and adopted the Breda Declaration. Complementing his earlier observation on the English Revolution's role in shattering the previously symbiotic relationship between church and state, White commented on the Restoration that:

> There was a strong conviction, held by many, both high and low in churchman-ship and high and low in society, that there should be one church and one church only in the land to provide cement and stability for a deeply disturbed society …there was a sense that the multiplicity of sects which had developed in the 1640s and 1650s had contributed to the unsettlement of society because so many of them also seemed to promote political instability.[17]

Thus, together with the Restoration of the monarchy went the restoration of the episcopal form of the establishment of the Church of England. At the same time, among other conditions of the Restoration, the Breda Declaration had promised a qualified liberty of conscience. Charles stated that, 'we do declare a liberty to tender consciences, and that no man shall be disquieted or called into question, for differences of opinion in matters of religion which do not disturb the general peace of the Kingdom'. Not all were assured of this, however, and in 1661 the Fifth Monarchist Thomas Venner led an uprising. This resulted in a wave of arrests of Dissenters and the introduction of the so-called 'Clarendon Codes' which restricted the practice of non-established Christians.

On the basis of fears about the possible re-emergence of a period of further social and political upheaval, and in order to guard against the threat of rebellion, the Corporation Act of 1661 required public officials to swear oaths of royal allegiance and supremacy. On pain of dismissal from office, these oaths required disavowal of the Presbyterian Solemn League and Covenant. Appointments or elections to public office remained valid only if, within one year of election or appointment, Holy Communion was taken according to the rites of the Church of England. Parliament then accepted a revised Book of Common Prayer and, on 19 May 1662, a further Act of Uniformity was passed which forced around one thousand clergy out of their livings along with the approximately seven hundred who had already been forced to resign immediately following the Restoration. The close connection between royalty, the Church of England and the state was thereby, during this period, reinstated.

In 1664, in the aftermath of the abortive Yorkshire Plot, the first Conventicle Act was passed. This made it illegal for more than five people over the age of sixteen (other than members of the same household) to meet together for worship except according to the formularies of the Book of Common Prayer. The restrictions upon 'Dissent' continued with the Five Mile Act of 1665, which required Dissenting clergy to take an oath accepting the ecclesiastical-political status quo, failing which they were forbidden to live within five miles of their place of ministry and were also forbidden to keep a school.

In 1667, a more severe Conventicle Act became law, although in 1672 the King issued a Declaration of Indulgence for Dissenters (to practise in public) and Catholics (to practise in private). However, this concession became part of the emerging conflict of powers between Crown and Parliament, and Parliament retaliated with the Test Act of 1673 that required public officials to receive the Lord's Supper at a parish church. That this Act was originally directed against a fear of Catholic sedition can be seen from its full name: An Act for Preventing Dangers Which May Happen From Popish Recusants. However, it also caught Dissenters within its scope. This was because, although the House of Commons also passed a Bill for the Ease of Protestant Dissenters, this was opposed by the Church of England bishops in the House of Lords, and Parliament was prorogued before the Bill could become law.

1678–81 was the period generally known in English history as that of the 'Popish Plot' and which therefore saw a rise in pressure against Catholics. This resulted, in 1685, in the exclusion of Catholics from Parliament. On 6 February, Charles' Roman Catholic brother, James II, ascended to the throne. The unsuccessful Monmouth Rebellion broke out and, in retaliation, the so-called 'Bloody Assizes' clamped down on Dissent. But on 10 March 1686, King James issued a pardon to all imprisoned for religion and, from November onwards, a family licence of nonconformity could be bought for 50 shillings. On 4 April 1687, James issued a first Declaration of Indulgence for Catholics and Dissenters. This was followed, on 27 April 1688, by a second in which James declared that he would work for toleration established by law. On 10 July 1688, a Catholic male heir was born.

4. *Dissent and Toleration*

a. *The 'Glorious Revolution'*

The events now generally known to English history as the 'Glorious Revolution' of 1689 followed. Due to a shared fear about the possible re-establishment of Roman Catholic supremacy, Anglicans sought the political support of Dissenters whose influence and practice they had hitherto tried to restrict. James fled the country and William and Mary of Orange were invited by Parliament to take the Throne. However, despite the alliance into which they had been wooed, Dissenting hopes for real equity were disappointed as Anglicans re-asserted their supremacy and the legal restrictions upon Dissenters were continued.

Therefore, although the period of the 'Glorious Revolution' is often popularly associated with the rise of toleration, it can alternatively be seen as ushering in a period that is characterized by Buchanan as 'the era of privilege'[18] which lasted from 1689 until the Reform Parliament of 1830. White comments on this period that, despite Dissenting support for the 'Glorious Revolution':

> Anglican treatment of Dissent over the thirty-five years down to the accession of George I (and even for several generations after that) was that of a body, even while growing less concerned for unanimity over doctrinal detail, which was consistently concerned for its own monopoly of all the political power it could preserve. In addition to this, no doubt, there was the sense that Dissent had been responsible for republican revolution and that society could only be safe if there were one church in the land to give the country its cement of faith, worship, and discipline.[19]

In the ensuing years, nonconformist Christians, Roman Catholics and Jews alike suffered civil disabilities and social exclusions because they did not follow the established religion. Such disabilities continued despite the passage of the Toleration Act of 1689 which, although it is often held up as an example of progressive legislation, was, in fact, not a measure for full toleration. Rather, the full title of the legislation illuminates its actual nature and scope. More precisely than the name by which it is generally known to history its full title, in fact, was An Act for Exempting Their Majesties' Protestant Subjects Dissenting from the Church of England from the Penalties of Certain Laws. This is because its scope was actually limited to Trinitarian Protestants adhering to the 39 Articles of the Church of England (excepting Articles 34, 35 and 36 on the tradition of the Church, public reading of the second *Book of Homilies* and episcopal ordination, together, for Baptists, with infant baptism).

The necessity for the payment of tithes remained, as did a sacramental test for public office. In connection with the licensing of religious meeting places there was still a requirement to take the oaths of supremacy and allegiance. Therefore, although it was an important historical development, rather than bringing about *religious liberty* for all, what the Act eventually produced was legal *toleration* for some categories of Christians. Unitarians were excluded from its terms of reform and Roman Catholics remained unable to be teachers, only had limited rights of ownership of land, and were liable to be penalized for not attending the Church of England parish church.

b. *Relaxation of Restrictions*

The eighteenth century was, in many ways, a period of relative religious calm and stability that saw a gradual improvement in the position of non-established religious groups. Some have claimed that this was due to an increase in religious indifference, although Monica Furlong points to recent research which suggests that such a reading of history may owe more to the later critique of Evangelicals and the Oxford Movement than to an accurate portrayal of the times.[20] During this period, John Locke and others argued for a broadly 'comprehensive'[21] national Church extending to what was seen as the widest possible range of toleration (again excepting Deists and Catholics).[22] A number of restrictions upon nonconformist and Roman Catholic religious practice were lifted.[23] In 1727, the Indemnity Act was passed, followed by the 1778 Catholic Relief Act that repealed the 1700 Act for the Further Preventing of the Growth of Popery. In 1779, the Dissenters' Relief Act repealed the requirement to subscribe to most of the 39 Articles of the Church of England.

In 1791, the Roman Catholic Relief Act allowed lay Catholics to hold some public offices and to become teachers, as well as allowing Roman Catholic places of worship to be licensed. Nevertheless, the 1812 Places of Religious Worship Act continued earlier legislative restrictions on nonconformist ministers, allowing them to teach and preach only upon making a declaration in front of a Justice of the Peace. The Act also confirmed that it was an offence to teach or preach in any premises with the doors locked or without the consent of the occupier.

But in 1812 the Conventicle Act and the Five Mile Act were repealed. In 1813, Unitarians were given the same privileges as other Protestant nonconformists and, in 1828, the Test Act and the Corporation Act were modified. Following this, Dissenting Protestants, upon taking a civil or court appointment, needed only to affirm that:

> I, A.B, do solemnly and sincerely, in the presence of God, profess, testify and declare upon the true faith of a Christian, that I will never exercise any power, authority or influence I may possess by virtue of the office of … to injure or weaken the Protestant Church, as it is by law established in England, or to disturb the said Church, in the possession of any rights or any privileges to which the said Church, or the said Bishops and clergy, are or may be by law entitled.[24]

The phrase 'upon the true faith of a Christian' had not been part of the originally proposed legislation, but had been inserted by the House of Lords on the motion of the Bishop of Llandaff. Its continuing disqualification of Jews, Deists and atheists highlights the limits of the toleration that had been achieved and it was only later in the nineteenth century that these groups saw significant progress in overcoming their social and legal disadvantages.

c. *Pressure for Equity*

As will be explored in greater detail in Chapter 2 the nonconformists, in particular, had been the source of much of the pressure on the Church of England's privileged legal status. In 1702, the General Body of the Three Denominations had been formed to promote religious equality before the law and, in 1732, the

Protestant Dissenting Deputies of churches in the London area was formed[25] to work for the repeal of the Test and Corporation Acts.

The nineteenth century saw an intensification of these developments. The Protestant Society for the Protection of Religious Liberty was founded in 1811 and worked with the Dissenting Deputies to secure the repeal of the Conventicle Act and the Five Mile Act. The Religious Freedom Society was founded in 1839, the English Voluntary Church Association and the Anti-Church Rates Conference in 1834 and the Church Rates Abolition Society in 1836. The most significant among these various campaigning groups was the Liberation Society. This was originally founded in 1844 under the name of The British Anti-State Church Association. In 1853, it changed its title to what became its full formal name of the Society for the Liberation of Religion from State Patronage and Control.

It was during the Reform Parliament, from 1830 onwards, that significant social, political and religious openings were created for Protestant Dissenters. Catholic disabilities also began, progressively, to be dismantled. As has already been noted, following the bloody end of Queen Mary's reign, from the time of the Elizabethan settlement onwards, Roman Catholics had been seen by the Anglican establishment as a political as well as a religious threat. While sharing disabilities with Roman Catholics, many nonconformists also concurred with this Anglican perception. As will be seen in Chapter 2, although nonconformists argued strongly for religious freedom and civil rights, some did exclude Roman Catholics from their more general arguments. Thus, in nineteenth-century English society, the progress of Roman Catholic emancipation was a key litmus test of the nature and extent of religious toleration and of the integration within the civil society and the state of people of diverse religious identity, belief and practice.

Under the terms of the 1829 Roman Catholic Relief Act, Catholics were re-admitted to Parliament. This followed the Roman Catholic O'Connell's inability to take his seat after his 1828 election to the Parliamentary seat of Clare in Ireland. The 1832 Roman Catholic Charities Act allowed Roman Catholics to hold property for charitable, educational or religious purposes on the same basis as nonconformists. At the same time, Catholics were forbidden to hold the post of Regent, Lord Chancellor or Lord Lieutenant of Ireland. It was also made illegal for a Catholic to interfere in the Church of England and for a member of the Jesuit order to enter the country without a licence from the Secretary of State.

5. *The Ending of Civic Disabilities*

a. *Reformism and Religion*

The Reform Parliament marks the beginning of Buchanan's third phase (1830–1920) of the establishment that he characterizes as one of 'Church self-discovery'.[26] It is, however, at least arguable that the principal cause of these changes was not really, as might be suggested by Buchanan's name for this period, an internal Anglican dynamic of re-evaluation. Rather, it is perhaps more accurate to see the changes that occurred as coming about due to a conjunction of forces connected with industrialization, the introduction of a widening electoral mandate, and the growth both in numbers and political significance of nonconformist

Christianity. Commenting on these developments, the legal academic St John Robilliard pointed out that 'The early story of the struggle for religious liberty is one of sects establishing an identity of their own, with their members being freed from the obligation of supporting a faith they did not hold. From the struggle for existence we pass to the struggle for equality, in many important fields, with the Established Church.'[27]

In this context, the religious Census of 1851[28] was of enormous symbolic and psychological significance. It demonstrated that the Church of England was no longer the Church of the vast majority of people of England. Although Monica Furlong notes that questions have recently been raised concerning the methodology and hence the results of this survey,[29] the impact of its results at that time is undoubted. Only slightly over half of the people worshipping on a Sunday were recorded as doing so in the established Church of England, while the relative strength of nonconformist Christianity was underlined. But, even more radically than this, the Census produced evidence that a large proportion of people were completely unchurched. It therefore called into question not only the appropriateness of the establishment of the specific form of Anglican Christianity relative to other Christian traditions, but also the more fundamental notion of England's identity as a 'Christian country'.

By 1836, nonconformists no longer had to get married in a church of the established Church of England. In 1844, the remaining provisions of the Test Act and the Corporation Act were repealed. In 1846, the Religious Disabilities Act removed the last restrictions on nonconformists; allowed Jews the same rights with respect to education, charities and property; and removed all former laws restricting Roman Catholics, with the exception of the new ones created in the 1829 Roman Catholic Relief Act. In 1850, Roman Catholic dioceses were re-established in England, although the 1851 Ecclesiastical Titles Act made it an offence for anyone to be called an Archbishop, Bishop or Dean of an area already having Church of England functionaries of that kind and name.

In 1853, the Braintree Rates case established that a parish could not, against the wishes of its voters, set rates for the financial support of the Church of England. The 1855 Liberty of Worship Act allowed congregations of more than 20 people to meet in private homes or (occasionally) in other buildings not having certification as places of worship. In 1855, the Places of Worship Registration Act put in place a system for the registration of places of worship, to which certain benefits were attached. In 1858, the Jews' Relief Act established for Jews the same civil rights that had been granted to Catholics in 1829 (including the taking of seats in Parliament). The exception to this was that it was specifically made an offence for a Jew to advise the Crown on any appointment to offices in the Church of England.

In 1854, the Oxford University Act abolished religious tests for matriculation for the award of the Bachelor of Arts degree, though not for higher degrees, and in 1856 the Cambridge University Act followed suit. In 1867 the Test Abolition Act abolished the oath of the Crown's supremacy in ecclesiastical matters for certain public offices, and Catholics were allowed to become Lord Chancellors of Ireland. In 1868, church rates were abolished following Gladstone's election victory gained with nonconformist support. In 1871, the University Tests Act removed religious tests for all degrees except Divinity, and tests were also removed for official University posts with the exception of the Professorship of Divinity. In 1880, the Government removed the right of established Church priests to conduct a funeral and allowed any Christian service to take place at the graveside.

The role, significance and form of oaths also brought into focus questions concerning the more general relationships between religion and the instruments of the state. Since 1749, Quakers had been allowed to affirm, rather than to swear an oath. In 1833, Joseph Pease, a newly elected Quaker MP, was allowed to take his Parliamentary seat on the basis of an affirmation rather than an oath. In 1854, this right was more generally extended, but it still excluded atheists. Between 1850 and 1855, the atheist Charles Bradlaugh, despite being elected four times, was not allowed to take his seat by oath or affirmation, until agreement was eventually reached. Following this, the 1868 Promissory Oaths Act, the 1871 Promissory Oaths Act, the 1869 Evidence Further Amendment Act, the 1870 Evidence Amendment Act and the 1880 Oaths Act made additional provisions for oaths or affirmations to be made without reference to religious beliefs.

b. *Debate on Disestablishment*

Three-quarters of the way through the nineteenth century not only the removal of specific religious disabilities, but also the more general possibility of the disestablishment of the Church of England, emerged more firmly onto the political agenda. In May 1871, following the disestablishment of the Church of Ireland in the 1869 Irish Church Act, the Congregationalist Member of Parliament Edward Miall introduced his first motion calling for disestablishment of the Church of England. Free Church leaders continued thereafter to press for disestablishment, and there were further Bills in 1886, 1889 and 1892, with Welsh disestablishment becoming Liberal Party policy in 1887. But, in many ways, the 1871 motion represented the peak of nonconformist agitation for a fundamental change in the nature of church–state relations.

It is arguable that the ensuing relative decline of the cause of disestablishment came about as individual civil disabilities were progressively removed from nonconformist Christians, thus removing a major part of the basis for the sense of felt injustice.[30] However, while the removal of some of the key disadvantages was undoubtedly influential in ameliorating the urgency and force of the Free Church criticism of the establishment, for the majority in the Free Churches, disestablishment was primarily a *theological* and *ecclesiological* imperative rather than an issue only of social equity. It was the potential for the state's control over aspects of the inner life of the Church of England, and therefore over matters of theology and ecclesiology, that more often lay at the heart of nineteenth- and twentieth-century debate over establishment as it took place between nonconformists and Anglicans.

As will be explored in greater detail in Chapter 2, a classical example of such theological and ecclesiological debate can be seen in the positions adopted by William Ewart Gladstone, who defended establishment, and of Revd Baptist Wriothesley Noel, who critiqued it from the perspective of a congregationalist ecclesiology. Therefore, even with the progress of civic equality and social inclusion, tensions and conflicts between the Free Church and established Church approaches remained. At the end of the nineteenth and the beginning of the twentieth century, the ongoing tensions coalesced around issues concerning the relationships between church and state in relation to the emerging national education system.[31]

For a long time, many nonconformists had opposed the introduction of such a system on the basis of voluntarist principles and the existence of their own educational initiatives which had been developed for those denied educational opportunity through their religious nonconformity. Gradually, however, nonconformists accepted the principle of state-funded and organized education. But they remained concerned about the particular forms proposed for this, believing them often to entail a privileging of the established Church of England. Thus the launch of a nonconformist campaign of civil disobedience against payment of what was argued to be 'denominational teaching on the rates' became the last great social and political struggle between nonconformists, the established Church and the state.

6. Changes in Church, Parliament and Crown

a. Church and State in Wales, Scotland and Ireland

Buchanan sees the 1920 Enabling Act as a 'hinge point in church–state relationships in England'.[32] He characterizes the era (1920–70) that it ushered in as 'the era of growing incredibility'.[33] The period commenced with significant changes relating to the relationship between religion(s), state and society in all four nations of the UK. The Welsh Church Act had been passed in 1914, and on 1 April 1920 the Anglican Church was disestablished in Wales. During the 1913 House of Lords debate on Welsh disestablishment, while arguing against disestablishment, Archbishop Cosmo Lang of Canterbury had developed a line of argument, variations upon which can still be heard today, when he set out the position that:

> The question before us is whether just there in that inward region of the national life where anything that can be called its unity and character is expressed, there is not to be this witness to some ultimate sanction to which the nation looks, some ultimate ideal it proposes. It is in our judgement a very serious thing for a state to take out of that corporate heart of its life any acknowledgment at all of its concern with religion.[34]

The Act was nevertheless passed. Changes also came into effect with a bearing on the relationships between religion, state and society in Scotland and in Northern Ireland. In the context of the partition of Ireland, section 5 of the 1920 Government of Ireland Act stated that no Northern Ireland law should be enacted 'so as either directly or indirectly to establish or endow any religion, or prohibit or restrict the free exercise thereof'. In Scotland, the 1921 Church of Scotland Act freed the Presbyterian Church of Scotland from all vestiges of Parliamentary control, while it continued to maintain its links with the Crown.

b. *The 'Prayer Book Crisis' in England*

In England, in 1919, the National Assembly of the Church of England (the Church Assembly) was brought into being as a forum for lay discussion of Church of England matters which, up until that time, had been discussed in Parliament. The clergy continued to be represented in the historic Convocations of York and of Canterbury and, in 1920, the Enabling Act recognized the role of the Assembly.

Despite the introduction of this measure of self-government, a major church–state controversy broke out in 1928–9 in which Evangelicals and Anglo-Catholics united in appeal to Parliament against changes to the Prayer Book that were proposed by the Church Assembly. Parliament's refusal to ratify the Assembly's proposals for such change underlined the Assembly's continuing dependence upon Parliament for approval of the Measures that it passed. It was perhaps this controversy, more than any other, which opened up internal Church of England questioning concerning the implications of establishment for the Church of England's own life and mission.

c. *Post-War Disruption*

The Second World War brought about a disruption to many of the pre-war characteristics of English life. Following the war, many of the pre-war traditions were brought into question, and the Church of England was by no means exempt from this general time of question and change. In his 1947 book *The Claims of the Church of England*, the Archbishop of York, Cyril Garbett, argued that while, 'At the moment Parliament has no desire to exercise active control over the Church or gratuitously to interfere in its concerns' the Church 'should not acquiesce any longer in a relationship with the State which might suddenly prove to be inconsistent in practice as well as in principle with religious freedom.'[35] Again, following a line of argument that one can still find echoed today, he did not take a position in favour of an immediate church-initiated disestablishment but, rather, proposed four major reforms.

The reforms that Garbett argued for included, first, a formula for the Crown to assent to changes of worship without Parliamentary approval needing to be sought. Second, the introduction of really spiritual Courts from which appeal to Civil Courts would only be possible in terms of reviewing the appropriateness of the process adopted by the spiritual Courts. Third, the right for the Church to be consulted on the appointment of bishops and archbishops. Finally, he proposed that Convocations should have the power to pass Canons.

In Garbett's view, such reforms would 'vindicate the freedom of the Church' but would also 'retain its connection with the state'. He concluded with the observation that, 'If however the Church cannot agree to these reforms or, if Parliament after due consideration refuses to accept them, then Disestablishment and Disendowment will be unavoidable.' In the light of the minimal progress made on these matters by the beginning of the next decade, in his later book *Church and State in England*, Garbett spoke of his 'grave heart-searching and discomfort' and his sense that disestablishment might, indeed, as a last option, become necessary.[36]

In the 1960s a number of the reforms advocated by Garbett were achieved. In 1963, the Ecclesiastical Jurisdiction Measure transferred legal disputes over the doctrine and ritual of the Church of England away from the Judicial Committee of the Privy Council to a new Court of Ecclesiastical Causes Reserved. In 1965, the Prayer Book (Alternative Services Measure) gave the Convocations and the House of Laity of the Church Assembly the authority to allow experimental services. In the light of the 1927–8 dispute over the Prayer Book, this development was both highly significant for, and symbolic of, a shift in the relations between the Church of England and the state.

However, no significant progress was made with regard to the issues surrounding the appointment of bishops. As Monica Furlong points out, in the latter part of the twentieth century, the principal Anglican concerns surrounding establishment have tended to focus on the role of the state in the appointment of Church of England bishops and archbishops.[37] For example, following the Second World War, renewed concern about the implications of establishment was aroused when, following the death of Archbishop William Temple in 1944, Bishop George Bell of Chichester was passed over for appointments to the sees of Canterbury and London. This was thought to have been connected with Bell's criticism of the carpet bombing of German cities and thus underlined concerns within the Church about the influence of political, rather than spiritual, considerations in episcopal appointments.

7. The Contemporary Period

a. The General Synod and the Appointment of Bishops
The sixth and final (1970–present) of Buchanan's phases of establishment was characterized by him as 'the end of pretence'.[38] Following the passage of the 1969 Synodical Government Measure, Buchanan saw this phase as beginning with the Queen's inauguration of the General Synod in November 1970. Although opposed by a minority of Conservative MPs who wanted to maintain Parliamentary control, the 1974 Worship and Doctrine Measure gave the Synod permanent control over matters of worship.

In 1976, the then Labour Prime Minister James (now Lord) Callaghan, agreed to delegate a large proportion of the process of appointing bishops and arch-bishops to a Crown Appointments Commission appointed by the General Synod. The principle was that the Commission would suggest two names to the Prime Minister who could choose either or neither. However, the Prime Minister's ultimate choice was preserved on the basis that, while episcopal seats continued to be reserved in the House of Lords, there remained a continuing need for political influence over the question of who would take up these seats. In 1984, too, the House of Commons rejected a Measure for further reforms in the appointment procedures for bishops.

b. Debate on Church and State
In the most recent period, Free Church and Roman Catholic critiques of the establishment have receded considerably compared with their nineteenth-century heyday. The historian John Wolffe notes that 'in striking contrast to the situation in the later nineteenth century, the debate about disestablishment in the later twentieth century – such as it was – was very much an internal Anglican affair'.[39]

In the twentieth century there were, in fact, four major internal Anglican reports examining the relationship between church and state as well as a number of others on aspects of canon law which is also significantly affected by the established status of the Church of England. The major reports were the Selborne Commission's *Report of the Archbishops' Committee on Church and State* (1916);[40] the Cecil Commission's *Report of the Archbishops' Commission on the Relations Between Church and State* (1935);[41] the Moberley Commission's *Church and State: Being the Report of a Commission Appointed by the Church Assembly in June 1949* (1952);[42] and, finally, the Chadwick Commission's report on *Church and State* (1970).[43]

Each of these reports advocated some modification to the forms of the relationship that pertained at the time, but none advocated disestablishment. In fact, until the 1970 *Church and State* report, the reports included no fundamental dissent from support for establishment. In this latter, however, two members of the Commission – Valerie Pitt and Peter Cornwell – recorded their dissenting view. Peter Cornwell later went on to write what was at one and the same time both a forceful and a measured Christian theological critique of establishment in his book *Church and Nation*.[44] Valerie Pitt also continued to maintain and explain her position in a series of pieces about establishment.[45]

Much of the self-criticism of the Church of England's established status has come from within its Anglo-Catholic and, to some extent, Evangelical wings, on the basis of the establishment being seen as inimical to one or the other emphasis within Christianity that is advocated by them. In a sense this is not surprising given that it has been argued that it has been the fact of establishment that has held these tendencies together in the same Church. Hobson, in fact, goes so far as to argue that what he describes as the 'incredible achievement' of the 'ecclesiological equivalent of getting the lion and the lamb to chum up' is 'unthinkable without the Church's establishment: an overarching political ideal was needed to make the fragile union work'.[46]

Among the Anglo-Catholics, early critiques had developed within the context of the rise and influence of the Oxford Movement. Newman had preached his Assizes Sermon on 14 July 1833 and he began publishing his famous *Tracts for the Times* in September 1834. Many of the concerns of the Tractarians were related to what they saw as a lack of apostolic freedom for the Church to determine its own principles and practices. In other words, they were protesting against Erastianism. Contemporary critiques continue from within the Anglo-Catholic tradition. A number of such critiques – by Simon Barrow, Jonathan Chaplin, Alan Ecclestone, Ken Leech, Chris Rowland, Trevor Huddleston, Tom Hurcombe and Valerie Pitt – were published in the Jubilee Group's edited collection on *Setting the Church of England Free: The Case for Disestablishment*. This was edited by Ken Leech, whose introduction to the collection declared that, 'The Constantinian era is over. The survival of an established Church in England is a quaint but dangerous anachronism.'[47] Elsewhere, in sharper language, Leech has argued that, 'As it stands, the Church of England is a compromised, captivated and Constantinian Church, a Church in bondage to Babylon ... For the Church to hide behind the structures of Caesar is a betrayal of the Gospel.'[48]

As far as Evangelicals have been concerned, while a few (such as Buchanan) have strongly criticized establishment, others have been among its staunchest defenders. This has been because of their concern to preserve the Protestant character of the Church of England against what, in their understanding, is a perceived threat of Romanization were the Church of England to be cut free from the constraints of Parliament and the Governorship of the monarch. Today, however, it is the Evangelicals who are in the ascendency in the Church of England and, therefore, there can often be a greater readiness among them to consider disestablishment than was perhaps the case in the past.

c. *The 'Special Relationship'?*

Significant numbers of Anglicans continue to hold the position that establishment is not the way of being the Church that they would choose to start from. However, since it exists, then they believe that one should try to make the best of the opportunities it provides for influence in the machinery of the state and the institutions of civil society. Popularly expressed, this kind of approach proceeds along the lines of the argument that, 'if something ain't broke, don't try to fix it'. Analogously to the British government's claim that it has a 'special relationship' with the USA through which it exercises influence, supporters of establishment argue that the 'special relationship' between church, state and society that establishment bequeaths means that an established Church can bring positive influence to bear upon the state.

Three recent Archbishops of Canterbury (William Temple, 1942–4; Michael Ramsey, 1961–74; and Robert Runcie, 1980-91) hinted at the possible coming of disestablishment, albeit without initiating it. However, Donald Coggan (1974–80), Geoffrey Fisher (1945–61) and George Carey (1991–2002), together with the last three Archbishops of York (Donald Coggan, 1961–74; Stuart Blanche, 1975–83; and John Habgood, 1983–95) have all strongly supported its continuance on the basis of arguments of this kind. The substance of some of these arguments will be explored in greater detail later in the book, and especially in Chapters 5 and 6. But, for example, the previous Archbishop of Canterbury, George Carey (who comes from the Evangelical tradition), spoke of the significance of the establishment of the Church of England in terms of:

> The continuing existence, within the stewardship of the Church of England, of a commitment to God and the spiritual dimension in the central institutions of our national life. There may be more than one opinion about how far these are symbolic rather than real and actual, but they are there nonetheless. Monarchs are crowned in the setting of a communion service by the Archbishop of Canterbury; each day's business in both Houses of Parliament begins with prayers; bishops still contribute to the debates and legislative programme of the nation in the House of Lords.[49]

Carey, in fact, intensified his defence of the establishment just prior to the end of his period of office at a time when there was then considerable speculation about the possibility of Rowan Williams being in line for appointment as Archbishop of Canterbury, in an 8 July 2002 debate in the General Synod of the Church of England about the procedures governing the appointment of bishops. The Synod debate had been initiated by the anti-establishment Bishop of Woolwich, Colin Buchanan, who proposed a motion (which was defeated) for a change to the current practice in which the Prime Minister's Office has a key role in the appointment of Church of England bishops and archbishops. In the debate, George Carey insisted that the establishment was secure for another quarter of a century and that it represented 'an essential part' of the fabric of the country.50

d. *Rowan Williams and the Future of Establishment*

As has previously been noted, Rowan Williams (who himself originally came from a family background in the Presbyterian Church in Wales) was a bishop in the Anglican Church in Wales, itself a disestablished Church, and has made a number of statements that seem supportive of disestablishment.

During a question and answer session at the Christian music festival Greenbelt, Williams was said to have stated that the establishment as it currently existed was a 'relic' and that 'the notion of the Monarch as the supreme governor has outlived its usefulness'. He was also reported as saying that establishment was 'not good for the Church' since it 'encourages a level of self-deception in the Church about how important it is, which in the long run may raise some sort of issue about credibility and integrity'.[51] Finally, he predicted 'disestablishment by a thousand cuts'.

However, following his appointment as Archbishop of Canterbury, Williams made it clear that although his positions as an individual theologian on a variety of issues (for example on homosexuality and Christian identity) are well known, he does not come into the role of the Archbishop of Canterbury pursuing a personal manifesto. Thus Williams' more recent statements on establishment have been less clear cut and, in the run up to his appointment, when what he had said at Greenbelt was reported, he issued a written statement seeking to 'clarify' in a more precise manner his earlier more conversational comments.[52]

The Church in Wales Press Release explained that the *Church Times* article appeared to contain 'a re-hash of comments made by Archbishop Rowan during a question and answer session at the Greenbelt festival in August 2000'. In the Press Release, Williams explains, 'It seems self-evident that the disestablishment of the Church of England is not something which is going to come all at once or in the immediate future.' He also states that this is a matter 'quite clearly not at the top of the agenda for the Church of England ...'. At the same time, he also acknowledged that '... with the pace of social change being what it is, this is a matter that is bound to need renegotiation and reconsideration in the decades to come. This is something that seems to be quite widely agreed in both church and society at large.'

Therefore, although Williams at least *appears* to have moved away from his previous verbal remarks that suggested a tendency towards recognising the logic of disestablishment, a recognition remains – albeit now expressed more in the passive voice of an *observer* rather the active voice of an *advocate* – that establishment is something that '... is bound to need renegotiation ... in the decades to come'.

The question that remains is whether, under the leadership of Rowan Williams as Archbishop of Canterbury, the Church of England will *itself*, in partnership with other key stakeholders in the future of relationships between religion(s), state and society, find the courage and vision necessary *actively* to *initiate* such a renegotiation. These stakeholders include the other Christian traditions and Churches of the UK; the other than Christian religions and their communities, groupings and organizations; inter-faith organizations, groupings and initiatives; the organizations and institutions of civil society; the political parties; and the Governments of both the UK and its devolved component parts.

e. *Possible Alternative Resources*

It is to the contribution to such a process that could be made from within the alternative perspectives on established religion that are located in the Baptist and Free Church traditions of Christianity that the following chapter turns. In this, some key 'notes' of Baptist history are outlined and highlighted. These include a theologically rooted commitment to religious liberty and an ecclesiological self-understanding of 'covenantal voluntarism'.[53]

Then, following a survey of the contemporary religious landscape of England and the UK, the contemporary experience of religious discrimination is examined. Finally, the closing chapters of the book argue that these key 'notes' of Baptist tradition offer significant resources for the reconceptualization of the Church in its relationship with the state and the society that is needed in this current post-Christian and 'three-dimensional' context. Furthermore it is argued that these key 'notes', in appropriately 'translated' forms, can connect with the value perspectives and self-interests of other key stakeholders in the future possible configurations between religion(s), state and society, and can do so in a way that is capable of positive facilitation of change.

Notes

1 A. Kee, *Constantine Versus Christ: The Triumph of Ideology* (London: SCM Press, 1982).

2 See A. Hastings, *Church and State: The English Experience* (Exeter: Exeter University Press, 1991).

3 J. Wolffe, ' "And There's Another Country ...": Religion, State and British Identities', in G. Parsons (ed.), *The Growth of Religious Diversity: Britain From 1945* (vol. 2; London: Routledge, 1994), pp. 85–121 (90).

4 C. Buchanan, *Cut the Connection: Disestablishment and the Church of England* (London: Darton, Longman & Todd, 1994), p. 11.

5 C. Buchanan, *Cut the Connection*, pp. 11–19.

6 S. Murray, *Post-Christendom: Church and Mission in a Strange New World* (Carlisle: Paternoster, 2004), p. 149.

7 At this stage in history, of course, the terms 'Protestant' and 'Catholic' need very much to be set within inverted commas, as an indication of the tendencies of individuals and groups rather than as terms that define solidly boundaried groups.

8 L. Paul, *A Church by Daylight: A Reappraisement of the Church of England and its Future* (London: Geoffrey Chapman, 1973), p. 22.

9 M. Furlong, *C of E: The State It's In* (London: Hodder & Stoughton, 2000), p. 51.

10 R. Hooker (1648), *Of the Laws of Ecclesiastical Polity* (A. McGrade (ed.); Book 1 and Book 8; Cambridge: Cambridge University Press, 1989), p. 130.

11 E. Sandys, cited in P. McGrath, *Papists and Puritans Under Elizabeth I* (London: Blandford Press, 1967), p. 1.

12 See W. Hudson, 'Who Are the Baptists?', *BQ* 16/7 (1955–6), pp. 305–12, and E. Payne, 'Who were the Baptists? (A Comment)', *BQ* 16/8 (1955–6), pp. 339–42 (342).

13 See W. Klaassen, *Anabaptism in Outline: Selected Primary Resources* (Scottdale: Herald Press, 1981).

14 See H. Bender, 'The Anabaptists and Religious Liberty in the 16th Century', *MQR* 29/2 (1955), pp. 83–100.

15 B. White, *The English Baptists of the Seventeenth Century* (London: Baptist Historical Society, 1983), p. 31.

16 C. Hill, *The World Turned Upside Down: Radical Ideas During the Revolution* (Harmondsworth: Penguin, 1975).

17 B. White, *English Baptists of the Seventeenth Century*, p. 94.

18 C. Buchanan, *Cut the Connection*, pp. 19–23.

19 B. White, *English Baptists of the Seventeenth Century*, p. 132.

20 M. Furlong, *C of E*, p. 62.

21 'Comprehensive' in the sense of a broad inclusivity.

22 J. Locke, *A Letter Concerning Toleration* (London: Awnsham Churchill, 1689).

23 See R. Barlow, *Citizenship and Conscience: A Study of the Theory and Practice of Religious Toleration in England During the Eighteenth Century* (Philadelphia: University of Pennsylvania Press, 1962).

24 Cited in D. Sparkes, 'Test Act of 1673 and Its Aftermath', *BQ* 25/2 (1973), pp. 74–85 (84).

25 B. Manning, *The Protestant Dissenting Deputies* (Cambridge: Cambridge University Press, 1952).

26 C. Buchanan, *Cut the Connection*, pp. 23–32.

27 St John A. Robilliard, *Religion and The Law: Religious Liberty in Modern English Law* (Manchester: Manchester University Press, 1984), p. ix.

28 See *Census of Great Britain, 1851, Religious Worship. England and Wales* (London: George E. Eyre and William Spottiswoode, 1853) reprinted in *British Parliamentary Papers, Population 10* (Shannon, Ireland: Irish University Press, 1970).

29 M. Furlong, *C of E*, pp. 86–7.

30 See D. Bebbington, *The Nonconformist Conscience: Chapel and Politics, 1870–1914* (London: George Allen & Unwin, 1982), p. 30.

31 See J. Murphy, *Church, State and Schools in Britain, 1800–1970* (London: Routledge & Kegan Paul, 1971).

32 C. Buchanan, *Cut the Connection*, p. 33.

33 C. Buchanan, *Cut the Connection*, pp. 33–45.

34 Cited in S. Lamont, *Church and State: Uneasy Alliances* (London: Bodley Head, 1989), p. 185.

35 C. Garbett, *The Claims of the Church of England* (London: Hodder & Stoughton, 1947), p. 196.

36 C. Garbett, *Church and State in England* (London: Hodder & Stoughton, 1950), p. 140.

37 M. Furlong, *C of E*, p. 237.

38 C. Buchanan, *Cut the Connection*, pp. 45–9.

39 J. Wolffe, ' "And There's Another Country …" ', p. 93.

40 The Selborne Commission, *Report of the Archbishops' Committee on Church and State* (London: SPCK, 1916).

41 The Cecil Commission, *Report of the Archbishops' Commission on the Relations Between Church and State* (London: Press and Publications Board, 1935).

42 The Moberley Commission, *Church and State: Being the Report of a Commission Appointed by the Church Assembly in June 1949* (London: Church Information Board of the Church Assembly, 1952).

43 The Chadwick Commission, *Church and State*.

44 P. Cornwell, *Church and Nation: The Case for Disestablishment* (London: Blackwell, 1983).

45 V. Pitt, 'The Protection of Faith', in T. Modood (ed.), *Church, State and Religious Minorities*

(London: Policy Studies Institute, 1997), pp. 36–9, and 'The Church by Law Established', in K. Leech (ed.), *Setting the Church of England Free: The Case for Disestablishment* (Croydon: Jubilee Group, 2001), pp. 48–58.

46 T. Hobson, *Against Establishment*, p. xi.

47 K. Leech, 'Introduction', in K. Leech (ed.), *Setting the Church of England Free*, p. 5.

48 K. Leech, letter, *The Guardian*, 9.1.2003.

49 G. Carey, 'A Church for the Nation', *This Church of England* (1994), pp. 4–5.

50 Reported in *The Guardian*, 9.7.2002.

51 Reported in *The Sunday Times*, 27.1.2002.

52 Church in Wales Press Release, 27.1.2002.

53 The terminology of 'covenantal voluntarism' is used here in preference to the more frequently used 'voluntarism'. This is on the basis that within the Baptist vision, a balanced understanding of the nature of the Church calls for an emphasis both on the voluntary nature of Christian belonging, and also its mutually binding obligations, with both of these being rooted in a recognition of the divine grace that understands them both and to which they are both a response.

Chapter 2

ALTERNATIVE THEOLOGIES AND ECCLESIOLOGIES
OF RELIGION(S), STATE AND SOCIETY

1. *The Roots and Distinctive Notes of the Baptist Vision*

a. *Establishment: Baptist and Free Church Responses*

Aside from the Prayer Book crisis, during most of the twentieth century there was often a tendency on the part of both supporters and critics of establishment to downplay its contemporary significance. But as we have seen in Chapter 1, during the nineteenth century extremely vigorous social and theological debates had taken place about the adequacy and appropriateness of established religion.

At that time, most of the pressure of change came from the Free Church, non-conformist traditions of Christianity. In contrast to this, for most of the twentieth century, it is noteworthy that nonconformist leaders and theologians have not criticized establishment so much and some, indeed, even began to speak out in its defence. As previously noted, this change may partly have been informed by the perception that the civic disabilities of the earlier centuries had become largely something of the past. It may also have been influenced by a growing perception of the common challenges to Christianity from secularism and the numerical decline experienced by all the Christian Churches in England and the UK, whether established or not. Although establishment has occasionally still been seen as an intra-Christian ecumenical impediment, Wolffe observes that:

> The Roman Catholics and the Free Churches appeared to regard it as an imper-
> tinence to press the point. Indeed, there often seemed a readiness to accept the
> establishment of the Church of England as a means to exercise a particular kind
> of ministry to the nation, on behalf of the wider Christian Church.[1]

For example, in the early 1960s, R. K. Orchard wrote an article addressing the issue of how far people in the Free Church traditions needed to take the 1662 Church settlement into account in the context of contemporary ecumenical Christian relations. He posed the question, 'Would we really welcome the disestablishment of the Church of England? Would we be wise if we did? Do we really consider that the severance of an official relationship between church and state would benefit the influence of the gospel on the life of our people as a nation?' Overall, he argued that these issues should be 'put in a new setting – not in the setting of an argument within Christendom – the setting in which all our present ecclesiologies arose – but in the setting of a world which does not know who is the source of true life; in short, in a missionary setting'.[2]

More recently, Bernard Thoroughgood of the United Reformed Church argued that, 'The responsibility of the national church is never self-preservation but a continuous watchman's role to alert the nation on behalf of those who can only raise a small voice themselves.'[3] At the same time, Thoroughgood had to acknowledge the gap between aspiration and reality in this respect when he noted that, 'Past history is not happy at this point.' Arguments for the retention of a minimal establishment on the basis of the Church of England fulfilling a particular ministry to the nation have also been advanced by the Roman Catholic Church historian Adrian Hastings.[4]

Some Free Church figures, such as the former Baptist Union President, Nigel Wright,[5] have, however, continued to press an alternative perspective derived from the Free Church tradition. It is such an alternative perspective that is also at the heart of the argument of this book. This is that there remain significant theological resources within the Free Church Christian traditions. It is with this alternative, Free Church, source of theological and ecclesiological history and vision that the present chapter is concerned. In particular, it draws upon the Baptist tradition, which, although relatively small in the UK, in global terms constitutes a very substantially sized Christian tradition.[6]

b. *The Main 'Streams' of Baptist History and Vision*
As the American Baptist theologian H. Moody puts it, 'In the evolution of the Christian community and in the spread of the Christian vision, various people chose different messages and emphases out of Christian doctrine and teaching, to lift up and on occasion to absolutise.'[7] Two central themes or key 'notes' of the Baptist tradition will be highlighted as forming the basis for envisioning a more appropriate configuration for the relationships between religion(s), state and society in England and the UK than that of establishment.

In highlighting these distinctive 'notes' of the Baptist vision of Christian theology and practice it is not being claimed that these are the *exclusive* property of the Baptist tradition. Such 'notes' can also be present to varying degrees in other traditions. However, within the Baptist tradition they do not just reflect the positions identified with a range of individuals or with particular groups within the tradition. Rather, they have been relatively *constant*, forming what the Baptist theologian and Principal of Regent's Park College, Oxford, Paul Fiddes, has recently described by the metaphor of 'tracks'. As Fiddes explains, 'To use this metaphor of the heritage of a Church community implies that there are pathways trodden in the past which still have defined meaning and relevance for the present, and for which the technical term is "tradition".'[8]

The two key themes focused on here are, first, a theologically rooted commitment to religious liberty and, second, an ecclesiology of 'covenantal voluntarism'. These themes, along with others, lie at the heart of the Baptist vision of Christianity and its particular refraction of the Christian vision as it emerges from a varied denominational history, and it is to the highlights of this history that we now turn.

The roots of the present-day organizational structure of the Baptist Union of Great Britain and Ireland date from a meeting of Calvinist Baptists which was held in Carter Lane Baptist Church, Tooley Street, Southwark, on Thursday, 25 June 1812, when a Particular Baptist Society was formed. In 1813 this became a 'Union of Baptist ministers and churches with Calvinistic doctrine and Congregational polity'. However, the present Union embraces not only the Calvinistic or 'Particular' Baptists, but also a 'General' Baptist stream that did not hold to a 'particular' atonement. In 1891, the General Baptists joined together with the previously existing Particular Baptist Union to create the ecclesial organization that is in continuity with the present-day Baptist Union.

The 'General Baptists' were the earlier of the two groups. They can trace their origins back to the Separatist congregation that, in 1606, began to meet in the home of Thomas Helwys. Helwys was a Nottinghamshire gentleman who, along with John Smyth, became one of the *Kirchenvater* of English Baptist life. Smyth was a Cambridge scholar and had been the Anglican Chaplain to the City of London. The congregation that they founded was constituted in 1606 or 1607 through the so-called 'Gainsborough Covenant'. According to the terms of this covenant as recorded later by William Bradford, its members 'joined themselves (by a covenant of the Lord) into a Church estate, in the fellowship of the Gospel to walk in all his ways, made known, or to be made known unto them, according to their best endeavours, whatsoever it should cost them, the Lord assisting.'[9]

With James I's accession to the throne, the congregation migrated to Amsterdam, where they developed contacts with the Waterlander Mennonites. In 1609, Smyth baptized himself and then the others of the group including Helwys. However, tensions developed as Smyth moved closer to the Mennonites and, under their influence, questioned the validity of his 'se-baptism'. Eventually a split occurred with the majority following Smyth, while Helwys and a smaller group continued to hold that they were an authentic Church and did not need to be in the sucession of the Mennonites in order to have a true baptism or ordination.

In 1611, Helwys' group drew up a *Confession of Faith* that became one of the basic Baptist confessions. Smyth died in 1612 and the majority of his group then joined the Mennonites, while Helwys and his group returned to England to found a church in Spitalfields, London. Helwys died in 1616, and little is then known about the history of his underground church apart from some materials that are available in Mennonite archives. But by 1644, at least 47 General Baptist congregations were in existence.

The 'Particular' Baptists sprang out of the Separatist congregations of 1630s London. As Barrie White says, 'The Calvinistic Baptists first appeared as a self-conscious group with the publication of their 1644 London Confession. This was to provide the basic theological platform for their programme of evangelism, church-planting, and organization of associations for the years down to the Restoration.'[10] The 1644 Confession was signed by representatives of seven congregations. It was basically a defence of Calvinistic orthodoxy, except that ministers were subordinated to the congregation, church and state were seen as separate and baptism was reserved to believers. This last article of faith appears to have grown out of the experience of Henry Jacob's congregation in London.

This congregation did not totally repudiate its connection with the Anglican Church but, by 1630, its members were questioning the baptism of their children in the parish church. Samuel Eaton was then baptized as a believer, and in 1640 Richard Blunt also raised a question about the appropriateness of baptismal mode in terms of a debate between 'dipping' or full immersion in water, and 'effusion' or sprinkling with water. Smyth's se-baptism in Amsterdam had been 'out of a basin' and not by total immersion. Blunt was sent to confer with believer-baptists in the Netherlands and, on his return in 1642, he baptized a number of people as believers by full immersion in water.

In the eighteenth century, much of the original General Baptist stream moved in the direction of Rationalism, Deism and Socinianism. In reaction to this, and influenced by the Evangelical Revival, in 1770 the Yorkshire General Baptist Dan Taylor (1738–1816) led a group of General Baptists to form the New Connexion of General Baptists. Through the influence of Andrew Fuller, the Particular Baptists also underwent a renewal that brought Particular Baptists closer to other Christians in the Evangelical tradition. However, it also led to disputes over the issue of whether the Communion Table should be open only to those who had been baptized on profession of faith. As a result of this a number of Baptist congregations that held to the 'closed table' withdrew from the Particular Baptist Associations and formed a Strict Baptist grouping. The remainder of the old General Baptists continued in existence into the twentieth century having very little contact with the mainstream of Baptists. They mostly co-operated with the Presbyterians and, although some joined the Baptist Union in 1916, the rest finally became a part of the Unitarian Church.

c. *The Key 'Notes' of Baptist Christianity*
It is from this diverse history and tradition, with its differing organizational structures and varied theological and ecclesiological emphases, that a number of constant and distinctive or key 'notes' of the Baptist vision of Christianity may be identified. For the sake of clarity, rather than as a claim to an exhaustive and absolutely precise definition, the author has previously[11] grouped these 'notes' under five shorthand headings: (i) the primacy of the scriptures (ii) liberty of conscience and religious practice (iii) the Church as a fellowship of believers (iv) the centrality of Christian witness and (v) the importance of discipleship. It is arguable that these 'notes' cohere together in a mutually reinforcing way, but for the purposes of this chapter and this book, the primary focus will be upon the second and third of the identified 'notes'.

In many ways the Baptist movement was what might today be described as a 'Restorationist' one. This is because it was seeking to recreate the original shape of the Church before what was seen as its Constantinian degeneration. Rather than allowing the Church to govern itself according to its scriptural foundation documents, secular rulers were seen as having attempted to order the life of the Church according to their own priorities. This, of course, had been the central issue at stake between the Puritans and the Elizabethan church polity that gave rise to the Separatism from which the earliest Baptist congregations sprang.

Such an approach to ecclesiology was, at the same time, undergirded by a general position that the scriptures were to be interpreted according to a predominantly Christological and soteriological hermeneutic. This approach accorded a relative primacy to the writings of the New Testament. This, in turn, was at least partly responsible for leading Baptists away from an attempt to recreate the theocratic patterns of the Old Testament. It thus reinforced a differentiation between the Church and the social order, and also provided a basis for seeking the restitution of what was believed to be a New Testament pattern of church life. This ecclesiological approach will be explored in greater detail later in the chapter. But such an understanding of the Church also rests upon a theologically prior conviction concerning the importance of religious liberty. It is therefore to the tradition's affirmation of faith as freely chosen and personally affirmed that this chapter first of all turns.

2. *A Theological Commitment to Religious Liberty*

a. *Religious Liberty: A Baptist 'Universal'*

The 'note' of the Baptist vision that is concerned with religious liberty is, in fact, the nearest to a Baptist 'universal' principle, affirmed by Baptists in all times and places, that can be found. In his study on *Protestantism and Progress*, Ernst Troeltsch, while acknowledging the rationalistic and utilitarian sources of the idea of toleration, also argued that its 'real foundations', especially in England, were to be found in the 'revived Anabaptist and Spiritualist movements, in combination with Calvinism of a radical tendency'.[12] In similar vein, in the course of the authoritative survey on *The Development of Religious Toleration in England*, W. Jordan argued that, 'The great Baptist apologists had made profoundly important contributions to the theory of religious toleration. They had systematised the thought of their predecessors and had broken new ground in their examination of the forces which had for so many centuries made religious devotion synonymous with religious bigotry.'[13]

In his article on 'The English Baptist Doctrine of Religious Toleration' Timothy George explained that 'In seeking to define themselves over against the radically pacifistic Anabaptists on the one hand, and the more "magisterially" orientated dissenters on the other, the first generation of General Baptists in England made a lasting contribution to the debate on coercion, toleration and religious liberty.'[14] Although this Baptist principle contributed towards the development of social, political and legal arguments for religious toleration, the Baptist vision was itself primarily concerned with a *theologically* rooted understanding of religious liberty.

It was therefore a position born neither of religious indifferentism nor of agnosticism, but rather was rooted in a positive conviction about the nature of faith and belief, and was based on a profound trust in the work of the Holy Spirit to further the truth without need for coercive measures. Furthermore, this principle of religious liberty was intimately related to a particular understanding of the nature of Christian existence and Christian community as a free, responsible and chosen destiny, rather than something which is either imposed, assumed or merely inherited. Thus George observed that, '... the Baptist idea of toleration was born out of the experience of persecution and martyrdom. This in itself did not make Baptists unique. Oppressed sects had long argued for their right to religious toleration.

What set the Baptists apart was the explicit avowal of universal religious tolera-tion.'[15]

Such an understanding was the result of pushing the logic of Separatism to its conclusion. The development of such a logic can be illustrated in the story of John Smyth's individual religious pilgrimage. In 1605, while a Puritan lecturer in London, Smyth wrote *The Patterne of True Prayer* in which he argued that:

> When there is toleration of many religions, whereby the kingdom of God is shouldered out of doors by the devil's kingdom: for without question the devil is so subtle that he will procure, through the advantage of man's natural inclina-tion to false doctrine and worship, more by thousands to follow strange religions than the truth of God's word: wherefore the magistrates should cause all men to worship the true God, or else punish them with imprisonment, confiscation of goods, or death as the quality of the cause requireth.[16]

By his 1609 *The Character of the Beast*, there were signs of a change in Smyth's position. He began to argue against infant baptism and, by the time he published his 1611 *Confession*, he was arguing that:

> The magistrate is not by virtue of his office to meddle with religion, or matters of conscience, to force and compel men to this or that form of religion: but to leave Christian religion free, to every man's conscience, and to handle only civil transgressions (Romans 13), injuries, and wrongs of men against man, in murder, adultery, theft etc, for Christ only is the king and lawgiver of the church and conscience (James 4 v. 12).[17]

b. *Classical Baptist Articulations of Religious Liberty*

In 1612 Thomas Helwys published *A Short Declaration of the Mystery of Iniquity*.[18] In an article on Helwys and this pamphlet, F. Clouts observed that, 'The Mystery of Iniquity was the first fully-developed defence of the theory of complete separ-ation of church and state to appear in England in the English language.'[19] There had been earlier advocates of toleration, such as Jacobus Ancontius; Sir Thomas Moore in his *Utopia*; John Hooper, the Bishop of Gloucester during the reign of Edward VI; and the Protestant (possibly Calvinist) lawyer Alberico Gentili (1552–1608). However, after surveying the history of the various contributions to development of religious toleration, it was Jordan's judgement that:

> Helwys gave to religious toleration the finest and fullest defence which it had ever received in England, if we except the thought of Jacobus Ancontius. And when we recall that Ancontius' work had been an isolated apology by a detatched observer, while Helwys drew his inspiration from the underlying religious philosophy of the sect of which he was a member, and gave to that sect a missionary impulse which was to fix its roots firmly in England, it would seem probable that his work was of greater historical significance than that of his predecessor.[20]

Helwys' book was addressed to King James with the intention of persuading him that restriction and coercion in matters of religion were contrary to Scripture. While affirming the King's temporal powers, Helwys did not plead with him about religious liberty so much as throw down a challenge to him on the question. This can clearly be seen from Helwys' inscription on a flyleaf of the copy of the book that was addressed to King James I in which, while ending with the words

'God save the King', Helwys addressed James in extremely robust manner stating
in plain and challenging words that:

> Hear O King and despise not the counsel of the poor, and let their complaints
> come before thee. The King is a mortal man and not God therefore hath no power
> over the immortal souls of his subjects to make laws and ordinances for them
> and to set Spiritual Lords over them. If the King have authority to make Spiritual
> Lords and Laws then he is an immortal God and not a mortal man. O King, be not
> seduced by deceivers to sin against God whom thou oughtest to obey, nor against
> thy poor subjects who ought and will obey thee in all things with body, life and
> goods or else let their lives be taken from the earth. God save the King.[21]

Helwys believed that religious coercion could become an excuse for people to try
and circumvent their individual responsibility and conscience. He also believed
magistrates and kings committed a grave sin when they forced the conscience of
an individual or group. Thus he eloquently argued:

> O Let the King judge is it not most equal, that men should choose their religion
> themselves seeing they only must stand themselves before the judgment seat of
> God to answer for themselves, when it shall be no excuse for them to say, we were
> commanded or compelled to be of this religion, by the king, or by them that had
> authority from him.[22]

Helwys paid for his courage and convictions with the loss of his liberty and finally
with his life. However, his early advocacy of religious liberty was soon followed
by other Baptists. In 1614, Leonard Busher published *Religion's Peace*,[23] described
as 'presented to King James and the High Court of Parliament then sitting, by
Leonard Busher, citizen of London', the title of which continued with the words:
*Wherein is Contained Certain Reasons against Persecution for Religion: Also a
design for a peaceable reconciling of those that differ in opinion.*

Busher argued that, 'if the believing should persecute the unbelieving to death,
Who should remain alive?'[24] It was his conviction that, '... persecution for difference in religion is a monstrous and cruel beast, that destroyeth both prince and
people, hindereth the gospel of Chist, and scattereth his disciples that witness and
profess his name'.[25] In 1615, this was followed by *Persecution for Religion Judg'd
and Condemn'd in a Discourse between an AntiChristian and a Christian*,[26]
and in 1620 by *An Humble Supplication to the King, Prince Charles and the
Parliament*[27] (thought to be authored by John Murton).

Murton's *An Humble Supplication* had an impact that crossed the Atlantic and
informed the history that, eventually, led to the constitutional entrenchment of
religious freedom in the United States of America. Roger Williams, who became
a Baptist and founded the first Baptist church in North America, used Murton's
pamphlet as a preface to his own, 1644, classic work on religious liberty, *The
Bloudy Tenent of Persecution for Cause of Conscience Discussed in a Conference
Between Truth and Peace*. Williams maintained that 'the blood of so many
hundred thousand souls of Protestants and papists, spilled in the wars of present
and former ages for their respective consciences, is not required or accepted by
Jesus Christ, the Prince of Peace'.[28] In further developing his position, Williams
put it thus in uncompromising words:

it is the will and command of God that, since the coming of his Son, the Lord
Jesus, a permission of the most Paganish, Jewish, Turkish or anti-Christian consciences and worships be granted to all men in all nations and countries: and that
they are to be fought against with the sword which is only, in soul matters, able
to conquer: to wit, the sword of God's spirit, the word of God.[29]

In terms of both theology and the practicalities of state, Williams argued that, 'true
civility and Christianity may both flourish in a state or kingdom, notwithstanding
the permission of diverse and contrary consciences, either of Jew or Gentile'.[30] By
contrast, Williams maintained that 'an enforced uniformity of religion throughout
a nation or a civil state confounds the civil and religious, denies the principles of
Christianity and civility, and that Jesus Christ is come in the flesh'.[31]

c. *Development of the Arguments for Religious Liberty*
The kind of perspective on religious liberty which contributed to the development
of religious freedom in North America, and was expressed by Roger Williams'
writing and work, also continued in England even following the Restoration of the
Monarchy and of the Church of England. In 1660, four Baptists from Kent (James
Blackmore, George Hammon, William Jeffrey and John Reve) issued from prison,
*An Humble Petition and Representation of the Sufferings of Several Peaceable
and Innocent Subjects Called by the Name of Anabaptists*. In this, they pointed up
the absurdity of requiring religion to mirror the position taken by rulers:

Thus, if we had lived in Turkey we must receive the Koran, and be a worshipper
of Mahomet; if in Spain, be a papist; in England, sometimes a papist, as in Henry
Eighth's days, a Protestant in Edward Sixth's, a papist again in Queen Mary's, and
a Protestant again in Queen Elizabeth's. And so for ever, as the authority changes
religion, must we do the same. But God forbid.[32]

Such an outlook was something not found only among individual Baptists, but
was also reflected in the Confessions produced by groups of Baptist churches.
Thus in the 1660 *General Baptist Confession* that was written in the light of the
Restoration of the Monarchy, article 24 argues:

That it is the will, and the mind of God (in these gospel times) that all men should
have the free liberty of their own conscience in matters of Religion, or Worship,
without the least oppression, or persecution, as simply on that account; and that
for any authority otherwise to act, we confidently believe is expressly contrary to
the mind of Christ who requires that whatsoever men would that others do unto
them, they should even so do unto others. Mat 7.12. and that the Tares and Wheat
should grow together in the field (which is the world) until the harvest (which is
the end of the world). Mat. 13.29, 30, 38, 29.[33]

Among the Particular Baptists, the 1677 *Confession of Faith* contained chapter 21,
'Of Christian Liberty and Liberty of Conscience'. While this had a more 'interior'
perspective than the clause from the 1660 *General Baptist Confession* quoted
above, it did state clearly that 'God alone is Lord of the Conscience'.[34] In the 1678
Orthodox Creed or a Protestant Confession of Faith, article 46 was 'Of Liberty
and Conscience'.[35]

d. *Religious Liberty 'Without Limits'*

Remarkably for their times, the early Baptists did not apply this element of their vision only to the diversities of Christian belief. For example, Thomas Helwys held to the position, astonishing for his seventeenth-century context, that freedom of religious conscience should also extend beyond the borders of Christianity, when he declared that:

> Our Lord the King is but an earthly king and he hath no authority as a King but in earthly causes, and if the King's people be obedient and true subjects, obeying all humane laws made by the King, our Lord the King can require no more: for men's religion to God, is betwixt God and themselves: the King shall not answer for it, neither may the King be judge between God and man. Let them be heretics, Turks, Jews, or whatsoever it appertains not to the earthly power to punish them in the least measure.[36]

Although this call for liberty for Jews, Turks and heretics is certainly startling it was not, in fact, entirely new. As Ernest Payne asked in making his case for an Anabaptist influence on the development of the English Baptists: 'Where did Helwys learn the things he set out in the *Mistery of Iniquity*? His references to Turks and Jews suggest a continental background.'[37]

The continental Anabaptist movement, with which the English Baptists had contact through their links with the Waterlander Mennonites of the Netherlands, had come into public light with the Zurich Disputation between Zwingli and Grebel. As the Anabaptist movement developed, the renunciation of the sword in religious matters came to be firmly fixed within its tradition. In 1534, Kilian Aurbacher, the Moravian Anabaptist, had written to Bucer in Strasbourg arguing in terms that seem to prefigure Helwys' terminology that, 'It is never right to compel one in matters of faith, whatever he may believe, be he Jew or Turk.'[38]

Although there is an ongoing debate within Baptist and Mennonite historiography as to the precise relationship between the Anabaptists and the English Baptist movement, the structural and linguistic similarities between Aurbacher's and Helwys' arguments are striking. They suggest that, at least with regard to religious liberty, English Baptist tradition stands in some degree of continuity with Anabaptist tradition. In addition, as the English Baptist historian W. Whitley pointed out, Helwys' call was not without a practical political model to point to since:

> In various parts of the continent there was toleration of diverse opinions; Transylvania, Poland, France with its Edict of Nantes; in the Netherlands there was not even an Established Church, much as the Dutch Reformed sought Establishment. James might see the incongruity of one form of government being established in Scotland, and another in England; he might be convinced that the solution was not uniformity, but disestablishment, liberty of conscience.[39]

Leonard Busher's *Religion's Peace*, as well as basing its arguments on theological and ecclesiological grounds, also challenged Christians by reference to historical descriptions of the Muslim treatment of both Christians and Jews in Constantinople. Thus Busher pointed out that:

> I read that a bishop of Rome would have constrained a Turkish emperor to the Christian faith, unto whom the emperor answered, 'I believe that Christ was an

excellent prophet, but he did never, so far as I understand, command that men should, with the power of weapons be constrained to believe his law: and verily I also do force no man to Mahomet's law.' And I read that Jews, Christians, and Turks are tolerated in Constantinople, and yet are peaceable, though so contrary the one to the other.[40]

From citing this practical example, Busher went on to use it in order to press the point by comparison upon the Christians of his time that:

If this be so, how much more ought Christians not to force one another to religion. AND HOW MUCH MORE OUGHT CHRISTIANS TO TOLERATE CHRISTIANS, WHEN THE TURKS DO TOLERATE THEM? SHALL WE BE LESS MERCIFUL THAN THE TURKS? OR SHALL WE LEARN THE TURKS TO PERSECUTE CHRISTIANS? IT IS NOT ONLY UNMERCIFUL, BUT UNNATURAL AND ABOMINABLE. YEA, MONSTROUS FOR ONE CHRISTIAN TO VEX AND DESTROY ANOTHER FOR DIFFERENCE AND QUESTIONS OF RELIGION. (capitalization in the original)

While the early Baptist commitment to the religious freedom of Jews and Turks was remarkable for its times, it could be argued that this might have been because, in the context of seventeenth-century England, these groups posed little immediate threat to the freedom and existence of Baptist Christians. However, the depth and tenacity of the Baptist commitment to religious freedom can be seen in their general determination to include Roman Catholics among those entitled to such freedom.

To understand the full significance of the Baptist position in this regard, it must be realized that English Protestants in general feared a possible ecclesiastical restoration of the Roman Catholic Church that they believed would threaten their own liberty. They also shared in a widespread perception that Roman Catholics were basically disloyal to the country and were thus seen as potential subversives. When one adds to this the substantial theological divergences between these two ecclesial bodies, then the fact that Baptists by and large remained true to their principles by including Roman Catholics within their stand for religious liberty is an item of convincing evidence concerning the theological grounding of these convictions.

There were some exceptions to this general rule. These included, for example, Christopher Blackwood, who made a proviso to his 1644 statement on religious liberty. This was to the effect that the godly ruler may, if Roman Catholics begin to outnumber others, 'command some of them out of the kingdom' for the safety of the nation. For those that remain, he also argued that the ruler 'may take such securement of them in point of arms, that they may be sure never to make any head'.[41] Also, in 1659, the noted Baptist theologian Jacob Tombs declared that he was against the toleration of Popery. However, even taking full account of such individual positions, George's study of the Baptist doctrine of toleration stressed that, 'These quotations should not be taken as representative of a major shift in the Baptist view of toleration. They clearly are exceptions to the larger Baptist consensus that continued to advocate unrestricted religious liberty.'[42]

The re-establishment of Roman Catholic dioceses in England in 1850, coupled with the rise of the Oxford Movement in the Church of England, led to fresh outbursts of anti-papal agitation and to fears that the civil government could no longer guarantee the Protestantism of England. In this situation, as Anne-Marie Petty-John LeBarbour argued in her doctoral thesis on 'Victorian Baptists: a Study in Denominational Development':

> While Baptists opposed Roman Catholicism as fanatically as any other group, they also opposed legal harassment. The Baptist Union formulated the official position: the delegates stated their abhorrence of the doctrinal and practical elements of the Roman system, but maintained that they had no desire for legal interference.[43]

An individual example of this apparent paradox can be found in Benjamin Evans' book *Modern Popery: A Series of Letters on Some of its More Important Aspects.* In the Preface to this book Evans explained that, while he 'is second to none in his unmingled hatred of their doctrines', nevertheless, 'to the civil rights of Romanists he is still an unwavering friend'.[44] In arguing against Catholic doctrine and beliefs Evans used extreme terminology at the level of doctrinal dispute that, 'To repress, to overthrow, entirely to annihilate deadly error, is the duty of all who love humanity, and the interests of truth and righteousness.' At the same time, he also argued that any approach taken to Catholics themselves, as people, should be undertaken only 'by moral means'.[45]

e. *Tensions: Religious Liberty and Religious Truth*

Of course, in practice it is not so straightforward to separate out ideological dispute and social civility. In addition, as evidenced in the conduct of the nineteenth-century 'Downgrade Controversy'[46] among Baptists, it has all too often been the case that affirmation of religious freedom for all in the wider society has not been matched by support for such freedom in the internal life of the Baptist movement and its congregations. As the Baptist theologian H. Wheeler Robinson acknowledged, 'Liberty within is a more difficult attainment than liberty without. Prejudices which we nurture within our own hearts are more subtle and dangerous than those whose folly and injustice we can see plainly when they belong to others.'[47] As M. Jordan highlighted in a reference to Thomas Helwys' *A Short Declaration of The Mistery of Iniquity*, although this contains a remarkably clear and prophetic plea for the religious liberty of Jews, Turks, heretics and all kinds of Christians, at the same time the same it:

> expressly dooms to everlasting perdition every man who had ever held the name, office or power of a bishop who had died without repenting of his error, every Puritan who remained in the Church of England, every Separatist who defended infant baptism, in short, everyone who in any single particular departed from the Divinely appointed Apostolic government of the Church.[48]

Thus, although it is argued that this 'note' of Baptist tradition is highly relevant and of great importance for the contemporary configuration of religion(s), state and society, in terms of its application to the internal life of the Church, the Baptist tradition is itself in need of ecumenical modification. But it remains significant that even in so sharp a critique of Catholic doctrine as that offered by Evans, the principle of religious freedom in society is still strongly advocated.

It is precisely because it sits alongside a passionate concern with religious truth and a strong impulse to bear witness to that truth that the centrality of the religious liberty element of the Baptist vision can be seen to be so important. Thus the Vision/Mission Statement of the global Baptist World Alliance contains a clause that gives expression to the commitment of its affiliated Baptist Unions and Conventions throughout the world to a theologically based affirmation of religious liberty when it clearly states that the Alliance shall uphold the claims of fundamental human rights '... including full religious liberty'.[49]

f. *Religious (and Other) Liberty and Toleration*
In the introduction to the book *Puritanism and Liberty*, A. Woodhouse maintained that 'the amazing importance of the struggle for religious liberty is due partly to the momentous issue with which it deals; but beyond that is the fact that it holds, as it were in solution, within itself all the rest of the struggle for liberty and equality'.[50] This connection between advocacy of religious liberty and other struggles for liberty can be seen in the social politics of such leading eighteenth-century Baptists as Robert Hall. Against the background of Napoleonic scares of the late eighteenth century, Hall wrote a number of radical works with titles such as *Christianity Consistent With a Love of Freedom*[51] and *An Apology for the Freedom of the Press and For General Liberty.*[52]

Although the struggle of Baptists together with other disadvantaged religious groups did lead to religious toleration in the social and political spheres, the goal was always that of liberty that went beyond a merely pragmatic and grudging toleration. The fundamental basis of the Baptist vision of religious liberty has always been a religious one. In contrast to mere toleration, religious liberty is something wider. As Philip Crannell maintained in an article on 'Tolerance and Company':

> The application of this principle of liberty is universal. Confucian, Mohammedan, Theosophist, 'Scientist', Agnostic, Fundamentalist, Modernist, Animist, Bahaist, Sunnite, Buddhist, Jew, Christian, Shintoist, Taoist (God of heaven, what a Babel!) – each single man of them, and one just as much as the other, entitled, as a matter of absolute right – not concession, permission, toleration – to a fair field 'and no favour', in the holding, maintenance, and advocacy of religion or non-religion.[53]

For the Baptist vision, the promotion of religious freedom has been, and is, a theologically grounded conviction and practice. While the promotion of religious liberty has opened up possibilities for religious toleration, the commitment to religious liberty is basically different from toleration. While in many social contexts toleration represents a significant advance, it continues to reserve to itself the right not to recognize other groups, and in fact, sometimes exercises this option. Toleration implies retention of imbalances in religious power and tends to be based upon political pragmatism rather than theological principle. In addition, as the Mennonite writer Harold Bender pointed out, it can be the product of religious indifferentism:

> It is a deeply disturbing fact that the victory for toleration in the seventeenth, eighteenth, and nineteenth centuries was to a large degree due not to the will of the dominant Christian Churches, Catholic or Protestant, but to the will of rulers exhausted by religious wars and determined to find a basis for peace in the European community which would transcend the warring religious parties;

or to the growing rationalism, secularism and materialism of the politically ever
more powerful upper middle class, which placed religion low in the scale of
cultural values and, in the words of Frederick the Great, was quite willing to
have everyone 'saved after his own fashion' – or in the words of Theodore Beza
a century and a half earlier, 'to go to hell in his own fashion'.[54]

The strength of the Baptist vision of religious liberty is that it is not a product
of religious indifference. Rather, it is theologically based. As a contemporary
theological resource, the Baptist tradition's commitment to religious freedom thus
provides a basis for Christian acceptance of the fact of religious plurality understood as a theological imperative. This contrasts with the approach of granting
recognition of such plurality merely as a grudging concession consequent upon
increasing pluralization of the social context and the privatization of religion.
The Baptist vision of a *theologically* grounded commitment to religious freedom
enables the possibility of maintaining distinctive and passionately held religious
convictions alongside a deep concern for the promotion of the religious rights of
others.

3. *An Ecclesiology of 'Covenantal Voluntarism'*

a. *A Critique and Alternative to Christendom*
The second distinctive note of the Baptist refraction of the Christian vision that
is highlighted in this book relates to the tradition's approach to ecclesiology. As
Hugh Martin's article on 'Protestantism and the State' points out, 'From the days
of Constantine onwards Church and State were not two societies, but two aspects
of one society, and Emperors and Popes were rival authorities within it.'[55] The
theological grounding of the idea of religious liberty challenged the medieval syn-
thesis of church and society embodied in the concept of the *corpus christianum*.
The meaning of this concept is clearly explained in Dale Brown's article on the
contemporary relevance of the radical Reformation, where Brown wrote that:

> This Latin phrase defines the medieval synthesis in which the Church and human
> society coincided numerically. The empire was regarded as holy; the church was
> the empire at prayer. The corpus christianum had emerged when the Emperor
> Constantine began to favour Christianity following three centuries of persecution.
> From the status of an illicit sect to a tolerated religion in the Edict of Milan in A.D.
> 313, Christianity became the only tolerated religion by 392 when the Emperor
> Theodosius forbade all pagan worship, public and private, under penalty of death.
> Unlike the traditional view espoused by Eusebius, which has seen Constantine's
> conversion as the glorious beginning of the Christianization of the world, the
> Radical Reformers located the fall of the Church in its alignment with the inter-
> ests of the State.[56]

But whereas the old ideal had been that of a universal Church, the new post-
Reformation Protestant one arose as a counterweight to papal power and took
shape in the form of a national Church with uniformity of practice and belief
(although there were exceptions to this, such as in Poland after the signing of the
Pax Desideratum of the Warsaw Confederation). In an article on 'The Struggle
for Religious Liberty', McGlothin points out about these Churches that, 'As in

the case of the Catholics infant baptism was retained as a means of making the Church and the State coterminous.'[57] McGlothin maintained that, with infant baptism, 'The primitive tribal or national conception of religion as the concern of society conquered Christianity, so that the defection of the individual in religious matters was equivalent to spiritual suicide for himself and the worst treason to society.'[58]

The Baptist vision of religious freedom, when coupled with the idea that the Church is a community of personally committed people who covenant together, challenged such a conception of the relationship between church and state. This vision also required a rejection of the principle and practice of *cujus regio, ejus religio*, being rooted in a vision of Christian existence as a free, responsible and chosen, and not a forcibly imposed or merely assumed destiny.

As noted in Chapter 1, among the 'Brownist' congregations of the mid-sixteenth century there had been English precursors to aspects of this Baptist vision. But, in Baptist theological vision and ecclesiological practice, the principle of a congregationally covenanted pattern of the Church was dramatically embodied by offering baptism only to those who could personally affirm their belief rather than to babies. The practice of believer's baptism symbolically undermined any geographical or social definition of the Church as a body that is co-terminal with a nation or state.

This was not primarily intended as a negative position, but rather it was intended to be an affirmation of a prior positive understanding of Christian existence as free, chosen and responsible. As Wheeler Robinson put it, in contesting infant baptism, Baptists have been 'testifying against much more than an isolated and relatively unimportant custom; they are testifying against the whole complex of ideas of which it was a symbol'.[59] Wheeler Robinson thus maintained that 'The Baptist stands or falls by his conception of what the Church is; his plea for baptism becomes a mere archaeological idiosyncrasy, if it be not the expression of the fundamental constitution of the Church.'[60]

b. 'Sectarian' Withdrawal?

One of the weaknesses of Baptist understandings of the Church is that they have sometimes resulted in a lack of engagement with the structures, responsibilities and concerns of the wider common life of society. However, it should be noted that this has historically been more of a danger to certain parts of the Anabaptist tradition than it was among mainstream English Baptists. Baptists and Anabaptists, for example, had a major divergence over the question of the office of the magistracy. The Anabaptist position was generally that a member of the Christian community could not hold the office of magistrate since this implied the use of the sword that Anabaptists viewed as being contrary to the Gospel imperatives concerned with leaving judgement to God. Baptists, on the other hand, allowed their members to hold the office of magistrate, while maintaining that they should not thereby become agents of compulsion in matters of conscience.

As George noted, 'This positive position on magistracy was reflected at three crucial points (1) a defence of the ethics of war (2) a recognition that coercion was the precondition of social order and religious toleration (3) a willingness to admit magistrates to church membership.'[61] By not seeing the exercise of 'the sword' of magisterial responsibility as incompatible with membership of the Christian Church, Baptists were affirming the importance of the involvement of Christians in matters of social and structural responsibility.

For example, Thomas Helwys had criticized the Dutch Mennonites for attacking the office of magistrate while living under the protection afforded by the Dutch rule of law, pointing out that this protection was lacking for many of their co-religionists in other countries. Referring to the Anabaptists' deliverance from the threat to their religious liberty posed by the Duke of Alva, Helwys wrote *An Advertisement or Admonition Unto the Congregations, which men call the New Fryelers in the Lowe Countries,* in which he argued that:

> Of all the people on earth none hath more cause, to be thankful to God for this blessed ordinance of Magistracy than you, and this whole country and nation, in that God hath by his power and authority given unto you magistrates who have so defended and delivered you from the hands of a cruel destroyer, and will you notwithstanding condemn this ordinance, and consider it a vile thing.[62]

What Baptists have generally rejected has been a state Church although, as in the case of their commitment to religious liberty, it should be noted that there have been some historical exceptions to the general rule. For example, Christopher Hill noted that, in the 1650s, Baptists were 'still quarrelling among themselves about the lawfulness of taking tithes – which means about the lawfulness of a state church; and some few Baptists had livings in, and acted as Triers for, the Cromwellian Church'.[63]

c. *Uniformity, Nonconformity and Disestablishmentarianism*

The restoration of the monarchy and the Act of Uniformity led to two centuries of rearguard action by those who wanted the old consensus to return. After the hiatus of the English Civil War, the Republic and the Protectorate, and during the post-Restoration years, this conception again reduced the social space of Roman Catholics and nonconformists. The Breda Declaration that preceded the Restoration contained a highly ambiguous affirmation of freedom 'for differences in matters of religion which do not disturb the general peace of the kingdom'. From 1660, the peace of the kingdom *was* perceived as being under threat, especially following the abortive Venner uprising of 1661, and so the freedom in principle afforded to difference in matters of religion was often, in reality, restricted by the constraints of political pragmatism.

Baptists were among the group of Dissenting Deputies of the nonconformist churches of London which was formed in 1732 to oppose the Test Act and the Corporation Act. But it was not until the nineteenth century that the great struggles for religious equality began to bring about significant changes in the status quo. As noted in the previous chapter, during the nineteenth century, together with other Dissenters, Baptists were in the forefront of the struggle for the abolition of religious discrimination. This struggle also included playing a major part in the campaign for the disestablishment of the Church of England. As a result of the extension of the political franchise, and the impact of this on electoral politics,

Baptists found that they could exercise a new political influence. They used this opportunity to move beyond the demand for a mere toleration to that of a full religious equality.

John Howard Hinton's motion at the 1838 Baptist Union public meeting led to the Baptist Union's first official avowal of the principle of 'voluntarism', and to the identification of the establishment of the Church of England as 'a violation of the law of Christ'.[64] LeBarbour says that during this period: 'Baptists viewed the extension of religious voluntarism throughout Britain as the primary political goal.'[65] Edward Steane, the Baptist Union General Secretary, became a founder member of the Church Rate Abolition Society and of the Religious Freedom Society. In 1844 a national conference of Baptists and other nonconformists formed the British Anti-State Church Association in which a number of leading Baptists were involved, including Joseph Angus and John Hinton.

In this context it is important to note that it was not only individual Baptists, even prominent ones, who were involved in these organizations. The Baptist Union itself also sent denominational representatives to such meetings. As Ernest Payne pointed out, 'it is not without significance that the Baptist Union, of which Hinton had then become co-Secretary, was the only representative body to send delegates to the conference held in London in April 1844, at which the British Anti-State Church Association was formed'.[66]

The Baptist commitment to the separation of church and state also spanned serious internal theological differences. For example, Charles Haddon Spurgeon, who was at the heart of the major internal conflict known as the 'Downgrade Controversy' that almost split the Baptist Union apart, allowed meetings of the Liberation Society to be held in the Metropolitan Tabernacle of which he was the minister. Spurgeon sent messages of support to their meetings even though he did later withdraw his support because he felt that the Society had become too secularized in its concerns.

In 1857, the Baptist newspaper *The Freeman* called the establishment of the Church of England 'the question of the time'[67] and urged that Dissenters should undertake earnest political work towards disestablishment. The first major focus of the disestablishment struggle was over the requirement to pay church rates. When the majority of parishioners present at a vestry meeting voted for their imposition, these rates were levied on all members of a parish for the upkeep of the parish church. Leading Baptists such as J. Mursell had been involved, in 1836, in the formation of the Voluntary Church Society that began to organize the struggle against the compulsory payment of such church rates.

LeBarbour's research reveals that, 'Petitions for the abolition of church rates were the most often passed political resolutions in the Baptist Union and the Associations' and that, 'Baptists worked through the Liberation Society to defeat church rates, sent delegates to a national conference held to oppose rates and their principal publications heartily supported abolition.'[68] Some Associations even advocated actions such as passive resistance. In 1853, the Braintree Rates Case established that a parish could not set rates against the will of its voters. In 1860 the Baptist Union sent a circular to all its congregations seeking support for a petition against church rates. In 1868, a Bill for the abolition of the compulsory collection of church rates was finally passed by Parliament.

As was noted in Chapter 1, other legal disabilities began to be remedied. In 1854, the Cambridge University Act abolished religious tests for matriculation and for the degree of Bachelor of Arts. However, such tests remained for higher degrees and reserved Fellowships were maintained for clergy. In response, and led by the Baptist W. S. Aldis, the Association at Cambridge for the Removal of Religious Disabilities from the Universities was founded to press for their abolition too. Samuel Morton Peto, a Baptist Member of Parliament, introduced the 1861 Burial Bill that took away the Anglican parish priest's right to conduct all burial services in the parish, and in 1880, a government Bill allowed any Christian service to take place at the graveside in parochial churchyards.

Baptists generally supported Gladstone's campaign for Irish disestablishment which was finally successful in 1869. When, in May 1871, the Congregationalist Edward Miall introduced his first parliamentary motion calling for the disestablishment of the Church of England, the Baptist Union enthusiastically moved a supporting resolution. Nevertheless, by the middle of the 1870s, anti-establishment fervour had generally subsided. *The Freeman* of 14 May 1875 said of the Liberation Society's Annual General Meeting of that year that, 'We doubt whether the Liberationists ever held an anniversary in which the Baptists took so little part as in the proceedings of last week.'[69] As LeBarbour comments: 'One of the most important reasons for dwindling Baptist interest in disestablishment was the fact that they had won most of the major fights against dissenting disabilities. Most of the old legal limitations had been removed, so self-interest no longer dictated a constant fight against establishment.'[70]

However, as we have already seen, Baptist convictions about religious liberty and the nature of the Church were not at root based on either self-interest or political pragmatism and so the latent conflict flared up again over the question of education. Baptists and other nonconformists had been shut out from educational opportunities and, as a consequence, had formed their own Dissenting Academies, founded on voluntarist principles of financial support. It was, therefore, not until well into the 1860s that Baptists had accepted the idea of a national education system. In accepting it, the 1868 Baptist Union Annual General Meeting passed a resolution affirming the possibility of the development of an equitable system of national education, but only on certain conditions. These included the principles that secular and religious instruction should be separate, that inspection and control should be limited to the secular department, and that efficiency in the secular department constituted the sole aim of government support.

W. E. Fraser's Education Bill failed to include measures for integrating the existing voluntary schools (which were largely Church of England) into the new national system of education, but rather proposed providing these schools with state financial subsidies. The Baptist Union appointed representatives to the National Education League and protested strongly against what was viewed as the extension of sectarian education at public expense. In 1869 the autumnal meeting of the Baptist Union resolved that the Government should confine itself to secular teaching and Baptists ranked among the firmest opponents of the government scheme.

The Freeman of 27 May 1870 stressed that Baptists had been the only denomination to decide, as a denomination, for secular education. *The Baptist Magazine* of

February 1873, however, did note that while a large majority accepted the secular platform, a small but 'influential minority believed that there should be undenominational religious instruction'. The struggles over education rumbled on into the twentieth century and were inflamed again by Balfour's 1902 Education Bill and the response to it of John Clifford's passive resistance campaign against the payment of public rates to subsidize church schools in which denominational teaching was taking place, during which 48 Baptists were among the nearly 200 passive resisters sent to prison for not paying their rates.

d. *'Covenantal Voluntarism'*

In terms of ecclesiology, Baptists wholeheartedly advocated the approach of voluntarism, the theological and ecclesiological roots of which were clearly expounded in Angus's essay on *The Voluntary System: A Prize Essay in Reply to the Lectures of Dr. Chalmers on Church Establishments*.[71] However, Baptists were not unaware of the dangers that can accompany this ecclesiological approach. For example, Angus's classic Baptist argument for the voluntary system that called such forms of church organization 'the Noblest Form of Social Life; the Representatives of Christ on Earth; the Dwelling Place of the Holy Spirit' also recognized that, in practice, voluntarism can lead to divisions, jealousy, isolation and exclusivity.[72] However, despite recognition of these dangers, the principles of voluntarism continued to be maintained.

The arguments advanced by the Hon. and Revd Baptist Wriothesley Noel gave another classical nineteenth-century expression to some of the issues that have been at stake in this element of the Baptist vision. Noel was the brother of the Earl of Gainsborough and an eminent Anglican Evangelical. He had been the minister of St John's Chapel in Bedford Row, but in 1848 he became a Baptist over the issue of the establishment and the practice of infant baptism. This event provoked widespread reverberations in the English Christian world. With no doubt at least some degree of partisan hyperbole, the February 1849 edition of *The Baptist Reporter* called Noel's secession 'the leading ecclesiastical event of the past year in this country'.[73]

Noel had begun to speak out on the establishment after Dr Chalmers of Edinburgh gave his 1838 London lectures on the issue. Chalmers did not maintain that establishment was in principle wrong, but he did argue that the Scottish establishment had become inimical to true religion. Because of this, in 1843, he led an Evangelical succession from the Church of Scotland. This led to a new stage in Noel's thinking. In his book, *The Case of the Free Church of Scotland*, he developed an argument that every lawful compact between a Church and a state must secure to church officers the liberty to obey Christ and to govern the Church according to His will.[74] In his 1845 book *The Catholic Claims: A Letter to the Lord Bishop of Cashel*, Noel likewise left open the question of whether establishment could ever be justified.[75] But, at the same time, he argued for the disestablishment of the Church of Ireland on the grounds that an overwhelming majority of the Irish population was not Anglican.

In November 1848, Noel left the established Church of England. The entire first edition of his *Essay on the Union of Church and State*,[76] which explained the

reasons for his decision, was sold out on the first day of its publication. Reflecting
on the life and significance of Noel, the historian David Bebbington called this
book 'the classic Baptist presentation of the disestablishment cause in the nineteenth century'.[77] As evidence of the classic nature of its arguments, it should
be noted that, fifty years after its publication, it was still being quoted by the
Liberation Society in its arguments for disestablishment.

Noel's book was a systematic consideration of whether it was the will of Christ,
as seen in the scriptures, that the Christian congregations of England should
receive the salaries of their pastors from the state and, as a result, be subordinate
to it. Noel tackled the issues raised by William Ewart Gladstone's 1839 defence
of establishment as set out in his book *The Church Considered in its Relations
with the State*[78] and modified in his 1840 *Church Principles Considered in Their
Results*.[79] Gladstone had entered politics in the 1830s as a defender of the Church
of England, believing that the state had a right to recognize and endow the Church
– in other words, to establish it. His early arguments in favour of establishment
might be summariszed as, 'it is written; it is natural; it is expedient; it is cus-
tomary'. Gladstone himself dismissed the arguments from custom but he had
made the 'natural' argument his own, believing that, like a good parent, the state
should educate its charges in theological truth.

By contrast, Noel argued that the scriptures are clearly not in support of establishment and that, in practice, church questions were settled by the party system
in Parliament and sometimes by the votes of the most irreligious of people. In fact,
on similar grounds, Gladstone himself came to change his mind on this issue, and
these changes led eventually to Baptists and other nonconformists looking back
on Gladstone's life and career with gratitude for the extension of liberties which
it brought to them. But, characteristically for the Baptist tradition, Noel regarded
the argument from scripture as the decisive one. Like Chalmers, he believed that
the Old Testament dispensation no longer provided an ecclesiastical model for the
present. But, unlike Chalmers, Noel believed that the New Testament did have
clear things to say and drew special attention to Jesus' words that 'My Kingdom
is not of this world', highlighting what he believed to be the implications of this for
the ordering of church and state. By focusing almost solely on the consequences of
the establishment for the life of the Church, Noel eschewed a major consideration
of the standard Tory argument that the establishment was good for the social and
political order.

Bebbington comments that, 'Noel contributed to a persistent strand in nonconformist arguments for disestablishment – a distinctively religious apologetic for
the principle of the gathered church, exercising its own discipline and paying its
own pastor.'[80] Noel's position was thus primarily concerned with the integrity of
the Church, although he did also append to his book a lengthy catalogue of the
detrimental results of establishment. In addition, Noel also allowed a section of
his book to be reprinted in tract form by the Liberation Society in 1866 as a part
of its struggle for Irish disestablishment. However, he was generally wary of the
degree of political involvement exhibited by such people as Edward Miall and J.
Mursell and, by contrast, based his own arguments on theological appeals to the
witness of the scriptures and the history of the Church.

4. *The Future of the Baptist Inheritance*

a. *'Notes' and 'Tracks' and Contemporary Options*

There have been individuals of all religious backgrounds and none, including those from within the established Church of England, who have argued for disestablishment. But such calls have often been *exceptions* to the general rule, whereas within the Baptist tradition, the critique has, historically, been more the *rule* than the exception. Within this, the Baptist tradition's theological commitment to freedom of religion and its ecclesiological orientation towards a 'covenantal voluntarism' has (together with that of the 'baptistic'[81] Mennonite tradition) been the most consistent and insistent.

However, as the contemporary Baptist theologian Paul Fiddes points out, the implications of 'tracks' or 'notes' in the Baptist tradition concerned with religious liberty and the nature of the Christian Church cannot simply be translated into a single model for the relationship between religion(s), state and society. Thus it would not be appropriate to argue that a necessary corollary of the Baptist inheritance in these matters is advocacy of an *absolute* separation of church and state as in the more Jeffersonian ('wall of separation')[82] view of the constitutional separation between church and state in the USA. As Fiddes points out, among Baptists in Europe, 'engagement of the Church in some corporate way with government is not *in principle* ruled out'.[83] What Fiddes suggests can, from a European Baptist perspective, be seen as illegitimate is summarized by reference to a document produced by the Division for Theology and Education of the European Baptist Federation, *What Are Baptists? On the Way to Expressing Baptist Identity in a Changing Europe.*[84] Fiddes argues that, in article 12 of this document, the particular approaches to the relationship between religion(s), state(s) and society(ies) that should be ruled out are those in which:

> (a) any kind of establishmnent in which Christian believers or a certain kind of Christian are privileged above other members of society; (b) a territorial view of religion in which a country or section of it is designated by government as the exclusive preserve of one Church; (c) any interference by civil government in church government, or in religious belief or practices.[85]

What Fiddes suggests is that, 'it should be the Baptist approach to ask how, in each situation, the relation between Church and State accords with the sovereign rule of God and the place of Christ as the only covenant-mediator in the Church'.[86] Therefore, just as defenders of the establishment would acknowledge that the direct historical inheritance of the establishment of the Church of England is no longer appropriate to the present situation of the Church of England and has already been modified from its historic original forms, so also the inheritance of the Free Church and Baptist traditions cannot *straightforwardly* be applied to present realities in the relationship between religion(s), state(s) and society(ies).

b. *Baptist and Establishment Inheritance: The Changing Context*

The contemporary socio-religious context has changed (in ways that will be more fully explored in following chapter) in comparison with the nineteenth-century heyday of the debates between establishment and disestablishment, as have the relationships between religions within it, and between religions and the wider society. The Christian Churches and their relationships with one another have also changed. The present age is an ecumenical one, in which the Churches are increasingly, in mutual critique, becoming prepared to learn from the strengths and weaknesses of their respective inheritances, and to forge a new future as 'Churches Together' in England and in the UK.

This ecumenical dialogue itself impacts upon the inheritance of the Free Church and Baptist traditions, bringing corrective change where necessary. However, it is also precisely within the same ecumenical process that it is important that the 'notes' of Free Church and Baptist tradition outlined in this chapter are brought to bear upon the Anglican tradition in England. In evolving an appropriate form for corporate Christian existence and for configuring the relationships between religion(s), state and society within a socio-religious reality characterized by Christian, secular and religiously plural dimensions, the theological resources of religious freedom and ecclesiological resources of 'covenantal voluntarism' could, it is argued, be particularly helpful.

To clarify why such resources might be helpful, the following chapter seeks to delineate the contours of religious believing and belonging in contemporary England and the UK. This is undertaken in order that any future reconceptualization and renegotiation of the relationships between religion(s), state and society might be rooted in an empirically based understanding of the present socio-religious context.

Notes

1   J. Wolffe, ' "And There's Another Country ..." ', p. 93.

2   R. Orchard, 'How Far Must We Still Take "1662" into Account in Ecumenical Relations Today', *BQ* 20/3 (1960–1), pp. 118–28 (126).

3   B. Thoroughgood, *The Flag and the Cross: National Limits and the Church Universal* (London: SCM Press, 1988), p. 47.

4   A. Hastings, *Church and State*.

5   N. Wright, 'The Need to Disestablish', *The Guardian*, 8.10.1990; *Power and Discipleship: Towards a Baptist Theology of the State* (The Whitley Lecture, 1996–7; Oxford: Whitley, 1996); *Public Truth or Private Option? Gospel and Religious Liberty in a Multi-Faith Society in the Light of the Resurrection* (Joppa Group Occasional Paper, 1999); and *Disavowing Constantine: Mission, Church and the Social Order in the Theologies of John Howard Yoder and Jürgen Moltmann* (Carlisle: Paternoster, 2000).

6   The Baptist World Alliance (see www.bwnet.org) has 211 Unions and Conventions in membership with it, representing around 46,500,000 baptized believers, with a wider worldwide circle of around 110,000,000 congregants.

7   H. Moody, 'Baptists and Freedom: Some Reminders and Remembrances of our Past for the Sake of our Present', *ABQ* 3/1 (1984), pp. 4–15 (5).

8   P. Fiddes, *Tracks and Traces*, p. 1.

9   William Bradford, *History of the Plymouth Plantation, 1620–1674.* (W.C. Ford (ed.); 2 vols.; vol. 1; Boston: Massachusetts Historical Society, 1912), p. 20.

10   B. White, *English Baptists of the Seventeenth Century*, p. 58.

11   These 'notes' were originally identified in the author's unpublished Master's thesis, P. Weller, 'The Theology and Practice of Inter-Religious Dialogue', and were then further developed in P. Weller, 'Freedom and Witness in a Multi-Religious Society. Part I', pp. 252–64; P. Weller,

'Freedom and Witness in a Multi-Religious Society. Part II', pp. 302–15; and P. Weller, 'Baptist Principles as they Relate to the Four Principles of Dialogue', pp. 53–68.

12 E. Troeltsch, *Protestantism and Progress: An Historical Study of the Relation of Protestantism to the Modern World* (Boston: Beacon Press, 1958 reprint edition of 1912 original).

13 W. Jordan, *The Development of Religious Toleration in England*. (2 vols.; London: George Allen & Unwin, 1932, 1936), vol. 1, p. 314.

14 T. George, 'Between Pacifism and Coercion: The English Baptist Doctrine of Religious Toleration', *MQR* 58/1 (1984), p. 30–49 (31).

15 T. George, 'Between Pacifism and Coercion', p. 40.

16 J. Smyth, *The Patterne of True Prayer: A Learned and Comfortable Exposition of or Commentarie Upon the Lord's Prayer*, *The Works of John Smyth*, (W. Whitley (ed.); 2 vols.; Cambridge: Cambridge University Press, 1915), vol. 1, p. 166.

17 J. Smyth, 'Confession', in *The Works of John Smyth*, W. Whitley (ed.), vol. 2, p. 748.

18 T. Helwys in R. Groves (ed.), *Thomas Helwys: A Short Declaration of the Mystery of Iniquity* (Macon, GA: Mercer University Press, 1998).

19 F. Clouts, 'Thomas Helwys and His Book, The Mistery of Iniquity', *RevExp* 41/4 (1944), pp. 372–87 (372).

20 W. Jordan, *The Development of Religious Toleration in England*, vol. 2, p. 274.

21 T. Helwys, in R. Groves (ed.), *Thomas Helwys: A Short Declaration of the Mystery of Iniquity*, p. vi.

22 T. Helwys in R. Groves (ed.), *Thomas Helwys: A Short Declaration of the Mystery of Iniquity*, p. 37.

23 L. Busher, *Religion's Peace: Or a Plea for Liberty of Conscience*, in E. Underhill (ed.), *Tracts on the Liberty of Conscience and Persecution, 1614–1667* (London: Hanserd Knollys Society, 1846), pp. 1–81.

24 L. Busher, *Religion's Peace*, p. 21.

25 L. Busher, *Religion's Peace*, p. 41.

26 *Persecution for Religion Judg'd and Condemn'd in a Discourse Between an AntiChristian and a Christian*, in E. Underhill (ed.), *Tracts on the Liberty of Conscience and Persecution, 1614–1667*, pp. 95–188.

27 *An Humble Supplication to the King's Majesty*, in E. Underhill (ed.), *Tracts on the Liberty of Conscience and Persecution, 1614–1667*, pp. 189–231.

28 R. Williams, *The Bloudy Tenet of Persecution for Cause of Conscience Discussed in a Conference Between Truth and Peace* (R. Groves (ed.); Macon, GA: Mercer University Press, 2001), p. 3.

29 R. Williams, *The Bloudy Tenet of Persecution for Cause of Conscience*, p. 3.

30 R. Williams, *The Bloudy Tenet of Persecution for Cause of Conscience*, p. 4.

31 R. Williams, *The Bloudy Tenet of Persecution for Cause of Conscience*, p. 4.

32 *An Humble Petition and Representation of the Suffering of Several Peaceable and Innocent Subjects Called by the Name of Anabaptists*, in E. Underhill (ed.), *Tracts on the Liberty of Conscience and Persecution, 1614–1667*, pp. 287–308 (301).

33 '1660 *General Baptist Confession*', in W. McGlothin (ed.), *Baptist Confessions of Faith* (London: Baptist Historical Society, 1911), p. 119.

34 '1677 *Confession of Faith*', in W. McGlothin (ed.), *Baptist Confessions of Faith*, pp. 215–89 (258).

35 *An Orthodox Creed or a Protestant Confession of Faith*, in W. McGlothin (ed.), *Baptist Confessions of Faith*, pp. 124–61.

36 T. Helwys, in R. Groves (ed.), *Thomas Helwys: A Short Declaration of the Mystery of Iniquity*, p. 53.

37 E. Payne, 'Who were the Baptists' (A Comment)', p. 342.

38 Quoted in J. Norman, 'The Relevance and Vitality of the Sect-Idea', *BQ*, 27/6 (1977–8), pp. 248–58 (251).

39 W. Whitley, 'Thomas Helwys of Grays Inn and of Broxtow Hall, Nottingham', *BQ* 7/6 (1934–5), pp. 241–55 (251).

40   L. Busher, *Religion's Peace*, p. 24.

41   C. Blackwood, *The Storming of the Antichrist, in His Two Last and Strongest Garrisons: of Compulsion of Conscience and Infants' Baptism* (London, 1644), no pagination.

42   T. George, 'Between Pacifism and Coercion', p. 49.

43   A.-M. LeBarbour, 'Victorian Baptists: A Study in Denominational Development' (unpublished doctoral dissertation, University of Maryland, 1977), p. 4.

44   B. Evans, *Modern Popery: A Series of Letters on Some of Its More Important Aspects* (London: Houlston & Stoneman, 1855), p. vi.

45   B. Evans, *Modern Popery*, pp. v–vi.

46   See W. Glover, 'English Baptists at the Time of the Downgrade Controversy', *Foundations* 1/3 (1958), pp. 41–51; and E. Payne, 'The Downgrade Controversy: A Postscript', *BQ* 28/4 (1979), pp. 146–158.

47   H. Wheeler Robinson, *The Life and Faith of the Baptists* (London: Carey Kingsgate Press, 2nd revision, 1946), p. 137.

48   M. Jordan, 'John Smyth and Thomas Helwys: The Two First English Preachers of Religious Liberty', *BQ* 12/4 (1946–8), pp. 187–95 (192).

49   Baptist World Alliance, *Together in Christ: Official Report of the Sixteenth Congress, Seoul, Korea, August 14th–19th* (McLean: Baptist World Alliance, 1990), pp. 194–200 (194–5).

50   A. Woodhouse (ed.), *Puritanism and Liberty: Being the Army Debates from the Clarke Manuscript, with Supplementary Documents* (London: J. M. Dent & Sons, 1838), pp. 81–2.

51   R. Hall, *Christianity Consistent with a Love of Freedom: Being an Answer to a Sermon Lately Preached by Revd. G. Chapman* (London: J. Johnson, 1791).

52   R. Hall, *An Apology for the Freedom of the Press and for General Liberty* (London: J. Johnson, 1793).

53   P. Crannell, 'Tolerance and Company', *RevExp* 24/1 (1927), pp. 24–44 (27).

54   H. Bender, 'The Anabaptists and Religious Liberty in the 16th Century', p. 83.

55   H. Martin, 'Protestantism and the State', *BQ* 12/6 (1946–8), pp. 309–17 (310).

56   D. Brown, 'The Radical Reformation: Then and Now', *MQR* 45/3 (1971). pp. 250–63 (251).

57   W. McGlothin, 'The Struggle For Religious Liberty', *RevExp* 8/3 (1911), pp. 378–94 (383).

58   W. McGlothin, 'The Struggle for Religious Liberty', p. 382.

59   H. Wheeler Robinson, *The Life and Faith of the Baptists*, p. 71.

60   H. Wheeler Robinson, *The Life and Faith of the Baptists*, p. 73.

61   T. George, 'Between Pacifism and Coercion', p. 37.

62   T. Helwys, quoted in T. George, 'Between Pacifism and Coercion', p. 38.

63   C. Hill, 'History and Denominational History', *BQ* 22/2 (1967–8), pp. 65–71 (68).

64   *Baptist Union Minutes, 1833–1842*, p. 147.

65   A.-M. LeBarbour, 'Victorian Baptists', p. 236.

66   E. Payne, *The Baptist Union: A Short History* (London: Carey Kingsgate Press, 1958), p. 84.

67   *The Freeman*, 4.2.1857.

68   A.-M. LeBarbour, 'Victorian Baptists', p. 239.

69   *The Freeman*, 14.5.1875.

70   A.-M. LeBarbour, 'Victorian Baptists', p. 249.

71   J. Angus, *The Voluntary System: A Prize Essay in Reply to the Lectures of Dr. Chalmers on Church Establishments* (London: Jackson & Walford, 1839).

72   J. Angus, *Christian Churches: The Noblest Form of Social Life; The Representative of Christ on Earth; the Dwelling Place of the Holy Spirit* (London: Ward & Co., 1862).

73   *The Baptist Reporter*, February 1849, p. 45 and p. 75.

74   B. Noel, *The Claims of the Free Church of Scotland* (London: James Nisbet & Co., 1844).

75   B. Noel, *The Catholic Claims: A Letter to the Lord Bishop of Cashel* (London: James Nisbet & Co., 1845).

76   B. Noel, *Essay on the Union of Church and State* (London: James Nisbet & Co., 1848).

77   D. Bebbington, 'The Life of Baptist Noel: Its Setting and Significance', *BQ* 24/8 (1971–2), pp. 389–411 (398).

78   W. Gladstone, *The State in its Relations with the Church* (London: John Murray, 1839).

79   W. Gladstone, *Church Principles Considered in Their Results* (London: John Murray, 1840).

80   D. Bebbington, 'The Life of Baptist Noel', p. 398.

81   The Baptist theologian J. McClendon, Jnr, refers to 'baptist' with a small 'b' in terms of a particular approach to Christian existence that is rooted in the radical Reformation. He argues that this inheritance can be seen in various contemporary ecclesial groupings including (but not always) those who currently call themselves 'Baptist', but also including some who do not use this self-description. See J. McClendon, Jnr, *Systematic Theology*, vol. 1: *Ethics* (Nashville: Abingdon Press, 1986).

82   After Thomas Jefferson who, in 1802, referred to the amendment as 'a wall separating church from state'.

83   P. Fiddes, *Tracks and Traces*, p. 263.

84   European Baptist Federation Division for Theology and Education, *What Are Baptists? On the Way to Expressing a Baptist Identity in a Changing Europe* (1992, revised in 1993 and received, though not formally accepted, by the Council of the European Baptist Federation in September 1992).

85   P. Fiddes, *Tracks and Traces*, p. 264.

86   P. Fiddes, *Tracks and Traces*, pp. 263–64.

Part II

ESTABLISHED RELIGION: RELIGIOUS AND POLITICAL CONTEXT

Chapter 3

The Changing Religious Landscape

1. Describing the Religious Landscape

a. Outlining the Contours

Thus far we have examined the historical inheritance of establishment together with the alternative theological and ecclesiological perspectives to be found in the Free Church and, more specifically, Baptist refractions of the Christian vision. The nature of both the inheritance of the establishment and of the alternatives to it were formed in very different social, political and religious circumstances to those that now obtain. This chapter is thus concerned with describing the current religious landscape in order that consideration of the most appropriate way forward for the configuration of the relationships between religion(s), state and society can be rooted in an empirical understanding of the contemporary religious scene.

b. Describing and Interpreting

In describing the contours of religion in England and the UK, the sections on individual religions in the UK and the section on the development of inter-faith initiatives draw upon and rework material from *Religions in the UK: Directory, 2001–3* that was edited by the present author.[1] At the same time, the descriptive material that predominates in most of the chapter is set within an *interpretative framework* that is advanced by the author.[2] Thus the particular use made of the descriptive data from *Religions in the UK*, the statistical data from the 2001 Census, and the figures on church community, membership and attendance taken from the *UK Christian Handbook: Religious Trends No. 4, 2003–2004*, is the responsibility of the author alone.[3]

2. Demography, Theology and Ecclesiology

a. Context and Content in Theology and Ecclesiology

The contemporary socio-religious context is substantially different from that which existed during the nineteenth-century higher-water mark of public debate concerning establishment and disestablishment. This change in *context* also means that the *content* of the debates between the inheritance of the establishment and its theological, ecclesiological and political alternatives will itself also be likely to have changed. It is, in fact, argued that it is the changed *circum*stances of the establishment which are a substantial part of what has created a moment of *kairos* in the present configuration between religion(s), state and society that calls for new theological and political *stances* to be adopted for the future.

The Baptist theologian J. McClendon, Jnr, sees the process of theological reflection as involving 'the discovery, understanding and transformation of the convictions of a convictional community, including the discovery and critical revision of their relation to one another and to whatever else there is'.[4] On this basis, the present chapter tries to trace some key dimensions of the 'whatever else there is' of social and historical reality that might inform the critical revision of the convictions of the Christian community in relation to establishment. Therefore, in order to evaluate the argument that the present is indeed a time that calls for change, it is important to identify key features that have changed in the contemporary contours of the English and UK religious landscape.

The rapid pace of global and national change that took place in the latter half of the twentieth century means that the world in which the Church now exists is, in many ways, a very different one than was the case in the years immediately following the Second World War. Furthermore, this has had significant implications for the development of Christian theology and practice.[5] The most dramatic contextual changes have occurred in connection with the collapse of the political power of colonialism and the movement of migrant and refugee populations into Europe.

b. *Migration and Religious Pluralization*

Prior to the Second World War, although some degree of religious plurality existed within European societies, including in the UK, this was primarily related to the internal diversities of the Christian tradition and the presence of the Jewish population. However, since the middle of the twentieth century, and especially in its last quarter, the religious composition of society changed radically, especially through the primary immigration of Hindus, Jains, Muslims, Sikhs and others.

Following the passage of the 1962 Commonwealth Immigrants Act, the flow of primary migration slowed down. At the same time, the original mainly male migrants were joined by spouses and children with the result that secondary immigration accelerated. As a consequence, the character of what could, by then, properly be called emergent 'communities' began to form as originally migrant minorities started to perceive themselves more in terms of settled groups than as a collection of visiting individual workers. Thus, increasing attention began to be paid to building the structures necessary for sustaining and developing an established internal community life and for relating to the wider society.

Due to the Africanization policies of the newly independent African states of the former British Empire and Commonwealth, the original migrant groups were, during the later 1960s and early 1970s, supplemented by the arrival from Tanzania, Kenya and Uganda of a significant number of East African people of Asian origins. However, with the passage of the 1981 Nationality Act and subsequent ever-tighter immigration regulations, further significant growth of these populations by means of migration was limited.

For governments, civil society and the Christian Churches in England and the UK, the issues arising from the presence of a plurality of people and religions that are other than 'Western' and Christian are now thoroughly existential rather than being something at one remove in other parts of the world. Such religious diversity is, in turn, overlaid upon the pre-existing processes of secularization that emerged from the nineteenth century, in which secular and humanist perspectives came to the fore, the acceleration of which had developed with renewed impetus during the early 1960s.

c. *Counting Religion: Christian, Plural and Secular*

Until the 2001 decennial Census, with the exception of Northern Ireland (where a religion question had been asked in the Census since the inception of the Northern Ireland state) there had been no generally comparable data available on the size of the various religious groups in the UK.[6] This meant that it had only been possible to build a picture of the religious landscape based on either the internal estimates of religious communities and/or projections related to an analysis of an assumed degree of overlap between religion and ethnicity.

The only extensive surveys of religion in England and the UK had been voluntary surveys such as the English Church census organized by the Christian organization, MARC Europe (and later by Christian Research).[7] But there had also been a number of sample studies on such questions as the nature and extent of religious belief, affiliation and practice of a kind that have formed a part of the British Social Attitudes Survey and the European Values Survey.[8]

The only previous official census relating to religion that was conducted in England took place in 1851.[9] In contrast with the 2001 Census, this earlier Census in fact focused on participation in public worship. What its results confirmed was the relative increase in numeric strength of the Free Churches and the Roman Catholic Church as compared to the Church of England. The 2001 decennial Census was the first one in which, throughout the UK, a question on religious affiliation was asked. To be more precise, a range of religion *questions* were asked, with both differing forms of question and pre-set options for response in the various parts of the UK.

Although closely related, the differing questions and responses offered mean that data relating to different parts of the UK may not be entirely comparable and this must be borne in mind when looking at any data presented on a UK-wide basis. Therefore, the National Statistics website includes a note of caution on this matter explaining that, 'Different versions of the religious identity question were asked in England and Wales, in Scotland and in Northern Ireland, to reflect local differences in the requirement for information.'[10] Thus, it may be that the use of the word 'belonging' in both the Scottish and Northern Irish forms of the question encouraged respondents to interpret the question in a 'harder-edged' way than the 'What is your religion' version of the question in England.[11]

Because of this, it is not straightforward to add the results of these differing questions together to arrive at data covering the UK as a whole,[12] although the National Statistics website's cautionary note does conclude that, 'results are comparable across the UK as a whole'. At the least, it is arguable that, even with problems of comparability, the Census results do, for the first time ever, enable at least *some* kind of general overview to be taken of current patterns of religious self-identification found in the contemporary religious landscape of the UK.

Table 3.1 sets out the results of the religious affiliation questions both for the UK as a whole and also as broken down into each country within the UK. Tables

Time for a Change

that incorporate Census data and information derived from this include absolute numbers taken from the appropriate official Census sources.[13] Apart from Table 3.1, which originally appeared in another source, the percentage calculations that appear in the Tables are based on original Census data but are calculations that are made by the present author and should therefore not be directly attributed to the Census.

Table 3.1: Religion Responses in the 2001 Census

Religion	England	Scotland	Wales	Northern Ireland	UK Total	UK (%)
Buddhist	139,046	6,830	5,407	533	151,816	0.3%
Christian	35,251,244	3,294,545	2,087,242	1,446,386	42,079,417	71.6%
Hindu	546,982	5,564	5,439	825	558,810	1.0%
Jewish	257,671	6,448	2,256	365	266,740	0.5%
Muslim	1,524,887	42,557	21,739	1,943	1,591,126	2.7%
Sikh	327,343	6,572	2,015	219	336,149	0.6%
Other Religion	143,811	26,974	6,909	1,143	178,837	0.3%
Total	38,190,984	3,389,490	2,131,007	1,451,414	45,162,895	76.8%
No religion	7,171,332	1,394,460	537,935	*	9,103,727	15.5%
Not stated	3,776,515	278,061	234,143	*	4,288,719	7.3%
No religion/ not stated	10,947,847	1,672,521	772,078	233,853	13,626,299	23.2%

* In Northern Ireland, separate statistics for those of 'No religion' and 'Not stated' are not available.
Table reproduced from *Inter Faith Update* 21, p. 3, the newsletter of the Inter Faith Network for the United Kingdom. Due to rounding, percentages may not total 100%.

From Table 3.1, religion would seem to remain a factor of at least some significance in the self-understanding of around three-quarters of the population of the UK (45,162,895 people or 76.8% of the population). Of these, the Census results show that as many as 42,079,417 people (or 71.6% of the population) continue to identify themselves in some way as 'Christian'. Thus the religious landscape of the UK is one in which religion in general, and Christianity in particular, still features strongly in at least some sense.

The Census results also show 9,103,727 people (or 15.5% of the population) who indicate they are of 'no religion'. Thus, in contrast with what was quite common in the years immediately following the Second World War, it would no longer be correct, in any unqualified way, to continue to describe the UK as a 'Christian society'. A more rounded portrayal of its religious profile would, rather, have to take account both of its continuing Christian inheritance and also of its contemporary 'secularity'.

Finally, though, of those who identify with any specific religion at all there are 3,083,478 people (or 5.2% of the total population) who identify with religions other than Christianity. While less than the numbers identifying themselves as 'Christian' or as of 'no religion', in absolute terms, this is still a substantial number of people. Taken as a proportion of those who indicated any specific form of religious identification at all, those of other than Christian religion are as many as 6.8% of the total.

Therefore, in order to achieve a balanced understanding and approach to a more appropriate basis for structuring the relationships between religion(s), state and society in England and the UK, the contemporary religious landscape of the UK should be seen as exhibiting contours that are 'Christian, secular and religiously plural'. Thus, the contemporary socio-religious reality of England and the UK might be described as 'three-dimensional' in contrast with a more 'one-dimensional' Christian inheritance[14] or the 'two-dimensional' religious–secular modifications made to that self-understanding during the course of the nineteenth and early twentieth centuries.

By outlining some principal features of the diversity of religious belief, practice, identity and forms of organization found in the contemporary religious landscape of England and the 'four-nations-state' of the UK within which it is located, this chapter traces how the transformation into this 'three-dimensional' socio-religious reality has occurred. Finally, an overview is provided of the emerging and accelerating development of inter-faith initiatives, organizations and structures as these engage with the 'three-dimensional' contours of this 'Christian–secular–religiously plural' socio-religious reality.

3. A Christian Inheritance

a. Christianity in the United Kingdom

The 2001 Census results underline not only that Christianity is historically important, but that it remains a significant dimension of UK life. As already noted, 42,079,417 people or 71.6% of the population as a whole (which is 93.2% of the population identifying itself with any specific religion at all) has identified itself in some way as 'Christian'. Table 3.2 shows the numbers of respondents identifying themselves as 'Christian' as an absolute number, as a proportion of the population as a whole and as a proportion of respondents who identify with any specific religion at all.

Table 3.2: Census respondents identifying as 'Christian' by country of the UK in 2001

Country	Total numbers of Christians	Percentage of total population	Percentage of population identifying with any specific religion at all
England	35,251,244	71.7%	92.3%
Scotland	3,294,545	65.1%	97.2%
Wales	2,087,242	71.9%	98.0%
Northern Ireland	1,446,386	85.8%	99.7%
United Kingdom	42,079,417	71.6%	93.2%

Source: Census, April 2001. National Statistics website: www.statistics.gov.uk. Crown copyright, 2004. Crown copyright material is reproduced with the permission of the Controller of HMSO. Percentages as shown are calculated by the present author on the basis of the original Census data.

There is, of course, an issue about the relationship of Census data on religion to religions as they are lived and practised. This is especially the case in the light of the apparent discrepancy between the Census data and results from the British

Social Attitudes Survey and the European Values Survey.[15] This is because in the results of the latter for Great Britain, self-identification with religion would seem to be less widespread than indicated in the Census results.

In the European Values Survey, respondents were asked about how important religion is in their life. Of respondents in Great Britain, 12.6% said 'very important' and 24.8% said 'quite important', while 33.0% said 'not important' and 29.7% said 'not at all'.[16] In the 2001 Home Office Citizenship Survey, from a list of 15 things, respondents were asked to identify which things would say something important about them if they were using these words to describe themselves and, overall, ranking the items in order of frequency, 'religion' was ranked 9th. However, there was considerable variation of response between different ethnic groups. Thus, among 'Asians' it was ranked as high as 2nd, while for 'Whites' it was as low as 10th.[17]

In this context, critics such as David Voas and Steve Bruce suggest that the relatively high results of the Census might say more about how respondents perceive the challenge to the inherited culture from those of other than Christian religions than about their own positive identification with Christianity. At the same time, even Voas and Bruce acknowledge that Christianity has a significance that goes considerably beyond the actual numbers of those who identify with it. Thus, as a result of its historical position, Christianity is extensively woven into much of the fabric of the historical, artistic, cultural, legal and other aspects of the heritage of the UK and its constituent parts.

At the same time, the composition of the population identifying as Christian is itself increasingly diverse and complex.[18] Census figures as broken down into denominational tradition are not available for the UK as a whole. This is because the form of the question as asked in England and Wales did not ask about Christian denominational traditions.[19] However, based on estimates and tables in Christian Research's *UK Christian Handbook: Religious Trends, No. 4, 2003/2004*,[20] 'community membership' of the Trinitarian[21] denominations for the year 2000 is as set out in Table 3.3.[22]

Table 3.3: Estimates of Christian 'Community membership' by denominational tradition in the UK in 2000

Denomination	Community by denomination	Community by denomination (%)
Anglican	28,300,000	67.5%
Baptist	500,000	1.2%
Catholic	5,800,000	13.8%
Independent	400,000	1.0%
Methodist	1,300,000	3.1%
New Churches	400,000	1.0%
Orthodox	500,000	1.2%
Pentecostal	400,000	1.0%
Presbyterian	2,900,000	6.9%
All Other Churches	1,400,000	3.3%
Total	41,000,000	100.0%

Source: From figures in P. Brierley (ed.), *UK Christian Handbook: Religious Trends No. 4, 2003/2004* (London: Christian Research, 2003), Table 2.2.3, p. 2.2. Percentages as shown are calculations by the present author based on original figures from Christian Research.

'Community membership' relates to the broadest form of identification with a religious group and therefore, arguably, most closely aligns with the kind of information about religion that is found in the Census data (as distinct from, for example, information relating to either to 'Church membership' or to 'Church attendance').

As can be seen in Table 3.3, there is a substantial proportion – in fact just over two-thirds – of those who, considered in terms of 'Community membership', identify in some way with Anglican Christianity.[23] However, when taking the more restrictive notion of 'Church membership',[24] and based on estimates by Christian Research for the year 2001, the relative positions of the denominational traditions in the UK set out in Table 3.4 are quite different. Considered in terms of 'Church membership', the proportion of all Anglicans is just below that of Catholic 'Church membership' and considerably below that of the combined 'Church membership' of the other Christian Free Church, Orthodox and Presbyterian traditions.

Table 3.4: Estimates of 'Church membership' by denominational tradition in the UK in 2001

Denomination	Church membership	Church membership (%)
Anglican	1,668,025	28.3%
Baptist	215,062	3.6%
Catholic	1,745,652	29.6%
Independent	187,497	3.2%
Methodist	343,696	5.8%
New Churches	136,054	2.3%
Orthodox	255,308	4.3%
Pentecostal	253,722	4.3%
Presbyterian	958,268	16.2%
Other Churches	139,983	2.4%
Total	5,903,267	100.0%

Source: From figures in P. Brierley (ed.), *UK Christian Handbook: Religious Trends No. 4, 2003/2004* (London: Christian Research, 2003), Tables 2.22.2–2.23.7, pp. 2.22–2.23. Percentages as shown are calculations by the present author based on original figures from Christian Research.

The position of Christianity in the UK and in its various denominational traditions needs to be set within an appreciation of the implications of the UK being a multinational state. Although there is a popular perception of the role of the Church of England that was reflected in *The Times* leader-writer's description of the Church as 'the British National Church',[25] this is constitutionally incorrect. Not only do different parts of the UK religious landscape have different demographic contours, there are also a range of different arrangements for defining the relationships between religious bodies, the state and society. This variety underlines the fact that the UK and its Christian religious traditions are themselves reflections of the national diversity that can be found in the three nations of England, Wales and Scotland, as well as among people of the province of Northern Ireland.[26] In relation to this wider diversity, of the four parts that comprise the UK, England has the broadest and most numerous variety of religious traditions and populations, followed by Scotland and Wales, and then by Northern Ireland.

Social and political issues relating to the unity and diversity of the UK have, over recent years, grown in significance. Tom Nairn's book on *The Break-Up of Britain*, for example, began with a chapter entitled 'The Twilight of the British State'.[27] These issues have partly been related to the trends towards internal political devolution within the UK that have accelerated since the coming into power of the New Labour government. The trends have also been matched by other, wider developments that were set in motion following the UK's accession to the European Community. However, all too often in debates relating to the establishment of the Church of England, the implications of this national Christian diversity for the role of one English Church being established in the particular way that it is within the multi-national state of the UK is not given sufficient weight. Therefore even before considering the impact of the wider, other than Christian diversity, there is a question as to how far the establishment of the Church of England reflects and reinforces an inappropriate English dominance within the UK as a whole.

b. *Christianity in England*
With regard to England, the 2001 Census showed that 35,251,244 people or 71.7% of the population (and 92.3% of the population of England identifying itself with any specific religion at all) identified themselves, in some sense, as 'Christian'. As has already been noted, and perhaps particularly in connection with the 'Christian' responses to the Census, the point should be taken seriously that the particular form taken by the religion question in England (and Wales) may have been encouraging of responses informed more by an affirmation of 'a cultural background rather than a current affiliation'.[28]

The Census question as asked in England and Wales did not differentiate the 'Christian' category of response. Therefore, the results of the 2001 Census do not provide any data on specific identification with the Church of England. The 1970 Chadwick Report on *Church and State* had claimed a nominal Church of England affiliation as high as 67.5% of the English population.[29] Although Valerie Pitt, as a dissenting member of the Committee, offered a critique of such figures,[30] it is likely that some form of identification with the Church of England may well be felt by larger sections of the population than is immediately apparent. Grace Davie, for example, argues that one needs to take account of the phenomenon of 'believing without belonging'[31] in the 'ordinary God'[32] of folk Christianity. Due to the historic position of the Church of England, it may well be that many of these 'believers without belonging' still see themselves as, in some sense, 'C of E'.

Table 3.5 gives Christian Research's 2001 estimates for 'community belonging' by denomination in England. It shows over three-quarters of the population who are aligned with a Christian tradition as being, in this broadest sense, in some way aligned with the Church of England. However, when looked at in terms of the more restrictive notion of 'Church membership' (as in Table 3.6, which gives Christian Research's estimates for this in 2001), Anglican Christianity represents only just over a third of the total Christian 'Church membership' in England. Examined in terms of 'religious participation' understood in terms of 'Church attendance', the 1989 *English Church Census* had noted that, of the 10% of the total population who were in church on the census Sunday, only 31% were Anglicans.[33] In other words, at the time the English Church Census was conducted, in relation to the population taken as a whole, active identifiers with the Church of England through regular attendance at weekly worship represented only 3.1% of the English population. Table 3.7 sets out Christian Research's figures for 'Church attendance' in 2000, with Anglican Christians now very nearly equalled in numbers by Roman Catholic 'Church attenders' and less than a third of the combined attendance of the Free Church, Orthodox, Pentecostal, Presbyterian and Roman Catholic traditions.

Table 3.5: Estimates of 'Community by denomination' in England in 2000

Denomination	Community by denomination	Community by denomination (%)
Anglican	27,200,000	79.8%
Baptist	300,000	0.9%
Catholic	4,100,000	12.0%
Methodist	1,100,000	3.2%
Orthodox	500,000	1.5%
Presbyterian	100,000	0.3%
Other Churches	800,000	2.3%
Total	34,100,000	100%

Source: From figures in P. Brierley (ed.), *UK Christian Handbook: Religious Trends No. 4, 2003/2004* (London: Christian Research, 2003), Table 2.2.3, p. 2.2. Percentages as shown are calculations by the present author based on original figures from Christian Research.

Table 3.6: Estimates of 'Church membership' by denominational tradition in England in 2001

Denomination	Church membership by denomination	Church membership by denomination (%)
Anglican	1,377,085	37.1%
Baptist	164,771	4.4%
Catholic	971,172	26.1%
Independent	106,964	2.9%
Methodist	308,319	8.3%
New Churches	127,624	3.4%
Orthodox	225,503	6.1%
Pentecostal	225,686	6.1%
Presbyterian	85,305	2.3%
Other Churches	124,387	2.3%
Total	3,716,816	Due to rounding, figures may not total 100%

Source: From figures in P. Brierley (ed.), *UK Christian Handbook: Religious Trends No. 4, 2003/2004* (London: Christian Research, 2003), Tables 2.22.2–2.23.7, pp. 2.22–2.23. Percentages as shown are calculations by the present author based on original figures from Christian Research.

Table 3.7: Estimates of 'Church Attendance' by Denomination in England in 2000

Denomination	Church attendance	Church attendance (%)
Anglican	1,063,300	29.9%
Baptist	280,000	7.9%
Catholic	990,400	27.9%
Independent	150,200	4.2%
Methodist	372,600	10.5%
New Churches	248,400	7.0%
Orthodox	25,600	0.7%
Pentecostal	216,400	6.1%
United Reformed	112,000	3.2%
Other Churches	94,800	2.7%
Total	3,533,700	Due to rounding, figures may not total 100%

Source: From figures in P. Brierley (ed.), *UK Christian Handbook: Religious Trends No. 4, 2003/2004* (London: Christian Research, 2003), Table 2.24.1, p. 2.24. Percentages as shown are calculations by the present author based on original figures from Christian Research.

c. *Christianity in Scotland*

Turning to Scotland, since the 1603 accession of James Stuart to the English Crown as James I of England and the ensuing union of the Westminster and Scottish Parliaments in 1707 there has, together with England and Wales, been a shared monarch and political system. However, Scotland has in many ways remained distinct. This has especially been the case in terms of its systems of law and education and has also applied in matters of religion.[34]

The Presbyterian Church of Scotland has been the established Church in Scotland and has had a strong historical role as a national Church, reinforcing the specifically Scottish aspects of life within the UK.[35] Indeed, until devolution brought about the restoration of the Scottish Parliament, the Kirk was sometimes seen as a kind of surrogate Scottish Parliament. But as noted in our earlier discussion of the terminology of 'establishment', although the Church of Scotland maintains a formal link with the Crown, its form of 'establishment' does not entail any legal restrictions upon its self-government. In particular, in contrast to the position of bishops of the Church of England, the state does not have any role at all in the appointment of the Church of Scotland's leaders.

While Scotland has also had a substantial presence of both Episcopalians and Roman Catholics, Catholicism has often been identified with Irishness and Episcopalianism with Englishness. Even as late as the mid-1980s it could still be written that, 'To be a Scot is to be a Presbyterian, even though that designation may say more of cultural identity than religious persuasion.'[36]

In the 2001 Census results for Scotland, 3,294,545 people or 65.1% of the population of Scotland (and 97.2% of the population of Scotland identifying itself with any specific religion at all) is recorded as in some way identifying itself as 'Christian'. Table 3.8 gives the breakdown by denomination of those identifying as 'Christian' in Scotland, in the 2001 Census. Considered in relation to 'Church attendance', based on estimates by Christian Research for the year 2001, Table 3.9 sets this out by denomination in Scotland.

Interestingly (given what have often appeared to be higher levels of religious participation in Scotland than in England) the total proportion of the population in Scotland identifying itself with any specific religion at all appears, according to the Census, to be lower than in England. As previously noted, however, it is possible this may relate to the 'harder-edged' form of the Census question as asked in Scotland which referred to 'belonging' to specific denominational traditions as compared with the more general form of the religion question asked in England and Wales.

Table 3.8: Census results by religious denomination for those identifying as 'Christian' in Scotland

Religious denomination	Total numbers	Percentage of Scotland population	Percentage of population of Scotland identifying as 'Christian'
Presbyterian	2,146,251	42.4%	65.1%
Roman Catholic	803,732	15.9%	24.4%
Other Christian	344,562	6.8%	10.5%
Total	3,294,545	*	100.0%

*Other Religions and Philosophies are 1.9% of the population. Those of 'No religion' are 27.5% and 'Not stated' are 5.5% of the population
Source: Census, April 2001. National Statistics website: www.statistics.gov.uk. Crown copyright, 2004. Crown copyright material is reproduced with the permission of the Controller of HMSO. Percentages as shown are calculated by the present author on the basis of the original Census data.

Table 3.9: Estimates of 'Church attendance' by denomination in Scotland in 2000

Denomination	Church attendance	Church Attendance (%)
Episcopal	19,500	3.2%
Baptist	24,800	4.1%
Catholic	211,200	35.1%
Church of Scotland	248,600	41.3%
Independent	45,000	7.5%
Other Presbyterian	22,600	3.8%
Other Churches	30,700	5.1%
Total	602,400	Due to rounding, figures may not total 100.0%

Source: From figures in P. Brierley (ed.), *UK Christian Handbook: Religious Trends No. 4, 2003/2004* (London: Christian Research, 2003), Table 2.24.3, p. 2.24. Percentages as shown are calculations by the present author based on original figures from Christian Research.

d. *Christianity in Wales*

With regard to Wales, until the recent creation of the Welsh Assembly, Wales had very little modern constitutional distinctiveness, but it has had a vigorous ancient culture and language, the latter having been revived during the 1960s through the campaigns of *Cymdeithas yr Iaith Gymraeg* (the Welsh Language Society). In terms of religion, following the 1920 disestablishment of the Church in Wales there has been no established form of religion in Wales.[37] As has already been noted, it is from the disestablished Church in Wales that the new Archbishop of Canterbury, Rowan Williams, comes (although it should be noted that, during his earliest years, his family identified with the Presbyterian Church of Wales).

Unlike Scotland, in Wales there has not been a single predominant religious tradition that has acted as a focus for national identity, although the multiplicity of nonconformist Free Churches have played a significant role in Wales's social, political and cultural life.[38] These Churches were often at the forefront of nineteenth- and early twentieth-century agitation for disestablishment in Wales and they have also played a major role in preserving and promoting the use of the Welsh language. Since disestablishment, the Church in Wales has also become more attuned to nationalist feeling.

In the 2001 Census results for Wales 2,087,242 people or 71.9% of the population of Wales (and 98% of the population of Wales identifying itself with any specific religion at all) is recorded as, in some sense, identifying itself as 'Christian'. Based on estimates by Christian Research for the year 2000, 'Church attendance' by denominational tradition in Wales is set out in Table 3.10. From this table it can be seen that while Anglicans form the largest single group in terms of 'Church attendance', this is less than the combined total of the Free Churches in Wales and less than a third of the overall Christian total.

Table 3.10: Estimates of 'Church attendance' by denomination in Wales in 2000

Denomination	Church attendance'	Church attendance (%)
Church in Wales	63,300	28.2%
Baptist	22,500	10.1%
Catholic	43,800	19.6%
Methodist	15,600	7.0%
Presbyterian Church of Wales	23,800	10.6%
Union of Welsh Independents	16,300	7.3%
Other Churches	39,500	17.7%
Total	223,800	Due to rounding figures may not total 100%

Source: From figures in P. Brierley (ed.), *UK Christian Handbook: Religious Trends No. 4, 2003/2004* (London: Christian Research, 2003), Table 2.24.2, p. 2.24. Percentages as shown are calculations by the present author based on original figures from Christian Research.

e. *Christianity in Northern Ireland*

In Northern Ireland there is also no officially established form of religion, with the episcopal Church of Ireland having been disestablished as long ago as 1871. In addition, the Northern Ireland Act specifically proscribed the establishment of any particular religion or religious tradition. However, at 1,446,386 or 85.8% of the total population (and 99.7% of the population of Northern Ireland that identified itself with any specific religion at all), the profile of Christianity in Northern Ireland is, in numerical terms, stronger than in any other part of the UK. Levels of 'Church attendance' in Northern Ireland are also relatively high although Christian Research does not publish estimates for these.

Christian Research does not publish figures on church attendance in Northern Ireland but, in response to the European Values Survey question on 'How often do you spend time in church, mosque or synagogue?', 28.7% of respondents from Northern Ireland said 'every week' and 11.7% said 'every month', while 14.7% said 'a few times a year' and 41.4% said 'not at all'.[39] In response to the question on 'Apart from weddings, funerals and christenings, about how often do you attend a religious service these days?', 6.34% said 'more than once a month', 16.9% said 'on special occasions' and 19.8% said 'never'.[40] Table 3.11 gives the breakdown by denomination of those identifying as 'Christian' in Northern Ireland, in the 2001 Census, which shows Catholics as the largest single group in the Province.

Table 3.11: Census results by religious denomination for those identifying as 'Christian' in Northern Ireland

Religious denomination	Total numbers	Percentage of Northern Ireland population	Percentage of the population of Northern Ireland identifying as 'Christian'
Catholic	678,462	40.3%	46.9%
Presbyterian Church in Ireland	348,742	20.7%	24.1%
Church of Ireland	257,788	15.3%	17.8%
Methodist Church in Ireland	59,173	3.5%	4.1%
Other Christian	102,221	6.1%	7.1%
Total	1,446,386	*	100.0%

*Respondents of 'Other religions and philosophies' are 5,028 or 0.3% of the population. Those of 'No religion/Not stated' (in Northern Ireland Census results these categories are not differentiated) are 233,8523 or 13.9% of the population.
Source: Census, April 2001. National Statistics website: www.statistics.gov.uk. Crown copyright, 2004. Crown copyright material is reproduced with the permission of the Controller of HMSO. Percentages as shown are calculated by the present author on the basis of the original Census data.

4. *Migration, Christian Diversification and the Growth of Religious Plurality*

a. *Christianity and Ethnic Diversity*

In general, throughout the UK, there is now a much wider diversity of Christian forms of both 'believing' and 'belonging' than was the case when the nineteenth-century debates about establishment were at their height. In part this has come about through ethnic diversification in the wider population. In this context, the migration, settlement and development of new Christian communities has further diversified the profile of Christianity in England beyond even its relatively (as compared with many other European countries) pluralistic Christian inheritance of Anglican, Presbyterian, Roman Catholic and Free Church traditions.

Considered in terms of ethnicity, as Table 3.20 later shows, 96.3% of 'Christian' respondents are 'White', 2.2% are 'Black or black British', 0.9% are 'Mixed', 0.3% are 'Asian' and 0.3% are of 'Chinese or other ethnic group'. As set out in Table 3.21, this means that 75.7% of all those classified as 'White' respondents identified as 'Christian', along with 71.1% of 'Black or black British' respondents, 52.5% of 'Mixed' respondents, 27.3% of 'Chinese or other ethnic group' respondents and 4.1% of 'Asian' respondents.

A significant proportion of migrants from African, and especially those from West African countries, brought with them forms of indigenous Christian life that were developed in African Independent Churches,[41] such as those of the Cherubim and Seraphim traditions.[42] In their home countries, many Caribbean Christian migrants were members of one of the traditional Christian denominations. Following their experience of racism within the traditional Churches of England[43] many black Christians formed independent congregations where they could practise Christianity in ways that could draw upon the integrity of their own Christian experience and leadership,[44] free of the racism they had experienced within the older ecclesial communities.

A number of the congregations formed by black Christians have grouped together to form denominations of their own, while others have linked up with international movements based abroad, particularly in the USA. In more recent times, Churches in this sector of Christianity also began to organize umbrella bodies to represent their interests in the wider Christian ecumenical scene. These include the African West Indian United Council of Churches, the Cherubim and Seraphim Council of Churches, the Council of African and African–Caribbean Churches (UK), the International Ministerial Council of Great Britain, the Joint Council for Anglo-Caribbean Churches, and the New Assembly of Churches.

Together with the Roman Catholic Church (which had not been a member of the former British Council of Churches), these groupings became involved in a new process of ecumenical development. Towards the end of the 1980s, this issued into the so-called new 'ecumenical instruments' that eventually formed into the present ecumenical structures operating at UK and Ireland, national, regional and local levels. These are Churches Together in Britain and Ireland; Churches Together in England; Action of Churches Together in Scotland; Churches Together in Wales (*Eglwysi Ynghyd Yng Nghymru*) and the Irish Council of Churches.

The Orthodox Christian population remains numerically small, although in the earlier part of the century it was strengthened by Russian emigrés following the Bolshevik Revolution in Russia and by economic migration from Greece and refugee migration from Cyprus. In more recent times, it has grown further through the arrival of refugees from the Balkans. Migration and refugee movements from Africa and Latin America have also added to the size of the Roman Catholic Christian community.

But for reasons other than migration, Christianity has undergone other significant transformations in which new forms of Christian life and organization have emerged either outside of, or overlapping with, the more traditional Christian Churches. This has, for example, occurred in the development of the so-called 'Restorationist' or 'New Church' movements which seek to recover a more authentic form of Christian life than they feel has been transmitted by the traditional Churches,[45] with such congregations increasingly being organized in wider groupings and networks.

b. *Religious and National Diversity*
Together with the inherited and developed Christian diversity are now new layers of ethnic, cultural and religious complexity deriving primarily, although not

exclusively, from New Commonwealth immigration. Tables 3.12–15 provide an overview of this religious diversity with reference to the different countries of the UK which show considerable differences with regard to the degree of religious plurality that is to be found in the different parts of the UK. Tables 3.16–19 detail these differences. In addition to differences by country, because of the differing patterns of migration and settlement, some areas within in each country are characterized by a more pronounced religious diversity than are others.

In each nation, the greatest diversity of religions is to be found in cities, metropolitan boroughs and some towns. The cosmopolitan nature of London means that religious as well as ethnic and linguistic diversity is at its widest there. Seaports such as Liverpool, Cardiff and London often have the oldest minority religious communities because trade led to the settlement, in such places, of seafarers from other countries and to the establishment of some degree of community life.[46] Particular local communities often have a considerable degree of homogeneity in respect of a number of factors including religion, ethnicity and national origins. With greater population mobility, such local homogeneity may, in the future, begin to diminish, although it is also likely that the broad differences will persist into the foreseeable future.

What is clear, though, is that, overall, there has been a significant change in the cultural and religious composition of the UK population. Across the UK as a whole, Christians still form the largest group, but this is now followed by Muslims, Hindus, Jews and Sikhs; then Buddhists; then, Bahá'ís, Jains and Zoroastrians; and, finally, by a range of other communities and groups. Table 3.16 shows that, of the four nations that comprise the UK, England has both the broadest and most numerous variety of religious traditions and communities. In this, as Table 3.14 shows 6.0% of the total population, and 7.7% of the population indicating identification with any religion at all, identify with a religion other than Christianity. Among these, Muslims form the largest religious minority followed by Hindus, and then by Sikhs, Jews, 'Other religions' and Buddhists.

Table 3.17 shows the figures and percentages for Scotland. Once again, as in England, Muslims make up the largest religious minority, although in Scotland this is followed by 'Other religions', and then by Buddhists, Sikhs, Jews and Hindus. In Table 3.18 for Wales, as in all other countries in the UK, Muslims form the largest religious minority. As in Scotland, this is followed by 'Other religions', but then by Hindus, Buddhists, Jews and Sikhs.

The figures and percentages for Northern Ireland are set out in Table 3.19. Although other than Christian forms of religious believing and belonging often seem to be invisible in Northern Ireland, and both the absolute and relative size of these groups is much smaller than in the rest of the UK, religious diversity does also exist here. In his book, *Another Ireland*, Maurice Ryan has highlighted some of the unexpected diversity that is to be found, both North and South of the border.[47] As in other parts of the UK, in Northern Ireland Muslims constitute the largest religious minority. As in Wales and Scotland, Muslims are followed by those of 'Other religions' and then, in Northern Ireland, by Hindus, Buddhists, Jews and Sikhs.

Table 3.12: Percentage of the total population of each country in the UK who identify with each religion

Country	Buddhists	Christians	Hindus	Jews	Muslims	Sikhs	Others
England	0.3%	71.7%	1.1%	0.5%	3.1%	0.7%	0.9%
Scotland	0.1%	65.1%	0.1%	0.1%	0.8%	0.1%	0.5%
Wales	0.2%	71.9%	0.2%	0.1%	0.8%	0.1%	0.2%
Northern Ireland	0.03%	85.82%	0.05%	0.02%	0.11%	0.01%	0.07%
United Kingdom	0.3%	71.6%	1.2%	0.5%	2.7%	0.6%	0.3%

Percentages are shown to two decimal points for Northern Ireland where, with rounding up to a single decimal point, the differences between the relatively small numbers identified with some religions would otherwise be invisible.

Source: Census, April 2001. National Statistics website: www.statistics.gov.uk. Crown copyright, 2004. Crown copyright material is reproduced with the permission of the Controller of HMSO. Percentages as shown are calculated by the present author on the basis of the original Census data.

Table 3.13: Total numbers of people identifying with specific religions

Country	Buddhists	Christians	Hindus	Jews	Muslims	Sikhs	Others
England	139,046	35,251,244	546,982	257,671	1,524,887	327,343	143,811
Scotland	6,380	3,294,545	5,564	6,448	42,557	6,572	26,974
Wales	5,407	2,087,242	5,439	2,256	21,739	2,015	6,909
Northern Ireland	533	1,446,386	825	365	1,943	219	1,143
United Kingdom	151,816	42,079,417	558,810	266,740	1,591,126	336,149	178,837

Source: Census, April 2001. National Statistics website: www.statistics.gov.uk. Crown copyright, 2004. Crown copyright material is reproduced with the permission of the Controller of HMSO. Percentages as shown are calculated by the present author on the basis of the original Census data.

Table 3.14: Other than Christian Populations by Country in the UK

Country	Total numbers of other than Christians	Percentage of total population	Percentage of total population identifying with a Religion
England	2,939,740	6.0%	7.7%
Scotland	94,945	1.9%	2.8%
Wales	43,765	1.5%	2.1%
Northern Ireland	5,028	0.3%	0.4%
United Kingdom	3,083,478	5.2%	6.8%

Source: Census, April 2001. National Statistics website: www.statistics.gov.uk. Crown copyright, 2004. Crown copyright material is reproduced with the permission of the Controller of HMSO. Percentages as shown are calculated by the present author on the basis of the original Census data.

Table 3.15: Percentage of the total population of each country in the UK identifying with any specific religion at all who identify with each specific religion

Country	Buddhists	Christians	Hindus	Jews	Muslims	Sikhs	Others
England	0.4%	92.3%	1.4%	0.7%	4.0%	0.9%	0.4%
Scotland	0.2%	97.2%	0.2%	0.2%	1.23%	0.2%	0.8%
Wales	0.3%	98.0%	0.3%	0.1%	1.0%	0.1%	0.3%
Northern Ireland	0.04%	99.65%	0.06%	0.03%	0.13%	0.02%	0.08%
United Kingdom	0.3%	93.2%	1.0%	0.6%	3.5%	0.7%	0.4%

Percentages are shown to two decimal points for Northern Ireland where, with rounding up to a single decimal point, the differences between the relatively small numbers identified with some religions would otherwise be invisible.

Source: Census, April 2001. National Statistics website: www.statistics.gov.uk. Crown copyright, 2004. Crown copyright material is reproduced with the permission of the Controller of HMSO. Percentages as shown are calculated by the present author on the basis of the original Census data.

Table 3.16: Census results for religions in England

Religion	Total numbers in England	Percentages of the total population of England	Percentages of the population of England identifying with any specific religion at all
Buddhist	139,046	0.3%	0.4%
Christian	35,251,244	71.7%	92.3%
Hindu	546,982	1.1%	1.4%
Jewish	257,671	0.5%	0.7%
Muslim	1,524,887	3.1%	4.0%
Sikh	327,343	0.7%	0.9%
Other religion	143,811	0.3%	0.4%
Total	38,190,984	(77.7%)	Due to rounding, figures may not total 100%
No religion	7,171,332	14.6%	–
Not stated	3,776,515	7.7%	–
No religion/ Not stated total	10,947,847	(22.3%)	–
Grand Totals	49,138,831	Due to rounding, figures may not total 100%	–

Source: Census, April 2001. National Statistics website: www.statistics.gov.uk. Crown copyright, 2004. Crown copyright material is reproduced with the permission of the Controller of HMSO. Percentages as shown are calculated by the present author on the basis of the original Census data.

Table 3.17: Census results for religions in Scotland

Religion	Total numbers in Scotland	Percentages of the total population of Scotland	Percentages of the population of Scotland identifying with any specific religion at all
Buddhist	6,830	0.1%	0.2%
Christian	3,294,545	65.1%	97.2%
Hindu	5,564	0.1%	0.7%
Jewish	6,448	0.1%	0.22%
Muslim	42,557	0.8%	1.3%
Sikh	6,572	0.1%	0.2%
Other Religion	26,974	0.5%	0.8%
Total	3,389,490	(67.0%)	Due to rounding, figures may not total 100%
No religion	1,394,460	27.6%	–
Not stated	278,061	5.5%	–
No religion/ Not stated total	1,672,521	33.0%	–
Grand Totals	5,062,011	Due to rounding, figures may not total 100%	–

Source: Census, April 2001. National Statistics website: www.statistics.gov.uk. Crown copyright, 2004. Crown copyright material is reproduced with the permission of the Controller of HMSO. Percentages as shown are calculated by the present author on the basis of the original Census data.

Table 3.18: Census results for religions in Wales

Religion	Total numbers in Wales	Percentages of the total population of Wales	Percentages of the population of Wales identifying with any specific religion at all
Buddhist	5,407	0.2%	0.3%
Christian	2,087,242	71.9%	98.0%
Hindu	5,439	0.2%	0.3%
Jewish	2,256	0.1%	0.1%
Muslim	21,739	0.8%	1.0%
Sikh	2,015	0.1%	0.1%
Other religion	6,909	0.2%	0.3%
Total	2,131,007	(73.4%)	Due to rounding, figures may not total 100%
No religion	537,935	18.5%	
Not stated	234,143	8.1%	
No religion/ Not stated total	772,078	(26.6%)	–
Grand Totals	2,903,085	Due to rounding, figures may not total 100%	–

Source: Census, April 2001. National Statistics website: www.statistics.gov.uk. Crown copyright, 2004. Crown copyright material is reproduced with the permission of the Controller of HMSO. Percentages as shown are calculated by the present author on the basis of the original Census data.

Table 3.19: Census results for religions in Northern Ireland

Religion	Total numbers in N. Ireland	Percentages of the total population of N. Ireland	Percentages of the population of N. Ireland identifying with any specific religion at all
Buddhist	533	0.03%	0.04%
Christian	1,446,386	85.83%	99.65%
Hindu	825	0.05%	0.06%
Jewish	365	0.02%	0.03%
Muslim	1,943	0.12%	0.13%
Sikh	219	0.01%	0.02%
Other Religion	1,143	0.07%	0.08%
Total	1,451,414	(86.13%)	Due to rounding, figures may not total 100%
No religion/ Not stated total*	233,853	(13.88%)	–
Grand Totals	1,685,267	Due to rounding, figures may not total 100%	–

*In Northern Ireland, separate statistics for those of 'No religion' and 'Not stated' are not available.

Percentages are shown to two decimal points to allow for comparison between religions since, with rounding up to a single decimal point, the differences between the relatively small numbers identified with some religions in Northern Ireland would otherwise be invisible. *Source*: Census, April 2001. National Statistics website: www.statistics.gov.uk. Crown copyright, 2004. Crown copyright material is reproduced with the permission of the Controller of HMSO. Percentages as shown are calculated by the present author on the basis of the original Census data.

c. *Religious Belief and Practice, Culture and Ethnicity*

With regard to Christianity it has already been noted that there is a problem about the relationship between Census data on religion and information about religious practice. This problem is compounded with regard to other than Christian religions where, in the main, only extremely broad estimates of religious practice are available and these are based on widely varying criteria. For example, in some religions regular attendance at a place of worship may be particularly important, while in others this may not be so central and there may also be a question about the meaning of 'regularity'. At the same time, it is likely that the 'active' proportion of those self-identifying as being of other than Christian religions could well be higher than the 'active' proportion among the population self-identifying as 'Christian'. This is because, in general terms, minority religious practice is often proportionately more frequent than that found among majorities. In the 2001 Home Office Citizenship Survey, 20% of those identified as Christians were involved in religious associated groups or clubs, while this was the case for 41% of those identified as 'Hindus' and 52% of those identified as 'Jews'.[48]

When examining religious diversity in the UK, the relationship between religion and ethnicity also needs to be considered. Some aspects of this relationship were discussed in the Introduction of this book. Table 3.20 shows Census data for England and Wales on religion by the ethnicity of respondents, while Table 3.21 shows data on ethnicity by the religion of respondents:

Table 3.20 : Religion by ethnicity of respondents in England and Wales

Ethnic group	Christian	Buddhist	Hindu	Jewish	Muslim	Sikh	Other	No religion	Not stated	All people	Base
White	96.3	38.8	1.3	96.8	11.6	2.1	78.4	94.5	90.9	91.3	47,520,866
Mixed	0.9	3.2	1.0	1.2	4.2	0.8	2.5	2.0	1.9	1.3	661,034
Asian	0.3	9.6	96.6	0.7	73.7	96.2	13.7	0.4	3.1	4.4	2,273,737
Black or black British	2.2	1.0	0.5	0.4	6.9	0.2	3.3	1.1	3.1	2.2	1,139,577
Chinese or other ethnic group	0.3	47.3	0.6	0.9	3.7	0.7	2.0	2.0	1.0	0.9	446,702
All People					Due to rounding, figures may not total 100%						52,041,916

Source: Census, April 2001. National Statistics website: www.statistics.gov.uk. Crown copyright, 2004. Crown copyright material is reproduced with the permission of the Controller of HMSO. Percentages as shown are calculated by the present author on the basis of the original Census data.

Table 3.21: Ethnicity by religion of respondent in England and Wales

Religious group	White	Mixed	Asian	Black or black British	Chinese or other ethnic group
Christian	75.7	52.5	4.1	71.1	27.2
Buddhist	0.1	0.7	0.6	0.1	15.3
Hindu	*0.02	0.9	23.5	0.3	0.7
Jewish	0.5	0.5	0.1	0.1	0.5
Muslim	0.4	9.7	50.1	9.3	12.8
Sikh	*0.01	0.4	13.9	0.1	0.5
Other	0.3	0.6	0.9	0.4	0.7
No religion	15.3	23.3	1.4	7.6	33.7
Not stated	7.7	11.5	5.5	11.1	8.6
All people	100	100	100	100	100
Base	46,520,866	661,034	2,273,737	1,139,577	446,702

* In this table, in two instances, percentages are shown to two decimal points to allow for comparison between religions since, with rounding up to a single decimal point, the differences between the relatively small proportions of ethnic groups in some religions would otherwise be invisible.
Source: Census, April 2001. National Statistics website: www.statistics.gov.uk. Crown copyright, 2004. Crown copyright material is reproduced with the permission of the Controller of HMSO. Percentages as shown are calculated by the present author on the basis of the original Census data.

Interpreting such data is not always straightforward other than in very broad terms. On the one hand, it is clear that there can often be a significant overlap between particular religions and particular ethnic groups. However, on the other hand, it is also clear, for example, that both Christianity and Islam in England and Wales have diverse ethnic profiles. Thus, as can be seen in Table 3.20, 11.6% of those identified as 'Muslim' and 96.3% of those identified as 'Christian' are also identified as 'White'; 4.2% of the 'Muslim' population and 0.9% of 'Christian' population are 'Mixed'; 73.7% of the 'Muslim' and 0.3% of the 'Christian' population is 'Asian'; 6.9% of the 'Muslim' and 2.2% of the 'Christian' population is 'Black or black British'; 3.7% of the 'Muslim' and 0.3% of the 'Christian' population is 'Chinese or other ethnic group'.

Of people identifying as 'Buddhists', 38.8% are recorded as 'White', which indicates the relative numerical importance of 'White' adherents within the overall 'Buddhist' population of England and Wales. However, although the numbers of 'White' adherents to Islam is increasing, it may also be that the 11.6% of 'Muslims' recorded as 'White' could include significant numbers of Arab and Middle Eastern respondents who opted for 'White' in preference to any of the other pre-set categories for Census response.

In broad terms, as can be seen from Table 3.21, in England and Wales the vast majority of those who are recorded as being of 'Asian' origins are also recorded as 'Muslim', 'Hindu' or 'Sikh' by religion. Nevertheless, at the same time, 4.1% of 'Asians' are recorded as 'Christians'. Only 1.4% of all 'Asians' indicate 'no religion' as compared with a relatively very high 33.7% of 'Chinese and other ethnic group' respondents, 15.3% of the 'White' population, and 14.8% of the population as a whole.

It is therefore to a more detailed delineation of the populations associated with these various groups that this chapter now turns. In doing so, as explained in the opening to this chapter, the following sections draw on the introductions to the various religions found in the directory, *Religions in the UK: Directory, 2001–3*.

5. The Muslim Population and Organizations

a. Muslim Numbers and History

The largest and most diverse[49] religious minority in both England and the UK are Muslims. Table 3.22 shows, by country of the UK, the numbers of people in the 2001 Census identifying themselves as, in some sense, 'Muslims'.

Table 3.22: Census respondents identifying themselves as 'Muslim' by country of the UK

Country	Total numbers of Muslims	Percentages of the total population of each country	Percentages of the population of each country identifying with any specific religion at all
England	1,524,887	3.1%	4.0%
Scotland	42,557	0.8%	1.3%
Wales	21,739	0.8%	1.0%
Northern Ireland	1,943	0.1%	0.1%
United Kingdom	1,591,126	2.7%	3.5%

Source: Census, April 2001. National Statistics website: www.statistics.gov.uk. Crown copyright, 2004. Crown copyright material is reproduced with the permission of the Controller of HMSO. Percentages as shown are calculated by the present author on the basis of the original Census data.

The largest group of Muslims in the UK have ancestral origins in the Indo-Pakistan subcontinent, having come to Britain either directly or via earlier migrations to East Africa. The vast majority of the remaining Muslim population have ethnic and national origins in countries such as Cyprus, Malaysia, Turkey, Iran and the Arab world, but there are also a growing number of white people who have embraced Islam.

The earliest Muslim presence in the UK was that of individuals who, during the period of expansion of the British Empire, arrived as servants, *ayahs*, visitors or settlers. Significant communities began to emerge in geographically local-ized areas during the nineteenth century, in particular when Muslim seafarers and traders from the Middle East began to settle around major seaports such as Liverpool and Cardiff, as well as Yemenis in North-East England.

After the First World War these local communities were supplemented by the further settlement of Muslims who had been demobilized from military service in the armed forces of the British Empire. But it was following the Second World War that the size, distribution and significance of the Muslim population of the UK significantly expanded. Once again, this occurred initially through the settle-ment of individual Muslims during the demobilization of the armed forces. But it was the migration, in the 1950s and 1960s, of workers from the Indo-Pakistani subcontinent to work in the mills and the factories during the years of post-war reconstruction and labour shortage, which led to Muslims becoming a permanent feature of the wider society of UK life. During the 1970s, as primary immigration was brought to a halt through increasingly restrictive immigration legislation, the community continued to expand through the migration of spouses and children. In the 1980s this continued through the refugee settlement of Muslims from the conflicts in Somalia, Bosnia and the Middle East.

b. *Muslim Ethnic and Religious Diversity*
As seen in Table 3.20, 73.7% of the 'Muslim' population are recorded as 'Asian', 11.6% as 'White', 6.9% as 'Black or black British', 4.2% as 'Mixed' and 3.7% as 'Chinese or other ethnic group'. As set out in Table 3.21, this means that 50.1% of all those recorded as 'Asians' are recorded as 'Muslim' as are 12.8% of 'Chinese or other ethnic group', 9.7% of 'Mixed', 9.3% of 'Black or black British' and 0.4% of 'White' people.

In addition to its ethnic diversity, the Muslim population of the UK can also be considered in relation to its various religious traditions. In the UK, as globally, both the Sunni and the Shi'a Muslim traditions[50] are present, with Sunnis being the majority here, as globally. Within the Sunni Muslim tradition there are a number of what might be called 'tendencies' or 'movements'.[51] In the UK, the majority of these groupings are of South Asian origin[52] such as the Barelwis, Deobandis, the Tablighi Jamaat and the Ahl-e-Hadith, each of which have their own emphases, networks, structures and organizations.[53] The Barelwi[54] movement is a devotional form of Islam that is particularly strong among Muslims of rural origin. Barelwis look to *sayyids* (descendants of the Prophet) and to *pirs* (spiritual guides) for spiritual authority, teaching, guidance and intercession with God. They also promote popular devotional practice at the shrines of *pirs* and defend the Islamic legitimacy of this practice. The Barelwi tendency is particularly strong in commu-nities with rural origins. The World Islamic Mission and the Jamaat Ahl-e-Sunnat

UK (an organization of *imams* and *ulama* within the Barelwi tendency) are two national organizations that have links with the Barelwi movement.

The Deobandi[55] movement promotes an interpretation of Islam in which the focus is on textual scholarship. Within this, study of the Qur'an, *Hadith* and *Shari'ah* (as interpreted in the tradition of the Hanafi school) is emphasized. In the UK, the Deobandi movement is strongest in Lancashire, West Yorkshire and the Midlands. The Dar-ul-Uloom seminary in Bury and the Jamiat-e-Ulama of Britain (an organization for Muslim scholars associated with the Deobandi movement) are two national organizations with links to this movement.

The Tablighi Jamaat[56] is generally within the Deobandi tradition and it is usually non-political. Its aim is to encourage other Muslims to practise the ritual aspects of Islam in a more fervent and regular way. Its centre of strength in the UK is in Dewsbury but it is also very active elsewhere in West Yorkshire, Lancashire and the Midlands.

Ahl-e-Hadith[57] is a movement whose followers claim to accept only the teachings of the Qur'an and the earliest teachings of the *Hadith*. The movement is sometimes known as *ghayr muqallidun* (not attached to any school of thought). Within the UK it is mainly concentrated in Birmingham and London and has around 35 branches that are nationally linked by the Markazi Jamiat Ahl-e-Hadith UK.

Also significant is the Jamaat-I-Islami.[58] In India and Sri Lanka this has operated as a religious movement, but in Pakistan and Bangladesh it has been a religio-political party. It was founded by Sayyid Abul A'la Mawdudi (1903–79) in 1941 in India. In the face of the secular impact of Western civilization it is committed to seeing the development of an Islamic ideology embodied in an Islamic state. Among the organizations in the UK which have a relationship with the thought of Mawdudi are the UK Islamic Mission which originally developed mainly among migrants from Pakistan and has a network of local branches throughout the country. In 1976, after the emergence of Bangladesh, Bengali Muslims established their own Dawat-ul-Islam movement.

Shi'a is an Arabic word which literally means follower or associate. Shi'a Muslims[59] believe that a succession (the descendants of Ali and Fatima, the Prophet's youngest daughter) of individual Imams (spiritual leaders) was instituted from within Muhammad's family in order to continue to give guidance to the community. Along with other Muslims, the Shi'a believe that the process of revelation was completed with Muhammad. However, they differ from other Muslims through their belief that there are also Imams or *Hujjah* (Proofs of God) who are specially selected by God to interpret the Qur'an, and that these leaders can provide authoritative contemporary guidance to the believers.

Shi'a Muslims all agree that Ali was the first Imam. There are then, however, differences of view concerning the succession. A minority are known as Seveners. The majority are known as Twelvers (or 'Ithna Asherites).[60] Examples of Twelver Shi'a Muslim organizations in the UK include the World Ahl ul-Bayt (AS) Islamic League and the World Federation of Khoja Shi'a Ithna-Asheri Muslim Communities. Ismailis are Shi'a Muslims who accept the leadership of the first six Imams and they are known as 'Seveners'[61] because they then claim primacy for the oldest son of the sixth Imam, Ismail. There are also Nizari Ismailis who are more generally known as Agha Khanis. The Aga Khan is accepted as their living Imam, and it is expected that he will choose a member of his family to succeed him. The Ismaili Centre in London is a key contact point for Ismaili Shi'a Islam.

The mystical dimension of Islam that is found in both the Sunni and Shi'a traditions is known as *Tasawwuf* (Sufism).[62] While also involving a commitment to the practical aspects of Islam embodied in the Shari'ah, Sufism emphasizes the inner or esoteric aspects of Islam. Members of Sufi Orders are likely to engage in such practices as meditation, chanting the names of God and ritual dancing. The global Sufi Orders include the Naqshbandi, the Qadiri, the Chishti and the Suhrawardi. In the UK, Sufis are active in most towns and cities with a substantial Muslim presence.

As well as organizations that are connected with particular movements, a variety of other organizations seek to link Muslims of particular ethnic or national backgrounds. These include, for example, the Sri Lanka Islamic UK Association and the Indian Muslim Federation UK. The Association for British Muslims was established as long ago as 1889 to assist indigenous British people who embrace Islam.

c. *Muslim Organizations and Places of Worship*
Religions in the UK lists 147 Muslim organizations that operate on a national or UK basis.[63] The directory also lists 19 regional Muslim organizations (of which 18 are in England and 1 in Wales)[64] and 953 local Muslim organizations (of which 894 are in England, 26 in Wales, 32 in Scotland, and 1 in Northern Ireland).[65] These local organizations include approximately 486 mosques (of which approximately 443 are in England, 21 in Scotland, 21 in Wales and 1 in Northern Ireland).[66] At city or county levels there a number of Islamic federations and councils of mosques such the Bradford Council of Mosques, the Lancashire Council of Mosques and the Federation of Muslim Organisations in Leicestershire.

On a national level in recent years some Muslims within the UK have begun to form explicitly political organizations, an example of which is the Islamic Party of Britain that was launched, in July 1989, by a group of mainly indigenous followers of Islam. Their declared aim was to work for a better future for Islam in the UK and for a radical change to economic injustice in society. In addition, in the wake of the 11 September attacks on the World Trade Centre and the Pentagon, radical Islamist groups such as Al-Muhajiroun and Hizb ut-Tahrir have attracted a substantial amount of media and other attention, disproportionate to their actual size and influence.

Over the past decade a number of organizations have attempted to provide a broad representative voice for Muslims of various traditions, movements and ethnic/national groups at a national level within the UK. These include the Imams and Mosques Council, the Union of Muslim Organisations and the Muslim Parliament of Great Britain. There have also been a number of Muslim organizations that were founded to campaign on particular issues of concern to Muslims, such as the UK Action Committee on Islamic Affairs. For a long time no single organization established itself as a generally accepted and authoritative national council, although in recent times the development of the Muslim Council of Great Britain has emerged as a body which has evidenced both organizational stability and broad representation.

6. *The Hindu Population and Organizations*

a. *Hindu Numbers and History*

Small numbers of Hindus have visited and worked in the UK for centuries. But it was not until the 1950s and 1960s that significant numbers settled here and the contours of an organized community began to emerge.[67] Some arrived directly from India, but between 1965 and 1972 others came from countries of previous migration (such as Kenya, Tanzania, Uganda, Zambia and Malawi) when the Africanization policies of these newly independent states resulted in ethnic Asians becoming economic migrants and/or refugees. Hindu migrants also came from Fiji, as well as from Trinidad and other Caribbean islands.[68] Table 3.23 shows the numbers of people in the 2001 Census who identified themselves as in some sense 'Hindus'.

Table 3.23: Census respondents identifying themselves as 'Hindu' by country in the UK

Country	Total numbers of Hindus	Percentages of the total population of each country	Percentages of the population of each country identifying with any specific religion at all
England	546,982	1.1%	1.4%
Scotland	5,564	0.1%	0.2%
Wales	5,439	0.2%	0.3%
Northern Ireland	825	0.1%	0.1%
United Kingdom	558,810	1.2%	1.0%

Source: Census, April 2001. National Statistics website: www.statistics.gov.uk. Crown copyright, 2004. Crown copyright material is reproduced with the permission of the Controller of HMSO. Percentages as shown are calculated by the present author on the basis of the original Census data.

b. *Hindu Ethnic and Religious Diversity*

In the UK as a whole, between around 55 and 70% of Hindus are thought to be of Gujarati background, between 15 and 20% of Punjabi origin. Other Hindus in the UK have ancestral origins in other parts of India such as Uttar Pradesh, West Bengal, and the Southern states, as well as in countries such as Sri Lanka. Thus the Hindu population is composed of many ethnic and linguistic groups, the most common of which are Gujarati, Hindi, Punjabi, Bengali and Tamil.

As seen in Table 3.20, 96.6% of those recorded as 'Hindus' are also recorded as being of 'Asian' ethnic origin, 1.3% are 'White', 1.0% are 'Mixed'; 0.6% are 'Chinese or other ethnic group' and 0.5% are 'Black or black British'. As set out in Table 3.21 this means that 23.5% of all those recorded as 'Asians' are also recorded as 'Hindu', as well as 0.9% of 'Mixed', 0.7% of 'Chinese or other ethnic group', 0.3% of 'Black or black British' and 0.02% of those recorded as 'White'.

Within the Hindu population as a whole, but especially among Gujaratis, caste or *jati* groups have important functions ranging from social networking to voluntary welfare support. Although in the UK these do not necessarily correlate with the social, economic or occupational status of individuals and families they do remain significant social, cultural and economic networks within many aspects of internal Hindu community life. Due to differential patterns of settlement *jati* groups can be found concentrated in specific localities including, for example, a concentration of Mochis in Leeds and Lohanas in Leicester and North London.

Sampradaya[69] or spiritual traditions also often have a linkage with a regional base in India. These include Swaminarayan Hindus[70] who, in the UK, are predominantly of Gujarati origin, and the Pushtimarg or Vallabha *sampradaya* whose members are largely Lohana by *jati*. There are also members of the ISKCON (The International Society for Krishna Consciousness,[71] the Arya Samaj and the Ramakrishna Mission and a large number of Hindu-related traditions and movements, including TM (Transcendental Meditation) and the Divine Life Society.

c. *Hindu Organizations and Places of Worship*

The earliest Hindu organizations in the UK were established in the late 1950s. A variety of different national, regional and local organizations have been developed since then. *Religions in the UK*, for example, records 42 Hindu organizations with a UK or national scope[72] and 18 regional ones (including 17 in England and 1 in Wales).[73] It also records 312 local groups (including 302 in England, 6 in Wales, 3 in Scotland and 1 in Northern Ireland).[74] These include approximately 131 Hindu *mandirs* (temples) (of which around 121 are in England, 3 in Scotland, 5 in Wales and 2 in Northern Ireland).[75]

There is no one national representative organization of Hindus in the UK, although the Hindu Council (UK), founded in November 1994, has developed an umbrella role in relation to the various national groupings. These include the National Council of Hindu Temples (UK) and the UK arm of the international organization, Vishwa Hindu Parishad (The World Council of Hindus) which also has local branches throughout the UK. At the local and regional levels there has been some development of representative groups such as the Hindu Council (Brent), the Hindu Council of Birmingham, the Leicester Gujarat Hindu Association, the Hindu Council of the North and the Hindu Resource Centre (Croydon).

7. *The Sikh Population and Organizations*

a. *Sikh Numbers and History*

The UK Sikh population is the largest outside the Indian subcontinent. Table 3.24 shows the numbers of people in the 2001 Census who identified themselves as in some sense 'Sikh'.

Table 3.24: Census respondents identifying themselves as 'Sikh' by country in the UK

Country	Total numbers of Sikhs	Percentages of the total population of each country	Percentages of the population of each country who identify with any specific religion at all
England	327,343	0.7%	0.9%
Scotland	6,572	0.1%	0.2%
Wales	2,015	0.1%	0.1%
Northern Ireland	219	0.01%	0.02%
United Kingdom	336,149	0.6%	0.7%

In this table percentages Sikh figures for N. Ireland are shown to two decimal points since, when rounding up to a single decimal point, the very small numbers identified as Sikhs would otherwise be invisible.
Source: Census, April 2001. National Statistics website: www.statistics.gov.uk. Crown copyright, 2004. Crown copyright material is reproduced with the permission of the Controller of HMSO. Percentages as shown are calculated by the present author on the basis of the original Census data.

One of the first Sikhs to live in the UK was an exiled young Sikh prince called Maharaja Dalip Singh, the son of Maharaja Ranjit Singh, who acquired the Elveden Estate in Norfolk. During the First and Second World Wars many Sikhs served in the British Indian armies and a number of ex-servicemen migrated to Britain particularly after the Second World War. But the vast majority of Sikh migrants arrived in the 1950s and 1960s.[76] Many came directly from the Punjab, although a significant minority also came, in similar circumstances to the Hindu migrants described above, from East Africa and other former British colonies.[77]

b. *Sikh Ethnic and Religious Diversity*
Most Sikhs are of Punjabi ethnic origin. A few are indigenous converts, although conversion is not common because Sikhism is not an actively proselytizing faith. Most Sikhs in the UK speak Punjabi, as well as English, with most *gurdwaras* running Punjabi language classes.

As can be seen in Table 3.20, 96.2% of those recorded as 'Sikh' are also recorded as being of 'Asian' origin, 2.1% are 'White', 0.8% are 'Mixed', 0.7% are 'Chinese or other ethnic group' and 0.2% are 'Black or black British'. As set out in Table 3.21, this means that 13.9% of all those recorded as 'Asians' are also recorded as 'Sikh', as are 0.5% of 'Chinese and other ethnic groups', 0.4% of 'Mixed', 0.1% of 'Black or black British' and 0.01% of 'Whites'.

Sikh religious teachings emphasize that there should be no distinctions between people and therefore reject the concept of *caste* (or *Jat*) as something that has no religious significance. However, social groups do continue to play a role in the life of the community and the names of such groupings are, for example, often reflected in the names of *gurdwaras*. Although they do not necessarily define who is allowed to attend a particular *gurdwara*, in practice the names used may indicate the background of those who do actually attend.[78]

c. *Sikh Organizations and Places of Worship*

Religions in the UK records details of 29 UK Sikh organizations (and 1 in Northern Ireland)[79] and 3 Sikh regional organizations (all of which are in England).[80] It also records details of 244 Sikh local organizations (of which 233 are in England, 4 in Wales, 6 in Scotland and 1 in Northern Ireland)[81] including details of approximately 170 *gurdwaras* in the UK (of which 159 are in England, 6 are in Scotland, 4 are in Wales and 1 is in Northern Ireland).[82] The majority of *gurdwaras* in the world, including in the UK, follow guidance from the Shiromani Gurdwara Parbandhak Committee (SGPC), Amritsar, which is based at the *Harmandir Sahib* (Golden Temple) complex at Amritsar in the Punjab. A major municipal grouping of *gurdwaras* (Sikh places of worship) is the Council of Sikh Gurdwaras in Birmingham. Councils of *gurdwaras* have also begun to emerge in a number of other towns and cities.

A range of national groups and organizations also exist, such as the Sikh Missionary Society, and a number of groups define themselves in relation to the political demand for an independent Sikh homeland of Khalistan. At a UK level the Network of Sikh Organisations (UK) facilitates co-operation among Sikhs.

8. *The Jewish Population and Organizations*

a. *Jewish Numbers and History*

Jewish people have had historical roots in England that go back for many centuries.[83] However, they suffered sporadic outbreaks of persecution until Edward I expelled them in 1290. Following the English Civil War and during the period of the Commonwealth, Menasseh ben Israel of Amsterdam successfully campaigned for the readmission of Jews to England.

Following the death of six million European Jews in the killing fields and the death camps of Second World War continental Europe, the community in the UK is now one of the largest in Europe.[84] At the same time, it is a population that is in decline, with the results of the 2001 Census confirming what had previously been indicated by internal community surveys. Table 3.25 shows the numbers of people in the 2001 Census identifying themselves as in some sense 'Jews'.

Table 3.25: Census respondents identifying themselves as 'Jews' by country of the UK

Country	Total Numbers of Jews	Percentages of total population	Percentages of the population of each country who identify with any specific religion at all
England	257,671	0.5%	0.7%
Scotland	6,448	0.1%	0.2%
Wales	2,256	0.1%	0.1%
Northern Ireland	365	0.02%	0.03%
United Kingdom	266,740	0.5%	0.6%

In this table percentages Jewish figures for N. Ireland are shown to two decimal points since, when rounding up to a single decimal point, the relatively small numbers identified as Jews would otherwise be invisible.

Source: Census, April 2001. National Statistics website: www.statistics.gov.uk. Crown copyright, 2004. Crown copyright material is reproduced with the permission of the Controller of HMSO. Percentages as shown are calculated by the present author on the basis of the original Census data.

b. *Jewish Ethnic and Religious Diversity*

Initially, the Jewish community was predominantly Sephardi, which refers to those Jews who originally migrated from Spain and Portugal. Today, however, the majority of Jews in the UK are descendents of the Ashkenazi stream of the community whose origins can be traced to two major migrations from Central and Eastern Europe. The first Ashkenazi migration occurred between 1881 and 1914, when the community was strengthened by a combination of economic migration in the face of restricted social and economic possibilities, and escape from the anti-Jewish pogroms occurring within the Russian Empire. This was followed, from 1933 onwards, by the arrival of refugees from persecution and the Holocaust in Germany and other Nazi-occupied European countries. Although there are differences of religious identity and practice between those Jews who are descendants of the Sephardi and those who are descendants of the Ashkenazi, in terms of religion the more significant differences are now to be found between the Orthodox and Progressive strands of Judaism.

As can be seen in Table 3.20, 96.8% of those recorded as 'Jews' are also recorded as 'White', 1.2% as 'Mixed', 0.9% as 'Chinese or other ethnic group', 0.7% as 'Asian' and 0.4% as 'Black or black British'. As set out in Table 3.21, this means 0.5% of all those recorded as being 'White', 'Mixed' and as 'Chinese or other ethnic group' are also recorded as being 'Jews', as are 0.1% of all those recorded as 'Black or black British' and of those recorded as 'Asians'.

With regard to religious traditions, in the UK the basic traditions of Judaism are those of Orthodox and of Progressive (including the Reform and Liberal movements).[85] The principal Orthodox organization is the United Synagogue, established in 1870, and the spiritual leader of many Orthodox Ashkenazi Jews is the Chief Rabbi of the Hebrew Congregations of the Commonwealth. Smaller Orthodox groupings also exist including the Federation of Synagogues, founded in 1887, and the Union of Orthodox Hebrew Congregations, established in 1926.

There are two Progressive traditions in the UK – the Reform and the Liberal. The first Reform synagogue, the West London Synagogue, was opened in 1840 while the Liberal movement began in 1902 with the founding of the Jewish Religious Union. The Liberal movement has declined numerically, and although separate Reform Synagogues of Great Britain and the Union of Liberal and Progressive Synagogues continue to exist, there is also a joint Council of Reform and Liberal Rabbis.

c. *Jewish Organizations and Places of Worship*

Across the Jewish community as a whole, there has been a dynamic expansion of organizational development servicing every aspect of community life, at national, regional and local levels.[86] *Religions in the UK* includes details of 88 national Jewish organizations[87] and 14 regional ones (including 13 in England and 1 in Scotland).[88] It also records details of 282 local ones (including 272 in England, 7 in Scotland, 2 in Wales and 1 in Northern Ireland)[89] including details of approximately 184 synagogues in the UK (including approximately 176 in England, 5 in Scotland, 2 in Wales and 1 in Northern Ireland). There are, in fact,[90] many more Jewish organizations than those recorded in *Religions in the UK*, details of which can be found in *The Jewish Yearbook*.[91]

In major areas of Jewish population, so-called Representative Councils were established to represent and reflect the breadth of the community. At a national level, the Board of Deputies of British Jews, founded in 1760, is the organization which is the Jewish communal body covering Jews of all religious traditions as well as Jewish secular and cultural organizations.

9. *The Buddhist Population and Organizations*

a. *Buddhist Numbers and History*

During the nineteenth century a significant degree of academic interest in Buddhism developed among indigenous scholars.[92] As a result, Buddhist texts were translated into English, and an increasing number of individuals became interested in Buddhist teaching. The earliest Buddhist missions to the UK were undertaken by indigenous people who became Buddhists outside of the country returning later, over the first two decades of the twentieth century, to lead Buddhist missions in the UK. This was followed by migratory and refugee movements of Buddhists into England.[93] Table 3.26 shows the numbers of people in the 2001 Census identifying themselves as in some sense Buddhists.

Table 3.26: Census respondents identifying as 'Buddhist' by country in the UK

Country	Total numbers of Buddhists	Percentages of total population	Percentages of the population of each country who identify with any specific religion at all
England	139,046	0.3%	0.4%
Scotland	6,830	0.1%	0.2%
Wales	5,407	0.2%	0.3%
Northern Ireland	533	0.03%	0.04%
United Kingdom	151,816	0.3%	0.3%

In this table percentages Buddhist figures for N. Ireland are shown to two decimal points since, when rounding up to a single decimal point, the relatively small numbers identified as Buddhists would otherwise be invisible.

Source: Census, April 2001. National Statistics website: www.statistics.gov.uk. Crown copyright, 2004. Crown copyright material is reproduced with the permission of the Controller of HMSO. Percentages as shown are calculated by the present author on the basis of the original Census data.

b. *Buddhist Ethnic and Religious Diversity*

In terms of ethnicity, Table 3.20 shows that 47.3% of Buddhists are also recorded as being of 'Chinese and other ethnic groups', 38.8% are 'White', 9.6% are 'Asian', 3.2% are 'Mixed' and 1.0% are 'Black or black British'. As set out in Table 3.21, 15.3% of all those recorded as 'Chinese and other ethnic groups' are also recorded as being 'Buddhist', as are 0.7% of 'Mixed', 0.6% of 'Asians', 0.1% of 'Black and black British' and 0.1% of people recorded as 'White'. In terms of major religious traditions, groups and organizations from both the so-called Southern Transmission of Theravada Buddhism (the way of the Elders)[94] and the Northern Transmission of Mahayana Buddhism (the great vehicle)[95] are found in the UK.

Mahayana Buddhist groups include Tibetan Buddhist[96] organizations. The first Tibetan Buddhist centre in the west was founded at Johnstone House in Dumfriesshire, in Scotland, in 1967 by Chogyam Trungpa, a former Abbot of the Surmang group of monasteries in Tibet and Akong Rinpoche, the former Abbot of the Drolma Lhakhang Monastery. The Centre is known as Kagyu Samye Ling and it is representative of the Kagyupa tradition which, together with the Gelugpa, is the strongest of the Tibetan traditions in Britain. The former tends towards a more direct mystical experience, while the latter is more graduated in its approach and is typified by the Manjushri Institute, founded in 1976 by pupils of Lama Thubten Yeshe.

There are a number of Buddhist groups that have recognizably Japanese origins such as the pacifist Nipponzan Myohoji Order that has a London Peace Pagoda, inaugurated in 1985, and also one in Milton Keynes. Among Sri Lankans, the London Buddhist Vihara was the first Buddhist monastery to be established outside of Asia. It was founded, in 1926, by Angarika Dharmapala. Among Thai Buddhists, the Buddhapadipa Temple is a focus of activity with resident monks selected by the Sangha Supreme Council of Thailand.

c. *Buddhist Organizations and Places of Worship*
Religions in the UK records details of 69 Buddhist organizations working at a national level[97] and 37 Buddhist regional organizations (including 34 in England, 1 in Wales, and 2 in Northern Ireland).[98] It also includes details of 237 Buddhist local organizations (including 204 in England, 16 in Wales, 15 in Scotland and 2 in Northern Ireland)[99] among which are approximately 148 Buddhist viharas, monasteries and other publicly accessible Buddhist buildings (including around 129 in England, 8 in Scotland, 10 in Wales, and 1 in Northern Ireland).[100]

At national level, the Buddhist Society is generally recognized among Buddhists as a national point of contact and information on all Buddhist traditions in the UK. In more recent times, a Network of Buddhist Organisations (UK) has also emerged.

10. *Other Religious Groups and Organizations*

a. *'Other Religions': Numbers and Types*
The data for 'Other religions' as recorded in the top level Census results covers all religious groups other than Buddhists, Christians, Hindus, Jews, Muslims and Sikhs (the latter having tick-box options in the Census questions on religion). It therefore includes Bahá'ís, Jains and Zoroastrians as members of generally accepted world religious traditions with significant communities in the UK, as well as followers of New Religious Movements and other religious groups. These include groups that have a disputed historical or doctrinal relationship with those world religious traditions that have significant communities in Britain; groups known to academics as 'New Religious Movements' and more popularly often referred to as 'sects' and/or 'cults'; as well as a whole range of 'New Age' and spiritual movements.

Table 3.27 shows the overall numbers of people in the 2001 Census who indicated they identified with religions that were 'Other' than the pre-set categories of responses listed in the Census questions on religion by ticking the 'other, please write in' boxes.

Table 3.27: Census respondents identifying as being of 'other' religions than the pre-set categories offered by the census questions on religion by country of the UK

Country	Total numbers of 'Other' religions	Percentages of total population	Percentages of the population of each country who identify with any specific religion at all
England	143,811	0.3%	0.4%
Scotland	26,974	0.5%	0.8%
Wales	6,909	0.2%	0.3%
Northern Ireland	1,143	0.1%	0.1%
UK	178,837	0.3%	0.4%

Source: Census, April 2001. National Statistics website: www.statistics.gov.uk. Crown copyright, 2004. Crown copyright material is reproduced with the permission of the Controller of HMSO. Percentages as shown are calculated by the present author on the basis of the original Census data.

b. *'Other Religions': Ethnicity*

As can be seen from Table 3.20, 78.4% of all those responding as 'Other religions' than those for which tick-boxes were provided are also recorded as being 'White', 13.7% as 'Asian', 3.3% as 'Black or black British', 2.5% as 'Mixed' and 2.0% as 'Chinese or other ethnic group'. As set out in Table 3.21, this means that 0.9% of all those recorded in the Census as being 'Asians' are also recorded as being of 'Other religions', as well as 0.7% of 'Chinese and other ethnic group', 0.6% of 'Mixed', 0.4% of 'Black or black British' and 0.3% of those recorded as 'White'.

Clearly, while giving some impression of the religious diversity that exists beyond the largest groups these overall figures for 'Other religions' do not convey much by way of the variety of religious life involved. Using data commissioned from the Office for National Statistics on the basis of the coding of 'write-ins' for the 'other religion' responses, statistics for Bahá'ís, Jains and Zoroastrians in England and Wales are, as set out, in Table 3.28.

Table 3.28: Census respondents coded as 'Bahá'ís', 'Jains' and 'Zoroastrians'

Religion	Total numbers in England	Total numbers in Wales
Bahá'ís	4,374	271
Jains	15,067	65
Zoroastrians	3,355	383

Source: Census, April 2001. Table M275 Religion (most detailed categories). Crown copyright, 2004. Crown copyright material is reproduced with the permission of the Controller of HMSO.

c. *Bahá'ís*

Bahá'ís have been present in the UK since 1899 and some of the early formative history of the religion took place in London. Shoghi Effendi (1897–1957), who became Guardian of the Faith and Interpreter of Scripture, lived here for some time.[101] Up until 1939 most Bahá'í activity in the UK centred upon England, but after the Second World War it also spread to the other nations in the UK.

Religions in the UK includes details of 8 Bahá'í organizations on a UK basis with 2 Scottish, 2 Welsh and 2 Irish organizations. In addition, it records details of 289 Local Groups (of which 178 are in England, 61 are in Scotland, 31 in Wales, and 20 in Northern Ireland)[102] and 125 Local Spiritual Assemblies (of which 105 are in England, 8 in Scotland, 8 in Northern Ireland, and 4 in Wales).[103] These groups are co-ordinated by a single national body, the National Spiritual Assembly of the Bahá'ís of the United Kingdom.

d. *Jains*

The majority of Jains can trace their historical and ethnic origins back to the Gujarat area of India. As with Hindus, some Jains migrated directly from India in the 1950s while others came in the 1970s and 1980s as a result of the Africanization policies being carried out in countries such as Kenya, Tanzania and Uganda where they, or their forebears, had previously settled. Some Jain groupings have membership that is specific to particular social groupings within the community such as the Navnat Vanik Association of the UK, representing Vaniks. In religious terms, there are two main traditions within Jainism, the Shvetambara (meaning 'white-robed')[104] and the Digambara (meaning 'sky-clad', in other words, naked).[105] The majority of Jains in the UK are Shvetambara, but the Digambara have the Digambar Jain Visa Mewada Association of the UK as a national organization.

On a UK level, *Religions in the UK* records details of 16 Jain organizations.[106] It also records 13 regional organizations (all of which are in England)[107] and 27 local organizations (also all of which are in England). This includes details of around 4 Jain *mandirs* (temples) in the UK (of which all are in England)[108] with Leicester being home to the only purpose-built Jain Temple catering for all the major traditions outside of India – the Jain Centre. Many individual UK Jains and local Jain organizations identify with either Jain Samaj Europe or the Institute of Jainology.

e. *Zoroastrians*

Zoroastrians in the UK are only a small community. The first Zoroastrians known to have visited Britain came in 1723 and a Zoroastrian family business called Cama and Company was the first Indian business to be launched, being founded in 1855. However, despite the small size of their community, Zoroastrians made an early and significant impact upon British social and political life. The majority are of Indian origin and are known as Parsees or Parsis. The first three Members of Parliament of Asian ethnic origin were all Parsis. The first of these, in 1892, was Dadabhai Naoroji, who was elected as a Member of Parliament for the Liberal Party.

The contemporary Zoroastrian community includes both Indian and Iranian elements. The Parsees or Parsis (Pars being a province of Iran) migrated from Persia to Sanjan in Gujarat, India, in 936 CE and, over the next thousand years, were joined by many more. Those who remained in Persia were known as the

Irani Zardushtis or simply as Iranis. The majority of Zoroastrians in the UK are of Parsi origin, though in more recent years an Irani presence has also developed as a result of refugee movements arising from the Iranian revolution.

Religions in the UK records details of two Zoroastrian organizations active at a UK level.[109] On a national level the first Zoroastrian organization in the UK was established in 1861. It was known as the Zoroastrian Trust Funds of Europe. Under the new name of the Incorporated Parsee Association of Europe it obtained rented premises for the conduct of Zoroastrian worship and, in 1925, it purchased a building. In 1969, and by then known as the Zoroastrian Association of Europe (Incorporated), it purchased a centre in West Hampstead, London. Since 1978, it has been known as the Zoroastrian Trust Funds of Europe (Incorporated).

There currently being no consecrated Zoroastrian Fire Temple in the UK, community worship takes place at Zoroastrian House in London and at the Zoroastrian Centre in Harrow. A new Zoroastrian Centre has recently been planned in which it is hoped to establish a fire temple. The World Zoroastrian Organisation is also based in London.

f. *Contested Groups: Ahmadiyyas and Namdharis*
In relation to groups that have a disputed relationship with the world religious traditions, these conflicting and sometimes mutually exclusive self-understandings can give rise to considerable tensions, and sometimes actual conflict, between those involved. Majority groupings see the integrity of their traditions and identity as being at stake, while minority groupings may feel discriminated against by the majority. It is possible that many of these may, in their response to the Census questions, have identified themselves with their historical 'parent' tradition even where the majority in that tradition would not wish to recognise them as legitimate members of it.

Among such disputed groups are, for example, the Ahmadiyyas. The Ahmadiyyas understand themselves to be Muslims, and therefore use the word Muslim in the titles of their organizations and literature. However, for others, to describe them as Muslim is unthinkable because of what is seen as a pivotal Muslim belief that the Prophet Muhammad is the final prophet, which the Ahmadiyyas are perceived to breach. Significantly, the Office for National Statistics' coded list of 'Other religions' in the Census responses does not highlight any use of the descriptor 'Ahmadiyya' which suggests that people within this group may well have used the 'Muslim' category of response in the Census.

Namdharis[110] understand themselves as Sikhs and, in fact, as very orthodox Sikhs. However, for others, the Namdhari belief in a continuing line of living human gurus is seen as incompatible with the Sikh Code of Conduct[111] of the Shiromani Gurdwara Parbandhak Committee in Amritsar. By contrast, the Code affirms that the line of human gurus ended with the tenth Sikh Guru and that the Sikh scriptures, the Adi Granth, now function as the Guru for the community, and hence is known as the Guru Granth Sahib. Again, the Office for National Statistics' coded 'write-ins' for 'Other religions' does not highlight any use of the descriptor 'Namdhari' which suggests that, in the Census, people within this group are likely to have used the 'Sikh' category of response.

g. 'Christian-Related'/Contested Groups

There are also groups that have a disputed relationship with the wider Christian tradition. These include the Church of Jesus Christ of Latter-day Saints,[112] popularly known as the 'Mormons', which understands itself to be a true, restored, Christian Church for the latter days. For Trinitarian Christians of the historic Christian Churches, to accept the Church of Jesus Christ of Latter-day Saints as being on a par with a variety of other Churches is problematic due to Mormons' rejection of the doctrine of the Trinity. Similar issues apply to the Jehovah's Witnesses[113] and the Christian Scientists[114] as well as to some other groups that, considered purely historically and sociologically, have a connection with the broader Christian tradition.

Where respondents from these disputed groups did not use the category 'Christian', but wrote the name of their group in under the write-in 'Other religion' option, a statistical breakdown is available from the Office for National Statistics' 'Table M275 Religion (most detailed categories)'. The figures for these groups are set out in Table 3.29. It should be noted that Christian Research gives higher 2001 estimates for some of these groups. This includes Christadelphians at 16,350 in England and 1,000 in Wales;[115] Christian Scientists at 6,000 in England and 150 in Wales;[116] Church of Jesus Christ of Latter-day Saints at 148,310 in England and 8,510 in Wales;[117] Jehovah's Witnesses at 109,288 in England and 7,430 in Wales[118] and Unitarians and Free Christians at 4,350 in England and 1,000 in Wales.[119] Even allowing that some of these figures may be over-estimates, the discrepancies with the data from the Census write-in responses would seem to suggest that significant numbers of respondents from these groups may well have simply ticked the box 'Christian' rather using the 'Other religion' write-in option.

Table 3.29: Census respondents of 'Christian-related/contested' groups

Tradition	Total numbers in England	Total numbers in Wales
British Israelites	30	0
Church of Jesus Christ of Latter-day Saints/Mormons	11,673	1,049
Christadelphians	2,123	245
Christian Scientists	556	22
Christian Spiritualists *	1,246	215
Jehovah's Witnesses	65,453	5,198
Unitarians **	3,604	383

* As distinct from those who responded as 'Spiritualists'.
** As distinct from those who responded as 'Unitarian Universalists'.
Both the above were coded by the Office for National Statistics as 'Other religions' and whose statistics therefore appear in this chapter in Table 3.34.
Source: Census, April 2001. Table M275 Religion (most detailed categories). Crown copyright, 2004. Copyright material is reproduced with the permission of the Controller of HMSO.

h. *Pagans*

In addition to the world religious traditions and the groups which have a disputed relationship with them, there are also those who follow the various traditions of contemporary pagan groupings.[120] Contemporary Paganism understands itself as inheriting the indigenous religious tradition and practice of these islands. In some regions of England and the UK, the original Pagan traditions remained strong in their own right, even after Christianity gained an ascendancy. In more recent times, this inheritance has also been redeveloped through the modern revivals and/or reinterpretations to be found among the neo-Pagan and deep ecology movements.

Paganism is not a single tradition, but consists of a loose network of people, sometimes working as individuals, and sometimes as part of groups, in a variety of Pagan traditions. A number of Pagans work concurrently in more than one tradition. The Pagan traditions include the Craft (or Wicca), Druidism, Odinism (Asatru), Shamanism, Women's Traditions, and Men's Traditions.[121] There are significant differences between these groups, but all Pagans share in a sense of the organic vitality of the natural world and women's spirituality is respected in all traditions. Table 3.30 sets out the numbers of Census respondents to the 'Other' tick-box with 'write-in' responses that were coded to a group that is actually related to Paganism.

Table 3.30: Census respondents coded to a group connected with Paganism

Tradition	Total numbers in England	Total numbers in Wales
Asatru	90	3
Celtic Pagan	460	48
Druidism	1,568	89
Pagan	28,943	1,714
Wicca	6,844	383
Totals of Pagan-related *	37,905	2,237

* 368 respondents in England and 38 in Wales were recorded under 'Animism' which may also be seen as related to Paganism. In addition, there were 95 responses in England and 3 in Wales that were recorded as 'ancestor worship' that could either relate to (see Table 3.33 below) forms of religion connected with people of Chinese descent and/or to Pagan-related traditions. Finally, it should be noted that 265 respondents in England and 13 in Wales were recorded as 'Heathens' (which is a form of Pagan tradition as well as a more general linguistic descriptor for 'irreligiousness') whom the Office for National Statistics coded among the overall figure for those of 'No religion'.
Source: Census, April 2001. Table M275 Religion (most detailed categories). Crown copyright, 2004. Copyright material is reproduced with the permission of the Controller of HMSO. This particular grouping together of various traditions and the linkage of them together with an overall Pagan-related table and total is the author's.

i. *New Religious Movements*
Then, there are also groupings of what the media often disparagingly refer to in an undifferentiated way as 'sects' or 'cults', but which are usually known in academic discourse by the less prejudicial terminology of 'New Religious Movements'[122] (often referred to by the abbreviation of 'NRMs'). Table 3.31 sets out the numbers of Census respondents whose responses were coded to such groups.

Table 3.31: Census respondents coded to a group often seen as a 'New Religious Movement'

Group	Total numbers in England	Total numbers in Wales
Hare Krishna	612	28
Scientology	1,757	24
Unification Church*	241	11

*Those using the write-in 'Unificationist' were actually coded by the Office for National Statistics to the overall 'Christian' data, but are listed here on the basis that they project a more 'independent' and 'universalist' role.

Source: Census, April 2001. Table M275 Religion (most detailed categories). Crown copyright, 2004. Copyright material is reproduced with the permission of the Controller of HMSO.

Unificationists have often popularly – and sometimes disparagingly – been referred to as 'Moonies', in reference to the founder of their movement, Revd Sun Myung Moon.[123] Today, the movement is more formally known in the UK by the name of Family Federation for World Peace and Unification. Scientology, founded by L. Ron Hubbard, is a movement that has had a considerable national and international profile, including debates over the extent to which it can be considered to be a religious organization.

j. *'Hindu-Related' Groups*
The International Society for Krishna Consciousness (ISKCON) – often popularly know as 'Hare Krishnas' after their chant – are an example of a movement which, having earlier been seen as a 'New Religious Movement' has, in recent years, become less marginalized within the wider society. As evidenced by the Bhaktivedanta Manor controversy it has also come to play a central part in the wider Hindu tradition and community.[124] It is therefore quite possible that a number of ISKCON members may have responded to the Census questions on religion using the tick box option of 'Hindu'.

There are, in fact, also a number of other groups that have some relationship with the Hindu tradition, although quite a number of these understand their own identity and role in more universalist terms. Table 3.32 sets out details on respondents coded to groups that can, in some way, be seen as 'Hindu-related' in some way but who were not coded to the overall 'Hindu' data in the Census.

Table 3.32: Census respondents coded to a group that can be seen as, in some way, 'Hindu-related'

Group	Total numbers in England	Total numbers in Wales
Brahma Kumaris	323	8
Divine Light Mission	18	3
Eckankar	417	9
Raja Yoga	253	8

Source: Census, April 2001. Table M275 Religion (most detailed categories). Crown copyright, 2004. Copyright material is reproduced with the permission of the Controller of HMSO.

k. *Religions of People of Chinese Descent*
Many Chinese may have chosen to tick the pre-set option of 'Buddhist' although the reality of Chinese religious life is often much more complex and multi-faceted

than can be reflected in a single 'tick-box' response. Table 3.33 sets out responses coded to traditions that may be seen as being related to the religious life of people with Chinese descent (though it is likely that 'white', indigenous, followers of Taoism will be included in the figures for this).

Table 3.33: Census respondents coded to traditions that may be seen as being related to the religious life of people of Chinese descent

Tradition	Total numbers in England	Total numbers in Wales
Chinese religions	141	7
Confucianist	80	3
Taoist	3,576	16
Tin Tao	4	0

As has previously been noted in Table 3.31, there were also 95 responses in England and 3 in Wales coded to 'Ancestor worship' which could relate to Chinese forms of religiosity and/or to 'Ancestor worship' in the context of Pagan-related traditions.

Source: Census, April 2001. Table M275 Religion (most detailed categories). Crown copyright, 2004. Copyright material is reproduced with the permission of the Controller of HMSO.

l. *Other Religious and Other Groupings*

There are, in addition, a range of other religious groups recorded from Satanism, which is often confused with Paganism, through Rastafarianism, to followers of various New Age practices. The latter may have more or less to do with religion, depending on the individuals involved.[125] These responses are set out in Table 3.34. Then, also coded as being among 'Other religions', are a variety of what might alternatively be seen as groups associated with being of 'No religion' or, at least, of philosophical alternatives to religion. These are set out in Table 3.35. Finally, in addition to all the above, there were 22,187 respondents in England and 610 in Wales whose responses to the 'write-in' for 'Other' have not been added to the specific coded groupings. There were also 17,894 respondents in England and 1,412 in Wales who indicated that they were of 'Other' but without giving a specific 'write-in' and who were therefore coded as 'Other religion (not described)'.

Table 3.34: Census respondents coded to 'Other' religious groups

Group	Total numbers in England	Total numbers in Wales
Church of All Religion	60	10
Deist	621	18
Druze	260	0
Free Church of Love	49	0
Mysticism	150	8
Native American Church	217	17
New Age	869	36
Occult	96	3
Own belief system	3,056	203
Pantheism	1,516	87
Rastafarian	4,592	100
Sant Mat	53	0
Santeri	21	0
Satanist	1,459	66
Spiritualist	30,124	2,280
Theism	489	16
Unitarian Universalist	30	0
Universalist	914	57
Vodun	208	5

Source: Census, April 2001. Table M275 Religion (most detailed categories). Crown copyright, 2004. Copyright material is reproduced with the permission of the Controller of HMSO.

Table 3.35: Census respondents coded to stances often associated with being of 'No religion'

Tradition	Total Numbers in England	Total Numbers in Wales
Free Thinker	571	15
Humanist	7,866	430
Internationalist	3	0
Rationalist	37	0
Realist	104	0
Secularist	11	0

Source: Census, April 2001. Table M275 Religion (most detailed categories). Crown copyright, 2004. Copyright material is reproduced with the permission of the Controller of HMSO.

11. *A Secularized Society?*

a. *Secularization Processes*

Having outlined the contemporary diversities of the religious landscape in the UK, it is important also to take account of the degree to which the UK is appropriately characterized as 'secular' as well as 'religiously plural'. Writing in the middle of the 1960s, when consciousness of the technological revolution was at its height, the scholar of comparative religion A. C. Bouquet referred to Karl Jaspers' theory of 'the axial age' that gave rise to the historic world religions of today. He observed that, 'And now, just as we Christians are beginning to know more about the religions of our neighbours, it looks as though all of us, whoever we are, are being faced with the arrival of a second axial age, the age of the scientific revolution, in which a far greater challenge to religion will have to be faced than ever before.'[126]

What is signified by the concept of secularization has clearly brought something distinctively and significantly challenging to all religions.[127] The development of secularity, the origins of which are to be found in the humanism of the Renaissance, has been partly a by-product of the Industrial Revolution and the urbanization of life that it brought. As a result of this, a sense grew that humanity was becoming increasingly insulated from the mysteries and unpredictabilities of natural life. The machine became the emblem of progress and its mechanical precision a symbolic ideal. With the loss of mystery, it seemed as though God was being banished and the world was becoming explainable solely in terms of itself. Darwinism seemed to offer a new protology and eschatology; anthropology questioned the uniqueness of claims about religious revelation; and with Freud, psychoanalysis began to explain human mysteries in terms of sexuality.

Technology began to shrink the world as air travel became ever faster, cheaper and more popular. Communication by satellite and the development of the mass media brought the whole world into the living rooms of ordinary British people. Human beings even left the earth in space flight. The first cosmonaut, Yuri Gagarin of the Soviet Union, declared that when he was in space he had seen no God. Christian theological and ecclesiological awareness of the challenges posed by secularity intensified in the 1960s. Some theologians, influenced by contemporary interpretations of Dietrich Bonhoeffer's ideas of 'religionless Christianity'[128] and Harvey Cox's 1965 book *The Secular City*[129] sought to incorporate the secular as part of the inner meaning of the Christian Gospel. However, for many other Christians the secular became seen as more of a threat, and certainly as something about which there was more concern than the continuation of established religion.

The meanings associated with the concept of secularization and the extent of the social reality that it attempts to describe and interpret are neither unified nor uncontested.[130] The sociologist of religion Bryan Wilson characterizes secularization as 'the process whereby religious thinking, practice and institutions lose social significance'.[131] Another definition, also from within the sociology of religion, comes from Peter Berger, who defines secularization as 'the process by which sectors of society and culture are removed from the domination of religious institutions and symbols'.[132] The definitions offered by both Wilson and Berger share an analysis of the role that religion plays in the public sphere rather than any argument concerning an absolute decline in religious belief and practice of a kind that, from the 1960s onwards, has often popularly been associated with the concept of 'secularization'.

b. *Statistics and 'No Religion'/'No Response'*
Scotland is the country of the UK the largest proportion of whose population – in fact over a quarter – stated in the Census that it is of 'No religion'. By contrast England, often thought to be less religious than the 'Celtic fringes', had the smallest proportion of its population who gave this response. But, as previously noted, it is possible that at least some aspects of these results reflect differences in the form of the questions asked in Scotland and in England and Wales.

Table 3.36 shows the numbers of people in the 2001 Census who indicated they were of 'No religion'. Since the religion question was a voluntary one, there were also those who did not answer the question. Table 3.37 shows the numbers of people in the 2001 Census who did not respond to the religion questions and were therefore recorded as 'Not stated'. If, as in Table 3.38, the responses of 'No religion' and 'Not stated' are merged into a single category, it is possible to argue that the proportion of those who are not religious may be substantially higher than indicated by those who specifically responded that they were of 'No religion'. However, since the religion question was a voluntary one, there is a real difficulty in interpreting the significance of the respondents who did not state a religion. It is, for example, not self-evident that these non-respondents should necessarily be seen as being of no religion. This is because other research has indicated that non-respondents to questions of this kind *may* include individuals with or without a strong religious identity but who, on principle, refused to answer such questions believing religious identification to be a private matter.[133] They may also have included individuals, religious or otherwise, who were concerned about the possible uses to which this data might be put (for example, Jews have often historically had concerns about the collection of such data) and, as a result, chose not to answer this question.

Table 3.36: Census respondents indicating 'No religion' by country of the UK

Country	Total numbers of 'No religion'	Percentage of total Population
England	7,171,332	14.6%
Scotland	1,394,460	27.6%
Wales	537,935	18.5%
Northern Ireland	*	*
United Kingdom	9,103,727	15.5%

* Note: For Northern Ireland, separate figures for 'No religion' and 'Not stated' are not available. Coded to the overall 'No religion' data were 373,973 respondents in England and 16,154 in Wales who had put 'Jedi' (after the Jedi Knights of the Star Wars films) as a write-in answer to the religion question and 9,835 respondents in England and 522 in Wales who indicated 'atheist'. Perhaps more problematically it also included 14,067 respondents in England and 842 in Wales who indicated 'agnostic'. As already noted in Table 3.30 above, it particularly problematically included the coding of the write-in response of 'Heathen' to the overall data for 'No religion'. *Source*: Census, April 2001. National Statistics website: www.statistics.gov.uk and Table M275 Religion (most detailed categories). Crown copyright, 2004. Crown copyright material is reproduced with the permission of the Controller of HMSO. Percentages as shown are calculated by the present author on the basis of the original Census data.

Table 3.37: Census respondents not answering the religion question by country of the UK

Country	Total numbers of 'Not stated'	Percentage of total population
England	3,776,515	7.7%
Scotland	278,061	5.5%
Wales	234,143	8.1%
Northern Ireland	*	*
United Kingdom	4,288,719	7.2%

* Note: For Northern Ireland, separate figures for 'No religion' and 'Not stated' are not available. *Source*: Census, April 2001. National Statistics website: www.statistics.gov.uk and Table M275 Religion (most detailed categories). Crown copyright, 2004. Crown copyright material is reproduced with the permission of the Controller of HMSO. Percentages as shown are calculated by the present author on the basis of the original Census data.

Table 3.38: Census respondents indicating 'No religion' or not responding to the religion question by country of the UK

Country	Total numbers of 'No religion' and 'Not stated'	Percentage of total population
England	10,947,847	22.3%
Scotland	1,672,521	33.0%
Wales	772,078	26.6%
Northern Ireland	233,853	13.9%
United Kingdom	13,626,299	23.2%

Source: Census, April 2001. National Statistics website: www.statistics.gov.uk and Table M275 Religion (most detailed categories). Crown copyright, 2004. Crown copyright material is reproduced with the permission of the Controller of HMSO. Percentages as shown are calculated by the present author on the basis of the original Census data.

c. *Religion, 'No Religion' and Belief in God*

While atheism and secularism as systematized epistemologies and integrated ways of life were once sponsored by the states and political systems that were given birth by Marxist-Leninist ideology, principled stances of atheism can now be found only among relatively small numbers of people. Thus, the 2001 Home Office Citizenship Survey shows that 'only four per cent of those not affiliated to a faith community stated that not having a religious affiliation was important to their identity'.[134] In contrast to ideological atheism and secularism, the challenges arising to religion from secularity today are not so much along the lines of the explicit ideological conflict that once faced religious believers in the Communist-ruled countries of Central and Eastern Europe. Rather, they are more to do with perceptions of the irrelevance of organized religions to the life concerns and perspectives of significant numbers of people.

Such secularity – in which many of those who are non-religious are indifferent to religion rather than antagonistic towards it – is very much a part of the plurality of contemporary England and the UK. At the same time, some who do not identify with any religion do have deeply felt concerns about allowing too prominent a role for religion in public life. In organized campaigning terms these concerns are expressed by the National Secular Society. However, such concerns are also likely to be considerably more widespread than among 'signed up' secularists, especially following 11 September and the renewed concerns about religious extremism to which it gave rise. In the European Values Survey, in response to the question on whether respondents agree or disagree with the statement that 'religious leaders should not influence government decisions', 20.3% of respondents from Great Britain indicated that they 'agree strongly' and 44.9% that they 'agree'; 19.1% said they 'neither agree nor disagree', with 12.1% saying they 'disagree' and 3.6% that they 'disagree strongly'.[135]

Christian orthodoxy has certainly declined[136] and there are those, such as Callum Brown, in his book of the same title, who speak of *The Death of Christian Britain*.[137] However, it is also arguable that a large proportion of the population continue to share many 'folk beliefs' that are related to Christianity, and the significance of this should not be underestimated. Therefore alongside those who do not affirm a religious belief or identity and those who do identify with 'particular religions', their movements and institutions, it is also important to take account of the phenomenon highlighted by Thomas Luckmann's book entitled *The Invisible Religion*. In this, Luckman critiqued the assumption often found in the secularization debate, 'that church and religion are identical'.[138]

David Hay's work on religious experience argues that religious experiences are far wider than what is suggested by statistics on religious membership and participation or by affirmations of religiously orthodox beliefs.[139] The concepts of 'folk religion' and 'implicit religion'[140] have also been used to delineate these areas of religious life. As noted in the Introduction to this book, Wolffe identifies four distinct categories, namely: 'conventional religion', 'civil religion', 'common religion' and 'invisible religion'.[141] What all these concepts have in common is that issues related to religion can still surface even where individuals do not have a very strong connection with a specific religious tradition.

The British Social Attitudes Survey, 1998, reflects something of this complexity with 21% of respondents saying that, 'I know God exists and I have no doubt about it', 23% saying that, 'While I have doubts, I feel that I do believe in God', and 14% saying that, 'I don't believe in a personal God, but I do believe in a Higher Power of some kind'.[142] In addition, 14% of respondents said, 'I find myself believing in God some of the time, but not at others', 15% that, 'I don't know whether there is a God and I don't believe there is any way to find out', and 10% that, 'I don't believe in God'.

In the European Values Survey, when asked a 'yes' or 'no' question about 'belief in God', 71.8% of respondents in Great Britain answered 'yes' and 28.2% answered 'no'.[143] When asked 'Which of these statements comes closest to your beliefs', 31% said 'personal God', 40.1% said 'spirit or life force', 18.7% said 'don't know what to think' and 10.2% said there is 'no spirit, God or life force'.[144] When the European Values Survey asked 'independently of whether you to go church or not' would you say you are 'a religious person', 41.6% of respondents in Great Britain affirmed this and 53.4% said they were 'not a religious person', while only 5% said they were 'a convinced atheist'.[145]

Overall, then, the nature and extent of religious belief, belonging, participation in worship and secularization is not straightforward to portray in a statistical way since the results obtained from various surveys are highly dependent on the form in which the questions are asked. However, it remains clear that all three dimensions of the 'Christian', 'secular' and 'religiously plural' aspects of the contemporary socio-religious reality form a significant part of the religious landscape of contemporary England and the UK.

12. *Inter-Faith Developments*

a. *Origins and Developments*

Alongside the development of a greater religious plurality and the continued spread of secular perspectives, the emergence of inter-faith initiatives and structures at all levels of society has been another important dimension of the changing religious landscape of England and the UK. Inter-faith initiatives generally began at a more international level.[146] But one the earliest initiatives in the UK was the Religions of the Empire Conference,[147] organized by Sir Denison Ross and held in conjunction with the British Empire Exhibition. The colonial and imperial projects of the nineteenth century turned out, in many ways, to have been a significant catalyst for growth in consciousness of religious diversity and plurality and for engagement with the challenges brought by this.

As already noted, one of the consequences of the colonial project was that substantial numbers of people of other than Christian religions migrated to the UK from former colonies. In addition, in the earlier period, a significant number of colonial administrators, members of the armed forces and Christian missionaries contributed to the dissemination in the UK of the texts, ideas and beliefs of a variety of religions. A number of these people also became involved in these early inter-religious initiatives.

b. *Perceptions: Syncretism and Good Relations*

In the earlier part of the twentieth century, these initiatives suffered from a suspicion among many Christian leaders that such organizations might be syncretistic. As a result, there was a tendency for them to be perceived either as organizations for inter-faith 'enthusiasts' or else as fora through which more socially and religiously marginalized religious traditions could find a public platform. However, alongside multi-lateral initiatives involving a range of different religions, other initiatives and organizations developed whose activity focused on relationships between two or three specific religions and, in particular, relationships between Christianity and one or two other religions. Such initiatives generally secured a greater degree of endorsement from the leaderships of the mainstream religious bodies within their sponsoring religions, a good example of this being in the field of Christian–Jewish relations.

Other than Christianity, Judaism is the world religious tradition that has had the longest settled community presence in the UK. Therefore it is perhaps not surprising that among the earliest of the organized inter-faith initiatives were those that were specifically concerned with Christian–Jewish relations. An early instance of this was the founding, in 1927, of the London Society for Jews and Christians, which emerged from an initiative of the Social Service Committee of the Liberal Jewish Synagogue, and the Society continues to hold regular meetings today. In 1942, partly as a response to the situation of Jews in Nazi Europe, a Council of Christians and Jews (CCJ) was formed.[148]

The challenge of living together in an increasingly religiously plural society has meant that 'mainstream' communities have themselves gradually needed to develop positive ways to interact and co-operate. In addition, of course, the presence and claims of other religions also pose profound philosophical and epistemological challenges to all religions. Therefore for both theological/philosophical and practical reasons, faith communities and organizations in the UK have been giving increasing attention to relationships with people belonging to other religious traditions.

For example, the ecumenical instrument of the Christian Churches in the UK, Churches Together in Britain and Ireland (CTBI), has a Churches' Commission for Inter-Faith Relations. A number of CTBI member Churches also have their own committees that focus on inter-faith matters. Similar initiatives have also begun to be taken from within the faith community bodies of other than Christian religions. These include, for example, the Sikh Council for Inter Faith Relations UK, formed in 1987; the Three Faiths Forum, a Jewish initiative for Jewish–Muslim–Christian relations; and the employment, by the Islamic Foundation in Leicester, of a staff member focusing on inter-faith issues.

c. *Local Initiatives*
As well as national bodies, the development of local inter-faith initiatives has been of particular significance for the contemporary religious landscape of England and the UK. Thus, the existence of a network of local CCJ groups has translated inter-faith initiatives from international congresses and national organizations down to the level of specific communities. But emerging in the last quarter of the twentieth century and spreading more rapidly towards the beginning of the twenty-first century, one of the most significant developments for inter-faith relations has been the development of other, wider, local inter-faith initiatives and groups in towns and cities throughout the UK. *Religions in the UK* records 30 inter-faith organizations operating at UK level, 1 at Welsh national level and 1 at Scottish national level. In addition, it includes details on over 94 local inter-faith groups throughout the UK (including 88 in England, 2 in Wales and 4 in Scotland).

By the time of the Inter Faith Network for the UK's 2003 report on *Local Inter Faith Activity in the UK: A Survey*,[149] nearly 140 local multilateral initiatives had been identified. The majority of these are to be found in localities characterized by a high degree of ethnic diversity and visible religious plurality. These include groups such as the Harrow Inter-Faith Council, the Wolverhampton Inter-Faith Group and others. However, there are also groups such as the Beaminster One World Fellowship and the West Somerset Inter Faith Group which have been formed in areas that are, at least apparently, less diverse.

Local inter-faith groups have a variety of histories, self-understandings and methods of working. These can include a desire for better understanding and appreciation of another religious tradition; an objective of social harmony and friendship; a wish on the part of participant groups to secure greater social and religious acceptance; or an imperative within one's own religion to work with others. In the early days of local inter-faith organizations and initiatives, one of the main needs was simply for information about one another's beliefs and practices, and a good deal of inter-faith activity was oriented towards this aim. There remains a continuing need for this, but inter-faith activity has also expanded and developed in a variety of ways with differing goals, participants and forms of organization as people from various communities of faith have responded to the challenges presented by a multi-faith society. As the *Local Inter Faith Guide: Faith Community Co-Operation in Action* explains it, local inter-faith initiatives can now be:

> places where members of the different faith communities come to know each
> other, learn more about their neighbours deeply held beliefs, and develop
> relationships of trust which can underpin co-operative work on social issues; a

resource for local government, hospitals, police forces and other bodies which
need information on particular faiths or a reliable pattern of contacts for consultation and partnership; of assistance to Local Authorities in allocating resources
more efficiently and with appropriate attention to the particular needs of faith
communities, for example in the areas of education and social services.[150]

The varied character of these local groups and the diverse approaches taken by
them is often reflected in the terminology used in their organizational names.
Some have used the word 'group' in their titles, such as the Derby Multi-Faith
Group. Such a title often indicates a more informal style of organization and an
individual basis of membership rather than attempting to be a more 'representative' body. At the same time, there are those, such as the Leicester Council of
Faiths and the Birmingham Council of Faiths, that see themselves as more formally structured attempts to maintain a balanced representation from among the
principal religious traditions. Such bodies tend to see a major part of their work
as being concerned with the interface with wider public life and, particularly, with
local government.

A number of local organizations, as for example the Tyne and Wear Racial
Equality Council Inter Faith Panel, originate in the work of local Racial Equality
Councils. As a result, such groups have a particular concern for the promotion
of better community relations. There are also groups such as Rochdale Interfaith
Action which have had an anti-racist focus on issues of immigration and family
reunification. Others, such as the Coventry Inter Faith Group, place a particular
emphasis on individual fellowship and meeting and may also include in their
membership people who are spiritual seekers.

Many, but not all, of such local inter-faith groups are affiliated to the Inter Faith
Network for the United Kingdom.[151] Those that are affiliated to the Network are
not branches of the Network. Rather, they exist independently, and in many cases
were founded before the Network was established. Their emergence and development is, however, supported and encouraged by the Network, which organizes
regular regional meetings for representatives of local inter-faith groups (including
those in membership of the Network and those not in membership), in order to
facilitate the sharing and exchange of local experience.

d. *The Inter Faith Network for the UK*

The inception and development of the Inter Faith Network for the UK has provided
a major catalyst in the transformation of inter-faith initiatives from what were, historically, relatively marginal initiatives into a central feature of the contemporary
religious landscape of England and the UK. The Network was founded in 1987.
Its aims are to advance public knowledge and mutual understanding of the teachings, traditions and practices of different faith communities in Britain, including
an awareness both of their distinctive features and of their common ground and to
promote good relations between persons of different religious faiths.

In total, at the time of writing the Network links over 100 organizations within
four different categories of affiliation.[152] These include representative bodies from
within the historic world religious traditions with significant communities in the
UK (namely, the Bahá'í, Buddhist, Christian, Muslim, Hindu, Jain, Jewish, Sikh

and Zoroastrian traditions). The representative bodies include organizations noted earlier in the chapter such as the National Spiritual Assembly of the Bahá'ís of the UK; the Network of Buddhist Organisations; the Churches' Commission on Inter-Faith Relations of Churches Together in Britain and Ireland; the National Council of Hindu Temples; Jain Samaj Europe; the Board of Deputies of British Jews; the Muslim Council of Britain; the Network of Sikh Organizations; and the Zoroastrian Trust Funds of Europe.

Also affiliated to the Network are national inter-faith organizations such as the Calamus Foundation, the Council of Christians and Jews and the World Congress of Faiths. The third category of affiliation is local inter-faith groups and councils. Finally, the Network also links a number of educational bodies, study centres and academic bodies that are concerned with the study of religions and the relationships between them. These include the Religious Education Council for England and Wales, the Community Religions Project of Leeds University and the Multi-Faith Centre at the University of Derby.

The Network provides information and advice to a wide range of organizations and individuals on inter-faith matters and on how to contact communities at both national and local level. It holds regular national and regional meetings and organizes seminars and conferences on a variety of issues and projects. These have explored such topics as the quest for shared values in a multi-faith society; young people and inter-faith relations; the role of the media in reporting on the religious life of Britain; and planning, registration and other issues relating to places of worship in a multi-faith society.

The Network is a forum for information, exchange and encounter. Its aim is to promote mutual understanding rather than to represent the views and positions of its member organizations to others. However, occasionally its officers have issued statements in relation to very important issues and events that have had a direct bearing on inter-religious relations in the UK such as during the first Gulf War, and with regard to aspects of the *Satanic Verses* controversy.

In 1991, the Network produced a formal *Statement on Inter-Religious Relations*[153] and in 1993 it issued a short code of conduct on *Building Good Relations Between People of Different Faiths and Beliefs.*[154] Both of these documents were drafted by multi-faith working groups and were endorsed by all the Network's member organizations. The Network also produced a longer document expanding on the Code of Conduct that was entitled *Mission, Dialogue and Inter-Religious Encounter.*[155]

The Network has had particular success in winning trust from 'representative' bodies and leaders from within the 'mainstream' world religious traditions with substantial communities in the UK. From its beginning, too, the Network endeavoured to facilitate the participation of the full range of religious communities in the public life of the UK. As time has gone on, the dimension of the Network's work in relation to government and public bodies has assumed greater importance. Thus the Network has encouraged government departments and other public bodies to consult faith communities on the development and implementation of policies and programmes that are of particular concern to them. This has been both a stimulus for, and a response to, the Government's own developing approach in these matters.

e. *Inter-Faith Initiatives and Public Life*

Over the past decade there has been a significant growth in interest on the part of Government and other public bodies in the potential of inter-faith mechanisms as a means of facilitating the interface between religion and public life. The earliest expression of this was the foundation, in 1992, of the Inner Cities' Religious Council (ICRC). The ICRC was created as part of Government's response to the issues raised by the Church of England's *Faith in the City* report.[156] With a membership drawn from the Christian, Hindu, Jewish, Muslim and Sikh communities, the ICRC marked an important stage in development of government practice along religiously inclusive lines in comparison with previous reliance upon the establishment of the Church of England, supplemented by mechanisms for consultation with other Christian Churches.

In recent years, local authorities have increasingly recognized the potential contributions that can be made by religious groups and inter-faith organizations in the context of Local Strategic Partnerships for economic and social regeneration. The groundwork for this was laid by the ICRC's sponsorship, during the 1990s, of regional and local consultancy to elicit the support of religious groups in urban regeneration. These developments have both been stimulated by, and given rise to, a range of good practice guides in which the Local Government Association has played a significant role. Thus, for example, in association with the Inner Cities Religious Council, the Active Community Unit of the Home Office, and the Inter Faith Network for the UK, the Association produced *Faith and Community: A Good Practice Guide for Local Authorities.*[157]

Therefore alongside the changing landscape of the religions themselves, the overall context for the relationship between religion(s), state and society has shifted, with inter-faith organizations moving from a peripheral to a more central role from the perspective of both faith communities, the Government and other public bodies. In this context, 'bottom-up' and 'community-based' inter-faith initiatives have developed that not only engage with issues in the relations between individual religions, but also deal with the interface between religions and the wider society in its secular, Christian and religiously plural dimensions. Increasingly, too, alongside these 'bottom-up' and 'internal' initiatives, Government and public bodies have become active initiators of 'external', sometimes more 'top-down' and 'managerial' initiatives of a religiously plural character.

As a consequence, within the 'three-dimensional' religious landscape of contemporary England and the UK, a range of new points of intersection are developing between Christianity, religious diversity and secularity. The implications of these developments for the central arguments of this book will be explored in greater detail in the concluding chapter. For now, however, their existence is to be noted as one increasingly important part of the overall contemporary religious landscape.

13. *The 'Three-Dimensional' Socio-Religious Reality*

a. *Reality 'In the Round'*

The religious landscape of contemporary English society and the UK state is one that now exhibits a very substantial diversity. Following the overview provided in this chapter it can be restated here that, in order to gain a rounded picture of this religious landscape, it is necessary to see it in 'three-dimensional' terms as 'Christian, secular and religiously plural'. Such a 'three-dimensional' socio-religious reality is necessarily much more complex than a 'one-dimensional' or a 'two-dimensional' one. Among other things, it poses questions about how far an establishment model for the relationship between religion(s), state and society that was developed within a basically 'one-dimensional' Christian socio-religious reality can any longer remain appropriate within this new context.

b. *'Three-Dimensional' Reality and 'One/Two-Dimensional' Approaches*

The present configuration for the relationship between religion(s), state and society embodied in the establishment of the Church of England is essentially a 'one-dimensional' one. In evaluating the degree of 'fit' between this inheritance and the contours of the contemporary religious landscape it is important to try to take account of the experience of those – whether of other than Christian religious traditions, or of secular perspectives – who do not 'fit' this inherited 'one-dimensional' profile.

The next chapter therefore examines the nature and extent of discrimination and unfair treatment on the basis of religion, with particular reference to people of various religions and to the countries of England and Wales. This is then followed by the opening section of Chapter 5, which specifically focuses on those aspects of discrimination on the grounds of religion that can be described as resulting in a structurally based 'religious disadvantage' for people of non-established religious groups and people of 'no religion'.

Notes

1 This chapter primarily has the function of sociologically, phenomenologically and organizationally describing the contemporary socio-religious context. In particular, when describing the various religions and their organizations in the UK, the chapter draws upon and reworks the introductions to the various religions and their organizations in the UK that are originally found in P. Weller (ed.), *Religions in the UK*, 2001. The sections on 'Inter-Faith Developments' as well as, to some extent, those on 'A Christian Inheritance' and on 'Migration, Christian Diversification and the Growth of Religious Plurality', also do this. The sections describing the various religions and their organizations in the UK refer to and discuss Census results on religious affiliation obtained from the 2001 decennial census as well as figures produced by Christian Research, *Religious Trends, No. 4, 2003/2004*.

2 While the author would ultimately argue that the *implications of the descriptions* are related to the *direction of the arguments* that are made, the two should, of course, formally be distinguished.

3 Thus neither the Inter Faith Network for the UK nor the Multi-Faith Centre at the University of Derby, nor the Office for National Statistics, nor Christian Research, should be assumed to agree with the *argument* that is made by the author when using their *descriptive* materials or citing their data.

4   J. McClendon, Jnr., 'What is a Baptist Theology?', *ABQ* 1/1 (1982), pp. 16–39 (20).

5   See P. Weller, 'Transformed for Dialogue: Social Context and Theological Development in Britain (part I)', *MC* n.s. 32/3 (1990), pp. 51–63; 'Transformed for Dialogue: Social Context and Theological Development (part II)', *MC* n.s. 32/4 (1991), pp. 46–54; 'Transformed for Dialogue: Social Context and Theological Development (part III)', *MC* n.s. 32/5 (1991), pp. 42–50; 'Transformed for Dialogue: Social Context and Theological Development (part IV)', *MC* n.s. 33/1 (1991), pp. 43–50.

6   See L. M. Barley, C. Field, B. Kosmin and J. Nielsen, *Religion* (Reviews of United Kingdom Statistical Sources, 20; Oxford: Pergamon Press, 1987) and P. Weller and A. Andrews, 'How Many of Them Are There?: Religions, Statistics and the 2001 Census', *WFE* 21 (1998), pp. 23–34.

7   P. Brierley, *'Christian' England: What the English Church Census Reveals* (London: MARC Europe, 1991).

8   See S. Harding, D. Phillips and M. Fogarty, *Contrasting Values in Western Europe* (London: Macmillan, 1986); S. Ashford and N. Timms, *What Europe Thinks: A Study of Western European Values* (Aldershot: Dartmouth, 1992); D. Barker, L. Halman and A. Vloet, *The European Values Study 1981–1990* (Aberdeen: Gordon Cook Foundation, 1993). For a specific exploration of the UK results from this study, see D. Gerard, 'Religious Attitudes and Values', in M. Abrams, D. Gerard and N. Timms (eds.), *Values and Social Change in Britain* (Basingstoke: Macmillan, 1985), pp. 50–92. For the results of the latest survey see L. Halman, *The European Values Study: A Third Wave. Sourcebook of 1999/2000 European Values Study Survey* (Tilburg: WORC Tilburg University, 2001). For a discussion of results from the latest EVS survey see Y. Lambert, 'A Turning Point in Religious Evolution in Europe', *JCR* 19/1 (2004), pp. 29–45.

9   For the results of the 1851 Census see *Census of Great Britain, 1851, Religious Worship. England and Wales*,1853.

10   See the National Statistics website at www.statistics.gov.uk. © Crown copyright. Crown copyright material is reproduced with the permission of the Controller of HMSO.

11   See P. Weller, 'Identity, Politics and the Future(s) of Religion in the UK: The Case of the Religion Question in the 2001 Decennial Census', *JCR* 19/1 (2004), pp. 3–21 and D. Voas and S. Bruce, 'The 2001 Census and Christian Identification in Britain', *JCR* 19/1 (2004), pp. 23–8. The question as asked in Northern Ireland was in three parts: 'Do you regard yourself as belonging to any particular religion?' This was then followed by 'What religion, religious denomination or body do you belong to?' and then by 'What religion, religious denomination or body were you brought up in?' In Scotland, the question was in two parts, starting with: 'What religion, religious denomination or body do you belong to?' followed by the question 'What religion, religious denomination or body were you brought up in?' In England, however, the question was the (– apparently! – more) straightforward 'What is your religion?'

12   See D. Voas, 'Is Britain a Christian Country?', in P. Avis (ed.), *Public Faith: The State of Religious Belief and Practice in Britain* (London: SPCK, 2003), pp. 92–105; and D. Voas and S. Bruce, 'The 2001 Census and Christian Identification in Britain'.

13   Source: National Statistics website: www.statistics.gov.uk. © Crown copyright Crown copyright material is reproduced with the permission of the Controller of HMSO.

14   Of course, in reality, the historical position was never as 'one-dimensional' as the Christendom theory purported. Until their expulsion under Edward I, there was a significant Jewish population in England, and indigenous Pagan religious traditions survived either independently or in various forms of admixture with Christian belief and practice.

15   See L. Francis, 'Religion and Social Capital'.

16   L. Halman, *The European Values Study: Source Book*.

17   Maria O'Beirne, *Religion in England and Wales: Findings From the 2001 Home Office Citizenship Survey* (Home Office Research Study, 274; London: Research, Development, Statistics Directorate, Home Office, 2004), pp. 18–19.

18   See P. Brierley, *Christian' England*; P. Brierley (ed.), *Religious Trends 4, 2003/2004*; R. Gerloff, *A Plea for British Black Theologies: The Black Church Movement in Britain in its*

Transatlantic Cultural and Theological Interaction, Parts I & II (2 vols.; Frankfurt am Main; Peter Lang, 1992); and P. Weller (ed.), *Religions in the UK*, pp. 203–6.

19 See P. Weller, 'Identity, Politics and the Future(s) of Religion in the UK', pp. 3–21. For Census respondents in Scotland, for the questions 'What religion, religious denomination or body do you belong to?' and 'What religion, religious body or denomination were you brought up in?' the categories offered for response relating to Christianity were, 'Church of Scotland', 'Roman Catholic' and 'Other Christian, please write in'. For Ireland, to the question, 'What religion, religious denomination or body do you belong to?' the categories of response that were offered were: 'Roman Catholic', 'Presbyterian Church in Ireland', 'Church of Ireland', 'Methodist Church in Ireland', and the general alternative, 'Other, please write in'. For England, by contrast, to the question 'What is your religion?' the only pre-set response offered for Christian was 'Christian (including Church of England, Catholic, Protestant and all other Christian denominations)'. Hence no Census data is available relating to Christian denomination on a UK basis.

20 P. Brierley (ed.), *Religious Trends No. 4, 2003/2004*.

21 Defined by P. Brierley (ed.), in *Religious Trends, No. 4, 2003/2004*, p. 2.3 as those with 'acceptance of the historic formulary of the Godhead as three eternal Persons, God the Father, God the Son and God the Spirit in one unchanging Essence'.

22 In this and other Tables drawing on Christian Research information, the absolute numbers are taken from Christian Research but are then used as the basis for percentage calculations made by the present author which should therefore not be attributed directly to Christian Research.

23 At the same time, however, these figures do not equate to 'Community membership' of the Church of England. This is because these figures are for Anglican Christianity throughout the UK rather than for the Church of England only, the Church in Wales, the Scottish Episcopal Church, as well as the Church in Ireland, also being Churches in the Anglican communion.

24 The definition used for 'Church membership' by Christian Research is 'Total number of adult (aged 15 and over) members/adherents'. See P. Brierley (ed.), *Religious Trends, No. 4, 2003/2004*, p. 0.6.

25 *The Times*, 8.7.1980.

26 See D. Jenkins, *The British: Their Identity and Their Religion* (London: SCM Press, 1975).

27 T. Nairn, *The Break-Up of Britain: Crisis and Neo-Nationalism* (London: Verso, 2nd edition 1997), pp. 11–91.

28 D. Voas, 'Is Britain A Christian Country?'.

29 Chadwick Commission, *Church and State*, pp. 72–4.

30 Chadwick Commission, *Church and State*, pp. 107–8.

31 G. Davie, 'Believing Without Belonging'.

32 G. Davie, 'An Ordinary God: The Paradox of Religion in Contemporary Britain', *British Journal of Sociology* 41/3 (1990), pp. 395–421.

33 P. Brierley, '*Christian' England*, p. 35.

34 See B. Asponwall, 'The Scottish Religious Identity in the Atlantic World, 1888–1914', in S. Mews (ed.), *Studies in Church History: Religion and National Identity* (Oxford: Blackwell, 1982), pp. 505–18; and C. Brown, *A Social History of Religion in Scotland Since 1730* (London: Methuen, 1987).

35 See P. Bisset, 'Kirk and Society in Modern Scotland', in P. Badham (ed.), *Religion, State and Society in Britain* (Lampeter: Edwin Mellen Press, 1989), pp. 51–65.

36 P. Bisset, *The Kirk and Her Scotland* (Edinburgh: Handsel, 1986), p. 3.

37 See P. Bell, *Disestablishment in Ireland and Wales* (London: SPCK, 1969).

38 See R. Jones, 'Religion, Nationality and State in Wales, 1840–1890', in D. Kerr (ed.), *Religion, State and Ethnic Groups* (Aldershot: Dartmouth, 1992), pp. 261–76.

39 L. Halman, *The European Values Study: Source Book*, p. 35.

40 L. Halman, *The European Values Study: Source Book*, p. 78.

41 See G. Ter Haar, *Halfway to Paradise: African Christians in Europe* (Cardiff: Cardiff Academic Press, 1998).

42 See J. Omoyajowo, *Cherubim and Seraphim: The History of an African Independent Church* (New York: Nok Publishers International, 1982).

43 See J. Wilkinson, *Church in Black and White: The Black Christian Tradition in 'Mainstream' Churches in England: A White Response and Testimony* (Edinburgh: Saint Andrew Press, 1993).

44 See R. Gerloff, *A Plea for British Black Theologies*.

45 See A. Walker, *Restoring the Kingdom: The Radical Christianity of the House Church Movement* (London: Hodder & Stoughton, 1985).

46 See P. Fryer, *Staying Power* (London: Pluto Press, 1984) and R. Visram, *Ayahs, Lascars and Princes: Indians in Britain, 1700–1947* (London: Pluto Press, 1986).

47 M. Ryan, *Another Ireland: An Introduction to Ireland's Ethno-Religious Minority Communities* (Belfast: Stranmills College, 1996).

48 M. O'Beirne, *Religion in England and Wales*, p. 45.

49 See Z. Badawi, *Islam in Britain* (London: Ta Ha, 1981); D. Joly and J. Nielsen, *Muslims in Britain: An Annotated Bibliography, 1960–1984* (Coventry: Centre for Research in Ethnic Relations, University of Warwick, 1985); I. Wahhab, *Muslims in Britain: Profile of a Community* (London: Runnymede Trust, 1989); C. Christie, 'The Rope of God: Muslim Minorities in the West and Britain', *New Community* 17/3 (1990), pp. 457–66; J. Nielsen, *Muslims in Western Europe* (Edinburgh: Edinburgh University Press, 1992), pp. 39–59; S. Raza, *Islam in Britain: Past, Present and Future* (Leicester: Volcano Press, 2nd edition, 1992).

50 See P. Weller (ed.), *Religions in the UK*, pp. 437–9.

51 See F. Robinson, *Varieties of South Asian Islam* (Research Paper No. 8; Coventry: Centre for Research in Ethnic Relations, University of Warwick, 1988) and A. Andrews, 'The Concept of Sect and Denomination in Islam', *Religion Today* 9/2 (1994), pp. 6–10.

52 P. Hardy, *The Muslims of British India* (Cambridge: Cambridge University Press 1972); F. Robinson, *Varieties of South Asian Islam*.

53 S. Raza, *Islam in Britain*, R. Geaves, *Sectarian Influences Within Islam in Britain: With Reference to the Concepts of 'Ummah' and 'Community'* (Department of Theology and Religious Studies Community Religions Project Monograph Series; Leeds: University of Leeds,1996).

54 See P. Weller (ed.), *Religions in the UK*, p. 138.

55 See P. Weller (ed.), *Religions in the UK*, p. 138.

56 See P. Weller (ed.), *Religions in the UK*, p. 438.

57 See P. Weller (ed.), *Religions in the UK*, p. 438.

58 See P. Weller (ed.), *Religions in the UK*, p. 438.

59 See P. Weller (ed.), *Religions in the UK*, p. 439.

60 See P. Weller (ed.), *Religions in the UK*, p. 439.

61 See P. Weller (ed.), *Religions in the UK*, p. 439.

62 See P. Weller (ed.), *Religions in the UK*, p. 439

63 See entry in P. Weller (ed.), *Religions in the UK*, pp. 449–66.

64 See entry in P. Weller (ed.), *Religions in the UK*, pp. 467–547.

65 See entry in P. Weller (ed.), *Religions in the UK*, pp. 467–547.

66 See entry in P. Weller (ed.), *Religions in the UK*, p. 32.

67 See D. Bowen (ed.), *Hinduism in England* (Bradford: Faculty of Contemporary Studies, Bradford College, 1981); R. Burghart (ed.), *Hinduism in Great Britain: The Perpetuation of Religion in an Alien Cultural Milieu* (London: Tavistock, 1987); T. Thomas, 'Hindu Dharma in Dispersion', in G. Parsons (ed.), *The Growth of Diversity: Britain From 1945* (London: Routledge, 1993), pp. 205–41; and K. Knott, 'Hinduism in Britain', in H. Coward, J. Hinnells and R. Williams (eds.), *The South Asian Religious Diaspora in Britain, Canada and the United States* (New York: State University of New York Press, 2000), pp. 89–107.

68 S. Vertovec, 'Caught in an Ethnic Quandary: Indo-Caribbean Hindus in London', in R. Ballard (ed.), *Desh Pardesh: The South Asian Presence in Britain* (London: Hurst & Co., 1994), pp. 272–90.

69 See P. Weller (ed.), *Religions in the UK*, pp. 312–13.

70 See R. Williams, *A New Face of Hinduism: The Swaminarayan Religion* (Cambridge: Cambridge University Press, 1984) and R. Dwyer, 'Caste, Religion and Sect in Gujarat: Followers of Vallabhacharya and Swaminarayan', in R. Ballard (ed.), *Desh Pardesh: The South Asian Presence in Britain* (London: Hurst & Co., 1994), pp. 165–90.

71   See S. Carey 'The Hare Krishna Movement and Hindus in Britain', *New Community* 10/3 (1983), pp. 477–86, and K. Knott, *My Sweet Lord: The Hare Krishna Movement* (Wellingborough: Aquarian Press, 1986).

72   See entries in P. Weller (ed.), *Religions in the UK*, pp. 317–22.

73   See entries in P. Weller (ed.), *Religions in the UK*, pp. 323–56.

74   See entries in P. Weller (ed.), *Religions in the UK*, pp. 323–56.

75   P. Weller (ed.), *Religions in the UK*, p. 36.

76   See W. Cole 'Sikhs in Britain', in P. Badham (ed.), *Religion, State and Society in Modern Britain* (Lampeter: Edwin Mellen Press, 1989), pp. 259–76; T. Thomas, 'Old Allies, New Neighbours: Sikhs in Britain', in G. Parsons (ed.), *The Growth of Religious Diversity* (vol. 1; London: Routledge, 1993), pp. 205–41; R. Ballard, 'The Growth and Changing Character of the Sikh Presence in Britain', in H. Coward, J. Hinnells and R. Williams (eds.), *The South Asian Religious Diaspora in Britain, Canada and the United States*, pp. 127–44.

77   P. Bhachu, *Twice Migrants: East African Sikh Settlers in Britain* (London: Tavistock, 1985).

78   These include *Bhatras*, who were originally associated with itinerant traders and, due to their pre-Second World War settlement in a number of British ports, founded some of the earliest *gurdwaras* in the UK. *Ramgarhias* were originally a community of blacksmiths, bricklayers, carpenters, engineers and technicians, many of whom migrated to East Africa at the end of the nineteenth century in order to assist in the development of the transport network there.

79   See entries in P. Weller (ed.), *Religions in the UK*, pp. 562–5.

80   See entries in P. Weller (ed.), *Religions in the UK*, pp. 566–85.

81   See entries in P. Weller (ed.), *Religions in the UK*, pp. 566–85.

82   P. Weller (ed.), *Religions in the UK*, p. 37.

83   J. Campbell, 'The Jewish Community in Britain', in S. Gilley and W. Sheils (eds.), *A History of Religion in Britain: Belief and Practice from Pre-Roman Times to the Present* (Oxford: Blackwell, 1994), pp. 427–48.

84   See A. Lerman, *The Jewish Communities of the World* (Basingstoke: Macmillan, 1989); J. Gorsky, 'Judaism in Europe', in S. Gill, G. D'Costa and U. King (eds.), *Religion in Europe: Contemporary Perspectives* (Kampen: Kok Pharos, 1994), pp. 14–33; J. Webber, (ed.), *Jewish Identities in the New Europe* (London: Littman, 1994).

85   See P. Weller (ed.), *Religions in the UK*, p. 380.

86   See M. Harris and R. Harris, *The Jewish Voluntary Sector in the United Kingdom: Its Role and Its Future* (London: Institute of Jewish Policy Research, 1997) and E. Slesinger, *Creating Community and Accumulating Social Capital: Jews Associating With Other Jews in Manchester* (London: Institute for Jewish Policy Research, 2003).

87   See P. Weller (ed.), *Religions in the UK*, pp. 391–401.

88   See P. Weller (ed.), *Religions in the UK*, pp. 402–31.

89   See P. Weller (ed.), *Religions in the UK*, pp. 402–31.

90   This was for particular reasons to do with the methodology of the 2001 edition of the directory coupled with the circumstances pertaining at the time of the finalization of the 2001 edition as these specifically affected the Jewish chapter of the directory

91   The *Jewish Yearbook* is published annually by *The Jewish Chronicle* newspaper.

92   P. Almond, *The British Discovery of Buddhism* (Cambridge: Cambridge University Press, 1988); D. Green, 'Buddhism in Britain: "Skilful Means" or Selling Out?', in P. Badham (ed.), *Religion, State and Society in Modern Britain*, pp. 277–91.

93   C. Humphries, *Sixty Years of Buddhism in England 1907–1967: A History and a Survey* (London: Buddhist Society, 1968); P. Oliver, *Buddhism in Britain* (London: Rider & Company, 1979); S. Batchelor, *The Awakening of the West: The Encounter of Buddhism and Western Culture* (London: Aquarian Press, 1994).

94   See P. Weller (ed.), *Religions in the UK*, p. 145.

95   See P. Weller (ed.), *Religions in the UK*, pp. 145–6.

96   See P. Weller (ed.), *Religions in the UK*, pp. 145–7.

97   See entries in P. Weller (ed.), *Religions in the UK*, pp. 158–68.

98   See entries in P. Weller (ed.), *Religions in the UK*, pp. 169–202.

99   See entries in P. Weller (ed.), *Religions in the UK*, pp. 169–202.

100   P. Weller (ed.), *Religions in the UK*, p. 37.

101   See Bahá'í International Community, *The Bahá'ís: A Profile of the Bahá'í Faith and its Worldwide Community* (New York: Bahá'í International Community, 1992).

102   See entries in P. Weller (ed.), *Religions in the UK*, pp. 121–5.

103   See entries in P. Weller (ed.), *Religions in the UK*, pp. 126–38.

104   P. Weller (ed.), *Religions in the UK*, p. 361.

105   P. Weller (ed.), *Religions in the UK*, pp. 361–2.

106   See entries in P. Weller (ed.), *Religions in the UK*, pp. 366–8.

107   See entries in P. Weller (ed.), *Religions in the UK*, pp. 369–73.

108   See entry in P. Weller (ed.), *Religions in the UK*, p. 37.

109   See P. Weller (ed.), *Religions in the UK*, p. 598.

110   See P. Weller (ed.), *Religions in the UK*, pp. 610–11.

111   See Shiromani Gurdwara Parbrandhak Committee, *Sikh Rehit Maryada* (Amristrar: Shiromani Gurdwara Parbrandhak Committee, translation available through the Sikh Missionary Society, n.d.).

112   See P. Weller (ed.), *Religions in the UK*, pp. 606–7.

113   See P. Weller (ed.), *Religions in the UK*, pp. 608–9.

114   See P. Weller (ed.), *Religions in the UK*, p. 605.

115   P. Brierley (ed.), *Religious Trends, No. 4, 2003/2004*, Table 10.2.2, p. 10.2.

116   P. Brierley (ed.), *Religious Trends, No. 4, 2003/2004*, Table 10.2.3, p. 10.2.

117   P. Brierley (ed.), *Religious Trends, No. 4, 2003/2004*, Table 10.2.6, p. 10.2.

118   P. Brierley (ed.), *Religious Trends, No. 4, 2003/2004*, Table 10.3.4, p. 10.2.

119   P. Brierley (ed.), *Religious Trends, No. 4, 2003/2004*, Table 10.4.6, p. 10.4.

120   V. Crowley, *Phoenix From the Flame: Pagan Spirituality in the Western World* (London: Aquarian, 1994); G. Harvey and C. Hardman, *Paganism Today* (London: Thorsons, 1996).

121   For brief descriptions of each, see P. Weller (ed.), *Religions in the UK*, pp. 613–14.

122   E. Barker, *New Religious Movements: A Perspective for Understanding Society* (Lampeter: Edwin Mellen Press, 1982); *New Religious Movements: A Practical Introduction* (London: HMSO, 1990).

123   See G. Chryssides, *The Advent of Sun Myung Moon: The Origins, Beliefs and Practices of the Unification Church* (Basingstoke: Macmillan,1991).

124   M. Nye, 'Hare Krishna and Sanatan Dharm in Britain: The Campaign for Bhaktivedanta Manor', *JCR* 21/1 (1996), pp. 37–56; and *Multiculturalism and Minority Religions in Britain: Krishna Consciousness, Religious Freedom and the Politics of Location* (Richmond: Curzon Press, 1990)

125   The sociologist of religion Steve Bruce characterizes 'New Age' as 'a milieu in which people acquire and absorb a variety of beliefs and practices that they combine into their own pockets of culture and attend to with differing degrees of seriousness'. For this description see S. Bruce, *Religion in Modern Britain* (Oxford: Oxford University Press, 1995), p.105.

126   A. C. Bouquet, *The Christian Faith and Non-Christian Religions* (London: James Nisbet & Co, 1958), p. 100.

127   See A. Gilbert, *The Making of Post-Christian Britain: A History of the Secularisation of Modern Society* (London: Longman, 1980) and A. Gilbert, 'Secularisation and the Future', in S. Gilley and W. Sheils (eds.), *A History of Religion in Britain: Belief and Practice from Pre-Roman Times to the Present* (Oxford: Blackwell, 1994), pp. 503–21.

128   D. Bonhoeffer, *Letters and Papers From Prison* (London: SCM Press, enlarged edition, 1971).

129   H. Cox, *The Secular City: Secularisation and Urbanisation in Theological Perspective* (London: SCM Press, 1965).

130   See D. Martin, *A General Theory of Secularisation* (Oxford: Blackwell, 1978); K. Dobbelaere, 'Secularisation: A Multi-dimensional Concept', *Current Sociology* 29/2 (1981), pp. 1–216 and K. Dobbelaere, 'Secularisation Theories and Sociological Paradigms: Convergences and Divergences', *Social Compass* 31 (1984), pp. 199–219; S. Bruce, *Religion and Modernisation:*

Sociologists and Historians Debate the Secularisation Thesis (Oxford: Oxford University Press, 1992); E. Barker, J. Beckford and K. Dobbelaere (eds.), *Secularisation, Rationalism and Sectarianism* (Oxford: Oxford University Press,1993).

131 B. Wilson, *Religion in Secular Society: A Sociological Comment* (Harmondsworth: Penguin, 1969), p. 14.

132 P. Berger, *The Social Reality of Religion: Elements of a Sociological Theory of Religion* (London: Faber & Faber, 1967), p. 107.

133 See P. Weller and A. Andrews, 'How Many of Them Are There?', pp. 23–34.

134 M. O'Beirne, *Religion in England and Wales*, p. 19.

135 L. Halman, *The European Values Study: Source Book*, p. 107.

136 See M. Abrams, D. Gerard and N. Timms (eds.), *Values and Social Change in Britain*; S. Ashford and N. Timms, *What Europe Thinks*; and D. Barker, L. Halman and A. Vloet, *The European Values Study.*

137 C. Brown, *The Death of Christian Britain: Understanding Secularisation 1880–2001* (London: Routledge, 2001).

138 T. Luckmann, *The Invisible Religion: The Problem of Religion in Modern Society* (New York: Macmillan, 1967), p. 27.

139 D. Hay, *Exploring Inner Space: Is God Still Possible in the Twentieth Century?* (Harmondsworth: Pelican, 1982) and *Religious Experience Today: Studying the Facts* (London: Mowbray, 1990).

140 E. Bailey, 'The Implicit Religion of Contemporary Society: An Orientation and Plea for its Study', *Religion* 2 (1983), pp. 69–83; E. Bailey, 'The Folk Religion of the English People', in P. Badham (ed.), *Religion, State and Society in Modern Britain*, pp. 145–58.

141 J. Wolffe, 'The Religions of the Silent Majority', p. 309.

142 British Social Attitudes Survey, National Centre for Social Research, cited in Office for National Statistics, *Social Trends 30: 2000 Edition* (London: Stationery Office, 2000), p. 219.

143 L. Halman, *The European Values Study: Source Book*, p. 86.

144 L. Halman, *The European Values Study: Source Book*, p. 94.

145 L. Halman, *The European Values Study: Source Book*, p. 81.

146 See M. Braybrooke, *Inter-Faith Organisations, 1893–1979: An Historical Directory* (Lampeter: Edwin Mellen Press, 1980); *Pilgrimage of Hope: One Hundred Years of Global Interfaith Dialogue* (London: SCM Press, 1992); *Faith in a Global Age: The Interfaith Movement's Offer of Hope to a World in Agony: A Personal Perspective* (Oxford: Braybrooke Press, 1995).

147 W. Hare (ed.), *Religions of the Empire: A Conference of Some Living Religions Within the Empire* (London: Duckworth, 1925).

148 This was followed, later, by an International Council of Christians and Jews (ICCJ). In 1946 an international conference of Christians and Jews was held at Lady Margaret Hall in Oxford and it was decided to plan for an International Council of Christians and Jews (ICCJ). Its tasks became all the more urgent as the full truth emerged concerning the Holocaust of European Jewry in the Nazi death camps. For various reasons the Council did not formally meet until 1975 in Hamburg, Germany, although from 1962 onwards an International Consultative Committee of organizations concerned with Christian–Jewish co-operation was in existence. The CCJ in this country is a member organization of the ICCJ, which holds regular international conferences and seminars.

149 Inter Faith Network for the UK, *Local Inter Faith Activity in the UK: A Survey* (London: Inter Faith Network for the UK, 2003), p. 7.

150 Inter Faith Network for the UK/Inner Cities Religious Council, *The Local Inter Faith Guide: Faith Community Co-Operation in Action* (London: Inter Faith Network for the United Kingdom in association with the Inner Cities Religious Council of the Department for the Environment, Transport and the Regions, 1999), pp. 5–6.

151 P. Weller, 'The Inter Faith Network for the United Kingdom', *Indo-British Review: A Journal of History* 20/1 (1994), pp. 20–6.

152 For a current list of affiliated organizations see the Inter Faith Network for the UK's website, at www.interfaith.org.uk.

153 Inter Faith Network for the UK, *Statement on Inter-Religious Relations* (London: Inter Faith Network for the United Kingdom, 1991).

154 Inter Faith Network for the UK, *Building Good Relations Between People of Different Faiths and Beliefs* (London: Inter Faith Network for the United Kingdom, 1993).

155 Inter Faith Network for the UK, *Mission, Dialogue and Inter-Religious Encounter* (London: Inter Faith Network for the United Kingdom, 1993).

156 Archbishop's Commission on Urban Priority Areas, *Faith in the City: A Call for Action by Church and Nation – The Report of the Archbishop of Canterbury's Commission on Urban Priority Areas* (London: Church House, 1985).

157 Local Government Association, *Faith and Community: A Good Practice Guide for Local Authorities* (London: Local Government Association, 2002).

Chapter 4

THE VARIETIES OF RELIGIOUS DISCRIMINATION

1. *The Changing Context of Religious Discrimination*

a. *Discrimination and Disadvantage in UK History*

As has been seen in Chapters 1 and 2, questions and issues relating to various forms of unfair treatment and discrimination on the basis of religion and belief have been very much a part of the history of religion in England and the UK. In the nineteenth century, many of these issues came to a head in terms of the struggle for individual rights and participation in civil society of nonconformist and Roman Catholic Christians, Jews, atheists and freethinkers.

b. *Contemporary Re-emergence of Religious Discrimination*

By the end of the twentieth and the beginning of the twenty-first century, issues relating to religion and discrimination were once again coming to the fore of public debate. In these recent debates there are some points of continuity with the past inheritance of conflict and debate over the role of established religion. At the same time, in comparison with the nineteenth century, the issues and debates are framed by what Chapter 3 has outlined as the greater general *secularity* of society and the increased *religious diversity* of those sectors that *do* affirm the significance in their lives of religious believing and/or belonging.

In outlining contemporary claims and debates concerning discrimination on the grounds of religion, this chapter draws extensively on the work and the results of the Religious Discrimination in England and Wales research project. This was the first systematic research project undertaken into the nature and extent of such discrimination. It was conducted between 1999 and 2001 by a research team[1] at the University of Derby, of which the present author was Project Director. The full results of its empirical research – that included both a postal questionnaire survey and fieldwork interviews in four localities in England and Wales – were published in the Home Office Research Study 220, *Religious Discrimination in England and Wales.*[2] Materials from this report are drawn upon in the section of this chapter that deals specifically with 'Religious Discrimination in England and Wales'.

Northern Ireland and Scotland were outside the terms of reference of the project's empirical work. Nevertheless, the project did publish an earlier *Interim Report*[3] that was based upon a literature review of published and other relevant materials that were available and/or submitted to the project. This included an overview of the changing context for religious discrimination, a literature review in relation to Scotland, and some examination of (especially the legal) situation in

Northern Ireland. The *Interim Report* is therefore also drawn upon in this opening section of this chapter and also in the sections that summarize the position with regard to religious discrimination in Scotland and Northern Ireland.

The chapter concludes by moving from material that reports the empirical findings of the project to sections that include more analytical reflection by the author. This part of the chapter commences with the section on 'Analytical Categories for Religious Discrimination'. It uses and develops an analytical framework originally developed by the project's *Interim Report* as a basis for understanding the varied dimensions and dynamics of unfair treatment and discrimination on the basis of religion. Specific examples are quoted and referenced from the project's empirical report but, apart from this, the contents of these sections should be distinguished from the empirical results of the Religious Discrimination in England and Wales project.

The opening chapter of this book outlined a history in which the experience of religious discrimination among Free Church and Roman Catholic Christians, Jews, atheists, humanists and freethinkers was closely connected with the social, political and legal implications of the existence of the establishment of the Church of England. This discrimination was embodied in law, but also permeated the structures and dynamics of the institutions of civil society and cultural life reflecting a 'one-dimensional' understanding of religion and society.

Reforms that took place during the nineteenth century gradually removed the vast majority of the civic disabilities from nonconformist and Roman Catholic Christians. Participation in the wider society was thus increasingly facilitated for people from non-established Christian traditions and, in due course, also for atheists, humanists, freethinkers and Jews. However, in the twentieth century discrepancies remained between the position in principle and the social realities as experienced in practice. This was particularly the case for Jewish people who, for much of the first half of the century, continued to face significant prejudice and discrimination. This was especially the case during the arrival of Jewish refugees from Czarist Russia and, later, from Nazi Germany, Austria and the occupied lands of Europe from which they had fled.[4]

However, by the 1960s, under the impact of secularization, the kind of nineteenth-century public debate that had raged around religious discrimination and the relationships between religion and public life had, in much of the UK, subsided. The exception to this, of course, was the ongoing Catholic–Protestant tension, conflict, and communalism to be found in Northern Ireland which, to some extent, also continued to be reflected in Scotland. While the main focus of this chapter will be on reporting claims of religious discrimination in England and Wales, it is also important to try to take account of the specificity of experience in Northern Ireland and Scotland. The experience of Northern Ireland and Scotland is important in trying to understand the differences and similarities involved in the more traditional forms for the debates on the relationship between religion(s), state and society in the UK and the newer forms of these debates following the religious diversification of the second half of the twentieth century.

2. *Religious Discrimination in Northern Ireland*

a. *Religion and the National Question*

In Northern Ireland, issues of religious discrimination have continued to be of major concern in the context of the wider political and national struggle between Nationalists and Unionists, Republicans and Loyalists. In this context, religion (of the Roman Catholic and Protestant Christian varieties) has melded with other aspects of ethnic and communal identity to maintain a high degree of social and political division.[5]

Since the foundation of the Irish Free State and the subsequent creation of the Republic of Ireland, Protestant social and political ascendency over Roman Catholics has been part of the basis for the continuation of the political unit of Northern Ireland within the UK. The Province was created in response to Unionist opposition to Irish independence and was established in six of the nine counties of the ancient Province of Ulster and until the introduction of direct rule from Westminster in 1972, the Province had its own Parliament at Stormont. Following the Civil Rights movement's focus upon the frustration of the nationalist minority in relation to their widespread experience of property disenfranchisement in local government and discrimination in employment, the Irish Republican Army (IRA) and, later, the Provisional IRA (PIRA) sought to bring an end to British rule using armed means.

While Protestantism has been closely aligned with Unionism, the Roman Catholic community in the North has generally been identified closely with the aspirations of Irish nationalism. Thus, in 1978 the former Roman Catholic Archbishop (later Cardinal) Tomas O'Fiaich called explicitly for British withdrawal from the North. At the same time, there has been a tension, and often also serious conflict, between militant Republicanism and the episcopal leadership of the Roman Catholic Church in Ireland, with many of the actions of the Provisional IRA having been condemned by the Catholic hierarchy.

In more recent times the Republican party, Sinn Fein, has joined the nationalist Social Democratic and Labour Party in adopting a political strategy in support of a 'peace process'. The Downing Street Declaration of the British and Irish Governments led initially to an eighteen-months ceasefire by the PIRA and the Loyalist paramilitary organizations, until the PIRA resumption of armed conflict in February 1996. Eventually, however, the Good Friday Agreement created conditions for the formation of the Northern Ireland Assembly and the restoration of a measure of devolved government in the Province. However, these arrangements have been subject to constant fragility and since midnight on 14 October 2002 the Assembly has been suspended, with the Secretary of State for Northern Ireland taking direct responsibility for Northern Ireland government departments.

In terms of religion, the majority in the North has been concerned about the marginalized position of Protestants in the Republic of Ireland. The continuing demographic decline of Southern Protestants has reinforced Northern Protestant fears about their potential position in a united Ireland especially in the light of the Roman Catholic Church's originally special position within the constitution of the Republic. Due to this, its teachings shaped legislation in areas of personal, social and, especially sexual morality.[6] However, in 1972 the 'special position' clause of the Irish Republic's constitution was abolished. Nevertheless, as Steve Bruce points out, for that strand of Unionism which supports or sympathizes with Ian Paisley's Free Presbyterian Church and the Democratic Unionist Party, 'Unionism is about avoiding becoming a subordinate minority in a Catholic state. Avoiding becoming a Catholic means remaining a Protestant.'[7]

b. *Religion and Law in Northern Ireland*
Until recently Northern Ireland was the only part of the UK that had specific legal instruments for tackling discrimination and unfair treatment on the basis of religion. Legislation on religious discrimination has existed in the jurisdiction of Northern Ireland, under the terms of the Northern Ireland Act, 1998, which has prohibited discrimination by Government or public bodies on grounds of religious belief or political opinion. The Fair Employment and Treatment (Northern Ireland) Order, 1998 also covered religious discrimination in employment and extended protection to cover the provision of goods, services and facilities.

3. *Religious Discrimination in Scotland*

a. *'Nationalized Monopolies' of Religion in Scotland*
In Scotland, the history of the relationship between religion and society has included attempts to create religious monopolies. Since the Reformation, there has been a series of sharp struggles for control within the established Presbyterian Church of Scotland. Initially, this was between those of Presbyterian and Episcopalian traditions, with the governance of the Church of Scotland changing frequently between 1560 and 1690. Even when the established Church became clearly Presbyterian, there was a succession of conflicts between Presbyterians of different traditions contesting control of that tradition. These conflicts revolved around the laxity or rigour of the leading party in the Church and/or around the issue of the church–state relationship. They led to various secessions from, and reunions with, what (even where they were opposed to its established status) most parties to these debates nevertheless continued to see as a Scottish national Church.[8]

However, in addition to these intra-Protestant tensions, following the Reformation in Scotland, the Roman Catholic Church found itself with a significantly reduced number of adherents. Numerical regrowth only took place following the nineteenth-century immigration of Irish Catholics. The ensuing popular association of Catholicism with Irish migration to Scotland has underpinned what, among non-Catholics, has sometimes been a sense of Catholicism being something of an alien intrusion into Scottish society. Due to the links of history and migration, especially in the urban centres of Scotland and in the west of the country, the conflicts in Northern Ireland have interacted with underlying domestic tensions along sectarian lines that have sometimes issued into outbursts of popular conflict.

b. *Anti-Catholicism in Scotland*

Public debate on these issues was focused in August 1999, when James MacMillan[9] used a speech he was giving at the Edinburgh Festival as an opportunity to highlight what he sees as 'anti-Catholic bigotry' in Scottish society. In the same month, an essay by Professor Patrick Reilly that highlighted 'anti-Catholic prejudice' gave rise to a series of letters in *The Herald*. Following this, a September 1999 readers' survey[10] for the newspaper examined the extent to which readers agreed with the statement that there were 'deep rooted anti-Catholic attitudes throughout Scottish society' and found that, of these respondents, 34% agreed, 13% agreed strongly, and 45% disagreed. The continuing undercurrent from the inheritance of historical Protestant–Catholic conflict is clear but, with regard to the position of the newer and wider ethnic and religious minority groups of contemporary Scottish society, comparatively little research has so far been carried out.

c. *Wider Religious Diversity in Scotland*

In a study of social exclusion in Scotland, conducted for the Scottish Office by William O'Connor and Jane Lewis, the presence of religious discrimination in Scotland was reported[11] along with discrimination based on ethnic identity, impairment and sexuality. Muslims spoke of being publicly ridiculed for their beliefs, in particular their choice of prayer times, and their abstinence from alcohol,[12] and it was noted that religious exclusion was 'perceived to be caused by society firmly rooted in Judeo-Christian tradition values'.[13] The report also discussed the links between religious and ethnic identities, highlighting the fluidity of these and noting the tensions caused by such dual identity, while underlining the desire, and right, of Muslims to be included in Scottish society.[14]

It is apparent that, in Scotland, there are some significant concerns about paying too much attention to questions of religion in public life, or to religious discrimination in particular. The are fears that such attention might lead to 'taking the lid off' sectarian issues in a way which might at best be unhelpful, and at worst divisive or even potentially destructive. However, even if these issues are too difficult to handle along their traditional Protestant–Catholic, Orange–Green fault lines, it could perhaps turn out that it is more possible to address them in the context of a broader consideration of religion, discrimination and equal opportunities in Scotland.

There is, in fact, already some evidence to suggest that the widespread discussion about the nature of Scottish identity that accompanied devolution of powers to the Scottish Parliament might have allowed new directions to be taken in respect of older tensions. For example, in the context of debating whether or not to include opportunities for prayer and reflection in Parliamentary time, the reformed Scottish Parliament took the creative and innovative step of initiating a religiously inclusive opportunity for prayer and meditation.[15] This compares with the Westminster Parliament where parliamentary prayers are still led only by representatives of the established Church of England.

4. *Varieties of Religious Diversity and Discrimination*

a. *'New Religious Movements'*

Apart from the continuing Protestant and Catholic communalist tensions, the majority of issues relating to religious discrimination that emerged into public consciousness and debate have been concerned with the practices of those minority Christian groups often perceived as 'sects' (such as the Jehovah's Witnesses, Christian Scientists and Mormons). Thus with regard to Jehovah's Witnesses and Christian Scientists there have, respectively, been disputes over child custody and medical treatment, while the commitment of Seventh Day Adventists to Sabbatarianism has sometimes resulted in difficulties relating to employment.

The highest-profile political and legal debates relating to claims of unfair treatment on the basis of religion have occurred in relation to more recent 'New Religious Movements',[16] such as Unificationists and Scientologists. These have included conflicts over the legitimacy of their claims to charitable status as religions. Similarly, lifestyle issues in relation to The Family and the followers of Bhagwan Rajneesh (more recently known as Osho) have led to debates over 'brainwashing', 'deprogramming', matters of personal freedom, family and social rights as well as to claims of biased media coverage. Especially in the political context of the European Union, there has been a high level of concern around the alleged nature and activities of some of the newer of the 'New Religious Movements'. This has led to periodic attempts within the European Parliament and in various national Parliaments, including in that of the UK, to restrict the activities of such movements.[17]

b. *Wider Diversity and Discrimination*

Legal cases dealing with matters such as these have highlighted often complex issues in the relationship between religious commitments and individual freedom, the rights of families, the responsibilities of professionals and the interests of the wider society, as well as the scope and interpretation of the law. Such issues have also continued to be raised for Evangelical and Charismatic Christians. From time to time, such conservative Christians have felt that social services and other secular caring professions, such as psychiatry, have acted with scant regard for the religious identity and values of those religiously orthodox individuals and families in their care.[18]

But it has been in the context of the growing plurality of society consequent upon the development of communities of faith rooted in originally migrant populations that issues related to religious discrimination have again emerged onto the public and political agenda in England and the UK as a whole. In the 1970s and early 1980s the politics of identity and diversity were cast primarily in terms of 'race' and 'ethnicity'. But by the closing decades of the twentieth century, religion began to re-emerge as a marker of individual and community identity for a significant number of people, especially among those in minority ethnic communities. In the context of wider global change, in his Demos booklet *The World's New Fissures: Identities in Crisis*,[19] Vincent Cable linked the growing importance of cultural and religious factors of self-identification and organization with the phenomenon of globalization.

In a world that is rapidly shrinking and becoming the 'global village' of Marshall McLuhan's 1960s prophecy, the old political polarities of left and right, and of identities based on nation-state formations, have weakened. Individuals and groups are looking for ways to connect the local and the global. Religions are prime exemplars of this possibility with their participative communities centred on localized groups in villages, towns and cities. At the same time, they are connected with wider transnational networks in which primary allegiance is owed to value systems that claim to transcend the national, ethnic and legal systems of all human societies. Therefore, in the closing decades of the twentieth century, a shift began to take place in which, in the context of a developing identity politics, religion once again emerged as a major factor in the public sphere.

c. *Discrimination and International Impacts*

As in relation to the historic position of Roman Catholic Christians and of Jews, it has often been the actual and perceived tensions between particular (national) and global (religious) forms of belonging that have formed the backcloth to these debates. This has particularly, although not exclusively, affected the Muslim population of England, the UK and the global 'Ummah'. In the long-running Rushdie controversy,[20] during the 1991 Gulf War,[21] as well as in the climate of fear and suspicion about 'Islamic terrorism' following the Al-Qaida Network's 11 September attacks on the World Trade Centre and the Pentagon,[22] Muslims frequently found themselves inheriting the historic mantle of being perceived as at least potential 'fifth columnists'. The research report on *Muslims in Britain*, written by Humayan Ansari, and published by the Minority Rights Group International, has graphically highlighted some of the experiences that arose from 11 September and its aftermath. In this, Ansari records that:

> Muslim adults and children were attacked, physically and verbally. They were punched, spat at, hit with umbrellas at bus stops, publicly doused with alcohol and pelted with fruit and vegetables. Dog excrement and fireworks were pushed through their letterboxes and bricks through their windows. They were called murderers and were excluded from social gatherings. One woman in Swindon was hospitalised after being beaten with a metal baseball bat; two Cambridge University students had their headscarves ripped off, in broad daylight, outside a police station; Saba Zaman, who, in July 2001, had her scarf pulled off and two of her ribs broken in Tooting, London, was stopped and searched by the police three times in two weeks following the terrorist attacks in the United States of America. In west London, an Afghan taxi driver, Hamidullah Gharwal, was attacked shortly after 11th September, and left paralysed from the neck down. Sikh men, whose beards and turbans created the impression that they were Muslims, were also abused. Vandals attacked mosques and Asian-run businesses around the country. Nine pigs' heads were dumped outside a mosque in Exeter. Many mosques were said not to have reported attacks because of fear of reprisals.[23]

For other religious minority groups, too, international and domestic events have heightened awareness of the significance of religion as a key marker of self-identification and as a basis for self-organization. Events of this kind have, for example, in relation to Sikhs, included the storming of the Golden Temple in Amritsar[24] and struggles over legislation affecting the wearing of turbans.[25] For Hindus, there has been the discrimination against Hindus that took place in Fiji following a coup by indigenous Fijians. There was also the significant impact on the consciousness of Hindus in the UK of the long-running conflict over planning consent for the use of Bhaktivedanta Manor for Hindu worship and festivals.[26]

d. *Discrimination, Ethnicity and Religion*

That such issues were likely to emerge had been presciently identified by Bishop John Taylor as long ago as a 1977 Church of England General Synod debate on the hard-hitting 1976 report, *The New Black Presence in Britain* published by the then British Council of Churches' Community and Race Relations Unit.[27] In that debate, Bishop Taylor argued that 'The existence of religious minorities presents us with both problems and opportunities which are distinct from those that arise in the presence of racial and cultural minorities, and should not be lost sight of or evaded.'[28]

The *Satanic Verses* controversy was a key example that confirmed Taylor's insight and foresight. It also marked a watershed in this trend, putting religion once again at the heart of a whole range of public debates with entails relating to law, politics, culture and religion.[29] As the veteran socialist politician Tony Benn expressed it at the outbreak of the controversy in 1989:

> Now, all of a sudden, arguments which had almost disappeared into the mists of time have to come into sharp focus and are hotly contested across the world, involving diplomatic relations, trade arrangements and stretching into the heart of religious communities where people of different religious convictions have to live side by side.[30]

The arguments involved have concerned notions of Islam as a 'foreign' religion and Muslims as potentially disloyal 'fifth-columnists'; the equation of Islam with fundamentalism and the sidelining of religious perspectives on public life; the cultural relativism and alternative scale of values held by the artistic and cultural elite of the wider society; the entrenched privilege of the legal protection accorded to the Christian religion and the lack of any equivalent protection for the beliefs and feelings of Muslims; and finally, despite their participation in the political system, the impotence of Muslims to bring about their desired results due to a lack of direct representation and the marginalisation of their concerns by the mainstream political parties and the majority of political activists.

The Rushdie controversy brought some, albeit in many cases grudging, recognition that Muslims are not going to privatize their religious beliefs and values in order to fit in with the wider society. If 'assimilation' to secularism is not going to work, then perhaps institutional mechanisms for the 'integration' of religions on the basis of their own self-understanding need to be considered. Thus, in the closing decades of the twentieth century, the prescience of Taylor's insight has been confirmed. Whether or not this is seen as a welcome development, these symbolically charged major social and political events and the debates associated with them indicate that an observable shift has been taking place in social and political realities.

In contrast to the nineteenth century, when these issues of religious discrimination began to emerge at the end of the twentieth century they have seldom been articulated in relation to the establishment of the Church of England. Rather, underlying the symbolically charged and high profile events and debates, the focus of concern has been upon claims of day-to-day experiences of unfair treatment in employment, education, the media and a whole range of other aspects of daily life. Many of these concerns, albeit to differing extents, have been articulated by people from across the spectrum of the religions including (albeit to a lesser extent) from among Christians. These concerns have related to the overall impact upon religious believers of the secular ethos of the wider culture and society. Also, religious discrimination has continued to be claimed by people from 'New Religious Movements'.

e. *Anti-Semitism and Anti-Judaism*

Anti-Semitism and anti-Judaism remain very much a part of a common European inheritance.[31] As the Runnymede Trust's 1994 report, *A Very Light Sleeper*[32] evidenced, the tone and content of debates on *shechita* slaughter, circumcision and other matters of importance to the Jewish community have underlined the persistence of anti-Semitism, and the extent of anti-Jewish attitudes and discrimination should not be underestimated. In the European Values Survey, for example, when asked to identify groups of people from among a list of those whom the respondents would 'not like to have as neighbours', as many as 6.1% of respondents in Great Britain chose 'Jews'.[33]

f. *Muslims, Religious Discrimination and Islamophobia*

But it has been Muslims (constituting the largest other than Christian religious minority in England and the UK) who have been at the forefront in arguing for recognition of the reality of religious discrimination and for the necessity of legislative measures to tackle it. Among the issues raised have been tensions between patterns of religious observance and the demands of employment; issues connected with observance of fasting in the month of Ramadan; the desire of significant sections of the community for Muslim voluntary aided schooling; matters of Islamic personal and family law in relation to the European legal systems;[34] the existence of blasphemy laws[35] that protect only one religion; and a variety of other similar matters.[36]

Throughout the 1990s a range of reports and initiatives began to highlight the issues involved. Work by the Policy Studies Institute evidenced that religion was becoming an increasingly significant factor in the identities of minority ethnic communities.[37] In 1996, the Inner Cities' Religious Council issued both a leaflet and a booklet entitled *Challenging Religious Discrimination: A Guide for Faith Communities and Their Advisers*.[38] In 1997, the Commission for Racial Equality produced a leaflet on *Religious Discrimination: Your Rights*,[39] which outlined, under the terms of the Race Relations Act, 1976, ways in which unfair treatment on the basis of religion could be addressed as 'indirect racial discrimination'. These leaflets and booklets from the CRE and the ICRC addressed the areas of housing, education, immigration, prison, police, employment, state benefits, health, home life and transport, illustrating both the provisions and the limitations of race relations legislation when people feel discriminated against on account of their religion.

As part of a survey investigating the theme of religion and integration of migrants, the Council of Europe Group of Consultants on Religious and Cultural Aspects of Equality for Immigrants visited a number of Muslim organizations in the UK. In reporting on a visit to the Ladies Job Club Mosque, Golden Hillock Road in Birmingham, the Consultants noted that 'A very strong association was perceived between discrimination based on colour and based on religion, especially with Muslim women wishing to maintain some form of acceptable Muslim dress, in particular the head scarf.'[40] They also noted that 'Muslims constantly run up against preconceptions of "trouble-making fundamentalists" based on immediate judgment of outward appearance, like colour and dress.' From their visit to the Yemeni Muadh Centre, in Camp Hill, Birmingham, the Consultants reported that, 'There was a perception of widespread media bias against ethnic minorities and Muslims especially.'[41] In 1997 many similar concerns and issues were systematically collected, highlighted and brought to public attention by the Runnymede Trust report, *Islamophobia: A Challenge for Us All.*[42]

5. *Religious Discrimination in England and Wales*

a. *The Project*
It was against the background and growth of such claims that the Religious Discrimination in England and Wales Research Project (1999–2001) was the first research study specifically of religious discrimination to be commissioned from within the UK Government.[43] The project was carried out by means of quantitative and qualitative research methods, with a postal questionnaire being sent to 1,830 religious organizations,[44] and fieldwork conducted in four localities[45] that included meetings and interviews with religious organizations, public, private and voluntary sector bodies, and also biographical interviews with individuals. The full findings of the project can be found in the project's empirical report published by the Home Office. In highlighting key aspects of its empirical findings, the present section draws upon that report.[46]

b. *Overall Findings*
In its overall findings, the project confirmed much of what had previously been reported in more fragmentary ways. Thus, in the findings from the project questionnaire, a consistently higher level of unfair treatment was reported by Muslim organizations than by most other religious groups. This was both in terms of the proportion of respondents indicating that some unfair treatment was experienced, and by the proportion indicating that these experiences were 'frequent' rather than 'occasional'. The majority of Muslim organizations also reported that their members experienced unfair treatment in every aspect of education, employment, housing, law and order, and in all the local government services covered in the questionnaire.

Hindu, and especially Sikh, organizations also reported a relatively high level of unfair treatment and tended to highlight the same areas of concern as Muslim organizations. Christian organizations in the survey were generally much less likely to report unfair treatment than Muslims, Sikhs and Hindus, and nearly all the unfairness they reported was 'occasional' rather than frequent. However, black-led Christian organizations and those representing groups such as Mormons and Jehovah's Witnesses were much more likely to report unfair treatment in nearly all walks of life than organizations in what are often seen as the 'mainstream' Christian traditions.

In the local interviews, such groups often described overt hostility similar to that experienced by some of the non-Christian minorities. Pagans and people from 'New Religious Movements' also complained of open hostility and discrimination, and of being labelled as 'child abusers' and 'cults', particularly by the media. Representatives from some of the religious traditions with relatively small numbers were concerned that their very existence went unrecognized. Sometimes this was because little was known or taught about them and they felt themselves to be misrepresented. At other times, they felt themselves to be deliberately excluded. Such groups felt like 'minorities within minorities' who were being ignored by schools, employers, policy makers and service providers, even though these institutions may be working hard to include and involve the larger religious minorities.

Ignorance and indifference were of particular concern across all religious groups. Ignorance and indifference do not, of course, in themselves constitute discrimination, but in organizational settings they can contribute towards an environment in which discrimination of all kinds (including that which is 'unwitting' and institutional) is able to thrive. This theme came up many times in the local interviews and was echoed in the postal survey. In the local interviews, those who actively practised their religion often said that they were made to feel awkward and that they experienced pressure to conform. They claimed that other people based their views on pre-conceived ideas and stereotypes and seemed to neither know nor care about the things that are central to the experience of those for whom religious identity constitutes an important, or the key, aspect of their lives.

c. *Seriousness of Religious Discrimination*

To gain a little more sense of the issues involved, it is instructive to look at the results of the project questionnaire where respondents from religious organizations in various religions were asked for their personal view[47] of the seriousness of any unfair treatment on the basis of religion. As can be seen from the results[48] set out in Table 4.1, representatives from Muslim organizations were more likely than those from other religions to identify 'very serious' problems in nearly every area, with only a minority of Muslim respondents saying each issue was 'not at all serious'. Media coverage, ignorance and hostility were the most likely to be identified as 'very serious'. In contrast, a clear majority of Buddhist respondents regarded most of the problems as 'not at all' serious, although they had more concern about ignorance and media coverage.

Table 4.1: Responses, by religion, to the question: 'How serious do you think the following problems/experiences are for people within your religion?'

Form of unfair treatment and religious group	Very serious	Quite serious	Not at all serious	Don't know	Total responses (100%)
Ignorance					
Buddhist	9%	36%	39%	15%	33
Christian	18%	55%	22%	5%	285
Hindu	21%	58%	9%	12%	33
Jewish	17%	49%	34%	0%	35
Muslim	42%	44%	5%	9%	66
Sikh	22%	63%	9%	6%	32
Indifference					
Buddhist	3%	13%	68%	16%	31
Christian	20%	46%	29%	4%	282
Hindu	15%	58%	24%	3%	33
Jewish	9%	35%	53%	3%	34
Muslim	30%	45%	13%	12%	60
Sikh	13%	53%	25%	9%	32
Hostility					
Buddhist	6%	13%	71%	10%	31
Christian	6%	25%	62%	7%	279
Hindu	35%	35%	13%	16%	31
Jewish	12%	32%	53%	3%	34
Muslim	37%	47%	8%	8%	60
Sikh	25%	47%	19%	9%	32
Verbal abuse					
Buddhist	6%	13%	71%	10%	31
Christian	6%	23%	63%	9%	279
Hindu	27%	36%	21%	15%	33
Jewish	12%	47%	38%	3%	34
Muslim	35%	40%	13%	13%	63
Sikh	36%	48%	12%	3%	33
Physical abuse					
Buddhist	3%	13%	71%	13%	31
Christian	4%	8%	75%	12%	277
Hindu	28%	17%	31%	24%	29
Jewish	11%	25%	58%	6%	36
Muslim	28%	38%	16%	18%	61
Sikh	23%	52%	23%	3%	31
Damage to property					
Buddhist	3%	6%	81%	10%	31
Christian	7%	25%	57%	11%	283
Hindu	47%	25%	9%	19%	32

Jewish	11%	40%	43%	6%	35
Muslim	30%	36%	19%	16%	64
Sikh	33%	48%	12%	6%	33
Policies of organizations					
Buddhist	7%	17%	70%	7%	30
Christian	3%	20%	59%	19%	273
Hindu	7%	38%	24%	31%	29
Jewish	12%	15%	68%	6%	34
Muslim	16%	43%	16%	25%	63
Sikh	10%	32%	32%	26%	31
Practices of organizations					
Buddhist	6%	16%	68%	10%	31
Christian	4%	20%	56%	20%	271
Hindu	10%	42%	26%	23%	31
Jewish	12%	15%	71%	3%	34
Muslim	21%	43%	16%	21%	63
Sikh	14%	34%	28%	24%	29
Coverage in the media					
Buddhist	6%	34%	47%	13%	32
Christian	19%	39%	35%	7%	275
Hindu	32%	29%	19%	19%	31
Jewish	11%	28%	58%	3%	36
Muslim	48%	38%	5%	9%	66
Sikh	21%	36%	27%	15%	33

Source: P. Weller, A. Feldman and K. Purdam, *et al.*, *Religious Discrimination in England and Wales* (Home Office Research Study 220; London: Research, Development, Statistics Directorate, The Home Office, 2001), pp. 106–7. Tables from this report are Crown copyright and are used by kind permission.

The majority of Christian respondents were, to some degree, concerned about indifference, ignorance and media coverage (although more often in terms of these being 'quite' serious problems rather than 'very serious' ones) but very few identified physical abuse. Sikh and Hindu respondents, on the other hand, identified hostility, verbal and physical abuse and damage to property to an extent similar to Muslim respondents. Most Jewish respondents picked out ignorance, verbal abuse and damage to property, although mostly as a 'quite serious' problem. Muslims, Hindus and Sikhs were the most likely to identify hostility, verbal and physical abuse and damage to property as 'very serious' or 'quite serious' problems, although violence did not seem a widespread issue within the local interviews.

With the exception of Buddhists, a clear majority of respondents from every religion regarded ignorance as a 'very serious' or 'quite serious' problem. Media coverage and indifference were both regarded as 'very serious' or 'quite serious' by the majority of respondents from every type of religious organization except Buddhist and Jewish. National and local organizations from within each religion highlighted broadly similar issues, but there were some variations. National Muslim organizations, for example, were more likely to identify ignorance and media coverage as 'very serious' than local Muslim organizations. Organizational policy and practice were generally less likely to be regarded as a serious problem, although more respondents indicated that they did not know the answer than for the other questions.

d. *Frequency of Religious Discrimination*

Respondents to the postal survey were also asked whether, in the last five years, problems such as ignorance, hostility and discriminatory practices had become more or less frequent. Respondents from Muslim organizations were the most likely to say that the situation had worsened, with the majority indicating that hostility, verbal abuse and unfair media coverage had become more frequent. Views on organizational policy and practice were fairly evenly divided. Most Christian and Jewish respondents thought that things had stayed much the same, but a substantial number of Christians thought that ignorance, indifference and unfair media coverage had become more frequent. Some religious groups perceived improvements over the last five years. The majority of Buddhist and Bahá'í organizations, for example, said that ignorance was now less frequent.

e. *Types and Sectors of Religious Discrimination*

As well as being experienced differentially by various religions, the findings of the Religious Discrimination in England and Wales Research Project also suggested that discrimination is much more likely to be experienced in some sectors of social life than in others. For example, education, employment and the media were the areas most often highlighted in the postal survey and local interviews. Among people from all religious traditions, the media were identified as the most frequent source of unfairness. Traditions with a large membership of people from ethnic minorities (in particular, Muslims, Sikhs and Hindus) also frequently reported unfair treatment in areas such as immigration, policing and prisons.

The postal survey also gave some fairly consistent indications about the role played by the attitudes and behaviour of individuals compared with the policies and practices of organizations. Although the attitudes of ignorance and indifference among colleagues and managers were of greatest and most widespread concern across the religions, concerns were also expressed about the policies and practices of organizations. In some areas of life (e.g. policing, prisons, immigration, health care, social services, transport) the attitudes and behaviour of staff were seen by organizations from most religions as a more frequent source of unfair treatment than the policies of the organizations providing the service. However, it was also the case that Muslim respondents, in particular, often felt that policies were at fault as well. In education and housing, pupils and neighbours or other tenants were often seen as the most likely source of unfair treatment. Nevertheless, respondent organizations from some religions were equally likely to single out teachers.

In the context of employment, Christian and Jewish organizations were mainly concerned about the attitudes and behaviour of managers and colleagues, whereas other religions were also concerned about policy and practice. In the media, the attitudes and behaviour of journalists and presenters, and the coverage given to particular religious communities and organizations, were seen as relatively frequent sources of unfairness by respondents from all religions.

f. *Ethnicity, Religion and Discrimination*

In the Introduction to this book it was noted that the relationship between religion and ethnicity, and religion and culture is a complex and often contested one.

In the Religious Discrimination in England and Wales Research Project interviews, a white, male, police inspector noted that '... an incident may start as a road rage incident and then move to racial insults, even if it wasn't initially motivated by race. There's the same problem with religion: it might begin as racial harassment but then elements of religion are brought into it.'[49] A Muslim woman stated that 'If someone throws two stones through someone's window, that's racism. If they throw two pigs heads [as did happen in this person's experience], it's about religion.'[50] However, an African–Caribbean race equality worker observed about this that 'I don't care what they threw, but why they threw anything at all – the whole gambit of "ifs". You're usually dealing with a multiplicity of issues.'[51]

Chapter 3 included two tables (Tables 3.20 and 3.21) that presented the relationship between religion and ethnicity in a numerical way as derived from the results of the 2001 Census questions on religion and ethnicity. The statistics in those tables show a relatively high overlap between sectors of the population considered in terms of religion and those considered in terms of ethnicity. However, presenting a *statistical* picture of the relationship between religion and ethnicity is one thing. The question of how that relationship is *understood* by people of diverse religious and ethnic backgrounds is another and much more complex matter. As a matter of principle, people in some religious traditions make no distinction between their religion and their ethnicity. Others have a strong wish to make such a distinction even when the religion and ethnicity of particular groups are closely aligned. Therefore in the project questionnaire survey, respondents from religious organizations were asked to say how far they personally[52] perceived ethnic or racial grounds as forming part of the reason for their experience of unfair treatment on the basis of religion.

The results[53] of the questionnaire on this issue as set out in Table 4.2 suggest that, perhaps not surprisingly, respondents from religions with a high proportion of ethnic minority members see a clear area of overlap between religious and racial discrimination. Thus it can be seen that all Sikh and a large majority of Muslim and Hindu respondents felt that ethnicity played at least some role in their experience of unfair treatment on the basis of religion. Most Jewish respondents felt the same, although opinions were more evenly divided. In contrast, nearly all the NRM/Pagan organizations felt that ethnic or racial grounds played no role at all.

Some Christian Churches have mixed or predominately black congregations, and some forms of Christianity are, in the UK, specifically associated with African or African–Caribbean traditions. It is perhaps not surprising, therefore, that a significant minority of Christian respondents (around one in three overall) felt that ethnic or racial grounds formed at least some part of the reason for dis-

Table 4.2: Responses to the question: 'How far do you think that in your religion ethnic or racial grounds are part of the reason for unfair treatment on the basis of religion?'

Religious group	Not part of the reason	A small part	A large part	The main reason	Don't know	Total
Baháʼí	8	6	3	2	4	23
Buddhist	14	2	5	4	4	29
Christian 'Black-led'	0	3	5	2	3	13
Christian: all other	165	46	19	5	29	264
Hindu	4	9	8	8	3	32
Jain	1	3	0	0	1	5
Jewish	5	9	8	7	6	35
Muslim	4	20	22	11	4	61
NRM/Pagan	20	0	2	1	1	24
Sikh	0	9	12	10	3	34
Zoroastrian	1	2	0	2	0	5

Source: P. Weller, A. Feldman and K. Purdam *et al.*, *Religious Discrimination in England and Wales* (Home Office Research Study 220, London: Research, Development, Statistics Directorate, The Home Office, 2001), pp. 106–7. Tables from this report are Crown copyright and are used by kind permission.

crimination. However, only the black-led Christian organizations were as likely as Sikhs, Muslims, Jews and Hindus to say that ethnicity or race was a large part, or the main reason for discrimination. From the write-in comments to the questionnaires, it seems that respondents from black-led groups often had other Christians in mind when thinking about the role of racial discrimination.

National and local organizations within each religion gave broadly similar views. However, ethnicity tended to play less of a role in the view of national Muslim organizations than it did from the perspective of local organizations. The number of respondents answering 'don't know' to this question may also be significant. The fieldwork interviews and the write-in comments from questionnaires suggest that people who experience unfair treatment do not always find it easy to pigeonhole discrimination into one category or the other, and may sometimes come up with contradictory views.

Religions with large numbers of visible minorities, such as Muslims, Sikhs and Hindus, reported the most discrimination overall, and research participants who belonged to these minority groups often identified a degree of overlap between religious and racial discrimination. Implicit or explicit references to racism were also common during the local interviews. Among Christians, black-led organizations were consistently more likely to say that their members experienced unfair treatment than Christian organizations generally. Many interviewees pointed to the artificiality of trying to separate religious and cultural identities.

However, there were also claims of unfair treatment from white people of British descent with no outward, visible signs of their religion. This suggests that such treatment can be a response to the nature of someone's beliefs and practices (for example, the hostility that is sometimes expressed towards groups that are often referred to as 'cults'). In other cases it may be the strength of belief and its effect on behaviour ('the more active you are, the more vulnerable you become') or the degree to which people seek to convert others. A number of interviewees pointed out that while there are those who see religion as an intrinsic or important part of their identity, the rest of society tends to think of religion as optional and may therefore assume that religious requirements can be straightforwardly negotiated.

Interviewees provided instances in which the rigid dividing line between religion and culture that is sometimes imposed by outsiders can prove awkward and divisive. For example, religious groups may have to present themselves as cultural groups in order to obtain local authority funding for the community services they provide. They feel uncomfortable about doing this, and people from religious organizations that are not associated with cultural minorities may feel discriminated against because they are unable to present themselves in this way. That there is some overlap between discrimination on the ground of religion and that of ethnicity is clear. That there may also be discrimination along the axis of religion is also clearly the case.

6. *Analytical Categories for Religious Discrimination*

a. *Differentiation of Religious Discrimination*
The concluding sections of the chapter move from reporting the empirical findings of the Religious Discrimination in England and Wales Research Project to reflection by the author, albeit utilizing analytical categories first developed in the project's *Interim Report*[54] and including the quotation and referencing of specific examples from the project's final report.

Overall, the terminology of 'religious discrimination' is perhaps best understood as a kind of convenient verbal 'shorthand' for 'discrimination on the basis of religion'. What is generally characteristic of such discrimination may, as in the Religious Discrimination project's empirical report, most inclusively be characterized as 'unfair treatment on the basis of religion'. The notion of 'fairness' is important here, in the sense that what is deficient is not an impossible to achieve abstract position of mathematical equality, but a sense and expression of basic equity.[55]

Thus, the use of the general term 'religious discrimination' signals the existence of those attitudes, actions, circumstances and dynamics in which, in relation to factors concerned with religion, an individual or group is treated less favourably than another individual or group either of a different religion, or of no religion. However, as with the parallel category of 'racial discrimination', together with the shared characteristics of such 'unfair treatment', it is also important to distinguish between its varied dimensions. Understanding how these dimensions differ from, and relate to, one another is important in order that the phenomena under consideration can be correctly described and understood. It is also critical because of the bearing that such description and understanding has in relation to the appropriateness of the possible range of policy and other responses to the nature of the issues involved.

With regard to 'race' and 'ethnicity' agendas, it has proved important to distinguish between 'racial prejudice', 'racial hatred', 'racial disadvantage', 'racial discrimination' (including 'direct' and 'indirect' racial discrimination) and 'institutional racism'. For example, individual prejudice is not the same as institutional discrimination. An attitude may not always lead to discriminatory actions, whereas actions within organizations can be discriminatory in their effect even in the absence of prejudicial attitudes on the part of individuals. Both can feed and sustain each other, but they may require different approaches in terms of appropriate and effective responses.

Therefore, when examining the reported experiences and perceptions that are often colloquially grouped together under the term 'religious discrimination' it can be illuminating to consider the parallel terminological, definitional and policy debates that have taken place in respect of 'race' and 'ethnicity'. In order to analyse the reported experiences of unfair treatment, the remainder of this chapter turns to the analytical categories developed for distinguishing between the various dimensions of religious discrimination that were employed in the *Interim Report* of the Religious Discrimination in England and Wales Research Project.

b. *Religious Prejudice*

The Religious Discrimination in England and Wales Research Project found that attitudes of ignorance and indifference were of major concern across the religions. These are related to what might be identified as 'religious prejudice'. Such prejudice is rooted in the stereotyping of particular religious groups. Stereotyping of this kind is, for example, deeply entrenched in relation to Muslims,[56] being rooted in the historical inheritance of conflictual relationships that have developed over many centuries involving the overlap of religion, politics and warfare. The abuse experienced by many Muslims, without differentiation as to their individual positions on the issues at stake when the *Satanic Verses* controversy was at its height, provides ample evidence of attitudinal prejudice.

Such religious prejudice, although it can wound and even emotionally scar individuals, does not necessarily of itself lead to discriminatory actions. However, as with racial prejudice, through decisions taken by individuals holding positions of power within the public, private and voluntary sectors it is possible for it to translate into actual behaviour that results in 'direct religious discrimination'. It can also result in 'indirect religious discrimination' through the exclusivity of employment and recruitment policies, practice and service provision. In the project's field interviews, religious prejudice was often identified as being manifested in an ignorance that was one of the most frequently cited reasons for unfair or discriminatory treatment on the basis of religion.

Although people of various different religions have lived side by side, sometimes for decades, many interviewees from minority religions and communities felt that members of the majority society did not know very much about them. One individual, for example, explained that a neighbour was 'shocked' to discover that Jews don't celebrate Christmas/Jesus.[57] A Zoroastrian youth reported that, when asked about her religion by other young people, she is often asked if she attends church. When she explained that her place of worship is in London they replied that 'it can't be a real religion if you only have one temple.'[58] A Jehovah's Witness commented that people seem to believe that Jehovah's Witnesses are 'uneducated and brainwashed'. He also drew attention to what he believed was a public perception of Jehovah's Witnesses being involved in a 'controlling American organization' despite the fact that a key aspect of their beliefs is concerned with the individual actively developing and following one's own conscience.[59] A Sikh noted that people think that wearing a kirpan is an indication that the wearer is aggressive or dangerous.[60]

Interviewees reported that those who are not religious often seem to exhibit considerable levels of fear and suspicion towards people who have a strong religious identity and commitment. It was noted that, especially where others have had a bad experience of a particular religious group or of individual religious people, they can tend to generalize this to all other members of that particular religious group, or even towards all religious groups. One person felt that there is a section of the general public who believe that those who have strong religious beliefs and distinctive practices are 'dangerous, clinging to old, outmoded ways, clinging to their identity', commenting that, 'people don't understand and are suspicious of those who don't want to conform, who want to keep their distinct identity and not completely integrate'.[61]

Ignorance manifested as prejudice may take the form of comments like, 'What's wrong with your head?', as a Sikh man reported he used to be asked, while taunts relating to the traditional clothing of Muslim women such as, 'Where's the fancy dress?' are not uncommon.[62] Frequently, those who were the recipients of what they experienced as offensive comments found it hard to know whether the ignorance and/or lack of common sense derived from a lack of interest, or whether it was rooted in a deep-seated hostility. Such hostility relates to another dimension and dynamic of 'religious discrimination' in which 'religious prejudice' shades over into what can, perhaps, best be identified as 'religious hatred'.

c. *Religious Hatred*

'Religious hatred' develops from an intensified form of 'religious prejudice' that congeals into a settled attitude of mind, emotion and will. When it is emotionally intense and/or informed by an ideology that justifies violent actions against individuals and groups perceived as unacceptable 'others', such 'religious hatred' can itself spill over into physical manifestations of intimidatory and violent behaviour towards religious minorities. Such hatred can be stimulated and nurtured by extreme racist and fascist groups.

The kind of 'religious hatred' that has traditionally been directed towards the Jews[63] has, in more recent times, also been directed towards Muslims as representatives of what is perceived to be an alien civilization that is fundamentally at odds with the British and European heritage. The reports of the enquiry teams[64] into the 2001 summer disturbances in the northern English towns of Burnley and Oldham underline the role of organized fascist activity in this, and especially with regard to its particular targeting of 'Muslims' as a specific category of 'undesirable other'.

In responses to the Religious Discrimination project questionnaire, as well as for Muslims, hostility and violence were also very real concerns for organizations representing Sikhs and Hindus. In the project fieldwork, Hindu interviewees explained that at one temple there had been damage to the cars of devotees and that, despite security arrangements, some worshippers had been physically attacked when seeking to attend the temple at festival times.[65] Jews also continue to be targets of such 'religious hatred', with attacks on synagogues and cemetries not being uncommon. Pagans and people from 'New Religious Movements' complained of open hostility and discrimination, and of being labelled as 'child abusers' and 'cults', particularly by the media.[66] In the field research, Pagans reported that they feel they have to take measures to keep their religious lives secret while at work. One said that, if confronted about his Pagan identity, he would need to lie. As a consequence, therefore, they feared they may be perceived as being suspect and dishonest and they were worried that negative stereotypes would be perpetuated if anyone found out.[67]

Thus 'religious hatred' and its effects can be very serious, threatening and destabilizing in their consequences for individuals and groups, leading to violence against both persons and property. However, even in the absence of 'religious prejudice' and 'religious hatred', the findings of the Religious Discrimination research project underline that more day-to-day and structural dimensions of unfair treatment on the basis of religion play as significant a role in the lives of many. Because of this, it is also important to take account of how the practices and policies of organizations work and how they result in either 'direct' or 'indirect' religious discrimination.

d. *Direct Religious Discrimination*

'Direct religious discrimination' occurs where there is deliberate exclusion of people from opportunities or services on grounds related to their religious belief, identity or practice. It includes, for example, decisions made by potential employers to exclude people from employment because of their specific religious belief, identity or practice. As has already been noted, until recently such discrimination was not illegal in the UK outside the specific context of Northern Ireland.[68] However, since the recent implementation of the European Union directives on discrimination in employment through the Employment Equality (Religion or Belief) Regulations, 2003, direct discrimination (as well as indirect discrimination, harassment and victimization arising from complaints of the discrimination or harassment) on the grounds of religion or belief is now illegal throughout the UK in the specific field of employment and vocational training (including the provision of further and higher education).

'Religious prejudice' and 'religious hatred' do not necessarily lead to 'direct religious discrimination', but they may result in harassment on the grounds of religion or belief. However, as with racial prejudice, it is possible for these to translate into directly discriminatory behaviour when they inform decisions taken by individuals holding positions of power within the public, private and voluntary sectors. For example, a Hindu educationalist recalled Sikh children being embarrassed by teachers who derided them and their hair by saying things like 'Why can't they chop off that bun?'[69] It was noted that because of the status and power of teachers, such negative and prejudicial attitudes on their part can have an adverse influence on the behaviour of other students. As a Jehovah's Witness explained it, 'If a teacher gives a student a hard time in the class, then you can guarantee that the other students will do so at lunchtime. The reality is that a six-year-old is not intellectually able to articulate his or her views when challenged by teachers.'[70]

However, as with discrimination on the basis of ethnicity, gender and disability, conscious and deliberate 'direct religious discrimination' is not the only, or perhaps in its effects even the most widespread, form of unfair treatment on the basis of religion. It is also important to take account of 'indirect religious discrimination'.

e. *Indirect Religious Discrimination*
'Indirect religious discrimination' can be understood in terms of the exclusionary effects of historical decisions, contemporary structures or patterns of behaviour and organization. Although not the result of deliberate intent, 'indirect religious discrimination' can, in its effects, be at least as significant, and perhaps even more so than 'direct religious discrimination'. This is because 'indirect discrimination' usually extends beyond individual instances affecting single persons to impact upon the experience and opportunities of whole groups.

Where policies and practices are not reconsidered in the light of a current wider religious plurality, historic patterns of behaviour and organization can result in discrimination against people of various religious traditions. This may occur independently of whether or not attitudes of 'religious prejudice' or 'religious hatred' are present, although aspects of 'religious disadvantage' (as explained below) will often play a part. Examples of 'indirect religious discrimination' often, for example, include culturally exclusive requirements and provisions in terms of diet, clothing and religious festivals. In the Religious Discrimination Project field-work a Sikh woman, who worked in a medium-sized bakery, related the following story through her son:

> For 8 years, it was never a problem. Then, for one and a half years they picked on this (Sikh) woman for wearing her bangle. Finally, they moved her to a different part of the [organization]. They said she must take it off, but she said no. Representatives from the Sikh temple had a meeting with Personnel to explain, but they said no because it was classed as jewellery.[71]

Other interviewees who knew of this story mentioned that tests were done to see if there were any bacteria in the bangle, but that these tests had negative results. They also made the point that the woman's apron sleeves covered the bangle. The controversy had knock-on effects for other Sikh women who came forward in support of this woman to state that they themselves also wore bangles. They, too, however, then became subject to harassment by other employees as well as by the management. The woman took her employer to an employment tribunal. The case was lost, but after years of fighting a special sleeve was developed, and the management and staff were required to attend diversity training.

A number of interviewees who commented on this case believed that it represented an instance of discrimination, especially as various religious community representatives made out a clear and convincing case on behalf of the women, and other employees of the company were allowed to wear wedding rings. At the same time, a white, male, employment tribunal representative (who was not associated with the case) commented about it that:

> knowing how diverse society is, sometimes situations are just unfair. People will have to be aware of say, hygiene regulations, and if they have to wear a bangle, they may have to do something else either within the organization or as a job. You have to find a balance ... the average employer couldn't really care less about religion unless it affects the running of her or his business which usually can be covered by race protections.[72]

f. *Religious Disadvantage*

'Religious disadvantage' is a structural expression of unfair treatment on the basis of religion that is linked with the fact that some religions have traditions of historical presence and rights of access to a range of social institutions that are not available to other religions. Such factors can impact significantly upon the possibilities of social inclusion that are open to religious minorities.

The focus on issues connected with the establishment of the Church of England and the issues arising from this that forms the central concern of this book was not a central feature of the Religious Discrimination in England and Wales Research Project. It was not, therefore, specifically covered in the project's questionnaire survey. Nevertheless, in the course of the project's fieldwork, a number of relevant issues were raised.[73] For example, a Roman Catholic respondent drew attention to the fact that, under the law, Roman Catholic Christians are still the only religious group to which a direct successor to the Throne is not allowed to belong. This interviewee believed that these legal constraints remained in force because of persistent perceptions and myths about Catholic disloyalty. He felt that such things would be considered an outrage if they were in force in respect, say, of black people, and argued that a failure to alter this legal position helped to perpetuate the myths. He noted that the Government had challenged the hereditary principle in relation to the composition of the House of Lords and he could not therefore see why the Act of Settlement should not be repealed.

In addition Christian clergy of various denominations among the project respondents[74] noted that Church of England cathedrals received money from local authorities for improvements whereas, in their perception at least, other historic Christian churches and places of worship did not seem to do so. It was accepted that Anglican cathedrals are often located in the town centre and may be seen as buildings of wider 'public interest', or even as tourist sites. However, a representative of the Roman Catholic Church reported that even though their own cathedral was one of the major sites in the city centre, it was not treated equitably in comparison with a Church of England cathedral.

In more general terms, interviewees from secular agencies as well as from Christian religious groups pointed out that there was an overall Christian 'default position' built into some existing laws.[75] Many felt that this amounted to unfair treatment of other religions and should be reviewed, although what might take the place of the default position was the subject of much more diverse comment.

Examples of such 'religious disadvantage' include the fact that Christianity, especially in its established forms, has a privileged presence in, and right of access to, a range of social institutions that is either not available, or only available on different terms, to non-established traditions.[76] This can, for example, be seen in the provisions made for religious chaplaincy services in public institutions such as prisons,[77] institutions of higher education,[78] the health service and the armed forces.

In each of these areas there are now often advisers of other faith traditions playing a role, and the research both by Gilliat and by Beckford and Gilliat referred to above has shown that the privileges of establishment can sometimes be used creatively to involve minority groups. However, this relies upon the approaches taken by individual personnel and is thus highly dependent upon these individuals rather than being structurally supported and embedded.

g. *Institutional Religionism*
The various forms of discrimination highlighted so far can come together in a complex and interrelated way that the project described in the admittedly less than elegant neologism of 'institutional religionism'. This terminology represents an attempt to describe the endemic and structurally embedded forms of discrimination that can occur within organizations and the services that they provide to the public. By analogy with the MacPherson Report's[79] analysis of 'institutional racism', this can be understood as the product of a combination of several factors into a mutually reinforcing environment and ethos. 'Institutional religionism' thus occurs in a context in which 'religious prejudice', 'direct' and 'indirect' religious discrimination all combine together, resulting in the failure of an organization to provide an adequate and professional environment and service.

7. *Religion, Belief and Discrimination*

a. *Religious Discrimination and Religious Identification*
The findings of the Religious Discrimination in England and Wales Research Project show that religious discrimination is of contemporary concern and forms a significant part of the life experience of many people who actively identify with a religion. Sometimes, it is also experienced by those who do not personally affirm a religious belief or belonging but are identified *by others* as belonging to particular religions on the basis of visible markers that are related to cultural assumptions. The project also included findings on unfair treatment *between* people in different religions.[80]

b. *Religious 'Invisibility'*
What was revealed by the project was a more general concern among religious individuals, organizations and communities who see their primary identity in terms of religion and who have frequently experienced a sense of their 'invisibility'. As a group of Bahá'ís observed in relation to their experience of unfair treatment on the basis of religion, 'it's not out and out discrimination; not as bad as what ethnic minorities experience, but there's a whole part of your life people

don't care about'.[81] This was highlighted in the image used by a youth interviewed in the course of the project's fieldwork who spoke of those who discriminate on the grounds of religion as having 'a brick in front of their eyes'.[82] Such 'invisibility' has been manifested in the frequent failure of individuals, organizations and the society as whole to take account of the distinctive needs, experience and legitimate expectations of religious individuals, communities and organizations. But it also relates to the relative invisibility of the positive contributions that such individuals, communities and organizations can make to the wider societies of which they are a part.

The 'invisibility' of religion highlighted by the image of the 'brick in front of their eyes' underlines the nature and scope of the problem of unfair treatment on the basis of religion. But the image also suggests the possibility that once the presence of this blockage is identified, it is possible to remove it. With a clearer perception of the role and significance of religion in the lives of individuals, communities and organizations, actions can be taken that will result in both challenge to, and remedy for, unfair treatment on the basis of religion.

c. *Measures for Inclusivity*

The findings of the Religious Discrimination in England and Wales Research Project underlined the need to develop positive measures that can be taken at all levels of society to promote greater inclusivity. Such measures are needed so that the distinctive contributions represented by all the religious traditions and communities in England and Wales will be welcomed and valued for what they can offer to the common good.

In many ways, the findings of the Religious Discrimination in England and Wales Research Project highlighted concerns and experiences that, to some extent, were common to people of all religious traditions and backgrounds in the context of what was viewed as a predominantly secular society. In such a society, it was felt that institutions in sectors such as education, employment and the media did not have an adequate understanding of the role and significance of religion in the lives of individuals and communities.

Thus, the findings of the project may, at first sight, seem to strengthen the position of those who argue against disestablishment on the basis that it would allow secularism to squeeze religion completely out of public life. At the same time, it was also clear from the results of the project that such discrimination and unfair treatment on the basis of religion was experienced differentially, with religious minorities bearing the brunt of this. Also, although it did not form a key part of the questions asked, the existence of 'religious disadvantage' as linked with establishment was identified.

In summary, the Religious Discrimination in England and Wales Research Project both highlights the relatively inequitable experience of people of other than Christian religious traditions (underlining the inappropriateness of an establishment which further reinforces this) while also showing that the option of a purely 'secularizing disestablishment' could further compound the problems experienced. Thus the need for a new way forward is underlined.

The project did not look specifically at the experience of those who are not religious, and yet their experience of discrimination related to religion and/or belief also remains a factor of considerable significance and importance. Thus, recent legal developments with regard to religion, law, human rights, discrimination and equal opportunities have sought also to highlight the needs and rights of those who are not religious. This includes the Human Rights Act, 1988 that, in drawing upon the European Convention for Human Rights and Fundamental Freedoms, addresses the freedom of both religion and belief. This is also the case with regard to the Employment Equality (Religion or Belief) Regulations, 2003.

Informed by such perspectives, a broader and more nuanced range of basic options is opened up for consideration – in relation to what might be the most appropriate contemporary relationship between religion(s), state and society in England and the UK – than the traditional alternatives of continued establishment or a secularizing disestablishment.

Notes

1 The other members of the team included Marie Parker-Jenkins (Associate Director), Kingsley Purdam (Research Officer), Alice Feldman (Field Officer) and Ahmed Andrews, Anna Doswell, John Hinnells, Sima Parmar and Michele Wolfe, together with (at various stages in the project) Karen Rowlingson, Martin O'Brien and Lynne Kinnerley.

2 P. Weller, A. Feldman and K. Purdam *et al.*, *Religious Discrimination in England and Wales*, 2001 which is © Crown Copyright, 2001. The report can be viewed electronically through the Research Development and Statistics Directorate's section of the Home Office website at: www.homeoffice.gov.uk/rds/pdfs/hors220.pdf. Contributions to the empirical report were also made by Ahmed Andrews, Anna Doswell, John Hinnells, Marie Parker-Jenkins, Sima Parmar and Michele Wolfe. The authors and contributors also express their acknowledgements to the fieldwork informants and questionnaire respondents, whose experiences and views form the basis of the research findings. The views expressed both in this part of the chapter and in the chapter as a whole are those of the author of the chapter, and not necessarily those of the authors of the project report, or of the Home Office, nor do they reflect Government policy.

3 The interim report was published in January 2000: P. Weller and K. Purdam *et al.*, *Religious Discrimination in England and Wales, Interim Report, January 2000*, which is © Crown Copyright, 2000. The text of the report can be accessed electronically through the Multi-Faith Centre at the University of Derby's MultiFaithNet website at, www.multifaithnet.org/projects/religdiscrim/reports.htm.

4 See S. Cohen, *That's Funny, You Don't Look Anti-Semitic: An Anti-Racist Analysis of Left Anti-Semitism* (Leeds: Beyond the Pale Collective, 1984).

5 See P. Badham, 'The Contribution of Religion to the Conflict in Northern Ireland', in D. Cohn-Sherbok (ed.), *The Canterbury Papers: Essays on Religion and Society* (London: Bellew, 1990), pp. 119–28; R. Comerford, M. Cullen and J. Hill, *Religion, Conflict and Coexistence in Ireland* (London: Gill & Macmillan, 1990); J. Hickey, *Religion and the Northern Ireland Problem* (Dublin: Gill & Macmillan, 1984); and B. McSweeney, 'The Religious Dimension of the "Troubles" in Northern Ireland', in P. Badham (ed.), *Religion, State and Society in Modern Britain*, pp. 68–83.

6 J. Fulton, 'State, Religion and Law in Ireland', in T. Robbins and R. Robertson (eds.), *Church–State Relations: Tensions and Transitions* (New Brunswick: Transaction Books, 1987), pp. 253–67.

7 S. Bruce, *God Save Ulster: The Religion and Politics of Paisleyism* (Oxford: Oxford University Press, 1986) p. 265.

8 For a critical look at the implications of this inheritance in a contemporary and culturally and religiously more plural Scotland, see A. Hunter and S. Mackie, *A National Church in a Multi-Racial Scotland* (Dublane: Scottish Churches' Council, 1986).

9 Cited in *The Scotsman*, 10.8.1999.

10 *The Herald*, 3.9.1999.

11 It should, however, be noted that the sample for this study was relatively small (with a total of 37 people taking part in phase one, of whom 7 were from minority ethnic groups, while phase two consisted of six workshops with organizations that work with, or represent, the six populations from which the sample had been drawn).

12 W. O'Connor and J. Lewis, *Experiences of Social Exclusion in Scotland: A Qualitative Research Study* (Research Programme Research Findings No. 73; Edinburgh: Central Research Unit, Scottish Office, 1999), p. 20.

13 W. O'Connor and J. Lewis, *Experiences of Social Exclusion in Scotland*, p. 18.

14 W. O'Connor and J. Lewis, *Experiences of Social Exclusion in Scotland*, pp. 64–5.

15 See S. Sutcliffe, 'Unfinished Business: Devolving Scotland/Devolving Religion', in S. Coleman and P. Collins (eds.), *Religion, Identity and Change: Perspectives on Global Transformations* (Aldershot, Ashgate, 2004), pp. 84-106.

16 See E. Barker, *New Religious Movements*; *New Religious Movements*; 'New Religious Movements in Europe', in S. Gill, G. D'Costa and U. King (eds.), *Religion in Europe*, pp. 120–40.

17 Such as, for example, that initiated in the 1980s by Richard Cottrell, MEP. See 'Interview: Richard Cottrell, MEP', *Update: A Quarterly Journal on New Religious Movements* 8/3–4 (1984), pp. 30–4.

18 See P. Weller, 'Religion, Ethnicity and the Development of More Inclusive Health Care', in L. Basford and O. Slevin (eds.), *Theory and Practice of Nursing: An Integrated Approach to Caring Practice* (Cheltenham: Nelson Thornes, 2003), pp. 376-91.

19 V. Cable, *The World's New Fissures: Identities in Crisis* (London: Demos, 1994).

20 See L. Appignanesi and S. Maitland (eds.), *The Rushdie File* (London: Fourth Estate, 1989); and M. Ahsan and A. Kidwai (eds.), *Sacrilege Versus Civility: Muslim Perspectives on the Salman Rushdie Affair* (Leicester: Islamic Foundation, 1991).

21 See T. Benn, 'Religion, War and the Gulf', in D. Cohn-Sherbok and D. McClellan (eds.), *Religion in Public Life* (London: Macmillan, 1992), pp. 29–37.

22 See C. Allen and J. Nielsen, *Summary Report on Islamophobia in the EU after 11 September 2001* (Vienna: European Monitoring Centre on Racism and Xenophobia, May 2002).

23 H. Ansari, p. 4.

24 See D. Singh Tatla, 'The Punjab Crisis and Sikh Mobilisation in Britain', in R. Barot (ed.), *Religion and Ethnicity: Minorities and Social Change in the Metropolis* (Kampen: Kok Pharos, 1993), pp. 96–109.

25 See A. Helweg, *Sikhs in England: The Development of a Migrant Community* (Delhi: Oxford University Press, 2nd edn, 1986).

26 See M. Nye, 'Hare Krishna and Sanatan Dharm in Britain', pp. 37–56; and *Multiculturalism and Minority Religions in Britain*.

27 British Council of Churches, *The New Black Presence in Britain: A Christian Scrutiny* (London: British Council of Churches, 1978).

28 Quoted in J. Wolffe (ed.) *The Growth of Religious Diversity: Britain From 1945. A Reader* (Sevenoaks: Hodder & Stoughton, 1993), p. 193.

29 See P. Weller, 'The Salman Rushdie Controversy, Religious Plurality and Established Religion in England'.

30 *The Guardian*, 7.4.1989.

31 See H. Cooper and P. Morrison, *A Sense of Belonging: Dilemmas of British Jewish Identity* (London: Weidenfeld and Nicolson, 1991); and T. Kushner (ed.), *The Jewish Heritage in British History: Jewishness and Englishness* (London: Frank Cass, 1992).

32 The Runnymede Trust, *A Very Light Sleeper: The Persistence and Dangers of Antisemitism* (London: Runnymede Trust, 1997).

33 L. Halman, *The European Values Study: Source Book*, p. 43.

34 See G. Speelman, 'Muslim Minorities and *Shari'ah* in Europe', in T. Mitri (ed.), *Religion, Law and Society: A Christian–Muslim Discussion* (Geneva: World Council of Churches, 1995), pp. 70–9.

35 As will be explored in greater detail in Chapter 5, the blasphemy laws in the UK protect only the sensibilities of Christians.

36 UK Action Committee on Islamic Affairs, *Muslims and the Law in Multi-Faith Britain.*

37 T. Modood, S. Beishon and S. Virdee, *Changing Ethnic Identities* (London: Policy Studies Institute, 1994).

38 Inner Cities' Religious Council, *Challenging Religious Discrimination: A Guide for Faith Communities and Their Advisers* (London: Inner Cities' Religious Council of the Department of the Environment, 1996).

39 Commission for Racial Equality, *Religious Discrimination: Your Rights* (London: Commission for Racial Equality, 1997).

40 Council of Europe Group of Consultants on Religious and Cultural Aspects of Equality for Immigrants, *Study* (Strasbourg: Council of Europe, 1996), p. 42.

41 Council of Europe Group of Consultants on Religious and Cultural Aspects of Equality for Immigrants, *Study*, p. 43.

42 Runnymede Trust, *Islamophobia: A Challenge for Us All* (London: Runnymede Trust, 1997).

43 The aims of the Project, as commissioned by the Home Office were, as set out in P. Weller, A. Feldman and K. Purdam *et al.*, *Religious Discrimination in England and Wales*, to: '1. assess the evidence of religious discrimination, both actual and perceived; 2. describe the patterns shown by this evidence including: its overall scale, main victims, main perpetrators, and the main ways in which it manifests; 3. indicate the extent to which religious discrimination overlaps with racial discrimination; 4. identify the broad range of policy options available for dealing with religious discrimination' (p. v).

44 628 questionnaires were returned (including 154 from national, 16 from regional, and 458 from local organizations).

45 The locations for the fieldwork were: Leicester (November–December 1999) Newham (January–February 2000), Blackburn (March–April 2000) and Cardiff (May–June 2000).

46 P. Weller, A. Feldman and K. Purdam *et al.*, *Religious Discrimination in England and Wales.*

47 As distinct from the view of the *organization*, which, in most other questions within the questionnaire, respondents were asked to try to reflect.

48 Because the following table presents the findings in percentage terms, only those religions with about 30 or more respondents are included for the question.

49 P. Weller, A. Feldman and K. Purdam *et al.*, *Religious Discrimination in England and Wales*, p. 124.

50 P. Weller, A. Feldman and K. Purdam *et al.*, *Religious Discrimination in England and Wales*, p. 17.

51 P. Weller, A. Feldman and K. Purdam *et al.*, *Religious Discrimination in England and Wales*, p. 17.

52 Again, as in Table 4.1 above, in this question (in contrast to most of the questions within the questionnaire) it was the *personal* view of respondents that was asked for rather than the respondent attempting to reflect the viewpoint of the organization on whose behalf they were responding.

53 Absolute numbers are used in this Table rather than percentages since the presentation of the figures in terms of percentages could be misleading given the relatively small sample sizes involved.

54 P. Weller and K. Purdam *et al.*, *Religious Discrimination in England and Wales, Interim Report, January 2000*, pp. 7–10.

55 The terminology of 'equity' was used within the project because, as explained in P. Weller and K. Purdam *et al.*, *Religious Discrimination in England and Wales, Interim Report, January 2000*, 'What is at stake in issues of discrimination is a basic sense of justice, which for most ordinary people is perceived in terms of "fairness". "Equity" aims at such "fairness"' (p. 103).

56 See N. Daniels, *Islam and the West: The Making of an Image* (2 vols.; Edinburgh: Edinburgh University Press, 1960, 1967); F. Hussain, *The Anti-Islamic Tradition in the West* (Leicester: Muslim Community Studies Institute, 1990); E. Said, *Orientalism* (London: Penguin, 1978); R.

Southern, *Western Views of Islam in the Middle Ages* (Cambridge, MA: Harvard University Press, 1962).

57 P. Weller, A. Feldman and K. Purdam, *et al.*, *Religious Discrimination in England and Wales*, p. 111.

58 P. Weller, A. Feldman and K. Purdam, *et al.*, *Religious Discrimination in England and Wales*, p. 111.

59 P. Weller, A. Feldman and K. Purdam, *et al.*, *Religious Discrimination in England and Wales*, p. 114.

60 P. Weller, A. Feldman and K. Purdam, *et al.*, *Religious Discrimination in England and Wales*, p. 114.

61 P. Weller, A. Feldman and K. Purdam, *et al.*, *Religious Discrimination in England and Wales*, p. 112.

62 P. Weller, A. Feldman and K. Purdam, *et al.*, *Religious Discrimination in England and Wales*, p. 112.

63 See Runnymede Trust, *A Very Light Sleeper*.

64 T. Cantle and the Community Cohesion Team, *Community Cohesion: A Report of the Independent Review Team Chaired by Ted Cantle* (London: Home Office, 2001) and J. Denham and the Ministerial Group on Public Order and Community Cohesion, *Building Cohesive Communities: A Report of the Ministerial Group on Public Order and Community Cohesion* (London: Home Office, 2001).

65 See P. Weller, A. Feldman and K. Purdam, *et al.*, *Religious Discrimination in England and Wales*, p. 68.

66 P. Weller, A. Feldman and K. Purdam, *et al.*, *Religious Discrimination in England and Wales*, p. 104.

67 P. Weller, A. Feldman and K. Purdam, *et al.*, *Religious Discrimination in England and Wales*, p. 42.

68 Jews and Sikhs had protection as racial or ethnic groups within the meaning of the Race Relations Act, 1976, where a 'common religion' was viewed as being part of an ethnic identity. But such protection was not available to Muslims per se, or to other people of other religions that were not viewed as 'ethnic groups', although religion could, under race relations legislation, be taken into account as a factor in establishing 'indirect discrimination' in relation to ethnicity.

69 P. Weller, A. Feldman and K. Purdam, *et al.*, *Religious Discrimination in England and Wales*, p. 23.

70 P. Weller, A. Feldman and K. Purdam, *et al.*, *Religious Discrimination in England and Wales*, p. 27.

71 P. Weller, A. Feldman and K. Purdam, *et al.*, *Religious Discrimination in England and Wales*, p. 41.

72 P. Weller, A. Feldman and K. Purdam, *et al.*, *Religious Discrimination in England and Wales*, p. 42.

73 P. Weller, A. Feldman and K. Purdam, *et al.*, *Religious Discrimination in England and Wales*, pp. 125–6.

74 P. Weller, A. Feldman and K. Purdam, *et al.*, *Religious Discrimination in England and Wales*, p. 83.

75 P. Weller, A. Feldman and K. Purdam, *et al.*, *Religious Discrimination in England and Wales*, p. 125.

76 J. Beckford and S. Gilliat, *The Church of England and Other Faiths in a Multi-Faith Society* (2 vols.; Coventry: University of Warwick, Department of Sociology, 1996); *The Church of England and Other Faiths in a Multi-Faith Society: Summary* (Coventry: University of Warwick Departmant of Sociology, 1996).

77 J. Beckford and S. Gilliat, *Religion in Prison: Equal Rites in a Multi-Faith Society* (Cambridge: Cambridge University Press, 1998).

78 S. Gilliat, *Higher Education and Student Religious Identity* (Exeter: University of Exeter, Department of Sociology, in association with the Inter Faith Network for the United Kingdom,

1999); S. Gilliat-Ray, *Religion in Higher Education: The Politics of the Multi-Faith Campus* (Aldershot: Ashgate, 2000).

79 Sir W. MacPherson, *Inquiry Into Matters Arising From the Death of Stephen Lawrence on 22nd April 1993 to Date, in order Particularly to Identify the Lessons to be Learned for the Investigation and Prosecution of Racially Motivated Crimes*, Published 24 February 1999.

80 See P. Weller, 'Unfair Treatment Between Religions: Findings of a Research Project in England and Wales', *Interreligious Insight* 1/2 (2003), pp. 62–71.

81 P. Weller, A. Feldman and K. Purdam, *et al.*, *Religious Discrimination in England and Wales*, p. 103.

82 P. Weller, A. Feldman, and K. Purdam, *et al.*, *Religious Discrimination in England and Wales*, p. 112.

Part III

ESTABLISHED RELIGION: A TIME FOR CHANGE

Chapter 5

HERITAGE, CONTEXT AND MODELS FOR CHANGE

1. *Establishment and the Constitution*

a. *Establishment Heritage and Religious Disadvantage*

The previous chapter explored the re-emergence into public and political discourse of 'religious discrimination'. Although the Religious Discrimination in England and Wales Research Project did not, in its fieldwork or questionnaire survey, specifically focus on matters to do with establishment, a number of particular issues relating to religious disadvantage were, nevertheless, highlighted by interviewees within the fieldwork.

b. *Establishment: Symbolic and Operational*

Although the Church of England does not act in this way today, the fact that it was historically involved in active suppression and persecution of other forms of religious life and expression is something that should not be glossed over too quickly. At the same time, there are those who argue that, although there might once have been a pressing case to reconfigure the relationships between religion(s), state and society, this is no longer an issue of current theological, ecclesiological or political relevance. This kind of stance is taken on the basis that what remains of establishment is, by comparison with its history, only a cosmetic piece of political archaeology, or a kind of historical embellishment in the 'heritage' theme park of national life inhabited by Beefeaters and town criers.

At the end of Chapter 2, reference was made to George Carey's question about the extent to which the connections between church and state embodied in the establishment are (by implication, *merely*) 'symbolic' rather than 'real' and 'actual'. Thus there are those who argue that if the establishment only has continuing significance in 'symbolic' terms, it is not worth the trouble of initiating the inevitable complexities involved in attempting a disentanglement. Arguably, however, such a position does not give sufficient weight to the 'real' and 'actual' influence of the 'symbolic'.

While the nineteenth-century constitutionalist Walter Bagehot drew a distinction between what he called the 'dignified' and the 'effective' parts of the constitution, the 'dignified' parts are not, in fact, 'merely' symbolic. They are themselves connected with the 'effective' constitution through the social power of the symbolic to shape and form assumptions at all levels of social and political life. It is in any case the argument of this book that the 'actual' and 'real' aspects of the establishment remain far more deeply woven into the social, cultural, religious, legal and political fabric of English society and the UK state than is usually allowed for.

In the absence of a written constitution, the establishment remains a very significant part of what Peter Hennessy has called 'the hidden wiring' of the constitution.[1] As Stewart Lamont explains, although 'The British Constitution has never been formulated as a single written document', nevertheless, 'the bond of the Church of England with the Crown and the parliament of England is clearly spelt out.'[2] Lamont argues that this bond still hangs upon 'three pegs' – namely, 'the appointment of bishops, parliamentary oversight of the Prayer Book; and the position of the sovereign'.[3]

c. *Establishment and the Monarch*

Established religion remains at the heart of the constitution by virtue of the symbiotic relationship that it maintains between the Supreme Governor of the Church of England and the Head of State of the United Kingdom of Great Britain and Northern Ireland. In the absence of a written Constitution, the monarchy has been a key point of reference that is often appealed to as transcending the parties of politics in a bond of common and foundational loyalty. It is this extra-political quality of the monarchy that is often lauded by traditionalist supporters of the institution.

The Crown's historical connection with religion is also seen by many of its defenders as undergirding this differentiation from politics. For some among these supporters it is, in addition, seen as providing a more ultimately transcendent significance for its role. An historic example of the extent to which this can be taken can be seen in the report of *The Times* newspaper on the death of King George VI. This spoke of 'the subtle connexion between the Throne and the faith of Englishmen' and 'the ancient partnership between the Church and State which has played so mighty a part in the making of England'. Finally, it summarized its view that, constitutionally, 'The spiritual and temporal headships' of the Crown are 'aspects of the same sovereignty.' It furthermore noted that 'the sentiments evoked by the death and accession of monarchs have a quality which it is not impiety to call religious' and that:

> It may be that modern theologians, rightly alert against the danger of allowing secular emotion to pass for religious belief, have lost their sense of the value of temporal loyalty as one approach to the understanding of religious truth. In this way, and always in the zealous practice of their faith, the Kings and Queens of England still play an indispensable part in the nation's spiritual life.[4]

Views of this kind are in direct line of inheritance from the Henrician and Elizabethan formulae and their respective Acts of Supremacy. The Preface to the Thirty Nine Articles of Religion of the Church of England declares of the monarch that 'We are Supreme Governor of the Church of England', and, in the coronation of Elizabeth II, this dimension of the monarchy was very much in evidence. More recently Ian Bradley has, from a Christian theological perspective, written a book called *God Save the Queen: The Spiritual Dimensions of Monarchy*, which he describes as 'strongly, indeed passionately, supportive of the institution of the monarchy and which seeks to explore and promote its spiritual dimension'.[5]

The connection between monarch and established Church is expressed in the coronation. In this, traditionally, the charge to the monarch is given by the Archbishop of Canterbury in a context of a service of Holy Communion in which 'priestly' dimensions of the monarchy are vividly expressed by the ritual and symbolic actions that are performed. Under the Act of Settlement, anyone coming to the throne must be in communion with the Church of England and, on taking the throne, the monarch must declare adherence to the Protestant faith and commitment to upholding the Protestant succession to the throne. The Act of Succession prevents anyone with a claim to the throne from embracing the Roman Catholic tradition of Christianity, while the Royal Marriages Act of 1772 prevents the succession of anyone who marries a Roman Catholic.

Within the present arrangements, the monarch has the power to give assent to all Church of England legislation, is the patron of many ecclesiastical livings and, on the advice of the Prime Minister, formally appoints bishops and archbishops of the established Church. Indeed, such has been the connection between established religion and the monarchy that even such critics of establishment as Colin Buchanan suggest that a link could appropriately be maintained between Church and Crown following the disestablishment for which he argues.

d. *Establishment and Parliament*

However, the UK is a constitutional monarchy, where the locus of authority does not reside in the monarchy as such, but in the 'Crown-in-Parliament'. It is therefore also in relation to Parliament and the Prime Minister of the day that both the privileges arising from establishment, as well as the constraints upon the Church of England's freedom that are linked with this, are thrown into particularly sharp relief. With the evolution of a constitutional monarchy, the monarch's constitutional supremacy over the Church of England has been exercised mainly through Parliament. The 1928 Prayer Book controversy was only the most dramatic expression of the remaining parliamentary control over the internal affairs of the Church of England. At the same time, although many legislative matters have in practice been devolved to the General Synod for initial formulation, the Crown-in-Parliament can still, in principle, overturn a decision of Synod.

The Synod's devolved powers enable it pass both Canons and Measures. 'Canons' concern church matters which used to be dealt with by the Convocations of Canterbury and York. Under the 1974 Church of England (Worship and Doctrine) Measure, it became possible for 'Canons' to be formulated by the General Synod without need of submission to Parliament, although they do require Royal Assent to become law. By contrast, a 'Measure' is 'a law, about a Church matter, that applies to the entire Church and will also, where necessary, bind others as well, because it has the force of an Act of Parliament and may even repeal or amend an Act dealing with an ecclesiastical matter'.[6] For a 'Measure' to come into force the Synod's Legislative Committee must submit it to Parliament's Ecclesiastical Committee, the latter of which consists of fifteen members of the House of Commons and fifteen of the Lords.

The Ecclesiastical Committee may then decide whether to put a 'Measure' before Parliament. Before being submitted for Royal Assent, the 'Measure' must be passed without amendment by both Houses of Parliament and this is by no means a certainty. For example, in 1975 the Incumbents (Vacation of Benefices) Measure was rejected by the Commons on the grounds that it was proposed that hearings be held in private and that incumbents would not always have a right to put their case. Thus, although the Church of England's General Synod is able to regulate many of its own affairs, this power formally remains a *devolved* rather than an *independent* one.

e. *Establishment and the Bishops*

The Archbishop of Canterbury and the Archbishop of York, together with the Bishops of Durham, London and Winchester and 21 of the most senior bishops in the Church of England have seats as 'Lords Spiritual' in the second chamber of Parliament, the House of Lords. Leading figures in other Christian confessions and religious traditions have been appointed to seats in the House of Lords – for example, the Church of Scotland minister Lord MacLeod of Fuinary; the Methodist Lord Soper, and Lord Jacobovits, the former Chief Rabbi. But their appointments have been on a purely individual basis in contrast to what has been the constitutional entrenchment of the places of Church of England bishops.

As noted earlier, Monica Furlong points out that within the Church of England itself, it has been in relation to the processes that surround the appointment of its episcopal leaders that most current discontent with establishment has been focused.[7] In this, both the constraints and privileges of establishment are clear due to the involvement of the Prime Minister in the appointment of bishops and the political significance of their reserved places in the House of Lords.

As part of its overall examination of the composition, role and function of the Second Chamber of Parliament, the recent Wakeham Royal Commission on Reform of the House of Lords examined the role and function of the Church of England bishops. The Commission's recommendations with regard to 'organized religion' included that of widening the representation of organized religion to take account both of the principal Christian traditions of England and other parts of the United Kingdom, as well as of other than Christian religions.[8] But the alternative recommended by the Commission still entailed continuation of Church of England representation on a different and special basis as compared with that for others although, at the time of writing, debate on this and other matters connected with reform of the Second Chamber still continues without resolution.

2. *Establishment and Law*

a. *'Special Protection' and the Blasphemy Laws*

During the *Satanic Verses* controversy, it was clarified that the scope of the common laws of blasphemy laws do not include Islam. Thus it remains the case that 'Christianities' in general, and members of the Church of England in particular, have a legal means to seek redress in the courts when they feel their religion is being maligned while Muslims are denied this recourse to law. All the while that the common law provisions remain, neither abolished nor reformed, they are arguably a continuing expression of the enshrined privilege in the structures of the state and of society for one section of one religious community as well as being a reminder of the exclusion of others.

In 1981, the Law Commission published its Working Paper No. 79 on *Offences Against Religion and Public Worship* in which the history of the common law offences were outlined and issues surrounding the desirability and practicability of creating new statutory offences were examined. In 1985, after receiving submissions on this *Working Paper* from many different organizations, the Commission published its Report No. 145 entitled *Criminal Law Offences Against Religion and Public Worship*. By a majority of three to two Commissioners the Report recommended abolition of the common law offences of blasphemy and blasphemous libel without replacement by statute law, on the grounds that, 'where members of society have a multiplicity of faiths or none at all it is invidious to single out that religion [the Church of England], albeit in England the established religion, for protection'.[9]

However, the two outvoted Commissioners felt so strongly that a new statutory offence should be enacted and extended to other religions that they produced a minority Note of Dissent that also appears in the Report. In this, they advocated the enactment of a new offence which 'would penalise anyone who published grossly abusive or insulting material relating to religion with the purpose of outraging religious feelings'. These dissenters included Lord Scarman, who later played such a significant role in race and community relations with his Committee of Enquiry into the disturbances of the summer of 1981.[10]

b. *Blasphemy Laws: Retention, Extension or Abolition*

As Wolffe says, 'The problem, in a nutshell, was whether the law should treat England as a secular society in which religion had no special protection; or as a multi-religious one in which all faiths were accorded some legal recognition.'[11] Issues around the blasphemy laws therefore link intimately with debates about secularization, secularity and secularism and in relation also to matters of religious, cultural and values plurality. In arguing that protection should be given to Islam under the blasphemy laws, the historian John Vincent commented in respect of the Law Commission's arguments for and against such extension that, 'The balance is still a fine one. The arguments have not changed, but the sociology has', citing the significantly changed composition of English society.[12]

As part of their response to the Rushdie controversy, the Inter Faith Network for the UK and the Commission for Racial Equality jointly organized two seminars. Among the papers at the first seminar was a presentation by Keith Ward, the Regius Professor of Divinity at the University of Oxford. This was of particular interest because, as well as being at that time chair of the inter-faith organization, the World Congress of Faiths, Ward had previously been a member of a working party which had been appointed by the Archbishop of Canterbury to report on the Law Commission proposals with regard to the blasphemy law.[13] As a member of that working party Professor Ward had supported the extension of the blasphemy laws to include other than Christian religions. In the seminar, however, Ward explained that he had since changed his mind on this issue.[14] But with regard to the stance adopted by the Archbishop's Working Party, Ward made the significant off-the-cuff comment that, 'while its members did not want legal protection for themselves on a personal basis, they did not think it would be right simply to surrender it'.[15]

Ward's comment epitomizes the contradictory position in which members of an established Church can find themselves when they resist the implications of an argument not because of logic or principle, but simply on the grounds of historical inheritance. The consequence of such a stance, apparently innocuous in its reasonableness, is vividly summarized by Rana Kabbani's reflection on the *Satanic Verses* controversy, when she pointed out that, 'Rushdie's book brought into the open the frustrations of a Muslim minority for whom the much-vaunted multicultural society was a sham.... Faced by the majority community, still overwhelmingly Christian in law and institutions if not in belief, Muslims felt powerless and unprotected.'[16]

3. *Establishment and Education*

a. *Establishment and Religiously Based Schools*
Central to the ways in which the establishment of the Church of England is embedded in the fabric of national life and civil society is its continuing entrenched role in the maintained education system. In this, it is responsible for a significant number of voluntary aided and controlled schools within the framework of the so-called 'dual system' of publicly maintained education in England. This profile is partly a consequence of the origins of education in England. Nevertheless, Christianity in general, and the Church of England in particular, is quite clearly in a position of privilege and power within this area of English social life. For a long time, there have also been both Roman Catholic and Jewish voluntary aided schools. More recently, these have been joined by a small number of publicly funded Muslim and Sikh schools.

In fact, both Anglican and Roman Catholic Churches have a large investment in education.[17] There are 4,500 primary schools (which is around a quarter of all primary schools in England) and 200 secondary schools which have Church of England foundations, and there are plans to add a further 100 secondary schools over the next five years. The Roman Catholic Church has 1,760 primary and 363 secondary schools.

There are important differences between Roman Catholic and Anglican Church schools, with many Anglican (and especially primary) schools effectively functioning as general neighbourhood schools. A number of these schools have promoted good practice in a multi-religious society, and perhaps have (because of a basic religious sympathy) sometimes been more sensitive to questions related to the faith and practice of Muslim, Hindu, and Sikh parents and children than have some county schools. Thus some parents of children of other religions have chosen to send their children to church schools rather than county schools on the basis that they believe these schools will provide some form of religious environment which, even though it is not that of their own religion, is viewed as being preferable to the framework provided by a secular school.

However, it is also important to examine the social implications of these religiously based schools within the context of a multi-religious society.[18] If

Christians and Jews have had access to public funds for religiously based schools, then if these are to continue others will, as a matter of equity, justly demand this for themselves as well, in order to create parallel institutions based on other religions. This has, in fact, happened, and a number of Muslim, Sikh and Hindu schools have recently been recognized as the Government has shifted its stance on these questions towards supporting their extension.

But it can also be argued that removing religious believers from the county schools can damage the potential for social mixing and mutual understanding that is provided by the county system. The danger is that religiously based schools might, in practice, contribute to a religious ghettoization in which children of one religion can grow up without ever meeting or knowing children of another religion in a society where differences of religion are often overlaid by differences in race or ethnicity.

The advocacy of an educational system without religious privilege, segregation or 'denominational teaching on the rates' which is part of the heritage of the Baptist tradition could therefore still be germane to the situation in England today. But so entrenched is the system of voluntary aided schools that, even to raise the question of whether Anglicans and Roman Catholics should reconsider their position in relation to these schools is to invite a storm of controversy of the kind that occurred some years ago when Christians Against Racism and Fascism merely asked this question in a discussion leaflet on *Church Schools in a Multi-Faith Society*.[19]

b. *Establishment, Agreed Syllabus Conferences and SACREs*

But beyond the question of voluntary aided schools as such, the Church of England has a specially entrenched position, which is enshrined in statute, with regard to the rest of the education system in England. This relates to the composition of the Agreed Syllabus conferences and the Standing Advisory Councils on Religious Education (SACREs). The former are responsible for drawing up the content of local Agreed Syllabi for Religious Education, while the latter govern the practice both of Religious Education and of Collective Worship in accordance with education legislation and other relevant guidance from the Department for Education and Employment.

While model syllabi have been drawn up nationally for the teaching of Religious Education, in local authority areas it is the Agreed Syllabus Conferences that formally determine the precise shape and content of such syllabi at local levels. In an Agreed Syllabus Conference, there are four component Committees. These must all, *collectively* and *separately*, reach agreement on content. One of these four bodies is composed exclusively of representatives of the Church of England, one of local authority nominees, one of professional teachers and one of other religious bodies, including both non-established Christian denominations and religious traditions other than Christianity to reflect the principal traditions of the area.

The Church of England also has a similar pattern of specially entrenched representation on the Standing Advisory Councils for Religious Education. SACREs were made obligatory for Local Education Authorities under the terms of the 1988 Education Reform Act in order to monitor the local provision of Religious

Education and the arrangements for collective worship. They also have powers to grant or withhold the 'determinations' which can release individual schools from the generally binding obligations concerning the nature of the majority of acts of collective worship.

Arguably, this pattern of representation reflects the substantial Anglican role in educational provision, particularly at the primary school level. However, no such privileged position is accorded to the Roman Catholic Church that also has a substantial number of schools, particularly at secondary level. Therefore in this respect, too, a relative Anglican privilege is enshrined.

4. *Establishment and Chaplaincy*

a. *Chaplaincy and Historical Inheritance*
In addition to its place within the education system, the historical and social positioning of the established Church means that it has an institutionalized presence in, and therefore access to, a wide range of other social institutions beyond the education system. For example, the Church of England often has an institutionalized role in local public life, as in civic and mayoral chaplaincies. There are also institutionally embedded chaplaincy arrangements in the prison and health services, the armed forces, education and other institutions.

b. *Chaplaincy and Change*
Change in the inherited pattern of chaplaincies is beginning to occur, particularly at local levels where arrangements may be more susceptible to individual influence. Other Christian denominations, and increasingly also other religions, may also have chaplains appointed within many social institutions and sectors. But in many cases, the Church of England presence is structurally built into the institutions concerned in a way that is not generally the case with regard to the other Christian denominations, and even less so with respect to the representatives of other than Christian religious traditions.

Research into *The Church of England and Other Faiths in a Multi-Faith Society* by Sophie Gilliat-Ray and James Beckford has demonstrated that a number of Anglican chaplaincies in the health and prison services have used their inherited position to open up new opportunities for contributions from other religious traditions.[20] However, such openings are still largely dependent upon the goodwill of the individuals who happen to be in post. In structural terms, chaplaincies continue to embody the entrenched position of established religion.

This is particularly so when chaplaincies are located in those sectors that are close to the machinery and instruments of the state as, for example, in the prison service and the armed forces. Thus, under the 1952 Prison Act, all prisons have Anglican chaplains. While in recent years the Home Office has appointed a Muslim Adviser to the Prison Service, the appointment has been on a different structural basis from that of the Anglican chaplains.

5. *The Nexus of Establishment*

a. *Establishment: Multiple Intersections*

From the preceding discussion it should be clear that the social and political significance of establishment is of much wider symbolic and operational effect than Lamont's constitutional 'pegs' might, on a superficial reading, suggest. This is because it is not only at the strictly constitutional points of intersection between the Church of England and the state that establishment is of contemporary import. The constitutional 'pegs' upon which establishment hangs have also given it a place of both privilege and constraint in relation to the wider structures of the state and the society. Therefore the significance of establishment also extends at the symbolic, structural and operational levels to embrace: aspects of the English legal system, educational provision, and the network of institutionalized public access and presence found in the chaplaincies of English public life and institutions.

As a consequence of the impact of the establishment, in the key sectors of the law, education and chaplaincies, religious disadvantage is, at least in some measure, experienced by all religious groups that are not established. Such disadvantage fuels, feeds into, focuses and overlaps with the wider, more generalized and day-to-day experiences of religious prejudice, direct and indirect religious discrimination, religious hatred and institutional religionism as highlighted in the previous chapter.

Examined in isolation, some of the individual implications of the inheritance of establishment may appear to be quaint historical quirks. But, in the context of a society that is both secularizing and pluralizing in terms of religious belief, practice and identification, those to do with the constitution, monarchy, Parliament, education, law and the machinery of government certainly lie at the heart of life of both English society and the UK state. These include: a connection of Englishness and Anglicanism; the continuance of blasphemy laws that protect only Christians and, more specifically, the rites and doctrines of the Church of England; the existence of entrenched political representation for the Church of England through the bishops in the House of Lords; the widespread presence of its voluntary aided and controlled schools; its privileged weighting in the groups that constitute Agreed Syllabus Conferences and Standing Advisory Councils on Religious Education; and its institutionalized presence in prison, hospital and armed services chaplaincies.

b. *Establishment: Symbolic and Operational Significance*

In this sense, established religion in England is not a collection of remnants of ecclesiastical and political 'archaeology'. Rather, through a conjunction of its symbolic, structural and operational functions, it permeates large swathes of social, religious, cultural, legal and political life in England. It continues to be of both symbolic and operational significance in the machinery of government, the structures of the state, and the monarchy, the law and the institutions of civil society. Both at the level of national symbolic self-understanding, and also in terms of its structural forms and operational channels, the social, political, cultural, legal and institutional strands of the establishment lie at the heart of the 'hidden wiring' of the constitution of the United Kingdom of Great Britain and Northern Ireland.

Cumulatively these dimensions of establishment both *reflect* and *give effect* to the role of the establishment of the Church of England. In this, the Church of England stands at the intersection of a complex constitutional nexus of the social, religious, cultural, legal and political strands which make up the ethos and constitution of the UK state and of English society as it has existed since the restoration of the monarchy. This privileges the Church of England in relation to other bodies, but also restricts its own freedom of choice and action and does not match the contemporary 'three-dimensional' socio-religious reality of England and the UK.

6. *Models for a Change to Establishment*

a. *Models, Basic Metaphors and 'Reality-Matching'*

In his book *Truth in the Religions: A Sociological and Psychological Approach* William Montgomery Watt stressed that, 'behind an important religious change there is usually to be found some economic or other material change'.[21] In connection with this Watt identifies the social and historical context as itself constituting what he calls the 'governing decision' that gives shape to other decisions in the theological and institutional spheres.

In relation to the particular theme of this book, the 'governing decision' has been the change from a 'one-dimensional' socio-religious reality to a 'three-dimensional' one. This means that the 'one-dimensional' inheritance or continuation of establishment (as explained in Chapters 1 and 2) is not appropriate to the current position, nor is the other 'one-dimensional' approach of a secularity that is blind to religion and seeks to confine it entirely to the public sphere. A new approach is called for if the structuring of the relationships between religion(s), state and society is to be appropriate to our contemporary 'three-dimensional' socio-religious reality.

The first major step in all political life is to search for basic metaphors that are used to explain our political existence to ourselves and to others. Constitutional arrangements – whether in written forms (as in the USA) or in unwritten forms (as in the UK) provide such 'basic metaphors'. The establishment of the Church of England and the nexus that it forms across swathes of social, religious, cultural, legal and political life has been one such 'basic metaphor' that has persisted while English socio-religious reality has moved from being 'one-dimensional' through 'two-dimensional' and into 'three-dimensional'. However, in various ways, the previous two chapters have underlined that there is an increasing discrepancy between this basic political metaphor and the contemporary religious landscape of England and the UK.

Establishment is a 'basic metaphor' that only a minority in the wider society now wish to uphold. Thus in an ICP poll for *The Guardian* newspaper, in response to the question, 'Do you think the Church of England should keep its special position as the only state recognised religion which means, for example, that the prime minister has the final say over who becomes Archbishop of Canterbury'?

48% were against this, while 36% were in support.[22] Support rose to 39% among the over-65-year-old respondents, while 50% of the 35-64 age group were against continuation of the 'special position' as were 54% of all respondents in Scotland. But establishment is also something that few appear to have the *will* to *change* even if they do not wish *actively* to support its continuance.

During the nineteenth century, and for much of the twentieth century, options in the debates over the appropriate form of configuration in the relationships between religion(s), state and society generally boiled down to two basic alternatives. These were either continuation of the establishment or else disestablishment of the Church of England through a secularizing separation of church and state. In addition, the debate concerning these alternatives was constructed primarily in terms either of divergent Christian theological traditions and/or between Christianity and that of the emergent secularity and sometimes secularism of modern society.

In the twenty-first century, however, both the socio-religious context itself *and* the possible alternative models have changed and developed. Aspects of the 'one-dimensional' (Christian) or 'two-dimensional' (Christian–secular) options of the nineteenth century still remain. But they now need also to be informed by interaction with the 'third dimension' (religious plurality) that has developed particularly in the latter part of the twentieth century and at the beginning of the twenty-first century. In this setting, variants on the traditional positions and also alternative new positions have emerged to reframe the debates around establishment that originally took place primarily at the intersection between Christian and secular inheritances.

b. *'Abolitionist/Disestablishment' Model*

The option of disestablishment as 'abolition' does, of course, remain. As in Ireland in the nineteenth century and Wales in the early twentieth century, such an approach would be to advocate and implement disestablishment of the Church of England without replacement, thus ending the 'special relationship' between Anglican Christianity and the structures and machinery of the UK state. Historically, such an outcome was fairly consistently argued for from among the Free Church Christian traditions in general and the Baptist tradition in particular. As previously explained this was primarily, although not exclusively, articulated on the basis of a positive and profoundly religious motivation and rationale rather than as an expression of any conviction that a secular settlement was ideologically preferable to a religious basis for society.

In particular, the Free Church and Baptist 'abolitionist' stance was informed by a theology that affirmed freedom of conscience in religious belief and practice rather than restriction for those of some religious groups and privilege for others. It was also based on an ecclesiology that saw the Christian Church as a fellowship of people freely covenanting together rather than a nation at prayer according to forms of worship imposed and/or authorized by Parliament. It was the combination of these theological and ecclesiological principles with an existential experience of social disadvantage that gave the nineteenth-century disestablishment movement its particular passion and its power.[23]

But, as has already been noted, as the nineteenth century progressed, the spe-cifically religious motivations of the Liberation Society declined and secularists took a more prominent part in its affairs. Where once its meetings had begun and ended in prayer, by the 1880s, this was no longer so.[24] At this point, the Free Church critique began to lose both much of its distinctiveness and also much of its force. Since the mid- to later part of the nineteenth century high-water mark of the Free Church inspired movement for disestablishment, the majority of 'aboli-tionist' arguments have been put forward on the basis of specifically ideologically secularist grounds (as, for example, by the National Secular Society) or on (at least ostensibly less ideological) more generally pragmatic grounds concerned with social and political equity.

Proposals of this kind have included those initiated by the former Labour Member of Parliament Tony Benn in his 1988 Private Member's English Church Bill. This was a very brief Bill for ceasing the legal establishment of the Church of England that would also have barred the monarch or the monarch's ministers from making future appointments to ecclesiastical office. In May 1991, Benn also proposed a Commonwealth of Britain Bill. This was a broader Bill concerned with what Benn argued was the need for wider political and constitutional change by means of introducing a written constitutional basis to UK political life. But it also included a section on 'Religious Freedom' in which the Church of England was to be disestablished, the laws of blasphemy abolished, and equality before the law of persons of all faiths was to be enacted.

In March 1993, the Social and Liberal Democrat MP Simon Hughes introduced a Private Member's Bill for disestablishment. In doing this he was building upon a position previously adopted at the 1990 Liberal Democrat Party Conference that, uniquely among modern British mainstream political parties, has supported disestablishment.[25]

In many respects such 'abolitionist' modern initiatives towards disestablish-ment seek to bring about disestablishment by, in effect, 'privatizing' religion and replacing it with a new 'one-dimensional' and 'secular' paradigm, rather than on the basis of reconfiguring the relationship so that there is a continued but dif-ferent public role for religion(s). Generally, however, religions cannot accept such a limitation upon the scope of their vision and relevance without their religious integrity becoming impaired. Furthermore, in societies that have tried to banish religion to the private sphere, the evidence would seem to be that such a policy is ultimately ineffective, that it impoverishes civic society, and that it also risks provoking the growth of reactive and aggressive forms of religious expression and organization.

c. *'Evolutionary Extension' Model*

An alternative model to that of a merely 'abolitionist' disestablishment leading to a *de facto* secular*ism* would be to see if it were possible to facilitate some form of 'evolutionary extension' of the existing establishment towards a greater inclu-sivity. Such an approach could, in many ways, build upon the kind of 'umbrella role' of 'ecumenical inclusivity' that the Church of England (especially through its bishops in the House of Lords) has, in recent years, offered as a channel for expressing the concerns and interests of other, non-established Christian groups. In such an approach, the Church of England, based upon its historic inheritance and continuing constitutional position, would be expected to act as facilitator for a wider range of religious communities and traditions to contribute to public life.

This would enable other than established religious communities to bring their religious traditions and concerns to bear indirectly upon political and institutional processes. It would seem to offer a way forward that, arguably, is consistent with the characteristic way in which English society and the UK state has tended to go about accommodating difference and diversity. In other words, as with 'common law', it would proceed on the basis of custom and precedent modified by pragmatic change rather than reifying the present arrangements or seeking radical change on the basis of a set of abstract 'first principles'.

Arguably, this approach would also articulate with the general shift in Free Church thinking on these questions that, as has previously been noted, already began to take place in the nineteenth century and accelerated during the twentieth century as nonconformist civic disabilities were gradually remedied and the traditional disestablishmentarian demand became more associated with secularist developments. In concert with this, the concerns of the Free Churches gradually began to change into pleas for accommodation within the existing system of established religion. As an example, Bebbington pointed out that the growth of this new approach was 'evident in the eagerness of nonconformists to play a part in state ceremonial',[26] citing the nature of Free Church protests around the service to mark Queen Victoria's Diamond Jubilee. Rather than being, as they might previously have been, about the involvement of established Church clergy in an event of state, by the time of the Jubilee these were more about the allocation to Free Church leaders of places on the steps outside St Paul's Cathedral.

An 'extended establishment' approach also resonates with the kind of arguments that have been articulated in defence of establishment by figures such as John Habgood, the former Archbishop of York. Habgood argued that societies with dominant and recognized religious traditions offer better possibilities for the affirmation of religious values in general, and for the creation of wider social space for all religious traditions (including religious minorities), than do societies without such dominant religious traditions. Thus, Habgood argued that what is epitomized by the establishment of the Church of England 'is that of a major cultural influence, Christianity, tolerating and affirming sub-cultures, while providing the general religious environment in which they can be accepted and understood'.[27] In his view, the continuing establishment of the Church of England does not necessarily entail Christian triumphalism or arrogance.

The Church of England has, in fact, already taken a number of steps towards showing how an even more 'open' and 'inclusive' version of establishment could develop pragmatically appropriate channels of communication and consultation within a plural society. Evidence to suggest that the Church of England can play a constructive role in facilitating communication at the interface between the Christian, secular and religiously plural dimensions of England and the UK's current socio-religious reality could be found during the *Satanic Verses* controversy. Commenting more generally on the role of the Anglican Bishop of Bradford during this controversy, the historian John Wolffe suggested that this illustrated 'one prognosis for the establishment' in which there were 'indications that there was potential for the established Church of England to find a new role in a multi-cultural society, as a bridge between the mutual incomprehensions of secular liberalism and minority religious conviction'.[28]

A number of Jewish leaders, including the previous Chief Rabbi, Lord Jacobovits, and the current Chief Rabbi, Dr Jonathan Sacks, have argued in support of the importance of the continued establishment of the Church of England as signifying an affirmation of values which go beyond the secular. Thus, in his 1990 Reith Lectures, Sacks argued that minorities ought to support the Church of England as a national institution, commenting that, 'It might seem paradoxical that one who speaks from within the Jewish tradition should seek to support institutions that are intrinsically Christian.' But he explained that he held this position on the basis that 'each of the many faiths that constitute culturally plural Britain is diminished by a weakening of the faith of the majority'[29] and also because, in his view, disestablishment would 'have the effect of signalling a further dissociation between religion and public culture and would intensify the dangers of a collapse in our moral ecology'.[30]

d. *The Model of 'Invention' (of a National Religious Council)*

The third basic possible model for change is one of neither 'abolition' nor 'evolutionary extension' of the current establishment of the Church of England, but rather, instead, the 'invention' of something completely new. This is, for example, the radical option proposed by the Scottish commentator Stewart Lamont following a review of various forms of church–state relations undertaken in his book, *Church and State: Uneasy Alliances*. On a theoretical level, the logic of the historical developments identified in the present book would seem to translate directly into the kind of new 'socio-religious contract' of the type proposed by Lamont. Specifically, Lamont proposed that Parliament should:

> set up a National Religious Council for the United Kingdom. Assuming that it is the democratic will to retain Christianity as the historic faith of the nation (and I believe that any poll would back such a view), then the majority of places on this Council would go to the Christian Churches. ... It would have places for the principal non-Christian faiths such as Islam, Judaism and Sikhism and could act as a liaison body between parliament and the religious bodies.[31]

He then went on to propose that such a body should primarily be 'consultative', but also that it could 'carve out an influential role for itself by organising assemblies on subjects of common concern to those of religious faith'. The creation of such a Council would, he claimed, 'simply be to give institutional form to a process which has been gathering force over the years'.[32]

There have, in fact, been some tentative moves that might seem to indicate the viability of something along these lines. Within the framework of the Inter Faith Network for the UK, a separate regular meeting – the Faith Communities Forum – was, in 2003, established for the national representative bodies from within faith community organizations. Also, within the Home Office, a Faith Communities Unit has been established in order to pull together government policy-making and liaison in relation to religions, and a Faith Communities' Liaison Group has also been established. This is based in the Home Office and is chaired by the Minister for Race Equality, Community Policy and Civic Renewal. It involves a number of other government ministers, as well as representatives from the main world religious traditions with significant communities in the UK. Finally, during 2003–4 the Government undertook a comprehensive review of its mechanisms for consultation with faith community bodies. In March 2004 this resulted in a report[33] that took an overview across the whole range of interaction between Government and the religious communities, aspects of which will be taken up and further explored in the final chapter.

However, none of these initiatives has either the formal status or the scope that a full Council of Faiths might have. From the side of the religious communities, any initiative towards such a Council would inevitably raise important and difficult questions concerning its representivity, legitimacy and accountability. On the part of Government it would raise issues concerning the kind of recognition to be accorded to such a Council as well as issues relating to it.

7. *Negotiating Change*

a. *Transitions and Negotiation Theory*

Recognizing a need for change, deciding on a direction for change and actually implementing change are three different things. Since it is impossible to move from one set of historical arrangements to another without a transitional process of some kind, any evaluation of the 'adequacy' of various models for change needs to include an evaluation of their *transitional* potential as well as of their ultimate appropriateness. Such an evaluation needs to take account of the *practical realism* of what is proposed as well as its theoretical coherence and/or persuasiveness as an abstract model.

In considering how change might actually be effected, it is arguably helpful to use an analytical framework developed in relation to general organizational change. 'Negotiation theory' provides such a framework. In its development, it has drawn on perspectives from a wide range of disciplines including anthropology, sociology, social psychology, political science and behavioural economics, each of which has resulted in a particular theorization along structural, psychological, cognitive or normative lines.

In particular, the 'social contextualist' approach to negotiation theory is of particular relevance to the present task. This draws upon all the insights found in more general 'negotiation theory' but also maintains the importance of 'conceptualising individuals as fundamentally and essentially social decision-makers'[34] and of taking into full account 'the impact of the social and organizational environments'.

Some particularly helpful insights that might inform the issues and dynamics involved in moving from the present 'one-dimensional' model for configuring the relationships between religion(s), state and society to alternatives that are more appropriate for a 'three-dimensional' socio-religious environment, are found in an essay by Samuelson and Messick entitled 'Let's Make Some New Rules: Social

Factors That Make Freedom Unattractive'.[35] This is found in Kramer and Messick's edited collection, *Negotiation as a Social Process*. In this essay, Samuelson and Messick highlight a number of key factors that are involved in negotiating change. They articulate these in terms of the 'transition costs' involved and the consequent tendency towards 'risk aversion' that makes agreement on change difficult to achieve. As they explain in detail:

> First, any change in a social institution will involve transition costs. Replacing the status quo with any alternative system will generally involve costs that simply maintaining the status quo avoids. Such transition costs tend to add to the attractiveness of what is relative to what might be. Second, people are generally familiar with the properties of the status quo, whereas the qualities of an alternative system may only be guessed at. There is, in short, less uncertainty about the status quo than about rival systems. Risk aversion would therefore cause one to view competing systems somewhat less favourably, even if the status quo's deficiencies were clear. Better to have a system whose flaws are known than one that might bring unpleasant surprises.[36]

b. *Change and Risk Aversion*

Such observations are particularly relevant bearing in mind the apparent reluctance of many, both inside and outside the Church of England, to question the current establishment arrangements and/or to try to envision new ones that might more appropriately replace these. The extent to which such reluctance to consider change can go can be seen in one of the arguments deployed by the majority of the Chadwick Commission on church and state in arguing their case for retaining the church–state link in its current form.

> We have not recommended a total severing of the historic links; first because we think such a proposal to be impractical in the present state of opinion; and second because even if such a programme was practicable, most of us would not like it, though we should not shrink from it if the state decided it to be either wise or politically necessary. The people of this country value various features of our polity, and will not favour too much tampering.[37]

Since the establishment of the Church of England is so deeply embedded in English society and the UK state, there can be a comforting familiarity about the known quality of this arrangement, even when its flaws and weaknesses are recognized and acknowledged. The extent of the 'transition costs' that may be involved in changing the establishment can be seen from the fact that, even in the context of quite acute tensions[38] between the Church of England and the Thatcher Government over a range of public issues, disestablishment did not appear on the Government's radical political agenda, despite that Government's readiness to take on a range of other traditional and powerful social institutions. As the historian John Wolffe observed, 'the majority of both church leaders and of Parliament seemed happy – or at least not unhappy – with the status quo. They had no desire to face the distraction and conflict that would almost certainly have resulted from any serious attempt to achieve radical change.'[39]

As Samuelson and Messick put it, 'Transition costs and risks of unfamiliarity will have to be compensated for if structural change is to occur. Other dimensions of evaluation must promise sufficient benefits to make the change worthwhile.'[40] They therefore go on to suggest that, in any negotiation of change, at least the 'dimensions of evaluation' of 'efficiency, fairness, freedom and self-interest'[41] should be brought to bear in assessing the potential benefits and costs of change and the various models for change that exist.

8. *Evaluating the Options*

a. *Efficiency*

The first of Samuelson's and Messick's 'dimensions of evaluation' is that of 'efficiency', which they define in terms of 'the extent to which an allocation system can provide satisfactory levels of a resource to a group without depleting the resource'.[42] Applying this principle to the future of established religion or its alternatives, the 'resource' involved is the social significance of religion, in its symbolic, structural and operational senses. On the basis of such an understanding, in moving away from the establishment model the potential for 'depleting the resource' is the risk of secularization, privatization and marginalization of religion.

In many societies, and for much of human history, religion has provided the integrative symbols of ultimate meaning within which the diversities of social life have been enabled to find their coherence. In European history, the Enlightenment signifies that process by which religious beliefs have been at least relativized and privatized as well as in many cases also eroded, and in which the elevation of individual subjectivity and the emancipation of social structures from religious control has been promoted. For much of the twentieth century, religion was challenged by one or another alternative ideology, with Marxism having been a particularly powerful force in the earlier part of the century. Today this ideology has lost its hold and challenge as Communist regimes in the former Soviet Union and Eastern and Central Europe have collapsed, while China appears to be taking a capitalist pathway in all but name.

Advocates of a 'secular' settlement for relationships between religion(s), state and society have often argued that it has been the rise of the secular spirit and its adoption by states and societies that has enabled religious absolutism to be overcome and a degree of religious co-existence to be developed. In the judgement of post-Enlightenment secular liberals, religions have been responsible for an enormous amount of bloodshed and human suffering and should therefore be marginalized from public life. There is undoubtedly considerable truth in the argument that the rise of the secular spirit in philosophy and art coincided with the rise of religious toleration. Therefore the argument that a secular state can better deal with the plural nature of modern societies than the inheritance of an established religion is a powerful one that needs to be considered carefully.

However, this stance can also exhibit a too easy moral superiority. This is because it can also cogently be argued that the formation of the modern nation-states and the operation of modern secular ideologies have led to just as much, if not more, human suffering than have states founded upon religion. The phenomenon of the secular nation-state can hardly be uncritically glorified in a century that has seen it give birth to Nazism and the gas chambers and Stalinism and the gulags. Seen in this light, the basis of the nation-state can understandably seem no less dangerous than religious fanaticism. Indeed, it is precisely because of this that many Christians support the continuation of the Church of England's establishment. For example, in a discussion with Bishop Colin Buchanan, Michael Alison MP, the Second Estates Commissioner and a leading proponent of the establishment contended that 'The state in all Western societies now is becoming increasingly secularised, increasingly the victim of pressure groups of every sort from every side. I think that the State needs the support and interaction with the Church more than ever before in our history.'[43]

The experience of disintegration evokes the poetry of W. B. Yeats and its perception that 'things fall apart, the centre cannot hold'. Such a perception reflects the early twentieth-century experience of many societies in the transition from traditionalist and agrarian forms to those of modernity and industrialization. In conditions of post-modernity,[44] non-centredness and relativism are often all that is now possible, whether by way of celebration or despair. Such relativism can then become both a symptom and a cause of 'things falling apart' that leaves the way open for an unrestrained capitalism to dominate social, political, cultural and economic life to the detriment of all other values.

As Leslie Newbigin put it, 'To acknowledge that ultimate symbol, to reverence the sacred, was the precondition for knowledge and understanding. If that is destroyed, things fall apart.'[45] It is for these reasons that many religious people of all religions (as well some traditionalists of no particular religious commitment) are often nervous about the 'abolitionist' option of a 'secularizing disestablishment'. For much of history 'unwritten agreements' relating to religious beliefs and values have been seen as necessary for the health of a successfully functioning society. It is this to which the Chief Rabbi, Jonathan Sacks, also referred in his book *The Persistence of Faith* when he argued that:

> as well as a physical ecology, we also inhabit a moral ecology, that network of beliefs, relationships and virtue within which we think, act and discover meaning. For the greater part of human history it has had a religious foundation. But for the past two centuries, in societies like Britain, that basis of belief has been profoundly eroded. And we know too much about ecological systems to suppose that you can remove an element and leave the rest unchanged. There is, if you like, a God-shaped hole in our ozone layer. And it is time that we thought about moral ecology too.[46]

The idea of a 'moral ecology' is a suggestive one, indicating that the values and structures of social life, like the elements of the physical ecology, either are being maintained in balance or are being eroded. The elements of such an ecology exist even if we are not consciously aware of them and only become so through the impact of the symptoms of an ecology which has been thrown out of balance. The experience of those societies in Europe where national and state religions were removed from public life and an attempt was made to replace them with a communist ideology might seem to give this argument some validity. Because the state has tendencies to claim absolute power for itself, the presence of an established religion offers an important institutionalized reminder that the state is not the only significant reality, that it does not represent the only form of authority, and that the authority that it does have is not absolute.

In England and the UK, examples of the creative possibilities for established religion to critique the Government of the day can be seen in the role played by the Church of England's report on *The Church and the Bomb*[47] at the time of heightened Cold War tensions following the decision to deploy Cruise and Pershing missiles in Western Europe. This made an important contribution to national debate of a kind that might not have taken place had the report not been produced from within an established Church. In addition, during the social ravages of monetarism and the uprisings/riots of the inner cities, the Church of England played another significant role by publishing its *Faith in the City*[48] report.

Finally, at a time of national and government triumphalism in the wake of the Falklands/Malvinas war, Robert Runcie as Archbishop of Canterbury (and himself a former Second World War army tank commander with impeccable military credentials) insisted on a service of memorial rather than of celebration. At this service, Runcie declared that God must never be claimed for any nation and spoke of war as springing from loyalty being offered to a God-substitute. It is because of examples such as these that people such as Laurence Targett have been able to assert that 'Christianity is, for us in Britain, the central possibility for a larger view of our civil life, so the central task must be the rediscovery of the Anglican tradition.'[49] However, for many people in England and the UK the socio-religious 'centre' provided by Christendom, let alone that of the Church of England, can no longer command widespread assent, although it may retain a certain sympathy if the only alternative is perceived to be an 'abolitionist' one leading to the possibility of a complete secularism.

b. *Fairness*

The second of Samuelson and Messick's 'dimensions of evaluation' for assessing the 'transition costs' involved in negotiated change is that of 'fairness' which is understood in relation to 'the degree to which distribution of the resource satisfies the principles of equality or equity'.[50] In principle, it is clear that an establishment of the Church of England unmodified (for example by 'evolutionary extension' to include other religions) does not facilitate a 'distribution of the resource' (in other words the symbolic and operational social significance of religion) in an 'equal' way. In addition, as was noted in the discussion of religious discrimination in the previous chapter, it may be the case that a precise mathematical equality is neither desirable nor achievable.

Arguably, in a society with a Christian inheritance and in which a comparatively large proportion of the population continues to identify in some way as Christian, a contextual and balanced understanding of 'equity' is needed more than a formal 'equality'. In this connection, it should be noted that even Lamont's proposal for a National Religious Council did not advocate a mathematical equality of places for different religions, but rather a weighted representation, designed to ensure an overall equity.

Despite the religious disadvantage experienced by all non-established religions there are, as we have already seen, those within the minority religious communities who do not identify this as a particular problem. Nevertheless, Tariq Modood has overstated the case when he comments that 'there is not a single statement by any minority faith organization in favour of disestablishment'.[51] There are, for example, clear Buddhist statements urging disestablishment.

As long ago as the aftermath of the *Gay News* trial, the Venerable Sangharakshita, the leader of the Friends of the Western Buddhist Order (FWBO), published a pamphlet that included calls for the abolition of the blasphemy laws and the disestablishment of the Church of England. In this, Sangharakshita argued that:

> There should be complete separation of Church and State. The Church of England should be disestablished '... the sovereign should not be required to be a member of the Anglican communion – or indeed to belong to any Christian denomination, or even to any religion, at all. Reference to the Deity should be expunged from the National Anthem.[52]

In addition to this explicit kind of opposition to the establishment, it is also at least open to question how far the statements of leading minority religion figures who support the establishment of the Church of England reflect the grassroots perspectives within their communities. In taking such positions minority religious leaders may, at least on occasion, be mirroring the previous experience of those late nineteenth- and early twentieth-century Free Church leaders for whom, as the disadvantages became ameliorated, they became more concerned with the positioning of their 'place at the table' rather than with the 'nature of the table' as such.

There are certainly those who are more marginal to the formal representative structures of their community background, such as Women Against Fundamentalism (WAF), who argue explicitly for disestablishment. Thus, for example, two of WAF's leading members, Gita Saghal and Nira Yuval-Davis, robustly critique establishment in the introduction to their book *Refusing Holy Orders*. In this they argue that, through establishment, 'Christianity ... is given an affirmed legal status as the ideological content of national culture.' Furthermore, they go on to argue that the implication of this is that:

> this construction assumes a correspondence between national and religious identity, which means that members of non-Established Churches, and especially non-Christians, can be only partial members of the British national collectivity. They are defined to a greater or lesser extent, as outsiders. Christianity, therefore, is one of the most important bases for inherent racism in the hegemonic notion of Englishness.[53]

c. *Freedom*

Samuelson and Messick's third 'dimension of evaluation' is 'freedom' defined in terms of 'the extent to which a system permits individuals to make resource use decisions for themselves'.[54] This criterion therefore relates to the proper autonomy of each group within a plural society.

In its *Church and State* report, the Chadwick Commission stated with regard to a possible 'total severing of the historic links' that, 'whilst most of us would not like it', nevertheless, 'we should not shrink from it if the state decided it to be either wise or politically necessary'.[55] In stating this, the Commission adopted a position that owes more to Erastian pragmatism than to theological principle. As a dissenting member of the Commission, Peter Cornwell pointed out that the disestablishment of the Anglican Churches in Ireland and the Anglican Church in Wales was something that was brought about by political decision from outside the Church. In contrast to these politically initiated disestablishments, Cornwell stressed that what he advocated was 'something different, a demand for disestablishment by the Church of England itself'.[56] Buchanan also argues that an internal initiation of disestablishment would be preferable to any externally imposed development on the basis that a move towards disestablishment initiated from within would reinforce the Church's spiritual freedom as a proactive rather than merely reactive body.[57]

Lamont's review of the relationship between church and state concludes that, 'The case for disestablishment is now both historical and constitutional, statistical and equitable, moral and theological – but it is also practical and political on the basis that it is better to make the change willingly from strength, and from faith in the future, than unwillingly from weakness.'[58] A willingness to face the inadequacy of establishment now, and out of a choice of 'freedom' instead of being driven by external necessity of dealing with any *post hoc* consequences of change brought about externally would arguably allow English society, the UK state and the Christian Churches to draw upon their own traditions in negotiating change. In Samuelson and Messick's terms it would facilitate the Church of England's making for itself a 'resource use decision'.

d. *Self-Interest*

The final 'dimension of evaluation' identified by Samuelson and Messick is that of 'self-interest', defined in terms of 'one's own view of how one's own resource status would be affected by an allocation system'.[59] For religious minorities, a contextual judgement needs to be made concerning which 'allocation system' – the current establishment or one or the other of its possible replacement models – is likely to deliver an improvement in their 'resource status'. Issues both of pragmatism and of principle are likely to be involved in such an evaluation. As has been acknowledged, at least at the level of official community leadership, there are those from within the minority communities who see sharing the current 'allocation system' of the establishment, even as junior and dependent partners in an 'extended establishment' approach, as the best way of increasing the 'resource status' of their traditions.

For the Church of England itself, when reflecting upon the possibility of change to its established status, the factor of 'self-interest' is also an important one. Taken in a straightforward way, since Anglicans derive privilege from the 'resource allocation' benefits that are associated with establishment, the criterion of 'self-interest' might necessarily seem to indicate continued Anglican support for establishment. In terms of a straightforward reading of the criteria of 'self-interest', Lamont's observation, that 'The erosion of religious belief by secular forces may be tempting many Christians to cling to establishment as a last straw lest the church blow away entirely in the wind of change',[60] clearly has validity.

However, even in terms of purely pragmatic 'self-interest', as Martin pointed out in his 'Protestantism and the State' article, 'The truth is that the attitude of Anglicans to the state has always been decided practically, as is the English way, in relation to historical developments and never in accordance with a consistent doctrine.'[61] This observation is confirmed by the position taken in the 1970 *Church and State* report noted above, in which its majority authors stated that they would not shrink from disestablishment if the State wanted it. This may be Erastianism of the worst sort, but it might also be an indication of an *ecclesiological pragmatism* that takes the social and historical context into theological account, thus allowing a recognition of the arrival of a moment of *kairos* for the previous historical model.

As long ago as 1947, Cyril Garbett argued that, 'The Church is drifting towards disaster if it allows year after year to pass without making a determined and sustained attempt to readjust a position inherited from ages when the Church and the Nation were one, but which now in a time of rapid change has become fraught with danger.'[62] There are, therefore, dimensions even of pragmatic 'self-interest' that might call for at least some adjustment to the form of the current arrangements for the relationships between religion(s), state and society.

However, in addition to 'straightforward' views of 'self-interest', it is arguable that the 'self-interest' of a religious group and its 'own view' of its 'resource status' can also be considered on different grounds than those which apply in other organizations. For religious organizations, 'self-interest' may be considered not only in terms of observable and enumerable but nevertheless 'penultimate' strengths and weaknesses. Rather, if they are to attempt to be true to themselves, then as well as this 'penultimate' form of 'self-interest', religious organizations will at least try to be guided by the 'ultimate' goals they are called to bear witness to, and which therefore form a part of their self-interest understood in an 'ultimate' way.

It was because of such a view of 'ultimate' self-interest that Lamont judged that any attempt to hold onto establishment as a 'last straw' in the face of the 'winds of change' is something that 'is not only dishonest to the secular majority but cowardly and unchristian in its vision'. Such perspectives could help to facilitate the Church of England in making a transition from its established status on the basis of a re-evaluation of its 'ultimate' kind of 'self-interest' informed by a theological and ecclesiological vision modified by Free Church and Baptist perspectives within a convergent ecumenical approach, rather than approaching the issues solely on the basis of a pragmatic calculation of potential costs and benefits.

As E. G. Ernst argues in his article on 'A Concept of Christian Evangelism in a Secular Society', 'the process of planning and structuring the life of Christianity in a society that does not assure or guarantee a Christian existence is part of the sociological essence of evangelism'.[63] From a different theological standpoint, Don Cupitt states that:

> Our argument suggests that it is neither practicable nor desirable to try to entrench Christianity in social structures in the future, in the way that was attempted in the past. No nostalgia, then, for Christendom. That kind of social embodiment of religion was never an entirely satisfactory expression of Christianity, for it reconciled faith and society at an unconscious and basically subChristian level.[64]

9. *Options for Change: Possibilities and Practicalities*

a. *Change and Complexity*

Samuelson and Messick's analysis of the factors and dynamics involved in the negotiation of change concludes that what is involved in making a choice between alternative systems is what they describe as 'a multiattribute utility problem'.[65] In other words, the 'dimensions of evaluation' which have been considered above are not to be evaluated in isolation but as a complex and unified whole. As explained by Samuelson and Messick, 'the attractiveness of each allocation system is represented by its weighted average, and group members compare overall attractiveness measures of the different systems in order to make choices or comparative evaluations of two or more systems'.[66] This is because the individual 'dimensions of evaluation' are not always correlated and, depending on the circumstances, a differential importance can be attached to each individual dimension.

It is the recognition of such complexity that leads to an understanding of why, in relation to the current establishment, what might abstractly appear to be a logic of change to the current establishment does not always command the support even of those who might be expected to support this (in other words, why many minority religious leaders might not advocate change). Samuelson and Messick, in fact, highlight 'two systematic factors' which influence perceptions of the 'allocation systems' and which determine a group's formulation of the 'overall attractiveness measures' in analysing a possible change. These are the 'relative importance attached to the dimensions' and the 'experience subjects have had with the system'.[67]

In terms of the 'relative importance attached to the dimensions' both secularists and religious believers opposed to the establishment recognize the inequality and inequity of the current arrangements. But at the same time, they are likely to give a different *relative weighting* to the functions of 'fairness' and 'efficiency'. Secularists are likely to be attracted to a model (the 'abolitionist' model of disestablishment without replacement) that is based on a high evaluation of the criterion of 'fairness', while many religious believers might find this less attractive on the grounds of concerns about 'efficiency'. In other words, they may be concerned about the danger, in any process of disestablishment, that the 'resource' of the symbolic and operational public influence of religion might thereby be 'depleted'.

b. *Experience of the Current 'Allocation System'*

The second systematic factor identified by Samuelson and Messick as influencing the 'overall attractiveness measures' when analysing the possibilities for change is the 'experience subjects have had with the system'.

We have already seen that there are those among the minority religious leaders whose 'experience ... with the system' is no longer only negative. However, an argument can be made that current trends within a multicultural and religiously plural society have the potential for tipping the balance of evaluation towards recognition of the need for change. As Lamont observed in relation to the *Satanic Verses* controversy, it 'will not be the last clash of culture and religious freedom which we will see in Britain. It is better by far to plan ahead of such events and enunciate the framework of tolerance and democracy which must be applied to any church/state bond rather than be forced to decide the issue over controversial cases.'[68]

At the same time, the creation of a National Religious Council of the kind proposed by Lamont would seem to be premature. Although Lamont argues that his proposal would 'simply be to give institutional form to a process which has been gathering pace over the years',[69] many religious traditions are not yet in a position to be represented in the way which would be required. To this extent, it may be that Lamont has allowed commitment to a vision to obscure judgement concerning the extent to which there may be a current basis in fact for the realization of this proposal. Additionally, outside of the context of a broader social and political upheaval of constitutionally revolutionary proportions, the *de novo* creation of such a Council is, in practice, unlikely to happen since the 'dimensions of evaluation' explored in the previous section are so complex for the parties involved that the 'risk aversion' to such an option is not likely to be overcome.

c. *The Adequacy of the Abolition, Extension or Invention Models*

In fact, subjected to close examination, none of the three models examined here would seem to be really appropriate for the current and future configuration of religion(s), state and society in England and the UK. But in recognizing this, the question still needs to be pressed as to whether it really is beyond the bounds of possibility to envisage other models for the task of 'integrating religious, social and political values in a multi-cultural society'? Are there models that would presuppose neither the predominance of one religious tradition in the public life of society, nor the exclusion of all religions? It was Michael Ramsey's view that the central questions about establishment and disestablishment are of a theological nature rather than being merely sociologically driven, which he expressed when he asked the question, 'What is it that the Church should do and be different from what it does and is at the present? If the doing of it calls for the altering of the parts, or the whole, of the state relationship, then we should be ready to pay the price.'[70]

Notes

1   P. Hennessy, *The Hidden Wiring: Unearthing the British Constitution* (London: Victor Gollancz, 1995).

2   S. Lamont, *Church and State*, p. 177.

3   S. Lamont, *Church and State*, p. 183.

4   *The Times*, 15.2.1953, cited in J. Wolffe (ed.), *The Growth of Religious Diversity: Britain From 1945. A Reader*, pp. 172–3.

5   I. Bradley, *God Save the Queen: The Spiritual Dimensions of Monarchy* (London: Darton, Longman & Todd, 2002).

6   St John Robilliard, *Religion and the Law*, p. 85.

7   See M. Furlong, *C of E*, p. 237.

8   Royal Commission on Reform of the House of Lords, *A House for the Future: A Summary* (London: Royal Commission on Reform of the House of Lords, 2000).

9   The Law Commission, *Offences Against Religion and Public Worship* (Working Paper No. 79; London: Her Majesty's Stationery Office, 1981), para. 2.54, pp. 28–9.

10   Lord Scarman, *The Scarman Report: The Brixton Disorders, 10–12th April, 1981. Report on an Inquiry by the Right Honourable Lord Scarman OBE, Presented to Parliament by the Secretary of State for the Home Department by Command of Her Majesty, November, 1981* (Harmondsworth: Penguin, 1982).

11   J. Wolffe, ' "And There's Another Country ..." '.

12   *The Times*, 2.3.1989.

13   See General Synod of the Church of England, *Offences Against Religion and Public Worship, G.S. Misc. 149* (London: General Synod of the Church of England, December 1981); and *Offences Against Religion and Public Worship, G.S. Misc. 286* (London: General Synod of the Church of England, February 1988).

14   K. Ward, 'Third Introductory Paper', in Commission for Racial Equality, *Law, Blasphemy and the Multi-Faith Society, Report of a Seminar* (London: Commission for Racial Equality, 1990), pp. 30–9.

15   Commission for Racial Equality, *Law, Blasphemy and the Multi-Faith Society, Report of a Seminar* (London: Commission for Racial Equality, 1990), p. 52.

16   R. Kabbani, *Letter to Christendom* (London: Virago, 1989) p. 8.

17   See *Education Guardian*, 16.3.2004.

18   See Commission for Racial Equality, *Schools of Faith: Religious Schools in a Multi-Cultural Society* (London: Commission for Racial Equality, 1990).

19   Christians Against Racism and Fascism, *Church Schools in a Multi-Faith Society* (Christians Against Racism and Fascism, 1982).

20   See J. Beckford and S. Gilliat, *The Church of England and Other Faiths in a Multi-Faith Society*, 1996; J. Beckford and S. Gilliat, *The Church of England and Other Faiths in a Multi-Faith Society: Summary Report*, 1996; and J. Beckford and S. Gilliat, *Religion in Prison*, 1998.

21   W. M. Watt, *Truth in the Religions: A Sociological and Psychological Approach* (Edinburgh: Edinburgh University Press, 1963).

22   Reported in *The Guardian*, 23.1.2002, based on a telephone poll conducted 18–20 January 2002.

23   See W.H. Mackintosh, *Disestablishment and Liberation: The Movement for the Separation of the Anglican Church From State Control* (London: Epworth Press, 1972).

24   D. Bebbington, *The Nonconformist Conscience*, p. 27.

25   See *The Guardian*, 17.9.1990.

26   D. Bebbington, *The Nonconformist Conscience*, p. 29.

27   J. Habgood, 'The Supermarket of Competing Faiths', *The Independent*, 3.6.1989.

28   J. Wolffe, ' "And There's Another Country ..." ', p. 102.

29   J. Sacks, *The Persistence of Faith: Religion, Morality and Society in a Secular Age* (London: Weidenfeld & Nicolson, 1991), pp. 97–8.

30   J. Sacks, *The Persistence of Faith*, p. 97.

31   S. Lamont, *Church and State*, p. 204.

32   S. Lamont, *Church and State*, p. 204.

33   The Home Office Faith Communities Unit, *Working Together: Co-Operation Between Government and Faith Communities. Recommendations of the Steering Group Reviewing Patterns of Engagement Between Government and Faith Communities in England* (London: Faith Communities Unit, The Home Office, 2004).

34   R. Kramer and D. Messick (eds.), *Negotiation as Social Process*, p. ix.

35   See C. Samuelson and D. Messick, 'Let's Make Some New Rules: Social Factors That Make Freedom Unattractive', in R. Kramer and D. Messick (eds.), *Negotiation as Social Process*, pp. 48–68.

36   C. Samuelson and D. Messick, 'Let's Make Some New Rules', p. 63.

37   Chadwick Commission, *Church and State*, p. 65.

38   See D. Baker, 'Turbulent Priests: Christian Opposition to the Conservative Government Since 1979', *Political Quarterly* 52 (1991), pp. 90–105.

39 J. Wolffe, ' "And There's Another Country ..." ', p. 93.

40 C. Samuelson and D. Messick, 'Let's Make Some New Rules', p. 63.

41 C. Samuelson and D. Messick, 'Let's Make Some New Rules', p. 63.

42 C. Samuelson and D. Messick, 'Let's Make Some New Rules', p. 63–4.

43 Reported in C. Buchanan, *Cut the Connection*, p.74.

44 See F. Jameson, *Postmodernism: or, The Cultural Logic of Late Capitalism* (London: Verso, 1991).

45 L. Newbigin, 'Blasphemy and the Free Society', *DCJIRE* 4/2 (1990), p. 17.

46 J. Sacks, *The Persistence of Faith*, pp. 26–7.

47 Board for Social Responsibility, *The Church and the Bomb* (London: Hodder & Stoughton, 1982).

48 Archbishop's Commission on Urban Priority Areas, *Faith in the City*.

49 Quoted in *The Independent*, 15.4.1989.

50 C. Samuelson and D. Messick, 'Let's Make Some New Rules', p. 64.

51 T. Modood, 'Minorities, Faith and Citizenship', *DCJIRE* 6/2 (1992), pp. 58–60 (59).

52 The Venerable Sangharakshita, *Buddhism and Blasphemy: Buddhist Reflections on the 1977 Blasphemy Trial* (London: Windhorse, 1978), p. 24.

53 G. Saghal and N. Yuval-Davis (eds.), *Refusing Holy Orders: Women and Fundamentalism in Britain* (London: Virago, 1992), pp. 12–13.

54 C. Samuelson and D. Messick, 'Let's Make Some New Rules', p. 64.

55 Chadwick Commission, *Church and State*, p. 65.

56 P. Cornwell, *Church and Nation*, p. 103.

57 See C. Buchanan, *Cut the Connection*, pp. 196–208.

58 S. Lamont, *Church and State*, p. 196.

59 C. Samuelson and D. Messick, 'Let's Make Some New Rules', p. 64.

60 S. Lamont, *Church and State*, p. 196.

61 H. Martin, 'Protestantism and the State', p. 314.

62 Quoted in J. Wolffe (ed.), *The Growth of Religious Diversity: Britain from 1945, A Reader*, p. 216.

63 E. Ernst, 'A Concept of Christian Evangelism in a Secular Society', *Foundations* 16/2 (1973), pp. 143–55 (148).

64 D. Cupitt, 'Christian Existence in a Pluralist Society', *Theology* 78 (September 1974), pp. 451–9 (459).

65 C. Samuelson and D. Messick, 'Let's Make Some New Rules', p. 65.

66 C. Samuelson and D. Messick, 'Let's Make Some New Rules', p. 64.

67 C. Samuelson and D. Messick, 'Let's Make Some New Rules', p. 64.

68 S. Lamont, *Church and State*, p. 205.

69 S. Lamont, *Church and State*, p. 204.

70 M. Ramsey, *Canterbury Pilgrim*, p. 176.

Chapter 6

THE *KAIROS* OF ESTABLISHMENT

1. *Context for Change*

a. *'Post-Christendom': The End of Monopolistic Approaches*

For those religious bodies and organizations that wish to stay connected with reality, the days of being able to ignore the impact of *either* the secularity *or* the plurality of religions in English and UK society are gone. All religions live alongside other religions and all are confronted with the challenges posed by secularity. The complexity of our contemporary religious landscape means that theologically, ecclesiologically and socially monopolistic ways of thinking and acting, whether in religious or secular terms, are neither viable nor appropriate.

As pointed out by Stuart Murray, a shift has taken place from a Christendom context to a 'post-Christendom' one or, in the terminology used in this book, there has been a change from a 'one-dimensional' socio-religious reality to a 'three-dimensional' one. As a consequence of these shifts, life in what must now be recognized to be a 'three-dimensional society' poses theological and ecclesiological questions that cannot adequately be framed by the historical shape of issues, addressed by the proposed solutions of yesterday, nor indefinitely postponed.

The establishment of the Church of England means that it has a relative institutional and cultural advantage in comparison with other religious – including Christian – bodies within English and UK society. At the same time, when challenging the establishment of the Church of England, it is important to recognize that, in recent years, it has often been facilitative of creating openings for the wider participation of religious minorities in civic and political life. It is also important not to *overstate* the significance of the establishment.

For example, the establishment of the Church of England does *not* mean that people of other religious traditions may not publicly propagate their beliefs and ways of life and invite others to embrace these. It also does *not* mean that educational opportunities or political representation are systematically and in principle closed to religious minorities. To this extent, the establishment of one religious tradition is not, in principle, incompatible with the relevant freedom of religion and belief clauses of the Universal Declaration on Human Rights, the European Convention on Human Rights and Fundamental Freedoms which derives from this, or the UK's Human Rights Act, 1988.

b. *Church and State in Plural Perspective*

However, although the significance of establishment should not be *overstated*, and while it does *not* have the social power and privilege that it *once* did, its existence *does* still matter and its continuation *is* still problematic. This is because it is both an *expression of,* and a *reinforcement for,* a 'one-dimensional' socio-religious model that is neither symbolically nor operationally adequate to the 'three-dimensional' religious landscape that characterizes contemporary England and the UK.

Up until now, however, very few critiques of establishment, whether by Anglicans, nonconformists, secularists or others, have really located debates about it explicitly within the setting of the religiously plural context.[1] Thus serious and sustained debate on the establishment either has generally been largely internal to the Church of England and/or has primarily been conducted in terms of the secular–religious interface. In this debate, secularists have argued against establishment on the basis that it represents an archaic and inappropriate historical 'hangover' that ought to be removed from a modern society.

Among religious people generally are many (including those from among the Free Churches whose traditions have previously stood against establishment) who have increasingly (albeit with either more or less conviction) argued that its continuance has turned out to have been not entirely negative. This has been on the basis that, in an age dominated by economic consumerism and short-term political pragmatism, establishment has served as an important institutionalized reminder that alternative values and dimensions of life still exist. It has therefore been seen as something of a bulwark against the advance of secularization and, in particular, against what is perceived as an ideological secularism.

Among the religious critics of establishment, such as Colin Buchanan and Theo Hobson, the implications of religious plurality for establishment receive only fleeting mention. Like most Christian writers who address the issue of the establishment at all, Buchanan and Hobson articulate the question primarily in terms of intra-Christian theological and ecclesiological issues. There are, of course, intra-Christian issues at stake in the debate and some of these will be explored in this chapter. But it is argued that it is precisely the new ethnic, cultural and religious plurality of post-war English and UK society that reframes the theological, ecclesiological, sociological and political context for the historical debates over establishment and gives fresh impetus and relevance to these debates.

Initially, as we have seen, the immediate consequences of pluralization were seen primarily in terms of the issues posed by diverse ethnicities. Thus, in the early phase of settlement and community development of substantial migrant and minority communities, very few observers or participants in the debates about this plurality or its consequences discerned the distinctive challenges that a new and broader *religious* plurality would bring. Rather, the assumption was often made that, as part of an expected broader assimilation taking place throughout generational change, religious identities and commitments might also be eroded. Now, however, it is clear that the more popularized versions of secularization theories have not come to pass. The religious dimensions of public life have changed but have most certainly not faded away. Rather, through religious pluralization, these issues have instead become both more *prominent* and more *complex.*

Therefore, it is now clear that if life in a 'three-dimensional' socio-religious reality is to be a viable project, then a commitment to creative dialogue between people of various religious backgrounds, between religious and secular people, and between both and the state, is a necsssity. As a part of this dialogue, religious people will need to learn to be not so ready to equate 'secular' with 'irreligious' in a moral sense, while secular people will need to learn not to make a simplistic equation between 'religion' and 'fundamentalism'.

2. *Theology, Institutions and Change*

a. *Theology and 'Reality-Matching'*

As a matter of *description*, theological and ecclesiological reflection cannot be undertaken within a closed circle of the Christian community in abstraction from its social and historical context. But, in addition, as a matter of *prescription*, the 'reality-matching' involved in evolving adequate theological and ecclesiological approaches requires sociological analysis. As the 1977 Assembly of the former British Council of Churches expressed it, 'the presence in Britain of significant numbers of people of faiths other than Christian is within God's gracious purposes'.[2] Thus the task of theology can no longer be conducted in an intellectually, morally or socially responsible way unless it proceeds within a perspective that takes full account of the reality of the diversity of religions and of their implications for Christian personal and corporate existence.

However, even if the discrepancy between the 'one-dimensional' socio-religious inheritance embodied in the establishment and the 'three-dimensional' contemporary reality is recognized, this does not automatically or necessarily lead to change. As Watt points out, 'The basic economic or material decision may ... be said to constitute a framework within which the life of an individual or a society has to be lived', but although 'it controls that life to some extent', nevertheless, 'it does not determine it in detail.'[3] Changed *circum*stances do not deterministically lead to new theological, ecclesiological and political *stances*.

Furthermore, for ecclesiology *simply* to reflect a change in the times may not be *theologically* appropriate. Thus, while the context for theology and ecclesiology needs to be taken very seriously, this is not the same as advocating a reductionist view that seeks completely to explain theology and ecclesiology in terms of the economic or material framework. Rather, in order for a more appropriate 'fit' to be developed between theological theory, institutional shape and contextual reality in the process of 'reality-matching', there remains a vital role for theological, ecclesiological and political debate.

As Robin Gill puts it in *The Social Context of Theology*, 'theological variables' can become 'social determinates'.[4] It is also precisely because of this relationship between 'theological variables' and 'social determinates' that establishment is not just a *reflection* of a 'one-dimensional' way of thinking and living but *also* reinforces such an approach. It is for this reason that it *does* need to be changed. It is also because of this relationship between 'theological variables' and 'social determinates' that the theological and ecclesiological resources of Baptist Christian tradition can make an important contribution to the development of a more appropriate contemporary embodiment for the relationships between religion(s), state and society than that of establishment.

b. *Personal Faith, Cumulative Tradition and Community*

As has previously been noted, in his classic book, *The Meaning and End of Religion*,[5] the historian and scholar of religion Wilfred Cantwell Smith famously questioned both the legitimacy and the usefulness of the concept 'religion'. He did so on the basis that the 'isms' and 'itys' ('Hinduism', 'Christianity', etc.) by means of which various expressions of religious life are often labelled and categorized represent unhelpful abstractions that are not adequate to historical reality. Instead, Cantwell Smith proposed that the study of religions could best be illuminated by considering the interplay between what he identified as, on the one hand, 'personal faith' and, on the other hand, 'cumulative tradition'.

Within the disciplinary fields that have been applied to the study of the phenomenon of religion, much attention has focused on either one or the other of these dimensions of religious life. Approaches from within the Psychology of Religion and Pastoral Theology have tried to delineate the contours of the 'personal faith' dimension. Linguistic and textual studies, and historical and sociological perspectives, have, in different ways, attempted to trace the development of the 'cumulative tradition'.

Cantwell Smith's approach is, in many ways, illuminating of the nature of religious believing and belonging. But its weakness perhaps lies in his own Protestant Christian background, the influence of which upon his thinking has led to what is arguably an over-individualized approach to religion in which there is a tendency to neglect the collective social embodiment of both 'personal faith' and 'cumulative tradition'. By contrast, in the context of ethnic and racial studies, political science and social geography, this collective social dimension of religious life has become more central to the way in which religion is engaged with and understood

'Community' is the now near-ubiquitous word of public discourse that has often been utilized to denote this dimension of religious life. Increasingly, however, in both social and political debates and in academic studies, the uses of this word have a tendency to mystify rather than clarify. This is because, if the description 'the X community' is used as anything other than a shorthand notation for a particular clustering of religious life, it can present a misleading picture of homogeneity. Such a picture can often be significantly at variance with the much more complex, multi-layered, sometimes fragmented and even fractured realities that the word 'community' seeks to denote. However, even if the word 'community' is in some way still serviceable to designate a dimension of religious life not captured by either 'personal faith' or 'cumulative tradition', there remains an element of religion that is still something other than that which is signified even by these three linguistic markers.

c. *Religious Institutional and Organizational Forms*

In a today neglected 1974 article (which however still resonates with the contemporary situation) on 'Communalism and the Social Structure of Religion', Trevor Ling argued that the study of religions ought to take more account of the structuring of 'personal faith' and 'cumulative tradition' into a variety of *institutional* forms. Therefore, referring to Cantwell Smith's schema of 'personal faith' and 'cumulative tradition' Ling noted that:

This pair of concepts, cumulative tradition and personal faith are offered, if I have understood correctly, as likely to produce a more realistic insight into the structure of what is commonly called Christianity. It is at this point that I am inclined to think that his scheme needs supplementing; one needs to know more about the structure of the vast intervening area of institutions and organizations that extends between the personal faith of the individual and the cumulative tradition.[6]

In agreement with Ling, it is the contention of this book that the *organizational forms* of a religion are a much more highly significant part of the *content* of a religion than they are often given credit for. Such organizational forms are a major part of what a 'community' consists of. They are significant nodes in the network of relationships between the bearers of 'personal faith' and they form key social and historical meeting-points between such 'personal faith' and the broader 'cumulative tradition'. They are thus one of the principal means through which 'cumulative traditions' and the bearers of 'personal faith' mediate and negotiate their reality with all other social realities. They therefore become the public face that the 'cumulative tradition' presents to the world.

To function effectively in contemporary society, religious organizations generally have to form themselves in certain identifiable ways in order that, within the wider social and legal frameworks, they can corporately be accountable for their actions and activities. Then, in turn, the laws, rules and regulations that emanate from the state at all its levels of its operation significantly impact upon, and also actively shape, the development of the 'cumulative tradition' and perhaps, through this, to some degree also the 'personal faith' of organizational members.

Superficially it might be thought that, due to their role of embodying tradition and legitimacy, the institutional structures of religions might be more resistant to change than the ideational bodies of systematic theology. Of course, there is such a thing as institutional self-interest (though in the previous chapter we have noted how, in the case of religious organizations, there can also be a dimension of 'self-interest' that can be understood in an 'ultimate' as well as a 'penultimate' way). But even taking full account of the more everyday understanding of 'self-interest' it can be acknowledged that, paradoxically, the challenge of the 'three-dimensional' socio-religious reality is most difficult to avoid for institutions. This is because institutions need to make practical decisions. This means that when a religious body like the Church of England is fully engaged with the socio-religious reality of which it is also a part, then theological and missiological questions can focus pressure for change in ways that are sometimes sharper and more insistent than within systematic theology.

The institutional forms of religious bodies, including those of the Christian Churches, are thus a profoundly disturbing point of intersection between inherited theological positions and the need to respond to practical questions in contemporary practice that arise from the changing situations in which the institutions must live. The development of theological understanding that results from fresh examinations of old issues and bold explorations of new ones is then taken up, at varying rates of progress, into institutional structures. The further changes in institutional understanding, practice and structures that subsequently emerge complete the circle and give yet another new impulse to the further development of theological understanding and institutional practice. As Watt explains in relation to this phenomenon:

> our time cannot be neatly divided into a period when we study the situation objectively and a period when we consider what to do about this situation we have studied. Often the two processes go on concurrently and influence one another. Even if they are not contemporaneous, the interests which are promoted by the activity also influence the study of the situation. It was for this reason that it was stated above that social and ideational factors are complementary.[7]

d. *Ecclesiology as a Corporate 'Doing of the Truth'*

On this basis one can characterize ecclesiology as a corporate attempt at a 'doing of the truth'. In this, the question of the appropriateness of particular ecclesiological forms is to be understood not so much in terms of abstract comparisons between the strengths and weaknesses of different ecclesiological models but more in terms of the achievement of a transformative and relational understanding. As Kenneth Cragg put it when reflecting specifically on Christian–Muslim relations, but in a way that could also be applied to the challenge of ecclesiology in a 'three-dimensional' socio-religious reality:

> The contemporary relationship of faiths is a 'doing' that is looking for 'knowledge', aware that the knowledge that may finally justify the doing can be had in no other way. Like Peter in the house of Cornelius, we may feel at once both compelled and compromised in being where we are.[8]

This is a theology and practice of inter-religious dialogue as 'faith in action seeking understanding' in which theological '*stances*' are always integrally related to social and historical '*circum*stances' and can therefore only adequately be understood in the light of those circumstances. Theology and ecclesiology must not only relate to the traditions and internal life of the Church, but must also be adequate to the total reality out of which they are formed and in which they operate. The adequacy of particular theologies and ecclesiologies determines their relevance and power. To the degree that they are out of synchronization with the experienced reality of a particular time and place, they will fail to make connections beyond the boundaries of the Christian community, and even within these borders they will lose much of their relevance and power.

The social context and content of the theology and practice of inter-religious dialogue may often have been recognized as a *starting-point* and motivation for theological reflection, but all too often they have not remained *integral* to that reflection and, in particular, not with regard to the institutional forms of Christianity. Thus there is an argument that, while in general terms much of the best theological reflection on the theology and practice of inter-religious dialogue in England comes from within the Anglican theological *tradition*, such reflection has not always been matched by institutional practice.

Some of the 'notes' of Anglican tradition that inform the positive contributions made by Anglicans in this field are set out in Ninian Smart's ten theses on Anglicanism and other faiths, published in his 1967 *Theology* article on 'The Anglican Contribution to the Dialogue of Religions'. After noting the many individual Anglican contributors to inter-religious dialogue, Smart went on to ask what he called 'the deeper question'. This was whether there is 'something in the spirit and circumstances of Anglicanism which gives it a special form of insight and a special bias in relation to the interplay between world faiths'.[9]

In its tradition of 'natural theology' and the balance that it seeks to achieve between scripture, tradition and reason, it needs to be acknowledged that the overall theological spirit of Anglicanism has made many important contributions to the challenge of Christian thinking and living in a multi-religious environment. However, as C. Norman, a past President of the Modern Churchmen's Union once pointed out, although Anglicanism often *speaks* with the voice of Athanasius and of Temple its *attitudes* and *actions* are frequently informed by Barth's position on the radical discontinuity between the Christian revelation and other religions.[10] Thus, acknowledgement of the creative contributions to the theology and practice of inter-faith dialogue made from within the Anglican tradition in England does not abrogate the problematic nature of establishment when considered in relation to the history of exclusion in which it has also played an active part.

e. *Theological Stances, Historical Circumstances and Structural Relations*

While the Church of England today does not seek the civil exclusion of other forms of worship, and it does often facilitate minority religious contributions, nevertheless, the public face of the Church of England remains one of institutional privilege in comparison with other forms of religious life in the country. This is manifest in terms of its relationship with Royalty, its access to government, its presence in Parliament, and its positions of institutional privilege in such social institutions as hospitals, prisons, schools and universities.

Although this position of privilege is now generally exercised in benign ways, it remains the case that this can very often be accompanied by either an 'attitudinal paternalism', albeit often unconscious and unintended, or, in the absence of personally paternalistic attitudes, by what might be described as a 'structural paternalism'. Thus an 'extended establishment' model can be expounded with an individual generosity and sensitivity of spirit (as in a recent piece by Michael Ipgrave,[11] the Inter-Faith Adviser to the Archbishops' Council of the Church of England, on the reinterpretation of *Fidei Defensor*). But a serious question still needs to be pressed about whether such an approach is, structurally, really adequate to the implications of coming to terms with a 'three-dimensional' socio-religious reality?

The kind of issues that are involved in this can be illustrated by Ipgrave's reference to a Lambeth Place lecture on 'Holding Together: Church and Nation in the Twenty-First Century' given by the former Archbishop of Canterbury, George Carey, in 2002. In his lecture, Carey argued for what he called an 'hospitable establishment' in the following terms: 'Hospitality requires a host. So it is part of our role, I believe, to seek to provide space and access, opportunity and the right atmosphere for the many dealings and interactions between faith communities and the wider society, however and wherever we can.'[12] While preferable to the historic exclusionism of establishment, the question does need to be asked about whether the structural relations implied by the word 'host', together with its implied corollary of 'guests', are really any longer appropriate to what is now a 'three-dimensional' socio-religious reality?

The use of such language and the policy approach that it reflected was once relatively commonplace in relation to the place of ethnic minorities in the context of citizenship and public life. But, in view of the common citizenship status of minority ethnic groups, such ways of expressing things would now no longer be seen as appropriate in the social and political context. Expressed sharply, one could ask whether, in the 'extended establishment' apologia for establishment there might be at least a hint of a stance that is, in religious terms, analogous to that reflected in the colonial argument of the 'white man's burden'? In the context of colonial relations such an approach used to be advanced as a more 'liberal' justification for the continuing structural power of whites within the colonial status quo. Could it also be that, whatever the personal *intentions* of those who argue for a more religiously inclusive and 'hospitable' approach to establishment, what is actually reflected in the 'extended establishment' approach is, in structural reality, an articulation of establishment as 'the Church of England's burden' in a multi-faith society?

The imagery is sharp, and it may overstate the case. But it is expressed in this way in order to try to drive home the often inadequately discussed point that, regardless of the *attitudes* and *actions* of individual Anglicans, or indeed of the Church of England itself, religious disadvantage is fundamentally a *structural* matter. In colonial structures, even where ethnic relations were exercised in ways that were helpful and supportive to those who were colonized, the structural issues still remained. In this sense at least, the existence of established religion *in itself* entails disadvantage for organizations and people from other Christian traditions and from other than Christian religions, no matter how benignly its privileges are exercised. As noted in the previous chapter, a whole range of privileges and constraints arising from establishment still remain enshrined in the law.

Of course, in part these structural arrangements simply recognize the historic and continuing importance of the Church of England's contribution to the education system in England. However, such arrangements do *not only reflect* these positions of numerical majority, which might arguably not be inappropriate in recognition of both historic and contemporary demographic realities. They *also* effectively give a *veto* to one religious group. Those who act within such committees may very well be, and often are, the epitome of accommodation of the needs and concerns of others, but the question of the *structural embeddedness of privilege* is not thereby rendered irrelevant and an issue of corporate equity still remains.

There is also the widespread and structurally embedded position of the Church of England in chaplaincies. In areas such as the armed forces and the prison service, the publicly funded position of Anglican Christianity specifically privileges it above other forms of religion, whether Christian or other than Christian. Once again, as recent research[13] by Warwick University has shown, the positions held by Church of England chaplains in the prison system can be, and reasonably frequently are, creatively used to make openings for the provision of pastoral support from, and for, people of other than Christian religious traditions. But the *structural* arrangements still embody a lack of inclusivity. Therefore even if, in particular instances, they result in positive co-operation, ultimately they are at best based upon a structural paternalism rather than upon structures that embody equity.

Contra Modood, in a 'three-dimensional' and increasingly religiously plural socio-religious context, the implications of the establishment to do with education, the law and pastoral services are *not* just of a 'minimal nature'. Rather, they have substantial consequences for individuals, and certainly for communities and organizations, of the other than established religious traditions. Cumulatively they are part of a nexus that continues to have wider symbolic and constitutional significance for a society that aspires to be multi-cultural and multi-faith.

When this overall situation is examined in the light of the significant social correlation that exists between religious and ethnic minorities, in a society in which racism is an experienced reality, the maintenance of such structural privilege is particularly problematic. This is especially the case in a setting within which the political discourse of racism is ever more frequently expressed in cultural and religious terms. In such a context, identification of 'Englishness' and 'Christianness' can reinforce the tendency to identify 'our' way of life with Christianity in a way that encourages policies, practices and attitudes that define English Muslims, Hindus, Sikhs, Jews and others as essentially 'alien'.

Where fault lines of religious difference and sometimes of tension also map onto cultural and ethnic differences, the maintenance of an established form of religion that is bound up with national symbols of self-definition that were originally developed in a more 'one-dimensional' context is at least potentially problematic. Under certain conditions of social crisis in which 'communal scapegoating' can develop and be exploited by extremist groups, such alignments also have the potential of becoming dangerous. Although such communalism is not at present generally characteristic of English society, there have been warning signs, as in the British National Party's recent electoral targeting[14] of 'Muslims' in towns such as Oldham and Burnley, where unemployment and poverty is high, and where racism is now expressed in strongly 'religionized' forms.

3. *'Covenantal Voluntarism' for a Plural Society*

a. *Ethical and Political Ecclesiology*

A contemporary critic of establishment and Church of England bishop, Colin Buchanan notes that: 'Anglicans have got so used to double-think in their apologias that it needs outsiders to blow the distorted thinking aside.'[15] Historically, the Free Churches have been the major 'outsider' source for a *religious* critique of established religion. As we have seen, in the nineteenth century they waged vigorous political and religious campaigns for disestablishment. As was also previously noted, some of the force of this campaign was rooted in the social disadvantage experienced by nonconformist Christians. But for many it was also a matter of *theological* principle, rooted in their understanding of the nature of the Church as a community of believers who have freely covenanted together.

In contrast to the context of the struggle against racism in apartheid South Africa, and the liberation struggles of the Church of the poor in Latin America, ecclesiological debate in Europe (or in Western Europe, at least) seems too often to have been conducted in strangely ahistorical and apolitical registers. An exception to this was, of course, the history of the Confessing Church in the Germany of the Third Reich. But this was an exception of the kind that highlights the more general rule. It is, however, the argument of this book that even in less extreme settings, the *social and political context* needs to become much more part and parcel of ecclesiological thinking and acting than has hitherto been the case.

It is in the full encounter with, and recognition of, the 'three-dimensional' nature of the current socio-religious context that the timely relevance to contemporary ecclesiology of the Baptist vision can be recognized. In such a setting, the issue of 'epistemological praxis' comes to the fore and questions of theological ethics need to be seen as being at the heart of both epistemology and practical ecclesiology. In this, the emphases on 'covenantal voluntarism' and liberty of religious belief and practice found in the Baptist vision of Christianity are key resources for a contemporary and corporate 'doing of the truth' in the religiously plural and secular society of contemporary England and the UK state.

The Baptist contribution to ecumenical ecclesiology is one that is expressed in a call to discipleship arising from the free commitment of Christian believers to Jesus as the determining point of reference for their lives. It therefore insists that the *shape* of the Christian community and its *style of witness* lie at the very heart of the *content* of theology and practice. Thus theological ethics needs to be understood as being at the heart of systematic theology. As a corporate expression of theological ethics, ecclesiology needs to be central to the theological task, rather than being relegated to an ethical addendum or a derivative postscript to theology proper. Thus, in this vision, matters of ecclesiology and institutional practice are 'first order' matters concerned with the appropriate corporate shape of Christian existence and witness in a 'three-dimensional' socio-religious environment.

b. *'Church-type' and 'Sect-type' Ecclesiologies*

In his *The Social Teaching of the Christian Churches*[16] Ernst Troeltsch outlined how a 'Church-type' and 'Sect-type' ecclesiology have existed side by side in tension throughout Christian history. In sociological terms the theological approach of the Free Church tradition can, in classical Weberian terminology, be understood as a 'Sect-type' Christianity which may be contrasted with the 'Church-type' that is characteristic of an established Church and which has been the dominant tradition in European Christianity.

In the 'Church-type' ecclesiology, belief may vary, but only within a commonly accepted institutional framework which tends to approximate its structure to that of the prevailing social system and thus does not so clearly define the boundaries between 'insiders' and 'outsiders'. This type of ecclesiology aims to suffuse society with grace, but has tended to result in social privileges for some religious communities coupled with restrictions upon others. This is the tradition of what Ling calls 'the national churches or State religions of Europe' which, he argues, are 'all alike examples of the religious organization that approximates in its structure to a social system' that embodies the 'consensus of coercion'.[17]

The 'Sect-type', on the other hand, proceeds on the basis of differentiation from the rest of society characterized as a mutually covenanted and voluntary membership, rooted in a common basis of belief. As a consequence, the 'Sect-type' does not seek to impose its belief on others outside of its community of faith. This in turn supports the proper autonomy of the Church in relation to the state, coupled with the freedom of the individual from coercion in matters of conscience and religion. In considering the 'Sect-type' approach Troeltsch concluded that, 'The essential meaning of the Free Church system ... is the destruction of the medieval and early Protestant idea of a social order welded together by one uniform State Church, and of one infallible authority with a uniform control of the whole civilization.'[18]

The ability to draw upon such ecclesiological traditions of voluntarism is of great significance at this time of *kairos* for both church and society. Since Free Church ecclesiology is theologically rooted in an affirmation of religious freedom expressed through a 'covenantal voluntarism', it is better placed to facilitate the development of equitable structures for the relationships between religion(s), state and society in a religiously plural and secular society than are establishment structures. Recognition of the future ecumenical importance of Free Church ecclesiology has come also from theologians such as Jürgen Moltmann, who, speaking from within the perspective of an 'established' German Lutheranism, explained his view that:

> Whatever forms the free churches in England, America, and then, since the beginning of the 19th century also in Germany have developed (there are, of course, dangers, mistakes and wrong developments enough here too), the future of the church of Christ lies in principle on this wing of the Reformation because the widely unknown and uninhabited territory of the congregation is found here.[19]

c. *Ecumenical Critique and Modification of 'Covenantal Voluntarism'*

At the same time, in order for a balanced ecumenical ecclesiology to be developed, it is necessary to recognize that the Free Church ecclesiological tradition, too, is in need of modification. Thus, as Keith Clements (the Baptist General Secretary of the Conference of European Churches) noted with regard to Moltmann's assessment, 'all this is as much a challenge to the general pattern of our conventional "gathered church" as it is to the more obviously institutionalised "established" or "catholic" churches'.[20]

Those in favour of establishment often argue that disestablishment would undermine the open orientation and national range of the Church of England, based as this is upon its parochial structure of care for all within the parish and the wide availability of the occasional offices of baptism, marriage and funerals. There is a concern that disestablishment would reduce the Church of England to a 'sect' ministering only to its own congregations rather than to society at large. Disestablishment, it is feared, might remove from the public sphere some of the remaining constraints and alternative sources of value in what is perceived to be a highly secularized society in which many traditional solidarities and moralities have been weakened by market liberalism and/or are open to religious extremism.

That this is not a necessary outcome of disestablishment can be illustrated by the case of the Church in Wales that has, arguably, *become more closely engaged with Welsh society* as a whole in the decades following its disestablishment.[21] At the same time, a more adequate congregationalism and voluntarism does need to take *better account* of the importance of the *social dimensions* of Christian discipleship than has sometimes historically been the case. Thus, the contribution that is to be made from the Free Church tradition will be through an '*ecumencially modified congregationalism*' that promotes living in full solidarity with the world rather than through a '*congregationalism of withdrawal*' from social responsibility.

Although the 'Sect-type' of ecclesiology can have the weaknesses noted above, on balance it would seem that this ecclesiological pattern is more appropriate to life in a multi-religious society composed of what Toynbee called the 'shot silk' strands rather than a 'patchwork quilt' pattern of contemporary religious life.[22] In a society of many convictions, this kind of ecclesiology supports the maintenance of a strong convictional community with a clear religious identity, while at the same time affirming the freedom of other religious communities to develop in the same way. As J. C. G. Norman notes, 'sectarianism challenges Christians and non-Christians alike to think through their beliefs and attitudes. It may be more comfortable to drift along lazily in a form of belief accepted by one's community, but creativity is stifled that way. The presence of dissent provokes thought.'[23]

d. *Disavowing Constantine in the 'Three-dimensional' Society*

Reflecting on the contemporary salience of the Baptist inheritance of religious liberty for life in a religiously plural society, Tony Peck argues that, 'Surely the greatest challenge on religious liberty facing all Christians is how they will view the increasingly plural, multi-faith society which is Britain today, and what contribution they might be prepared to make to it.'[24] In relation to the 'secularity' of contemporary society, Ernst writes that a benefit of adopting the Free Church vision of the nature of the Church is that, 'Christians, when freed from the expectation of dominating the social order, and freed from the urge to gather everyone out of the world into the Church, may be able to live with corporate identity and integrity as whole persons within the secular world.'[25]

The convergence of social, historical, theological and institutional factors that have produced what it is argued here is a contemporary *kairos* for the establishment of the Church of England means that the establishment patterns of Christian existence in England can no longer be intellectually or morally sustained or justified. These patterns were based on premises that are no longer pertinent to contemporary church and society, but were rooted in a context that has since been radically transformed by the twin impacts of secularization and religious pluralization.

In the light of these changed circumstances, the Christian Churches in England and the UK and, specifically, the established Church of England, are challenged no longer to rely upon what Stuart Murray calls 'the vestiges of Christendom'.[26] Or, as Nigel Wright puts it in a phrase that echoes the title of his book, there is a need to 'disavow' the Constantinian inheritance.[27] In practical terms, this means it is necessary to find new ways of making a contribution to the wider society than those which rely upon the social, political, legal and constitutional institutionalization of position and role conferred by the inheritance of the establishment.

But critique alone is not sufficient. For the Christian Churches (including particularly the established Church of England), to consider taking positive steps towards divesting themselves of this inheritance, and to learn to rely more upon the inherent power of that to which they seek to bear witness, requires an alternative theological and ecclesiological vision. The Baptist theological and ecclesiological vision offers resources that can contribute to the development of such an alternative vision because it makes a very basic 'methodological contribution' that gives a far more prominent place to theological ethics and to ecclesiology than has hitherto been the case. It posits the *context* and *content* of the *social and political* relations of religious communities as an integral part of the central tasks of Christian theology and practice, maintaining that these relations form an inseparable part of the form and content of Christian witness. At the same time, rather than promoting a mere 'adaptation' of the Church to prevailing social trends, it can provide an integrated theological basis for contemporary British Christian attempts to come to terms with the 'three-dimensional' socio-religious reality.

Through its affirmation of religious liberty and its congregational ecclesiology, the Baptist vision provides a theological basis for a critical engagement with the 'three-dimensional' socio-religious reality as the arena for Christian life and witness. Within this approach, contemporary socio-religious realities can be engaged with while remaining deeply rooted in the constant point of reference provided by the Scriptures in the corporate process of attempting to discern the truth. Religious liberty in church and society is advocated on theological grounds. A congregational ecclesiology is supported that does not make inappropriate social claims within a religiously plural context. The continuing importance of Christian witness is affirmed. Finally, a theological ethics is promoted that is rooted in the call to believers' discipleship.

4. *Principles for a Change*

a. *Wider 'Translation' of the Baptist Vision*
Having argued for the importance within the Church of the alternative ecclesiolo-gical resources offered by the Free Church and specifically Baptist traditions, it might have been possible to conclude the book on this relatively clear-cut point addressed to the Christian Churches in terms of theology and ecclesiology alone. However, since it is argued that theology and ecclesiology need to engage not only with the Christian Church, but also with those of other religious traditions and none, it is important to try to go a little further than this. It has so far been argued that the Free Church and Baptist theological and ecclesiological principles that have been highlighted are those that will enable Christians more effectively to engage with such a 'three-dimensional' context. It is therefore important to see if it is possible to develop these principles into resources that are capable of making a contribution to debate beyond Christian circles.

The final sections of this chapter therefore seek to suggest ways in which such Christian theological and ecclesiological resources might be translated into wider social and political 'principles for a change' and then to offer at least an outline of some scenarios of how change might actually occur. This cannot, of course, be done here in any systematic way. As was noted in the Introduction, if change is actually to occur, intra-Christian debates will need to be brought into conjunction with a wider engagement with, and evaluation of, the issues involved. Thus the *detailing* of any actual proposals for change and, even more so, the *implementation* of any such change, will require contributions from all key stakeholders in these matters. But some key points are presented here as offering, it is hoped, a starting point for initial consideration, reflection and decision.

In identifying 'principles for a change' both possible senses of this phrase are intended. As 'principles *for a change*' a number of key propositions are identified that should inform both the *direction* and the *content* of any change in the present configuration for the relationships between religion(s), state and society. This contrasts with the kind of arguments often put forward to defend the current arrangements and which tend to proceed on grounds of historic inheritance and/or contemporary pragmatism rather than on the basis of principle.

This is not to imply that there are no principled arguments for supporting established religion. But the evidence also points to the fact that very few, if any, of those who continue to support establishment do so on the basis of arguing that they would wish to begin from this starting point if it were not already an historical given. In fact, since support for establishment tends to be pragmatic, if establishment *did* become seen (either by the government or by the Church of England itself) as something that *ought* to change, resistance to change might *not* be as strong as if support for establishment were based more on principle.

In presenting its 'principles for a change' as an attempt to translate key Baptist and Free Church theological and ecclesiological resources into impulses that can be more broadly engaged with by people of all religions and none, this section outlines seven propositions. These are neither exclusively theological nor political principles, but they are informed and shaped by an attempt at both theological and political discernment. They are not presented on the basis of any claim to them being 'universal principles' in terms of either geography or metaphysics. They are put forward – hence the original terminology of 'propositions' – on the basis of the author's personal, religious, academic, and professional engagements and reflection, over the past quarter of a century or so, on the specifically English, UK and European context for the relationships between religion, state and society. Whether, and/or how far, these principles might be seen to have a validity beyond that of the author's own argument and experience will need to be decided on the basis of an appraisal of the principles in the light of the experience and understanding of others.

b. *'Headlines' Towards Change*

As presented, these principles or propositions are, in a way, the equivalent of newspaper headlines. Thus they are intended to provoke reaction as 'debating principles'. As 'debating principles' there is much that could be said in relation to them by way of qualification. As propositions they do not claim to be either a detailed survey or the last word. They paint on a broad canvas, standing back a little from the detailed histories and variations that exist within the English and

UK context. But, in order to facilitate and provoke debate and discussion, and to uncover the presuppositions that underlie particular positions on the relationships between religion(s), state and society, it is important to offer some succinct formulations as well as to articulate some more developed arguments. Others can then react to these and affirm or disagree with them on the basis that such debate is a precondition for any actual change to be possible.

The principles presented here are, however, meant not only to be 'debating principles'. They are also intended to be 'working principles' in the sense of informing a *direction* of social and religious change to which they might themselves actively *contribute*. In other words, these principles are not intended to remain insulated in theoretical debate. Rather, they are intended to have at least the potential of being 'principles *for* a change' that are translatable into religious and social *impulses* that might help to bring about a reconfiguration in the nature and form of the relationships between religion(s), state and society in England and the UK.

c. *'Working Principles' for Religion(s), State and Society Relationships*[28]
Principle 1: The Need for a Reality Check
National and political self-understandings that exclude people of other than Christian religious traditions, either by design or by default, are, historically speaking, fundamentally distorted. Politically and religiously such self-understandings are dangerous and need to be challenged.

Principle 2: The Importance of Religious Inclusivity
Religious establishments as well as other traditions and social arrangements that provide particular forms of religion with privileged access to the social and political institutions need to be re-evaluated. There is a growing need to imagine and to construct new structural forms for the relationship between religion(s), state(s) and society that can more adequately express an inclusive social and political self-understanding than those which currently privilege Christianity.

Principle 3: The Imperative for Religious Engagement with the Wider Community
Religious communities and traditions should beware of what can be seductive calls from within their traditions to form 'religious unity fronts' against what is characterized as 'the secular state' and what is perceived as the amorality and fragmentation of modern and post-modern society.

Principle 4: The Need to Recognize the Specificity of Religions
Religious traditions and communities offer important alternative perspectives to the predominant values and power structures of states and societies. Religions are a reminder of the importance of the things that cannot be seen, touched, smelled, tasted and heard, for a more balanced perspective on those things which can be experienced in these ways.

Principle 5: The Importance of Not Marginalizing Religions from Public Life
A tendency to assign religions to the private sphere will impoverish the state by marginalizing important social resources and might unwittingly be encouraging of those reactive, backward- and inward-looking expressions of religious life that are popularly characterized as fundamentalisms.

Principle 6: The Need to Recognize the Transnational Dimensions of Religions
Religious communities and traditions need to pre-empt the dangers involved in
becoming proxy sites for imported conflicts involving their co-religionists in other
parts of the world. But because they are themselves part of wider global communities of faith, religions have the potential for positively contributing to a better
understanding of the role of the states and societies of their own countries within
a globalizing world.

Principle 7: The Imperative of Inter-Religious Dialogue
Inter-religious dialogue is an imperative for the religious communities and for
the states and societies of which they are a part. There is a need to continue the
task of developing appropriate inter-faith structures at all levels within states and
societies and in appropriate transnational and international structures.

d. *Public and Private, Common and Particular*
In general, the principles outlined above are an attempt to reframe the kind of presuppositions that have traditionally informed the classical alternatives in support
of establishment (whether of a traditional Anglican kind, or more recent 'extended
establishment' variety) or in proposing an alternative, secularizing, disestablishment. In doing so, it is hoped that they might also open up the possibility of new
thinking and acting in relation to the intersections between religion(s), state and
society.

The commonly accepted social-scientific and modernist model of society that
seeks to maintain a clear distinction between the 'public' and the 'private' spheres
as a means of managing a plural society has become increasingly problematic.
In fact, definitions of the boundaries between the 'public' and the 'private' are
themselves political definitions and therefore subject to change. In the latter part
of the twentieth century the classically sharp definitions of these boundaries
have already been challenged by the advocacy of the slogan 'the personal is the
political' found in the women's movement. Just as feminist theory critiqued the
assignment of women's experience to only the private sphere, by the opening of
the twenty-first century it should also be clear that religion, too, will not accept a
position of assigned privatization. This means that both the appropriateness and
the utility of the classical distinction between 'public' and 'private' need to be
questioned.

A different way forward might be to distinguish between 'common' and 'particular' cultures. In this approach, by 'particular cultures' is meant the cultures
of families and ethnic and religious groups, which tend to be more fixed and
enduring (though also subject to the process of change due to their interaction
with the wider social environment). By contrast, the notion of 'common culture'
represents not the *external imposition* of a set of dominant values or of a religious
tradition, but an *emergent, pragmatic* and *corporate* product resulting from a
process of *negotiation* governed by agreed practices and procedures. It thus represents an understanding reached at any given point in time which has a reasonable
degree of stability but which, at the same time, is always subject to revision as part
of the flux of public and democratic dialogue in a plural society.

By taking seriously the contribution to a fluid 'common' sphere of the relatively more fixed 'particular' cultures (including religions), some of the potential
dangers that could arise from having a 'naked public square'[29] in a society in
which traditional symbolisms have been removed without a dominant replacement might be ameliorated. Rather, through common commitment to the process
of dialogue the stability of the 'particular' and the fluidity of the 'common' could
achieve some measure of balance.

Religions contribute at many levels to the wider society and cannot allow
themselves to become individualized and privatized without denying their fundamental self-understandings. The integrity of religions demands that they do not
betray their inheritance of making truth-claims that relate to the public sphere.
While a religion will often be *personal*, to attempt to make it *only* applicable
in a 'private' sphere is to undermine its integrity. Thus, in both conceptual and
operational terms, replacement of the 'public' and 'private' dichotomy, through
distinguishing instead between 'common' and 'particular' cultures, offers a more
inclusive way forward.

Simultaneously, the 'common' demands an approach to integration based on an
emerging shared culture, rooted in a mutual commitment to dialogue rather than
simply promoting an accommodation of minority streams to a majority one. Such
a 'common' culture needs to be seen as the product of negotiation between all the
'particulars' in which each of the 'particulars' is thereby affirmed in its integrity,
but no particular becomes the sole arbiter of the emergent 'common' culture.

At first sight, this might appear to be a merely semantic adjustment. But when
translated into the substance of social policy and practice, such an approach
demands and *facilitates* a change of perspective and approach to one in which the
'particularistic' vision of each religious tradition and community is acknowledged
in its holistic entirety. This, in turn, enables the 'particular' religions to be true
to themselves in terms of their wider than personal reference while not being
excluded from a contribution to, and participation in, the 'common' sphere. In
doing so, it thereby avoids the confinement of religion to the private sphere that
is so feared by supporters of the establishment as the likely consequence of any
purely negative move towards disestablishment within a paradigm framed by
'public' and 'private' sphere thinking.

5. *Context for Change: Policies, Laws and International Obligations*

a. *Religions, Civil Society and government*
The previous section set out and discussed a range of *principles* for change in relation to the social and political construction of 'public' and 'private', or 'common'
and 'particular'. In the present section, we move on to examining some key aspects
of the present *context* for change with regard, especially, to the frameworks for the
relationships between religion(s), state and society currently being created in the
context of government policy development, laws and international obligations.

In contrast to a secularist approach that allows space for religion only in a
so-called 'private' sphere, in recent years government and public bodies at local,
regional and national levels in England and the UK have increasingly been

recognizing the significance of religious groups as key players within 'civil society'. In comparison with other parts of the 'third', 'civic' or 'voluntary' sector, religious people, plant, organizations and communities (and especially those of the traditional religious traditions of England and the UK) are rich in resources.[30] Thus in a context where Governments of all kinds are more modest about what can be done centrally and recognize their need of partners, it has increasingly been recognized that to exclude religious organizations from partnership in public life limits the effectiveness of both service delivery and policy development. As the Local government Association's *Faith and Community* report puts it, 'Among the typical resources which faith groups and local interfaith structures can offer as part of the voluntary and community sector are local networks, leadership and management capacity, buildings with potential community use, and volunteers.'[31]

b. *Local Strategic Partnerships*

The consequence of this general shift in approach can be seen in the creation of Local Strategic Partnerships, originally initiated in 88 target areas, identified by the UK government as the most deprived local authority areas in terms of social and economic needs. Many such Partnerships – promoted by government guidance – now seek to involve religious groups as part of the voluntary and community sector with which they must work.

In Local Strategic Partnerships (LSPs), elected councillors and council officers engage with representatives of 'civil society' from the private, public and voluntary and community sectors in partnership work to create a vision for the area and to help co-ordinate and organize better services. While the elected authorities retain local political power, LSPs are necessarily involved in local strategic planning. As a consequence, bodies that participate in such Partnerships can have an impact on defining the strategies that then inform the criteria by which the Neighbourhood Renewal Fund is applied.

But the openings created for religious group participation bring new challenges. Because of other policy imperatives, LSPs try to proceed on the basis of equitable and transparent approaches to involvement in their work. Thus where the Board of an LSP has only one or two places available for religious representation, the question is highlighted as to how such representatives might be identified, both in terms of who these representatives should be and also what should be the mechanism for identifying such people.

Nevertheless, where Local Inter Faith Councils already exist that have sought to work with a 'three-dimensional' agenda rather than being concerned only with intra- and inter-faith matters, their role and strategic significance has been enhanced. Where inter-faith initiatives of this kind have not previously existed, the shift in social policy towards the inclusion of the contribution of religious groups gives a new impetus to their potential creation. As the guidance document on *Community Cohesion* puts it:

> The development of effective local interfaith structures, bringing together representatives of different faith communities in a local authority area, can provide a valuable framework both for promoting mutual understanding and co-operation

between them and as a mechanism for consultation by the local authority and other public bodies. Local authorities can provide valuable encouragement and support for the launching of initiatives of this kind in areas where they have yet to be established and also in helping to sustain existing local inter-faith structures.[32]

As part of these developments, in addition to its *Faith and Community* report, the Local government Association (in association with the Home Office, the Commission for Racial Equality and the Inter Faith Network for the UK) produced *Guidance on Community Cohesion*[33] in which the role of religious groups was addressed. Finally and most recently, the Inter Faith Network for the UK (in association with the Local government Association, the Home Office, and the Inner Cities' Religious Council of the Office of the Deputy Prime Minister) has produced some good practice guidelines for local authorities and religious groups entitled, *Partnership for the Common Good: Inter Faith Infrastructures and Local government.*[34]

c. *Regional Initiatives*

To some degree, a parallel process of development to that which has been happening within local authorities can also be discerned as *beginning* to take place at regional levels in England. As Regional Development Agencies and Regional Assemblies begin to assume a greater economic, social and political importance, similar dynamics of engagement can also be identified at regional level with regard to the participation of, and engagement with, religious groups. For example, the East of England Churches Network has called together the East of England Faith Leadership Conference through contacts with inter-faith groups and fora. There is also an East of England Faiths Agency that was set up by invitation to representatives from the inter-faith groups in the region.

In the East Midlands, a Faiths Forum for the East Midlands has been formed to work alongside the East Midlands Churches Assembly in providing a context for support and accountability in relation to the other than Christian faith representation on the East Midlands Assembly. In North-West England the North West Development Agency hosts a regional Faith Officer, while the Yorkshire and Humber Assembly has produced a guide to the region's faith communities under the significant title of *Religious Literacy.*[35]

At the same time, while, at the level of local authority areas, minority religious organizations often have reasonably well-developed structures and networks, by and large, and certainly in comparison with the well-established structures of the Christian Churches, their regional level profile and organization is, at best, very patchy. Even within the relatively well-developed Jewish organizational context, Jewish Representative Councils tend to operate at city rather than county levels. Among other minority traditions, there are city-level bodies such as the Birmingham Council of Gurdwaras. There are also a few emergent bodies at county level, such as the Federation of Muslim Organisations in Leicester, and the Lancashire Council of Mosques.

However, regional levels of organization parallel to that of Church of England dioceses, United Reformed Church provinces and the like do not yet exist. It may also be that such equivalents will never really be developed for some religions since it is arguable that regional infrastructures of these kinds can be developed and sustained only on the basis of a wider geographical presence (encompassing both rural as well as urban areas) and greater economic and human resources than are available to many minority groups. Thus, while effective channels of communication, representation and accountability are being created at the level of local authorities, at regional levels the asymmetry between the Christian Churches and other religious communities, groups and organizations makes this much more challenging.

d. *National Level*

At national level, although the presence and profile of other than Christian religious traditions, communities and groups is more organized than at regional levels, the issue of representation is still far from straightforward. Thus, for example, in Chapter 3 it was noted that within the Muslim community a range of different bodies aspiring to a national role have emerged over the years and the Muslim Council of Britain has only recently emerged as a body with a reasonably wide constituency of support. But it is not totally representative as, indeed, even Together Churches in Britain and Ireland (CTBI) is not fully representative in relation to the totality of the Christian community (since important sectors of Evangelical Christianity aligned with bodies such as the Evangelical Alliance are not within the CTBI).

Thus, the challenges and issues involved in developing appropriate religiously inclusive structures for engagement between religions, government and society at national and UK levels remain complex and multi-faceted. Nevertheless, as long ago as 1991, the Inter Faith Network for the UK's *Statement on Inter-Religious Relations* argued that, 'We need to find ways of more adequately reflecting both our common citizenship and our religious diversity in the framework of our national life.'[36] The outcomes of the recent Review of the government's Interface with Faith Communities, published in the report, *Working Together: Co-Operation Between government and Faith Communities*,[37] marked an important step along this road in terms of what has been achieved, but also in noting what still needs to be done. Thus, in the Foreword to *Working Together*, the Home Secretary, David Blunkett, acknowledges that, 'Previously the record of government engagement with faith communities has been patchy.'[38]

As Blunkett explained it, one of the main aims of the report was 'to draw on good practice that already exists, and the perspective of faith community representatives, to offer a set of recommendations that are designed to make these processes even more effective and widespread across government.'[39] There is nothing at present at the English or UK level that really resembles Lamont's proposal for creating a National Religious Council. But in recent years there have been a number of important initiatives which indicate that important contextual changes have been under way, both with a view to operationalizing a greater religious inclusivity in social policy developments, and also in reflecting greater diversity in symbolic occasions of national importance.

The early existence and work of the Inner Cities Religious Council (ICRC) has already been mentioned. The ICRC is chaired by a government minister (originally from the Department of the Environment) from the Office of the Deputy Prime Minister. It was designed to foster partnership between government and faith communities in tackling urban social and economic problems and it has stimulated a range of local and regional activities in relation to this agenda.[40] Through its work in relation to encouraging religious group participation in urban regeneration schemes, and by the input of its government Department sponsor into the debate on inclusion of a religious question in the 2001 Census, the ICRC made a significant contribution to changing the national inter-faith landscape.

Over a number of years there had already been wider involvement in a limited number of events of symbolic importance and also having a religious dimension. This included the Commonwealth Day Observance, held annually at Westminster Abbey, and the annual Week of Prayer for World Peace initiated in 1974 and observed each October. But during the last decade of the twentieth century and the first years of the twenty-first century, such inclusivity has accelerated, deepened and spread. Thus, in addition to the historic presence of Christian and Jewish faith leaders in the annual remembrance ceremony held at the Cenotaph for those killed in major conflicts, in the year 2000 Buddhist, Hindu, Muslim and Sikh representatives also took part for the first time. Towards the end of the 1990s, preparations for marking the new millennium were undertaken by the so-called Lambeth Group. This worked on a religiously inclusive basis to develop guidelines for religious involvement in observance of the new millennium and provided advice on the planning of a Faith Zone in the Millennium Dome in a way that reflected both the Christian inheritance of the UK and also its religious plurality.

To mark the Millennium, in January 2000, a special event known as the Shared Act of Reflection and Commitment by the Faith Communities of the UK took place in the House of Lords. This was, in fact, the first ever event of its kind hosted by a UK government and was arranged for the government by the Inter Faith Network. It highlighted values that were held in common by the religious traditions represented at it. Faith leaders from all the world religious traditions with significant communities in the UK contributed to the event, which was broadcast on national television. The Prime Minister spoke and the event concluded with leaders from all the religions present joining in a Shared Act of Commitment which formed its centrepiece and was also used in a number of subsequent Millennium events held in different parts of the UK. As a symbolic event, the Act of Commitment embodied both the *actual changes* that had occurred in the religious landscape of the UK and also the growing recognition of the *implications* of these changes.

Most recently, from within the government itself has come recognition of the need for greater co-ordination of its activities in relation to faith communities. Therefore, in 2003 the Religious Issues section of the Home Office Race Equality Unit was reconstituted into the Faith Communities Unit. As described in the report *Working Together*:

> The Faith Communities Unit is presently developing its outreach to faith communities so that the government better understands the impact of its policies on them, and is increasingly engaging with these communities to encourage their participation at all levels in civil society. It meets with representatives of faith communities, faith-based groups and undertakes visits to places of worship and

community projects. It also seeks to promote dialogue between faith communities.[41]

One of the first tasks of the Faith Communities Unit was to provide support to the
Review of the government's interface with faith communities that produced the
Working Together report. One of options discussed in this report was the potential
need for, and the possibility of, creating a national Faith Communities Forum to
act as a single point of reference and consultation across the machinery of government. In evaluating arguments for and against this option,[42] the conclusion was
reached that 'the case for a new Forum is not proven, that its establishment would
be premature and that more flexible arrangements are preferable'.[43]

At the same time, it was also stated that the review's Steering Group 'should,
when it reconvenes in 2005 to carry out the proposed evaluation of impact,
consider in the light of experience over the coming year whether any additional
machinery or forum is required at that juncture'.[44] Thus, perhaps significantly for
the overall argument of this book, the decision not to proceed with the creation of
a central Forum was not taken on the basis of *principle*, but as a current *pragmatic
evaluation* of the balance of developments and possibilities at the present time,
which would be subject to review in the light of further experience.

e. *Legal Instruments for a Religiously Plural Society*

Policy developments taking place at local, regional, national and UK levels and
explored in the previous section are key parts of the current 'context for change' in
terms of their relationship with the ways in which government and public bodies
are now beginning to go about consulting with and involving religious groups in
strategic partnerships for service delivery and policy implementation. However,
government policy can and does change. While this is also the case with the law,
and also even for the frameworks provided by international obligations, both are
generally more enduring than the policies of particular governments. Therefore in
considering the contemporary context for change it is important to take account
of legal developments of a national and international nature that have a bearing on
the relationships between religion(s), state and society in England and the UK.

As explored in Chapter 5, the end of the twentieth and the beginning of the
twenty-first century have seen a significant growth in concern about discrimination on the grounds of religion. This has been because of the nature of the reported
experiences among people of various religions, but also because, in contrast with
the position in Northern Ireland, until recently it has not been illegal to discriminate on the grounds of religion in England, Wales or Scotland.

As has already been noted, apart from Jews and Sikhs being viewed as 'religio-
ethnic' groups, and the possibility of matters of religion forming one dimension
of a matter of 'indirect discrimination', the scope of the Race Relations Act did
not permit it to be used to tackle religious discrimination. However, in 2003, and
as a response to a European Directive on discrimination in employment deriving
from the Amsterdam Treaty of the European Union, new legal rights were introduced with regard to employment, religion and belief.[45] These rights are set out in
the Employment Equality (Religion or Belief) Regulations, 2003, which, for the
first time in England, Wales and Scotland, make discrimination on these grounds

illegal. In the context of employment (and also vocational training – see below), the Regulations prohibit direct discrimination on grounds of religion or belief (except for genuine and determining occupational requirements) as well as indirect discrimination (except for objective justification that is both appropriate and necessary). They also prohibit harassment, as well as victimization on grounds of pursuit of issues relating to discrimination or harassment on the grounds of religion or belief. Because the remit of the Regulations includes vocational training, students as well as employees of further and higher education institutions[46] fall within the scope of the Regulations.

Although – in contrast to discrimination on the grounds of race, gender and disability – it is still not illegal to discriminate on the grounds of religion or belief in the provision of goods and services, the introduction of these Regulations marks a step forward in the evolution of legal frameworks appropriate to a religiously plural and secular society. In a key area of social life that has a central bearing on the life chances of individuals and communities these Regulations both codify expectations of behaviour and provide individuals with means of redress supported by the possibility of legal proceedings and sanctions.

It is also the case that beyond the legal requirements within which they must now operate, many organizations are also now positively trying to take religion into account in developing their equal opportunities policies and practice. To assist in this the Arbitration, Conciliation and Advisory Service (ACAS) has produced a guidance booklet on *Religion or Belief and the Workplace: A Guide for Employers and Employees.*[47] At the same time, although discrimination in employment was one of the main areas of concern identified in the Religious Discrimination in England and Wales Research Project, the media and education were the other two principal foci for concern. The Regulations do not apply to these except in relation to matters of employment and training. There are therefore still substantial areas of social life within which it is not, in England, Wales and Scotland, illegal to discriminate on the grounds of religion or belief. Thus there are many who are still pressing for the introduction of wider legislation on religious discrimination, either alongside other anti-discrimination legislation or as part of an overall Human Rights approach.

f. *International Obligation Frameworks for a Religiously Plural Society*
Since the accession of the UK to the European Union there is an increasing need to set debates about religion and equity in a wider setting. In particular, there is a need to take account of the impact of the economic, social and political project of the European Union. However, also important is the wider European context of the Council of Europe and, within this, of the provisions of the European Convention for the Protection of Human Rights and Fundamental Freedoms.

One aspect of recent legal developments relating to religious discrimination has been that they have been framed with regard to discrimination on the grounds of 'religion' but, also, of 'belief'. In other words, alongside the concern for the rights of religious believers has also been one for the position of secular people, atheists and agnostics who can also experience discrimination and unfair treatment as a consequence of their beliefs. Such even-handedness is, in fact, in itself required under the terms of the Human Rights Act, 1998 which, in this respect, also reflects the requirements of the European Convention for the Protection of Human Rights and Fundamental Freedoms (ECHR). In defending the freedom of 'thought, conscience and religion', the Convention does so while seeking to strike a balance between religious and secular perspectives that have been in historic tension in European history and societies.

In comparison with the European Union, the Council of Europe has historically been more concerned with issues of culture, having as a part of its mission the safeguarding and realization of the spiritual and moral values that are seen as being the common heritage of its member states. The work of the European Court of Human Rights is, of course, based upon Article 9 of the ECHR that guarantees freedom of thought, conscience and religion. This is, in turn, related to Article 18 of the Universal Declaration of Human Rights which enshrined the principle of religious freedom among the universal human rights. Article 9 of the ECHR states that: 'Everyone has the right to freedom of thought, conscience and religion; this right includes freedom to change his religion or belief and freedom, either alone or in community with others and in public or in private, to manifest his religion or belief, in worship, teaching, practice and observance.'

Article 9 rights are among a number of 'qualified rights' in the Convention, which means that these freedoms may, in some circumstances, be limited or denied by the state parties to the Convention. However, it is not the nature or validity of the beliefs themselves which may be subject to interference by states, but only their *manifestation*. The qualifying proviso to the rights proclaimed in Article 9 is that, 'Freedom to manifest one's religion or beliefs shall be subject only to such limitations as are prescribed by law and are necessary in a democratic society in the interests of public safety, for the protection of public order, health or morals, or for the protection of the rights or freedoms of others.' In addition, any such state interference must be 'necessary in a democratic society', 'prescribed by law', and proportionate to the legitimate aim being pursued by the state, the burden of proof to justify any restriction lies with the state concerned.

International law has often seemed distant from the practical day-to-day concerns of citizens and the UK does not have a written Constitution. However, the Human Rights Act, 1988, brought about a major innovation by enshrining the ECHR into domestic law. This meant that, for the first time, within domestic law there were now positive rights with regard to religion, including protections for freedom of thought, conscience and religion, the right to change these, and (subject to some limitations) the right to manifest them.

The limitation of the Act is that it relates only to 'public authorities'. However, it does allow individuals engaged in legal proceedings against public authorities in the domestic courts and tribunals, to rely on the rights guaranteed by the ECHR without having to fight a lengthy and costly process only in the European courts once all domestic avenues have been exhausted. Now it is the case that government and all bodies acting as 'public authorities' must examine the degree to which their current policies and practices, and their future proposals, are in conformity with the rights upheld by the Convention. Thus the Human Rights Act has created a significantly new legal context that will require fresh and systematic consideration of issues of how public policy and law impact upon religion across a wide range of areas.

By contrast with the Council of Europe, until recently the European Union has given comparatively little attention to issues arising from the relationships between religion(s), state and society in the European space. While its founders did have a wider vision than the purely economic, its institutions began with a project based primarily upon economic co-operation and convergence. Only more recently has this project's acknowledged sphere of competence become further enlarged in terms of the provisions of the Social Chapter and the Amsterdam Treaty.

Nevertheless, we have already seen how Article 13 of the latter itself gave the impetus to the UK necessarily to bring in legislation in relation to equality of treatment in the sphere of employment. In future years, it is likely that the impact of both the EU law and international obligations adopted within the framework of the Council of Europe will come to have an increasingly important influence upon the relationships between religion(s), state and society in England and the UK. As Jean-Paul Williame's essay on 'Churches, Laicité, and the European Union' has pointed out:

> explicit programmes to harmonise church–state relations in the various member states are not on the European Union's or the Council of Europe's agenda. These relations are so bound up with each nation's distinctive historical, cultural and religious traditions that any moves towards harmonisation in this area would be interpreted as a direct threat to countries' national identity.[48]

At the same time, Williame notes that, 'Nevertheless, the process of European integration does interfere with and call into question the relevant national traditions' and this is because 'Bodies such as the European Court of Human Rights and the European Parliament are gradually developing patterns of law from which church–state relations are by no means totally exempt.'

6. Kairos, *Crisis and Discernment*

a. *Context and Principles for Change*

The two previous sections of this chapter have attempted to sketch in some of the key frameworks for change provided by current developments in policy, law and international obligations. In addition to the overall changes in the religious landscape outlined in Chapter 3, these further contextual changes have created a significantly new environment within which impulses and principles based upon the Baptist vision could operate in relation to questions affecting the relationships between religion(s), the state and society.

b. *Inter-Faith Relations: From the 'Margins' to the 'Mainstream'*

Within these frameworks we have seen how, from beginnings in which inter-faith activities, initiatives and organizations were often seen as 'fringe' activities, they have now become much more 'mainstream' and 'central'. In this they are now a necessary part of the life and witness of all religious communities. At the same time, from the perspective of government and other public bodies, they have become increasingly important mechanisms in the interface with religious traditions and their communities.

As the Preamble to *Working Together* expresses it, 'There has been a sea-change in the consultation of faith communities.'[49] In relation to the overall argument of this book that the establishment of the Church of England needs to be replaced with more equitable alternatives, the developments outlined above contain significant signs of hope. In the current readiness of government and other public bodies (in contrast to the 'exclusionist' traditions of secularizing disestablishmentarianism) not only to countenance but also to *encourage* the contributions of religions to public life, new opportunities have been opened up for religious groups. Furthermore, in the tendency for such policy initiatives to embody a stance that aspires to deal with religions across the board, the development of mechanisms embodying more equity, inclusivity and participation is being facilitated.

Opportunities of this kind do also, however, bring with them new dangers and temptations of which it would be wise for religious groups to be aware. In summary, one might characterize such temptations in terms of the danger of a new 'multi-faith neo-Constantinianism'.

c. *New Opportunities and the Dangers of a 'Multi-Faith Constantinianism'*

The modern, liberal and democratic capitalist state, seeking to govern on the basis of consent, needs social partners for dialogue, consultation, policy implementation and service delivery. Depending upon one's political perspective, these are needed either for the proper and inclusive functioning of its ideals, or else in order to incorporate – and thus potentially to neutralize – potential sources of alternative values and perspectives. In the ambiguous nature of historical, social and political reality, it is probable that a mixture of such dynamics is at work.

At the beginning of the twenty-first century, religions in England and in the UK find themselves in a surprising position in comparison with their general experience of only a decade or so ago. Instead of having to press for their claims to participate, in many instances religions are now being actively wooed. Just as when the Christians of the Roman Empire suddenly found themselves in imperial favour, this raises a set of new questions about how best to relate to these new opportunities. From having to deal with a predominantly 'secularist' approach of exclusion of religion from the public sphere, religious groups are once again having to work out best how to be engaged with government and public bodies without becoming inappropriately co-opted.

Government wants religions as partners for practical and political purposes. Religions will offer partnership to government, public bodies and wider society because of the ultimate and the unconditioned that are at the wellsprings of their tradition and which they are concerned to express in history. But potentially dangerous distortions can occur if the ultimate is made subservient to the penultimate, or the unconditioned to the conditioned. In connection with this, government can have a tendency to want dialogue in ways that are 'safe', and/or are concerned with 'safe' topics. Thus, for example, government wants values for social cohesion, but what about values that disturb the status quo in the service of social justice? Or, even more sharply, in the service of economic justice? Finally, the agendas of national and local government are often shaped by the demographics of the populations with which they deal. Since the inclusion of the religious affiliation question in the 2001 Census and the publication of its results, there is likely to be an increasing trend towards the 'quantification' of religion in policy-making. Within this, however, there can be a tendency towards marginalization of smaller religious groups.

Thus, alongside taking up the opportunities presented by government-initiated and supported 'top-down', 'external' and 'managerial' mechanisms for the interface between the religions and public life, it remains important for 'bottom-up', 'internal' and 'community based' initiatives to continue to flourish. Keeping both kinds of initiative in creative tension is likely to be of benefit to both as well as to the overall framework for relationships between religions and public life. In connection with this, the *Working Together* report notes that the Government itself thinks that it is 'important that views advanced by faith-based organisations are authentic and independent and reflect the commitment of their members'.[50]

Thus, for example, at local level it is important that the vigour of the 'bottom-up' inter-faith initiatives that led to the original development and spread of local inter-faith initiatives, groups and councils is maintained. At national level, in parallel to the work of the ICRC, the Faith Based Regeneration Network, UK has been created as a 'bottom-up' or 'voluntary' network. This was established in 2001 'by and for practitioners who identify with faith traditions or who work with or for faith community organizations'. Its membership is drawn from individuals across nine faith traditions in the UK, adding Bahá'í, Buddhist, Jain and Zoroastrian involvement to that represented in the ICRC. Its vision is 'to enable faith based regeneration practitioners to learn and gain inspiration from each other, across the different faith traditions in the UK, and establish a common voice to communicate with government and other relevant authorities about regeneration and community development issues'.[51]

On a wider front, within the framework of affiliation offered by the Inter Faith Network for the UK there is now a new Faith Communities Consultative Forum. This consists of national faith representative bodies affiliated to the Network together with the Northern Ireland Inter Faith Forum, the Scottish Inter Faith Council and the Inter Faith Council for Wales. This Forum 'provides a forum for faith communities' representative bodies to address issues of common concern, both in the area of their mutual relations and in the area of faith and public life; and promotes the development of closer working relations between them.'[52] At the same time, this is not a National Religious Council since, for example, the Terms of Reference of the Forum preclude it from issuing statements on behalf of the faith communities collectively as well as from taking policy decisions on their behalf.

d. *If Something Can be Done Better, Why Not Try ...?*
Although the changes and development in policy, legal and constitutional context set out above are of considerable import and scope, it remains the case that the

Christian Churches in general, and the established Church of England in particular, still continue to have a position of privileged access to many English institutions and the British state. Thus, despite the potential dangers of a 'multi-faith neo-Constantinianism', it remains the case that the new ways forward need to be risked if church, state and society are to be able to move beyond the 'one-dimensional' establishment arrangements that are no longer adequate to the contemporary socio-religious reality.

During the nineteenth century, the ending of civil disabilities and the development of wider social and political participation did not occur as the product of an automatic evolutionary process based on social and economic developments. While these factors played their part, the removal of civil disabilities related to religious identity and belonging demanded organized struggle and campaigning on the part of those who were adversely affected by them. Reflecting on the developments towards religious equality that took place in the nineteenth century, the legal academic St John Robilliard commented that: 'The early story of the struggle for religious liberty' was, in the first instance, based upon groups who experienced discrimination and disadvantage, 'establishing an identity of their own'. And then, 'From the struggle for existence we pass to the struggle for equality.'[53]

In the contemporary context, such campaigning is generally absent, and critique from spokespeople of minority religious faiths is relatively muted. In the light of this one could concede that Tariq Modood has a valid point when he argues that 'it is dishonest to suggest that religious equality and the empowerment of new minority faiths *begins* with a critique of establishment'[54] (emphasis mine). One could even perhaps go further with Modood and acknowledge that contemporary establishment has something of a *minimal* nature and that, in terms of historical process and pragmatic outcomes, in recent years its effects have been more *benign* than *malign*. *However*, while one could concede to Modood that challenging the establishment of the Church of England is not a task of the *first importance* in creating a more inclusive society, such challenge is not a *luxury* and it *may* turn out to be of *considerable importance*. This is because, in speaking of the 'minimal nature' of the establishment, Modood and others have too easily avoided *structural* issues and, therefore, have underestimated the significance of establishment as a social, religious, cultural, legal and political nexus.

Finally, to concede either or both of the above points is not necessarily to concede that, from the perspective of equity, inclusivity and participation, the continued establishment of the Church of England represents the *best* or *most appropriate* way forward. The argument that 'if something ain't broke don't try to fix it' has only limited validity. There is also the argument that 'if something can be done *better and more equitably*, why remain satisfied with the way it is currently done'. Thus the degree to which equity, inclusivity and participation are embodied in the current arrangements for configuring the relationships between religion(s), state and society is something that continues to need interrogation.[55]

Equity is, of course, not necessarily concerned with mathematical equality – which it is anyway doubtful can be obtained in the social and political sphere – but with basic fairness. It is arguable that the inheritance of the nineteenth-century struggles over religious discrimination has bequeathed a reasonably equitable position with regard to the civic rights of *individual* believers, at least with regard to those who belong to the generally acknowledged world religious traditions.

However, such *equity* can exist alongside relatively minimal forms of *inclusivity* and *participation*. In addition, individual equity does not really address *corporate*, *institutional* and *structural* dimensions of religious disadvantage, especially in interactions with the organs of state and the mechanisms of the law, with wider public bodies and with key social institutions. It is for these reasons that it is still maintained that it is indeed a 'time for a change' to the establishment.

e. *'Unresolved Ambivalences' as 'Implicit* Kairos*'*

As the historian John Wolffe observes, reflecting on the present situation in the UK, 'The unresolved ambivalences of a multi-national and multi-religious Britain in which institutional links remain between the state and particular religious groups are both an intriguing historical paradox and a challenging contemporary dilemma.'[56] It is this 'historical paradox' and 'challenging contemporary dilemma' in the setting of the 'three-dimensional' socio-religious character of England and the UK that this book argues has indeed brought about a moment of *kairos* with regard to the future of establishment of the Church of England.

As noted earlier, Colin Brown explains the Greek word *kairos* as a word that: 'characterises a critical situation, one which demands a decision ... Positively it implies opportunity ... or advantage; negatively, danger'.[57] The recognition of a particular *chronos* as a *kairos* comes about through a conjoining of factors and trends in socio-economic change, theological reflection and institutional developments. It is *not* the argument of this book that disestablishment will come about as a *necessary* historical consequence of social developments in the sense of a deterministically inevitable future. However, it *is* the argument of this book that a *kairos* has arrived for the future of established religion in England. A *kairos* is a point in time in which alternative possibilities clarify themselves and a clear decision is called for.

From his Scottish perspective, and reflecting on what seemed to be a puzzling relative lack of challenge to the continuation of the establishment of the Church of England on the part of English Christians both within and outstide the Church of England, Lamont commented that, 'The answer may be that there has been no crisis to focus the issue ...'[58] At the time of writing there is no explicit crisis for establishment of a kind that would be recognized by all and which could, for example, occur in connection with a constitutional crisis linked with issues to do with succession to the Throne. Currently, the *kairos* which this book argues does exist for the establishment of the Church of England is of a more 'implicit' kind that requires *discernment* rather than of an 'explicit' kind that *forces* itself upon the attention of all. Nevertheless, this book has put forward both evidence and arguments that key factors and parameters that have a bearing upon the continuation of the establishment and the range of possibilities for replacing it are in the process of shifting.

f. *Anticipatory Discernment*

Although the institution of the Monarchy maintains a strong hold on the popular imagination, in the past decade it has been under considerable pressure from negative publicity and there has been growing discussion of the republican option. In particular, because of the intertwining of constitutional, legal, royal and religious dimensions, the public issues relating to the relationship between Prince Charles and Camilla Parker-Bowles still have the potential to develop into a wider constitutional crisis.[59] Were such a constitutional crisis to occur in connection with the succession, then establishment of the Church of England would be unlikely to escape the focus of wider public debate and controversy, and so a more explicit crisis for the establishment could come about more rapidly and unexpectedly than anyone at present anticipates is likely.

It is also possible that the question of establishment may eventually be forced as a result of political policy developments. Although New Labour in government has slowed the pace of the constitutional reforms it began (for example, with regard to reform of the House of Lords), the growing electoral strength of the Liberal Democrats means that constitutional questions with a bearing upon the establishment may yet re-emerge onto the political agenda outside of the context of a specific constitutional crisis.

But instead of the 'passive' and 'Stoic' stance of waiting for the possibility of such externally initiated changes, it is the argument of this book that it would be better if initiatives for change could be generated from *within* the Church of England itself *in dialogue* with other Christian Churches, religious groups, the wider civil society and the state. To undertake such initiatives now on the basis of *anticipatory discernment* of the implicit *kairos* of establishment that can already be identified would enable a proactivity of approach that would be unlikely to be possible in the instance of any more externally triggered move towards disestablishment.

7. *Towards a New Socio-Religious Contract*

a. *'Unpicking the Hidden Wiring': 'Risk Aversion' and the Necessity of Change*

By reason of the same argument that establishment is not irrelevant and remains an important nexus in the interrelationships between religion, state and society, in advocating proactive steps to unravel this 'hidden wiring' of the constitution, there is a clear need to proceed with caution. This is because it is possible that undoing one or more of the threads of the 'hidden wiring' may turn out to have unintended consequences. Due to the embedded nature of the configuration of religion(s), state and society, any consideration of the possibilities for change suffers from what Samuelson and Messick called 'risk aversion', even when the inequity and inefficiency of the current arrangements are recognized.

It is the element of *risk* that has been a key factor in why the need for a change to establishment has not, in practice, always been supported by those who might logically seem likely to offer their support. In any change there is always an element of risk. However, while the reality of the risk needs to be recognized, it is necessary to move towards change in a measured way based upon theological principle as well as a sober evaluation of contextual factors.

If a more politically and religiously adequate basic 'social metaphor' than that of the establishment is to be evolved, the 'three-dimensional' complexity of the society's cultural and religious diversity means that people and institutions of all religions and none need to contribute to a broad dialogue about possible alternatives. In his analysis of pluralism, Jonathan Sacks indicates that dialogue of this kind implies:

> significant restraints on all sides. For Christians it involves allowing other voices to share in the conversation. For people of other faiths it means coming to terms with a national culture. For secularists, it means acknowledging the force of commitments that must, to them, seem irrational. For everyone, it means settling for less than we would seek if everyone were like us, and searching for more than our merely sectional interests. In short, for the common good.[60]

Challenging the establishment cannot be a 'sufficient' project. This is because, as an essentially negative position, disestablishment in and of itself would not necessarily promote wider religious equity, inclusivity and participation. As Michael Ramsey's 'quo tendimus?' question reminds us, in thinking about establishment and disestablishment it is important not only to think about these two alternatives, but about the question of *direction*. In this context, just as the double-think of a 'one-dimensional' establishment approach needs blowing apart, so too do alternative 'one-dimensional' secularist paradigms and political presuppositions which tend to exclude religion(s) from public participation.

Thus, while establishment does need to be challenged, it will also not do, with Keith Porteous Wood, Executive Director of the National Secular Society, to argue that, 'Religion should be relegated to the realm of the private conscience, the home and the place of worship.' Porteous Wood argues that if this happened, then, 'in that way all sense of disadvantage would be removed',[61] but his use of the word '*relegated*' indicates what the practical outcome of such an approach would be. By contrast, it is the argument of this book that while the current form of the establishment needs to be argued against, religion(s) *should* have a rightful place in public life and should *not* be relegated to the private sphere. Indeed, as previously argued, in a society committed to finding a way forward for more adequately conceptualizing and actualizing structures enabling the full contribution and participation of *all* its members, it is likely that the classical modernist distinctions between 'public' and 'private' domains will need at least to be modified.

b. *No Backdoor Route to 'Re-Religionizing'*
At the same time, it is also important for equity, inclusivity and participation that any such developments do take full account of the rights of atheists, agnostics and humanists. The report of the Council of Europe's consultants noted 'a suspicion in some quarters that some historically established churches may be seeking to exploit the presence of the new religions and their desires to regain some of the territory lost to the secular state and society'.[62]

The historic struggles for the rights to question and not to believe are important social gains. From the perspective of a theology informed by the Baptist vision, they are arguably, though perhaps ironically, also *religious* gains. This is because they are a part of the principle of religious identity being something that is freely affirmed, owned or rejected rather than being merely a product of history and convention. Furthermore, secular perspectives have, historically, also brought important critiques to bear upon religion. While affirming the principle articulated by the Inter Faith Network that 'Society is impoverished when religious perspectives on life are excluded or marginalized'[63], as I have argued elsewhere, in European history there is also ample evidence that, 'Religions can become dangerous when secular perspectives on life are excluded or marginalized.'[64]

Pragmatically, too, if those who affirm a religious identity wish to have their struggle against discrimination on the grounds of religion taken seriously as part of an agenda to create a pluralist society rather than as part of a nostalgic campaign to re-establish a society ruled by religious conformity, then all people – whether majority Christians, minority Muslims, Hindus, Sikhs and others, and atheists, agnostics and humanists – will need to recognize the benefits that can accrue to all in tackling religious inequity.

Finally, it is, of course, critical that that the Christian Churches, and in particular the Church of England, should become fully engaged in re-evaluating the present configuration of religion(s), state and society. As has been noted, the Church of England's historic position on establishment tends to have been governed rather more by pragmatic concerns than by principled theological and ecclesiological positions. As previously noted, it is perhaps this very pragmatism which might allow for a free reconsideration of its own role as argued for by Anglicans opposed to the establishment.

However, even if pragmatism continues to play a significant role in any Anglican re-evaluation of establishment, it is unlikely that any willing change could take place without significant theological and ecclesiological debate. It is within such theological debate that Free Church, and specifically Baptist, Christian perspectives (modified by the Anglican vision of commitment to the public sphere as a corrective to the Free Church temptation of sectarian withdrawal) bring theologically informed resources and impulses to bear.

On the basis of taking into account all three dimensions of our contemporary 'three-dimensional' socio-religious reality, there is a need to dare to imagine and to construct what might be more equitable ways to engage the participation of all. A combination of such initiatives legitimated by the state and public bodies alongside the continued development of local inter-faith councils and inter-faith initiatives emerging from within a vigorous wider voluntary sector, offers the most constructive way forward.

c. *'Worked Parallel Alternatives'*

Discussion in the previous chapter of Lamont's proposal for the creation of a National Religious Council concluded that this would be premature. The *Working Together* report also concluded this – at least for the immediate future – with regard to the possible creation of a central Faith Communities Forum. However, in relation to the engagement of government departments with faith communities, the *Working Together* report also clearly stated that, 'While the Church of England is the Established Church in England, it should not be accorded privileged status in such consultations.'[65]

In the light of this, it is important for multi-faith and religious–secular 'worked parallel alternatives' to be evolved and negotiated at every level of society. In the first instance, such alternatives would be *complementary* to the establishment and exist in *parallel* to it as, initially, *additional* ways for structuring the relationships between religion(s), state and society. But by their very existence and operation these 'parallel worked alternatives' could *gradually*, but also *fundamentally* and *structurally*, *challenge* the existing structures of the establishment while, in the interim, relationally working *with* them in order to bring change in an evolutionary and organic way.

Eventually, as the range and scope of such initiatives both *broadens* and *deepens* they could, *in practice*, begin to establish their credentials in terms of both legitimacy and utility. Then, in due course, it is at least possible that the *benefits* of such structures might begin to seem to outweigh the *risks* involved for all the stakeholders in religion(s), the wider society and government. This could, in turn, enable all parties to move towards the possibility of negotiating the general acceptance of such *alternative* ways for symbolizing, structuring and operationalizing the relationships between religion(s), state and society.

The construction of such multi-layered structures would be consistent with the evolutionary tendency of constitutional change in England and the UK. As such, it could lead to a position where the ending of establishment comes to be seen as a natural development on the basis of the further development of real and practically functioning – albeit untidy and ambiguous – alternatives. In this, stakeholders would no longer be faced with a choice between a currently known establishment and a set of purely theoretical alternatives. Within such an approach, it is possible that, on a practical level, at least some 'intermediate goals' for convergence might be found with the increasing numbers of those within the Church of England who advocate an 'extended establishment'.

In the meantime, should any more dramatic unravelling of the current constitutional nexus take place through a constitutionally and politically explicit type of *kairos* that could occur in connection with the death of the present monarch, then developments suggested here would offer some precedent and experience to draw upon. This would ameliorate the dangers of a purely state imposed and probably secularizing disestablishment of the kind feared by advocates and defenders of the establishment. In the meantime, the negotiated evolution of both 'emergent' and 'managerial' forms of multi-faith and secular–religious 'parallel worked' structures could at least act as *signposts* for the possibility of alternative ways forward.

Whether the present 'three-dimensional' reality is welcomed or feared, it must be recognized that all three of these dimensions are now an inescapable part of the contemporary social and political fabric of England and the UK. Reconfiguration of an inherited pattern in the relationships between religion(s), state(s) and society that has both deep historical roots and extensive contemporary ramifications is not straightforward. Nor is it without danger, for the Church of England itself, for the Christian Churches more generally, for other religions, and for the wider society and state. However, it is the conviction and argument of this book that impulses derived from Baptist tradition can contribute resources that could facilitate a collective recognition that the present might indeed be 'time for a change'.

These resources enable the kind of combination of pragmatism and principle that is necessary for creating the theological and political courage needed to initiate a debate about such change. They can also facilitate the kind of practical steps that are required for moving in the direction of a more equitable and inclusive pattern for the future. In doing so, they can empower religious groups to be *active initiators* in the reconfiguration of the relationships between religion(s), state and society. They can also facilitate new *stances* being taken in a way that is informed by theological principles, perspectives and impulses, rather than leaving change to be shaped primarily by a more passive and reactive pragmatism driven by present or future external *circum*stances alone.

8. *Footnotes for the Future*

In considering the relationships between religion(s), state and society in England and the UK, the words of Proverbs that, 'Where there is no vision, the people perish'[66] serve as a timely reminder of the importance of seizing *kairos* moments rather than letting them pass by. At the same time, it is the case that *Kairos* moments bring danger as well as opportunity. One reaction to the transformations that have so far occurred in the social, historical and institutional realities would be to retreat into patterns of life and thought that are no longer adequate to the contemporary 'three-dimensional' socio-religious reality.

However, while such patterns may seem to offer security, the possibility of maintaining them is, in reality, an illusion and can also be an expression of moral irresponsibility which, under certain conditions, could even contain the seeds of religious bigotry and conflict. In considering both the inheritance of the establishment and the implications of what might replace it, the words of Jesus provide a test that is both politically pragmatic and morally ultimate. The evaluative yardstick of 'By their fruits you will know them'[67] needs to be applied carefully and rigorously both to inherited structures and to imagined and developing new ones alike.

Finally, for Christian Church and inter-religious initiatives, in all their dealings with the governmental 'powers that be', the injunction of Jesus to be 'Be wise as serpents and as gentle as doves'[68] stands as a reminder of the *Spannungsfeld* (field of tension) within which Christians are called to live when dealing with the wider society. Throughout history there have been many different ways in which Christians have sought to live out their personal and corporate vocation. In replacing one model with another, it is important that both of the poles of the tension between the prophetic and the pastoral identities of the Church are maintained so that the Church can fulfil its responsibility to live in 'critical solidarity' with the wider world.

Bearing in mind these scriptural 'warnings' and drawing upon the ecumenically transformed contribution of Baptist theology and ecclesiology there is no reason to fear the challenges involved in seeking a more equitable, inclusive and participatory way for reconfiguring the relationships between religion(s), state and society. Rather, when approached with a confidence informed by facilitative and equitable theological and ecclesiological resources, the undoubted difficulties entailed in finding a new way forward need not be experienced as a *set of problems to be solved* so much as a *liberative opportunity to be celebrated and explored.*

Notes

1 See T. Modood (ed.), *Church, State and Religious Minorities* (London: Policy Studies Institute, 1997).

2 See K. Cracknell, 'Within God's Gracious Purposes: Inter-Faith Dialogue in Britain', *Ecumenical Review* 37/4 (1985), pp. 452–61 (453).

3 W. M. Watt, *Truth in the Religions*, pp. 18–19.

4 See R. Gill, *The Social Context of Theology*, 1975.

5 W. Cantwell Smith, *The Meaning and End of Religion.*

6 T. Ling, 'Communalism and the Social Structure of Religion', in J. Hick (ed.), *Truth and Dialogue: The Relationship Between World Religions* (London: Sheldon Press, 1974), pp. 59–76 (72).

7 W. M. Watt, *Truth in the Religions*, p. 9.

8 K. Cragg, 'Christian–Muslim Dialogue', *Anglican Theological Review* 57 (1975), pp. 109–20 (117).

9 N. Smart, 'The Anglican Contribution to the Dialogue of Religions', *Theology* 70 (1967), pp. 302–9.

10 C. Norwood, 'The Religion the World Needs', *MC* 35/3 (1945), pp. 102–13 (105).

11 M. Ipgrave, '*Fidei Defensor* Revisited: Church and State in a Religiously Plural Society', in N. Ghanea (ed.), *The Challenge of Religious Discrimination at the Dawn of the New Millennium* (Leiden: Martinus Nijhoff, 2003), pp. 207–22. Unusually for pieces on establishment coming from an Anglican provenance, this does also take some account of the Baptist inheritance in matters of religious freedom and the nature of religious belief.

12 G. Carey, 'Holding Together: Church and Nation in the Twenty-First Century' (www. archbishopofcanterbury.org).

13 J. Beckford and S. Gilliat, *Religion in Prison.*

14 An example of British National Party electoral literature entitled 'Winning for White Oldham, Winning for You', and which concludes with the words '*Nick Griffin and the BNP* or the pro-Muslim Labour party? Make up your own mind *and think of your family as you vote British National Party*', can be found in Commission on British Muslims and Islamophobia, *Addressing the Challenge of Islamophobia: Progress Report, 1999–2001* (London: Commission on British Muslims and Islamophobia, 2001).

15 C. Buchanan, *Cut the Connection*, p. 103.

16 E. Troeltsch, *The Social Teaching of the Christian Churches* (2 vols.; London: George Allen & Unwin, 1931).

17 T. Ling, 'Communalism and the Social Structure of Religion', p. 71.

18 E. Troeltsch, *The Social Teaching of the Christian Churches*, 1912, p. 656.

19 J. Moltmann, *The Open Church: Invitation to a Messianic Lifestyle* (London: SCM Press, 1978), p. 117.

20 K. Clements, 'Moltmann on the Congregation', *BQ* 28/3 (1979–80), pp. 101–9 (106).

21 See P. Chambers, 'Religion, Identity and Change in Contemporary Wales', in S. Coleman and P. Collins (eds.), *Religion, Identity and Change*, (Aldershot: Ashgate, 2004), pp. 69–83.

22 A. Toynbee, *An Historian's Approach to Religion* (London: Oxford University Press, 1956), p. 139.

23 J. Norman, 'The Relevance and Vitality of the Sect-Idea'.

24 T. Peck, 'Grace and Law: Baptists and Religious Freedom: Historical Antecedents and Contemporary Context', *BQ* 29/7 (2002), pp. 315–27 (324).

25 E. G. Ernst, 'A Concept of Christian Evangelism in a Secular Society'.

26 S. Murray, *Post-Christendom: Church and Mission in a Strange New World*, pp. 188–200.

27 N. Wright, *Disavowing Constantine.*

28   As explained in footnote 12 in the Acknowledgements section of this volume, an earlier version of these propositions was initially developed with regard to the relationships between Christians, Jews and Muslims in Europe. Later, they were developed for religion(s), state(s) and society in Europe more generally. In the present text, they are slightly modified from earlier published versions and have additional summary headings for each principle. Bibliographical details and acknowledgements of the earlier published versions are found in this volume's Acknowledgements.

29   R. Neuhaus, *The Naked Public Square: Religion and Democracy in American Public Life* (Grand Rapids: Eerdmans, 1984).

30   See G. Smith, *Faith in the Voluntary Sector: A Common or Distinctive Experience of Religious Organisations* (Working Papers in Applied Social Research, No. 25; Manchester: Department of Sociology, University of Manchester, 2003); D. Finneron and A. Dinham, *Building on Faith: Faith Buildings in Neighbourhood Renewal* (London: Church Urban Fund, n.d.); and T. Reith, *Releasing the Resources of the Faith Sector: A Faithworks Report* (London: Faithworks, 2003).

31   Local government Association, *Faith and Community: A Good Practice Guide,* paragraph 3.4, p. 7.

32   T. Cantle and the Community Cohesion Team, *Community Cohesion: A Report of the Independent Review Team Chaired by Ted Cantle*, paragraph 2.1, p. 3.

33   ˙Local government Association, in association with the Home Office, the Commission for Racial Equality and the Inter Faith Network for the UK, *Guidance on Community Cohesion* (London: Local government Association, 2002).

34   Inter Faith Network for the UK (in association with the Local government Association, the Home Office, and the Inner Cities' Religious Council of the Office of the Deputy Prime Minister) *Partnership for the Common Good: Inter Faith Infrastructures and Local government* (London: Inter Faith Network for the UK, 2003).

35   Yorkshire and Humber Assembly, *Religious Literacy: A Practical Guide to the Region's Faith Communities* (Wakefield: Yorkshire and Humber Assembly, 2002).

36   Inter Faith Network for the UK, *Statement on Inter-Religious Relations*, paragraph 3.

37   Home Office Faith Communities Unit, *Working Together: Co-Operation Between government and Faith Communities. Recommendations of the Steering Group Reviewing Patterns of Engagement Between government and Faith Communities in England* (London: Faith Communities Unit, Home Office, February 2004).

38   Home Office Faith Communities Unit, *Working Together*, Foreword.

39   Home Office Faith Communities Unit, *Working Together*, p. 8.

40   J. Lewis and E. Randolph-Horn, *Faiths, Hope and Participation: Celebrating Faith Groups' Role in Neighbourhood Renewal* (London: New Economics Foundation and Church Urban Fund, 2001).

41   Home Office Faith Communities Unit, *Working Together*, p. 90.

42   Home Office Faith Communities Unit, *Working Together*, p. 80.

43   Home Office Faith Communities Unit, *Working Together*, p. 81.

44   Home Office Faith Communities Unit, *Working Together*, p. 81.

45   In line with the provisions of the European Convention on Human Rights and Fundamental Freedoms, the Regulations relate to both 'religion' (as generally understood) and 'belief' (meaning any settled philosophical system or orientation) governing an individual's life.

46   The Equality Challenge Unit has therefore produced *Implementing the New Regulations Against Discrimination: Practical Guidance* (London: Equality Challenge Unit, 2003) as guidance for managers and institutions.

47   Arbitration, Conciliation and Advisory Service, *Religion or Belief and the Workplace: A Guide for Employers and Employees* (London: ACAS, 2003).

48   J.-P. Williame, 'Churches, Laïcité, and the European Union', in *Pluralismes Religieux et Laïcité dans L'Union Européen* (Brussels: Free University of Brussels, 1994), quoted in unofficial translation in the report of the Council of Europe Group of Consultants on Religious Aspects of Equality of Opportunities for Immigrants, *Study*, paragraph 2.2.3.

49 Home Office Faith Communities Unit, *Working Together*, p. 8.

50 Home Office Faith Communities Unit, *Working Together*, p. 79.

51 R. Ahmed, D. Finneron and H. Singh, *Tools for Regeneration: A Holistic Approach for Faith Communities* (London: Faith Based Regeneration Network, UK, 2004), p. 71.

52 Home Office Faith Communities Unit, *Working Together*, p. 75.

53 St John Robilliard, *Religion and the Law*, p. ix.

54 T. Modood, 'Minorities, Faith and Citizenship', p. 59.

55 See P. Weller, 'Equity, Inclusivity and Participation in a Plural Society', pp. 53–67.

56 J. Wolffe ' "And There's Another Country … " ', p. 118.

57 C. Brown (ed.), *The New International Dictionary of New Testament Theology*, vol. 3, p. 833.

58 S. Lamont, *Church and State*, p. 190.

59 See G. Austin, *Affairs of State: Leadership, Religion and Society* (London: Hodder, 1995).

60 J. Sacks, *The Persistence of Faith*, p. 68.

61 K. Porteous Wood, in T. Sulaiman, 'Religion and the State – The Observer Debate on Religion and the State', *The Observer*, 12.8.2001.

62 Inter Faith Network for the United Kingdom, *Statement on Inter-Religious Relations*, paragraph 2.2.2.

63 Inter Faith Network for the United Kingdom, *Statement on Inter-Religious Relations* (London: Inter Faith Network for the United Kingdom, 1991), para 4.

64 P. Weller, 'Inter-Faith Roots and Shoots', p. 52.

65 Home Office Faith Communities Unit, *Working Together*, p. 24.

66 Proverbs 29.18.

67 Matthew 7.20.

68 Matthew 10.16.

BIBLIOGRAPHY

Abrams, M., D. Gerard and N. Timms (eds.), *Values and Social Change in Britain* (Basingstoke: Macmillan, 1985).

Ahmed, R., D. Finneron and H. Singh, *Tools for Regeneration: A Holistic Approach for Faith Communities* (London: Faith Based Regeneration Network, 2004).

Ahsan, M., and A. Kidwai (eds.), *Sacrilege Versus Civility: Muslim Perspectives on the Salman Rushdie Affair* (Leicester: Islamic Foundation, 1991).

Allen, C., and J. Nielsen, *Summary Report on Islamophobia in the EU after 11 September 2001* (Vienna: European Monitoring Centre on Racism and Xenophobia, May 2002).

Almond, P., *The British Discovery of Buddhism* (Cambridge: Cambridge University Press, 1988).

Anderson, B., *Imagined Communities: Reflections on the Origin and Spread of Nationalism* (London: Verso, 1983).

Andrews, A., 'The Concept of Sect and Denomination in Islam', *Religion Today* 9/2 (1994), pp. 6–10.

Angus, J., *Christian Churches: The Noblest Form of Social Life; the Representative of Christ on Earth; the Dwelling Place of the Holy Spirit* (London: Ward & Co., 1862).

—— *The Voluntary System: A Prize Essay in Reply to the Lectures of Dr. Chalmers on Church Establishments* (London: Jackson & Walford, 1839).

Ansari, H., *Muslims in Britain* (London: Minority Rights Group International, 2002).

Antes, P., 'Islam in Europe', in S. Gill, G. D'Costa and U. King (eds.), *Religion in Europe: Contemporary Perspectives* (Kampen: Kok Pharos, 1994), pp. 46–67.

Appignanesi, L., and S. Maitland (eds.), *The Rushdie File* (London: Fourth Estate, 1989).

Arbitration, Conciliation and Advisory Service (ACAS), *Religion or Belief and the Workplace: A Guide for Employers and Employees* (London: Arbitration, Conciliation and Advisory Service, 2003).

Archbishop's Commission on Urban Priority Areas, *Faith in the City: A Call for Action by Church and Nation – The Report of the Archbishop of Canterbury's Commission on Urban Priority Areas* (London: Church House, 1985).

Ashford, S., and N. Timms, *What Europe Thinks: A Study of Western European Values* (Aldershot: Dartmouth, 1992).

Asponwall, B.,'The Scottish Religious Identity in the Atlantic World, 1888–1914', in S. Mews (ed.), *Studies in Church History: Religion and National Identity* (Oxford: Blackwell, 1982), pp. 505–18.

Austin, G., *Affairs of State: Leadership, Religion and Society* (London: Hodder, 1995).

Avis, P. (ed.), *Public Faith? The State of Religious Belief and Practice in Britain* (London: SPCK, 2003).

Badawi, Z., *Islam in Britain* (London: Ta Ha Publishers, 1981).

Badham, P. (ed.), *Religion, State and Society in Modern Britain* (Lampeter: Edwin Mellen Press, 1989).

— 'The Contribution of Religion to the Conflict in Northern Ireland', in D. Cohn-Sherbok (ed.), *The Canterbury Papers: Essays on Religion and Society* (London: Bellew, 1990), pp. 119–28.

Bahá'í International Community, *The Bahá'ís: A Profile of the Bahá'í Faith and its Worldwide Community* (New York: Bahá'í International Community, 1992).

Bailey, E., 'The Implicit Religion of Contemporary Society: An Orientation and Plea for its Study', *Religion* 2 (1983), pp. 69–83.

— 'The Folk Religion of the English People', in P. Badham (ed.), *Religion, State and Society in Modern Britain* (Lampeter: Edwin Mellen Press, 1989), pp. 145–58.

Bainton, M. (ed.), *Anthropological Approaches to the Study of Religion* (London: Tavistock, 1990).

Baker, D., 'Turbulent Priests: Christian Opposition to the Conservative Government since 1979', *Political Quarterly* 52 (1991), pp. 90–105.

Ballard, R., *Desh Pardesh: The South Asian Presence in Britain*, (London: Hurst & Co., 1994).

— 'The Growth and Changing Character of the Sikh Presence in Britain', in H. Coward, J. Hinnells, and R. Williams (eds.), *The South Asian Religious Diaspora in Britain, Canada and the United States* (New York: State University of New York Press, 2000), pp. 127–44.

Baptist World Alliance, *Together in Christ: Official Report of the Sixteenth Congress, Seoul, Korea, August 14th–19th* (McLean: Baptist World Alliance, 1990).

Barker, D., L. Halman and A. Vloet, *The European Values Study 1981–1990* (Aberdeen: Gordon Cook Foundation, 1993).

Barker, E., *New Religious Movements: A Perspective for Understanding Society* (Lampeter: Edwin Mellen Press, 1982).

— *New Religious Movements: A Practical Introduction* (London: HMSO, 1990).

— 'New Religious Movements in Europe', in S. Gill, G. D'Costa and U. King (eds.), *Religion in Europe: Contemporary Perspectives* (Kampen: Kok Pharos, 1994), pp. 120–40.

Barker, E., J. Beckford and K. Dobbelaere (eds.), *Secularisation, Rationalism and Sectarianism* (Oxford: Oxford University Press, 1993).

Barley, L.M., C. Field, B. Kosmin and J. Nielsen, *Religion* (Reviews of United Kingdom Statistical Sources, 20; Oxford: Pergamon Press, 1987).

Barlow, R., *Citizenship and Conscience: A Study of the Theory and Practice of Religious Toleration in England During the Eighteenth Century* (Philadelphia: University of Pennsylvania Press, 1962).

Barot, R. (ed.), *Religion and Ethnicity: Minorities and Social Change in the Metropolis* (Kampen: Kok Pharos, 1993).

Basford, L., and O. Slevin (eds.), *The Theory and Practice of Nursing: An Integrated Approach to Caring Practice* (Cheltenham: Nelson Thornes, 2003).

Batchelor, S., *The Awakening of the West: The Encounter of Buddhism and Western Culture* (London: Aquarian Press, 1994).

Bebbington, D., 'The Life of Baptist Noel: Its Setting and Significance', *BQ* 24/8 (1971–2), pp. 389–411.

— *The Nonconformist Conscience: Chapel and Politics, 1870–1914* (London: George Allen & Unwin, 1982).

Beckford, J., and S. Gilliat, *The Church of England and Other Faiths in a Multi-Faith Society* (2 vols.; Coventry: Department of Sociology, University of Warwick, 1996).

— *The Church of England and Other Faiths in a Multi-Faith Society: Summary Report* (Coventry: Department of Sociology, University of Warwick, 1996).

— *Religion in Prison: Equal Rites in a Multi-Faith Society* (Cambridge: Cambridge University Press, 1998).

Bell, P., *Disestablishment in Ireland and Wales* (London: SPCK, 1969).

Bender, H., 'The Anabaptists and Religious Liberty in the 16th Century', *MQR* 29/2 (1955), pp. 83–100.

Benn, T., 'Religion, War and the Gulf', in D. Cohn-Sherbok and D. McClellan (eds.), *Religion in Public Life* (London: Macmillan, 1992), pp. 29–37.

Berger, P., *The Social Reality of Religion: Elements of a Sociological Theory of Religion* (London: Faber & Faber, 1967).

Bhachu, P., *Twice Migrants: East African Sikh Settlers in Britain* (London: Tavistock, 1985).

Bisset, P., *The Kirk and Her Scotland* (Edinburgh: Handsel, 1986).

— 'Kirk and Society in Modern Scotland', in P. Badham (ed.), *Religion, State and Society in Britain* (Lampeter: Edwin Mellen Press, 1989), pp. 51–65.

Blackwood, C., *The Storming of the Antichrist, in His Two Last and Strongest Garrisons: of Compulsion of Conscience and Infants' Baptism* (London, 1644).

Board for Social Responsibility, *The Church and the Bomb* (London: Hodder & Stoughton, 1982).

Bonhoeffer, D., *Letters and Papers From Prison* (London: SCM Press, enlarged edition, 1971).

Bouquet, A., *The Christian Faith and Non-Christian Religions* (London: James Nisbet & Co., 1958).

Bowen, D. (ed.), *Hinduism in England* (Bradford: Faculty of Contemporary Studies, Bradford College, 1981).

Brackney, W., *Voluntarism: The Dynamic Principle of the Free Church* (Wolfville: Acadia University, 1992).

— *Christian Voluntarism: Theology and Praxis* (Grand Rapids: Eerdmans, 1997).

Bradford, W., *History of the Plymouth Plantation, 1620–1674* (W. C. Ford (ed.); 2 vols; Boston: Massachusetts Historical Society, 1912).

Bradley, I., *God Save the Queen: The Spiritual Dimensions of Monarchy* (London: Darton, Longman & Todd, 2002).

Braybrooke, M., *Inter-Faith Organisations, 1893–1979: An Historical Directory* (Lampeter: Edwin Mellen Press, 1980).
— *Pilgrimage of Hope: One Hundred Years of Global Interfaith Dialogue* (London: SCM Press, 1992).
— *Faith in a Global Age: The Interfaith Movement's Offer of Hope to a World in Agony: A Personal Perspective* (Oxford: Braybrooke Press, 1995).
Brierley, P., *'Christian' England: What the English Church Census Reveals* (London: MARC Europe, 1991).
Brierley, P. (ed.), *UK Christian Handbook: Religious Trends No. 4, 2003/2004* (London: Christian Research, 2004).
British Council of Churches, *The New Black Presence in Britain: A Christian Scrutiny* (London: British Council of Churches, 1978).
Brown, C. (Callum), *A Social History of Religion in Scotland Since 1730* (London: Methuen, 1987).
— *The Death of Christian Britain: Understanding Secularisation 1880–2001* (London: Routledge, 2001).
Brown, C. (Colin) (ed.), *The New International Dictionary of New Testament Theology* (3 vols.; Exeter: Paternoster Press, 1978).
Brown, D., 'The Radical Reformation: Then and Now', *MQR* 45/3 (1971), pp. 250–63.
Bruce, S., *God Save Ulster: The Religion and Politics of Paisleyism* (Oxford: Oxford University Press, 1986).
— *Religion and Modernisation: Sociologists and Historians Debate the Secularisation Thesis* (Oxford: Oxford University Press, 1992).
— *Religion in Modern Britain* (Oxford: Oxford University Press, 1995)
Buchanan, C., *Cut the Connection: Disestablishment and the Church of England* (London: Darton, Longman & Todd, 1994).
Burghart, R. (ed.), *Hinduism in Great Britain: The Perpetuation of Religion in an Alien Cultural Milieu* (London: Tavistock, 1987).
Busher, L., *Religion's Peace: Or a Plea for Liberty of Conscience*, in E. Underhill (ed.), *Tracts on the Liberty of Conscience and Persecution, 1614–1667* (London: Hanserd Knollys Society, 1846), pp. 1–81.
Cable, V., *The World's New Fissures: Identities in Crisis* (London: Demos, 1994).
Campbell, J., 'The Jewish Community in Britain', in S. Gilley and W. Sheils (eds.), *A History of Religion in Britain: Belief and Practice from Pre-Roman Times to the Present* (Oxford: Blackwell, 1994), pp. 427–48.
Cantle, T., and the Community Cohesion Team, *Community Cohesion: A Report of the Independent Review Team Chaired by Ted Cantle* (London: Home Office, 2001).
Cantwell Smith, W., *The Meaning and End of Religion* (London: SPCK, 1978).
Carey, G., 'A Church for the Nation', *This Church of England* (1994), pp. 4–5.
Carey, S., 'The Hare Krishna Movement and Hindus in Britain', *New Community* 10/3 (1983), pp. 477–86.
Cecil Commission, *Report of the Archbishops' Commission on the Relations Between Church and State* (London: Press and Publications Board, 1935).
Census of Great Britain 1851 Religious Worship. England and Wales (London: George

E. Eyre and William Spottiswoode, 1853), reprinted in *British Parliamentary Papers, Population 10* (Shannon, Ireland: Irish University Press, 1970).

Chadwick Commission, *Church and State* (London: Central Information Office, 1970).

Chambers, P., 'Religion, Identity and Change in Contemporary Wales', in S. Coleman and P. Collins (eds.), *Religion, Identity and Change* (Aldershot: Ashgate, 2004), pp. 69–83.

Christians Against Racism and Fascism, *Church Schools in a Multi-Faith Society* (Christians Against Racism and Fascism, 1982).

Christie, C., 'The Rope of God: Muslim Minorities in the West and Britain', *NC* 17/3 (1990), pp. 457–66.

Chryssides, G., *The Advent of Sun Myung Moon: The Origins, Beliefs and Practices of the Unification Church* (Basingstoke: Macmillan, 1991).

Clements, K., 'Moltmann on the Congregation', *BQ* 28/3 (1979–80), pp. 101–9.

Clouts, F., 'Thomas Helwys and His Book, The Mistery of Iniquity', *RevExp* 41 (1944), pp. 372–87.

Cohen, S., *That's Funny, You Don't Look Anti-Semitic: An Anti-Racist Analysis of Left Anti-Semitism* (Leeds: Beyond the Pale Collective, 1984).

Cohn-Sherbok, D. (ed.), *The Salman Rushdie Controversy in Inter-Religious Perspective* (Lampeter: Edwin Mellen Press, 1990).

— *The Canterbury Papers: Essays on Religion and Society* (London: Bellew, 1990).

Cohn-Sherbok, D., and D. McClellan (eds.), *Religion in Public Life* (London: Macmillan, 1992).

Cole, W., 'Sikhs in Britain', in P. Badham (ed.), *Religion, State and Society in Modern Britain* (Lampeter: Edwin Mellen Press, 1989), pp. 259–76.

Comerford, R., M. Cullen and J. Hill, *Religion, Conflict and Coexistence in Ireland* (London: Gill & Macmillan, 1990).

Commission for Racial Equality, *Law, Blasphemy and the Mutli-Faith Society, Report of a Seminar* (London: Commission for Racial Equality, 1990).

— *Religious Discrimination: Your Rights* (London: Commission for Racial Equality, 1997).

— *Schools of Faith: Schools in a Multi-Cultural Society* (London: Commission for Racial Equality, 1990).

Commission on British Muslims and Islamophobia, *Addressing the Challenge of Islamophobia: Progress Report, 1999–2001* (London: Commission on British Muslims and Islamophobia, 2001).

Connor, W., 'Ethno-National Versus Other Forms of Group Identity: The Problem of Terminology', in N. Rhoodie (ed.), *Intergroup Accommodation in Plural Societies: A Selection of Conference Papers with Special Reference to the Republic of South Africa* (London: Macmillan, 1978), pp. 44–83.

Cooper, H., and P. Morrison, *A Sense of Belonging: Dilemmas of British Jewish Identity* (London: Weidenfeld & Nicolson, 1991).

Cornwell, P., *Church and Nation: The Case for Disestablishment* (London: Blackwell, 1983).

Cottrell, R., 'Interview: Richard Cottrell, MEP', *Update: A Quarterly Journal on New Religious Movements* 8/3–4 (1984), pp. 30–4.

Council of Europe Group of Consultants on Religious and Cultural Aspects of Equality of Opportunities for Immigrants, *Study* (Strasbourg: Council of Europe, 1996).

Coward, H., J. Hinnells and R. Williams (eds.), *The South Asian Religious Diaspora in Britain, Canada and the United States* (New York: State University of New York Press, 2000).

Cox, H., *The Secular City: Secularisation and Urbanisation in Theological Perspective* (London: SCM Press, 1965).

Cracknell, K., 'Within God's Gracious Purposes: Inter-Faith Dialogue in Britain', *The Ecumenical Review* 37/4 (1985), pp. 452–61.

Cragg, K., 'Christian–Muslim Dialogue', *Anglican Theological Review* 57 (1975), pp. 109–20.

Crannell, P., 'Tolerance and Company', *RevExp* 24/1 (1927), pp. 24–44.

Crowley, V., *Phoenix from the Flame: Pagan Spirituality in the Western World* (London: Aquarian, 1994).

Cupitt, D., 'Christian Existence in a Pluralist Society', *Theology* 78 (1974), pp. 451–59.

Daniels, N., *Islam and the West: The Making of an Image, 1000–1300AD,* (2 vols; Edinburgh: Edinburgh University Press, 1960).

Davie, G., 'Believing without Belonging: Is This the Future of Religion in Britain?', *Social Compass* 37 (1990), pp. 455–69.

— 'An Ordinary God: The Paradox of Religion in Contemporary Britain', *British Journal of Sociology* 41/3 (1990), pp. 395–421.

Denham, J., and the Ministerial Group on Public Order and Community Cohesion, *Building Cohesive Communities: A Report of the Ministerial Group on Public Order and Community Cohesion* (London: Home Office, 2001).

Dobbelaere, K., 'Secularisation: A Multi-Dimensional Concept', *Current Sociology* 29/2 (1981), pp. 1–216.

— 'Secularisation Theories and Sociological Paradigms: Convergences and Divergences', *Social Compass* 31 (1984), pp. 199–219.

Durkheim, E., *The Elementary Forms of the Religious Life* (New York: Free Press, 1947).

Dwyer, R., 'Caste, Religion and Sect in Gujarat: Followers of Vallabhacharya and Swaminarayan', in R. Ballard (ed.), *Desh Pardesh: The South Asian Presence in Britain* (London: Hurst & Co., 1994), pp. 165–90.

Edge, P., and G. Harvey (eds.), *Law and Religion in Contemporary Societies: Communities, Individualism and the State* (Aldershot: Ashgate, 2000).

Equality Challenge Unit, *Implementing the New Regulations Against Discrimination: Practical Guidance* (London: Equality Challenge Unit, 2003).

Ernst, E., 'A Concept of Christian Evangelism in a Secular Society', *Foundations* 16/2 (1973), pp. 143–55.

European Baptist Federation Division for Theology and Education, *What Are Baptists? On the Way to Expressing a Baptist Identity in a Changing Europe*

(European Baptist Federation Division for Theology and Education, 1992; revised in 1993).

Evans, B., *Modern Popery: A Series of Letters on Some of Its More Important Aspects* (London: Houlston & Stoneman, 1855).

Fiddes, P., *Tracks and Traces: Baptist Identity in Church and Theology* (Studies in Baptist History and Thought, 13; Cumbria: Paternoster Press, 2003).

Finneron, D., and A. Dinham, *Building on Faith: Faith Buildings in Neighbourhood Renewal* (London: Church Urban Fund, n.d.).

Fitzgerald, T., *The Ideology of Religious Studies* (Oxford: Oxford University Press, 2000).

Francis, L., 'Religion and Social Capital: The Flaw in the 2001 Census in England and Wales', in P. Avis (ed.), *Public Faith? The State of Religious Belief and Practice in Britain* (London: SPCK, 2003), pp. 45–64.

Fryer, P., *Staying Power: The History of Black People in Britain* (London: Pluto Press, 1984).

Fulton, J., 'State, Religion and Law in Ireland', in T. Robbins and R. Robertson (eds.), *Church–State Relations: Tensions and Transitions* (New Brunswick: Transaction Books, 1987), pp. 253–67.

Furlong, M., *C of E: The State It's In* (London: Hodder & Stoughton, 2000).

Garbett, C., *The Claims of the Church of England* (London: Hodder & Stoughton, 1947).

— *Church and State in England* (London: Hodder & Stoughton, 1950).

Geaves, R., *Sectarian Influences within Islam in Britain: With Reference to the Concepts of 'Ummah' and 'Community'* (Community Religions Project Monograph Series; Leeds: University of Leeds Department of Theology and Religious Studies, 1996).

Geertz, C. 'Religion as a Cultural System', in M. Bainton (ed.), *Anthropological Approaches to the Study of Religion* (London: Tavistock, 1990), pp. 1–46.

General Synod of the Church of England, *Offences Against Religion and Public Worship, G.S. Misc. 149* (London: General Synod of the Church of England, December 1981).

— *Offences Against Religion and Public Worship, G.S. Misc. 286* (London: General Synod of the Church of England, February 1988).

George, T., 'Between Pacifism and Coercion: The English Baptist Doctrine of Religious Toleration', *MQR* 58/1 (1984), pp. 30–49.

Gerard, D., 'Religious Attitudes and Values', in M. Abrams, D. Gerard and N. Timms (eds.), *Values and Social Change in Britain* (Basingstoke: Macmillan, 1985), pp. 50–92.

Gerloff, R., *A Plea for British Black Theologies: The Black Church Movement in Britain in its Transatlantic Cultural and Theological Interaction, Parts I & II* (Frankfurt am Main: Peter Lang, 1992).

Giddens, A., *The Consequences of Modernity* (Stanford: Stanford University Press, 1990).

— *Modernity and Self-Identity: Self and Society in the Late Modern Age* (Stanford: Stanford University Press, 1991).

Gilbert, A., *The Making of Post-Christian Britain: A History of the Secularisation of Modern Society* (London: Longman, 1980).

— 'Secularisation and the Future', in S. Gilley and W. Sheils (eds.), *A History of Religion in Britain: Belief and Practice from Pre-Roman Times to the Present* (Oxford: Blackwell, 1994), pp. 503–21.

Gill, R., *The Social Context of Theology: A Methodological Enquiry* (London: Blackwell, 1975).

Gill, S., G. D'Costa and U. King (eds.), *Religion in Europe: Contemporary Perspectives* (Kampen: Kok Pharos, 1994).

Gilley, S., and W. Sheils (eds.), *A History of Religion in Britain: Belief and Practice from Pre-Roman Times to the Present* (Oxford: Blackwell, 1994).

Gilliat, S., *Higher Education and Student Religious Identity* (Exeter: University of Exeter, Department of Sociology, in association with the Inter Faith Network for the United Kingdom, 1999).

Gilliat-Ray, S., *Religion in Higher Education: The Politics of the Multi-Faith Campus* (Aldershot: Ashgate, 2000).

Gladstone, W., *The State in its Relations with the Church* (London: John Murray, 1839).

— *Church Principles Considered in Their Results* (London: John Murray, 1840).

Glover, W., 'English Baptists at the Time of the Downgrade Controversy', *Foundations* 1/3 (1958), pp. 41–51.

Gorsky, J., 'Judaism in Europe', in S. Gill, G. D'Costa and U. King (eds.), *Religion in Europe: Contemporary Perspectives* (Kampen: Kok Pharos, 1994), pp. 14–33.

Green, D., 'Buddhism in Britain: "Skilful Means" or Selling Out?', in P. Badham (ed.), *Religion, State and Society in Modern Britain* (Lampeter: Edwin Mellen Press, 1989), pp. 277–91.

Group of Consultants on Religious and Cultural Aspects of Equality of Opportunities for Immigrants, *Study* (Strasbourg: Council of Europe, 1996).

Groves, R. (ed.), *Thomas Helwys: A Short Declaration of the Mystery of Iniquity* (Macon, GA: Mercer University Press, 1998).

— (ed.), *Williams, R, The Bloudy Tenent of Persecution for Cause of Conscience: discussed in a conference between truth and peace. Who, in all tender Affection, present to the High Court of Parliament, (as the result of their Discourse) these, (among other Passages) of highest consideration* (Macon, GA: Mercer University Press, 2001).

Gustafsson, G., 'Church–State Separation: Swedish Style', in J. Madeley and Z. Enyedi (eds.), *Church and State in Contemporary Europe: The Chimera of Neutrality* (London: Frank Cass, 2003), pp. 51–72.

Habgood, J., *Church and Nation in a Secular Age* (London: SPCK, 1983).

— Letter to the editor, *The Times*, 1.3.1989.

— Quoted in 'Runcie Group May Seek Law Change to Protect Religions', *The Independent*, 2.8.1989.

— 'The Supermarket of Competing Faiths', *The Independent*, 3.6.1989.

Hall, R., *Christianity Consistent with a Love of Freedom: Being an Answer to a Sermon Lately Preached by Revd. G. Chapman* (London: J. Johnson, 1791).

— *An Apology for the Freedom of the Press and for General Liberty* (London: J. Johnson, 1793).

Halman, L., *The European Values Study: A Third Wave. Source Book of the 1999/2000 European Values Study Surveys* (Tilburg: WORC Tilburg University, 2001).

Harding, S., D. Phillips and M. Fogarty, *Contrasting Values in Western Europe*, (London: Macmillan, 1986).

Hardy, P., *The Muslims of British India* (Cambridge: Cambridge University Press, 1972).

Hare, W. (ed.), *Religions of the Empire: A Conference of Some Living Religions Within the Empire* (London: Duckworth, 1925).

Harris, M., and R. Harris, *The Jewish Voluntary Sector in the United Kingdom: Its Role and its Future* (London: Institute for Jewish Policy Studies, 1997).

Harvey, G., and C. Hardman, *Paganism Today* (London: Thorsons, 1996).

Hastings, A., *Church and State: The English Experience* (Exeter: Exeter University Press, 1991).

Hay, D., *Exploring Inner Space: Is God Still Possible in the Twentieth Century?* (Harmondsworth: Pelican, 1982).

— *Religious Experience Today: Studying the Facts* (London: Mowbray, 1990).

Helweg, A., *Sikhs in England: The Development of a Migrant Community* (Delhi: Oxford University Press, 2nd edn, 1986).

Hennessy, P., *The Hidden Wiring: Unearthing the British Constitution* (London: Victor Gollancz, 1995).

Hick, J. (ed.), *Truth and Dialogue: The Relationship Between World Religions* (London: Sheldon Press, 1974).

Hickey, J., *Religion and the Northern Ireland Problem* (Dublin: Gill & Macmillan, 1984).

Hill, C., 'History and Denominational History', *BQ* 22/2 (1967–8), pp. 65–71.

— *The World Turned Upside Down: Radical Ideas During the Revolution* (Harmondsworth: Penguin, 1975).

Hinnells, J., *Zoroastrians in Britain: The Ratanbai Katrak Lectures* (Oxford: Oxford University Press, 1996).

Hobson, T., *Against Establishment: An Anglican Polemic* (London: Darton, Longman & Todd, 2003).

Home Office Faith Communities Unit, *Working Together: Co-Operation Between Government and Faith Communities. Recommendations of the Steering Group Reviewing Patterns of Engagement Between Government and Faith Communities in England* (London: Faith Communities Unit, The Home Office, February 2004).

Hooker, R. (1648), *Of the Laws of Ecclesiastical Polity* (A. McGrade (ed.); Book 1 and Book 8; Cambridge: Cambridge University Press, 1989).

Hudson, W., 'Who Are the Baptists?', *BQ* 16/7 (1955–6), pp. 305–12.

Humphries, C., *Sixty Years of Buddhism in England 1907–1967: A History and a Survey* (London: Buddhist Society, 1968).

Hunter, A., and S. Mackie, *A National Church in a Multi-Racial Scotland* (Dunblane: Scottish Churches' Council, 1986).

Hussain, F., *The Anti-Islamic Tradition in the West* (Leicester: Muslim Community Studies Institute, 1990)

Inner Cities' Religious Council, *Challenging Religious Discrimination: A Guide for Faith Communities and Their Advisers* (London: Inner Cities' Religious Council of the Department of the Environment, 1996).

Inter Faith Network for the UK, *Statement on Inter-Religious Relations* (London: Inter Faith Network for the UK, 1991).

— *Building Good Relations Between People of Different Faiths and Beliefs* (London: Inter Faith Network for the United Kingdom, 1993).

— *Mission, Dialogue and Inter-Religious Encounter* (London: Inter Faith Network for the United Kingdom, 1993).

— *Local Inter Faith Activity in the UK: A Survey* (London: Inter Faith Network for the UK, 2003).

— *Inter Faith Update* 21 (2003), pp. 1, 3.

Inter Faith Network for the UK/Inner Cities Religious Council, *The Local Inter Faith Guide: Faith Community Co-operation in Action* (London: Inter Faith Network for the United Kingdom in association with the Inner Cities Religious Council of the Department for the Environment, Transport and the Regions, 1999).

Inter Faith Network for the UK in association with the Local Government Association, the Home Office, and the Inner Cities' Religious Council of the Office of the Deputy Prime Minister, *Partnership for the Common Good: Inter Faith Infrastructures and Local Government* (London: Inter Faith Network for the UK, 2003).

Ipgrave, M., '*Fidei Defensor* Revisited: Church and State in a Religiously Plural Society', in N. Ghanea (ed.), *The Challenge of Religious Discrimination at the Dawn of the New Millennium* (Leiden: Martinus Nijhoff, 2003), pp. 207–22.

Jameson, F., *Postmodernism: or, The Cultural Logic of Late Capitalism* (London: Verso, 1991).

Jenkins, D., *The British: Their Identity and Their Religion* (London: SCM Press, 1975).

Joly, D., and J. Nielsen, *Muslims in Britain: An Annotated Bibliography, 1960–1984* (Coventry: Centre for Research in Ethnic Relations, University of Warwick, 1985).

Jones, P., and N. Pennick, *A History of Pagan Europe* (London: Routledge, 1995).

Jones, R., 'Religion, Nationality and State in Wales, 1840–1890', in D. Kerr (ed.), *Religion, State and Ethnic Groups* (Aldershot: Dartmouth, 1992), pp. 261–76.

Jordan, M., 'John Smyth and Thomas Helwys: The Two First English Preachers of Religious Liberty', *BQ* 12/4 (1946–8), pp. 187–95.

Jordan, W., *The Development of Religious Toleration in England* (2 vols.; London: George Allen & Unwin, 1932, 1936).

Kabbani, R., *Letter to Christendom* (London: Virago, 1989).

Kee, A., *Constantine Versus Christ: The Triumph of Ideology* (London: SCM Press, 1982).

Kerr, D. (ed.), *Religion, State and Ethnic Groups* (Aldershot: Dartmouth, 1992).

Klaassen, W., *Anabaptism in Outline: Selected Primary Resources* (Scottdale: Herald Press, 1981).

Knott, K., *My Sweet Lord: The Hare Krishna Movement* (Wellingborough: Aquarian Press, 1986).

— 'Hinduism in Britain', in H. Coward, J. Hinnells and R. Williams (eds.), *The South Asian Religious Diaspora in Britain, Canada and the United States* (New York: State University of New York Press, 2000), pp. 89–107.

Kramer, R., and D. Messick (eds.), *Negotiation as Social Process* (London: Sage, 1995).

Kushner, T. (ed.), *The Jewish Heritage in British History: Jewishness and Englishness* (London: Frank Cass, 1992).

Lambert, Y., 'A Turning Point in Religious Evolution in Europe,' 19/1 (2004), pp. 29–45.

Lamont, S., *Church and State: Uneasy Alliances* (London: Bodley Head, 1989).

Law Commission, *Offences Against Religion and Public Worship* (Working Paper No. 79; London: Her Majesty's Stationery Office, 1981).

— *Criminal Law Offences Against Religion and Public Worship* (Report No. 145; London: Her Majesty's Stationery Office, 1985).

Lawton, R., (ed.), *The Census and Social Structure* (London: Frank Cass, 1978).

LeBarbour, A.-M. 'Victorian Baptists: A Study in Denominational Development' (unpublished doctoral dissertation, University of Maryland, 1977).

Leech, K. (ed.), *Setting the Church of England Free: The Case for Disestablishment* (Croydon: Jubilee Group, 2001).

— 'Letter to the Editor', *The Guardian*, 9.1.2003.

Lerman, A., *The Jewish Communities of the World* (Basingstoke: Macmillan, 1989).

Lewis, J., and E. Randolph-Horn, *Faiths, Hope and Participation: Celebrating Faith Groups' Role in Neighbourhood Renewal* (London: New Economics Foundation and Church Urban Fund, 2001).

Liberation Society, *The Case for Disestablishment* (London: Society for the Liberation of Religion from State Patronage and Control, 1884).

Ling, T., 'Communalism and the Social Structure of Religion', in J. Hick (ed.), *Truth and Dialogue: The Relationship Between World Religions* (London: Sheldon Press, 1974), pp. 59–76.

Local Government Association, *Faith and Community: A Good Practice Guide for Local Authorities* (London: Local Government Association Publications, 2002).

Local Government Association, in association with the Home Office, the Commission for Racial Equality and the Inter Faith Network for the UK, *Guidance on Community Cohesion* (London: Local Government Association, 2002).

Locke, J., *A Letter Concerning Toleration* (London: Awnsham Churchill, 1689).

Luckmann, T., *The Invisible Religion: The Problem of Religion in Modern Society* (New York: Macmillan, 1967).

Lyttle, J., quoted in, 'Primates' concern for Muslims', *The Church Times*, 4.8.1989.

MacEvoy, D., 'The Segregation of Asian Immigrants. A note', *Scottish Geographical Magazine* 94/1 (1978), pp. 180–2.

Mackintosh, W. H. (ed.), *Disestablishment and Liberation: The Movement for the Separation of the Anglican Church From State Control* (London: Epworth Press, 1972).

MacPherson, W., Sir, *Inquiry Into Matters Arising From the Death of Stephen Lawrence on 22nd April 1993 to Date, in order Particularly to Identify the Lessons to be Learned for the Investigation and Prosecution of Racially Motivated Crimes*, published 24 February 1999.

McClendon, J., Jnr, 'What is a "Baptist" Theology ?', *ABQ* 1/1 (1982), pp. 16–39.

— *Systematic Theology*, vol. 1: *Ethics* (Nashville: Abingdon Press, 1986).

McDermott, M., and M. Ahsan, *The Muslim Guide* (Leicester: Islamic Foundation, 1980).

McGlothin, W., 'The Struggle for Religious Liberty', *RevExp* 8/3 (1911), pp. 378–94.

— (ed.), *Baptist Confessions of Faith* (London: Baptist Historical Society, 1911).

McGrath, P., *Papists and Puritans Under Elizabeth I* (London: Blandford Press, 1967).

McSweeney, B., 'The Religious Dimension of the "Troubles" in Northern Ireland', in P. Badham (ed.), *Religion, State and Society in Modern Britain* (Lampeter: Edwin Mellen Press, 1989), pp. 68–83.

Madeley, J., and Z. Enyedi (eds.), *Church and State in Contemporary Europe: The Chimera of Neutrality* (London: Frank Cass, 2003).

Manning, B., *The Protestant Dissenting Deputies* (Cambridge: Cambridge University Press, 1952).

Martin, D., *A General Theory of Secularisation* (Oxford: Blackwell, 1978).

Martin, H., 'Protestantism and the State', *BQ* 12/6 (1946–8), pp. 309–17.

Mews, S. (ed.), *Studies in Church History: Religion and National Identity* (Oxford: Blackwell, 1982).

Mitri, T. (ed.), *Religion, Law and Society: A Christian–Muslim Discussion* (Geneva: World Council of Churches, 1995).

Moberley Commission, *Church and State: Being the Report of a Commission Appointed by the Church Assembly in June 1949* (London: Church Information Board of the Church Assembly, 1952).

Modood, T., 'Minorities, Faith and Citizenship', *DCJIRE* 6/2 (1992), pp. 58–60.

Modood, T. (ed.), *Church, State and Religious Minorities* (London: Policy Studies Institute, 1997).

Modood, T., S. Beishon and S. Virdee, *Changing Ethnic Identities* (London: Policy Studies Institute, 1994).

Moltmann, J., *The Open Church: Invitation to a Messianic Lifestyle* (London, SCM Press, 1978).

Moody, H., 'Baptists and Freedom: Some Reminders and Remembrances of our Past for the Sake of our Present', *ABQ* 3/1 (1984), pp. 4–15.

Murphy, J., *Church, State and Schools in Britain, 1800–1970* (London: Routledge & Kegan Paul, 1971).

Murray, S., *Post-Christendom: Church and Mission in a Strange New World* (Carlisle: Paternoster, 2004).

Nairn, T., *The Break-Up of Britain: Crisis and Neo-Nationalism* (London: Verso, 2nd edn, 1997).

Neuhaus, R., *The Naked Public Square: Religion and Democracy in American Public Life* (Grand Rapids: Eerdmans, 1984).

Newbigin, L., 'Blasphemy and the Free Society', *DCJIRE* 4/2 (1990), pp. 12–18.

Nielsen, J., *Muslims in Western Europe* (Edinburgh: Edinburgh University Press, 1992).

— 'State, Religion and Laïcité: The Western European Experience', in T. Mitri (ed.), *Religion, Law and Society: A Christian–Muslim Discussion* (Geneva: World Council of Churches, 1995), pp. 100–10.

Noel, B., *The Claims of the Free Church of Scotland* (London: James Nisbet & Co., 1844).

— *The Catholic Claims: A Letter to the Lord Bishop of Cashel* (London: James Nisbet & Co., 1845).

— *Essay on the Union of Church and State* (London: James Nisbet & Co., 1848).

Norman, J., 'The Relevance and Vitality of the Sect-Idea', *BQ* 27/6 (1977–8), pp. 248–58.

Norwood, C., 'The Religion the World Needs', *MC* 35/3 (1945), pp. 102–13.

Nye, M., 'Hare Krishna and Sanatan Dharm in Britain: The Campaign for Bhaktivedanta Manor', *JCR* 21/1 (1996), pp. 37–56.

— *Multiculturalism and Minority Religions in Britain: Krishna Consciousness, Religious Freedom and the Politics of Location* (Richmond: Curzon Press, 1990).

O'Beirne, M., *Religion in England and Wales: Findings From the 2001 Home Office Citizenship Survey* (Home Office Research Study, 274; London: Research Development and Statistics Directorate, Home Office, 2004).

O'Connor, W., and J. Lewis, *Experiences of Social Exclusion in Scotland: A Qualitative Research Survey* (Research Programme Research Findings, 73; Edinburgh: Central Research Unit, The Scottish Office, 1999).

Office for National Statistics, *The 2001 Census on Population, CM4253* (London: Her Majesty's Stationery Office, 1999).

— *Social Trends 30: 2000 Edition* (London: Stationery Office, 2000).

Oliver, P., *Buddhism in Britain* (London: Rider & Company, 1979).

Omoyajowo, J., *Cherubim and Seraphim: The History of an African Independent Church* (New York: Nok Publishers International, 1982).

Orchard, R., 'How Far Must We Still Take "1662" into Account in Ecumenical Relations Today', *BQ* 20/3 (1960–1), pp. 118–28.

Parsons, G., (ed.), *The Growth of Religious Diversity: Britain From 1945* (2 vols.; London: Routledge, 1993, 1994).

Parsons, G., 'Deciding How Far You Can Go', in G. Parsons, (ed.), *The Growth of Religious Diversity: Britain From 1945* (vol. 2; London: Routledge, 1994), pp. 5–21.

Paul, L., *A Church by Daylight: A Reappraisement of the Church of England and its Future* (London: Geoffrey Chapman, 1973).

Payne, E., 'Who were the Baptists? (A Comment)', *BQ* 16/8 (1955–6), pp. 339–42.

— *The Baptist Union: A Short History* (London: Carey Kingsgate Press, 1958).

— 'The Downgrade Controversy: A Postscript', *BQ* 28/4 (1979), pp. 146–58.

Peck, T., 'Grace and Law: Baptists and Religious Freedom: Historical Antecedents and Contemporary Context', *BQ* 29/7 (2002), pp. 315–27.

Pitt, V., 'The Church by Law Established', in K. Leech (ed.), *Setting the Church of England Free: The Case for Disestablishment* (Croydon: Jubilee Group, 2001), pp. 48–58.

— 'The Protection of Faith', in T. Modood (ed.), *Church, State and Religious Minorities* (London: Policy Studies Institute, 1997), pp. 36–9.

Porteous Wood, K., in T. Sulaiman, 'Religion and the State – The Observer Debate', *The Observer*, 12.8.2001.

Race, A., and I. Shafer (eds.), *Religions in Dialogue: From Theocracy to Democracy* (Aldershot: Ashgate, 2002).

Ramsey, M., *Canterbury Pilgrim* (London: SPCK, 1974).

Raza, S., *Islam in Britain: Past, Present and Future* (Leicester: Volcano Press, 2nd edn, 1992.

Reith, T., *Releasing the Resources of the Faith Sector: A Faithworks Report* (London: Faithworks, 2003).

Rhoodie, N. (ed.), *Intergroup Accommodation in Plural Societies: A Selection of Conference Papers with Special Reference to the Republic of South Africa* (London: Macmillan, 1978).

Robbins, T., and R. Robertson (eds.), *Church–State Relations: Tensions and Transitions* (New Brunswick: Transaction Books, 1987).

Robilliard, St John A., *Religion and the Law: Religious Liberty in Modern English Law* (Manchester: Manchester University Press, 1984).

Robinson, F., *Varieties of South Asian Islam* (Centre for Research in Ethnic Relations, Research Paper, No. 8; Coventry: University of Warwick, 1988).

Royal Commission on Reform of the House of Lords, *A House for the Future: A Summary* (London: Royal Commission on Reform of the House of Lords, 2000).

Runcie, R., *Windows onto God* (London: SPCK, 1983).

Runnymede Trust, *A Very Light Sleeper: The Persistence and Dangers of Antisemitism* (London: Runnymede Trust, 1997).

— *Islamophobia: A Challenge for Us All* (London: Runnymede Trust, 1997).

Rushdie, S., *The Satanic Verses* (London: Viking Penguin, 1988).

Ryan, M., *Another Ireland: An Introduction to Ireland's Ethno-Religious Minority Communities* (Belfast: Stranmills College, 1996).

Sacks, J., *The Persistence of Faith: Religion, Morality and Society in a Secular Age* (London: Weidenfeld & Nicolson, 1991).

Saghal, G., and N. Yuval-Davis (eds.), *Refusing Holy Orders: Women and Fundamentalism in Britain* (London: Virago, 1992).

Said, E., *Orientalism* (London: Penguin, 1978).

Samuelson, C., and D. Messick, 'Let's Make Some New Rules: Social Factors That Make Freedom Unattractive', in R. Kramer and D. Messick (eds.), *Negotiation as Social Process* (London: Sage, 1995), pp. 48–68.

Sangharakshita, Venerable, *Buddhism and Blasphemy: Buddhist Reflections on the 1977 Blasphemy Trial* (London: Windhorse, 1978).

Scarman, Lord, *The Scarman Report: The Brixton Disorders, 10–12th April, 1981. Report on an Inquiry by the Right Honourable Lord Scarman OBE, Presented to Parliament by the Secretary of State for the Home Department by Command of Her Majesty, November, 1981* (Harmondsworth: Penguin, 1982).

Scharf, M., *Belief and Exclusion: Combating Religious Discrimination in Europe: The First ENAR Approach* (Brussels: European Network Against Racism, March 2003).

Selborne Commission, *The Report of the Archbishops' Committee on Church and State* (London: SPCK, 1916).

Shadid, W. and Van Koningsveld, S. (eds.), *Muslims in the Margin: Political Responses to the Presence of Islam in Western Europe* (Kampen: Kok Pharos, 1996).

Shorter, A., *Towards a Theology of Inculturation* (London: Cassell, 1988).

Shiromani Gurdwara Parbandhak Committee, *Sikh Rehit Meryada* (Amritar: translation through the Sikh Missionary Society, n.d.).

Shortt, R., *Rowan Williams: An Introduction* (London: Darton, Longman & Todd, 2003).

Singh Tatla, D., 'The Punjab Crisis and Sikh Mobilisation in Britain', in R. Barot (ed.), *Religion and Ethnicity: Minorities and Social Change in the Metropolis* (Kampen: Kok Pharos, 1993), pp. 96–109.

Slesinger, E., *Creating Community and Accumulating Social Capital: Jews Associating With Other Jews in Manchester* (London: Institute for Jewish Policy Research, 2003).

Smart, N., 'The Anglican Contribution to the Dialogue of Religions', *Theology* 70 (1967), pp. 302–9.

Smith, G., *Faith in the Voluntary Sector: A Common or Distinctive Experience of Religious Organisations* (Working Papers in Applied Social Research, 25; Manchester: Department of Sociology, University of Manchester, 2003).

Smyth, J., *The Patterne of True Prayer: A Learned and Comfortable Exposition of or Commentarie Upon the Lord's Prayer*, in *The Works of John Smyth* (W. Whitley (ed.); 2 vols; Cambridge: Cambridge University Press, 1915).

— 'The Character of the Beast', in *The Works of John Smyth* (W. Whitley (ed.); (2 vols; Cambridge: Cambridge University Press, 1915).

Southern, R., *Western Views of Islam in the Middle Ages* (Cambridge, MA: Harvard University Press, 1962).

Sparkes, D., 'Test Act of 1673 and Its Aftermath', *BQ* 25/2 (1973), pp. 74–85.

Speelman, G., 'Muslim Minorities and *Shari'ah* in Europe', in T. Mitri (ed.), *Religion, Law and Society: A Christian–Muslim Discussion* (Geneva: World Council of Churches, 1995), pp. 70–9.

Sutcliffe, S., 'Unfinished Business: Devolving Scotland/Devolving Religion', in S. Coleman and P. Collins (eds.), *Religion, Identity and Change: Perspectives on Global Transformations* (Aldershot: Ashgate, 2004), pp. 84–106.

Ter Haar, G., *Halfway to Paradise: African Christians in Europe* (Cardiff: Cardiff Academic Press, 1998).

Thomas, T., 'Hindu Dharma in Dispersion', in G. Parsons (ed.), *The Growth of Diversity: Britain From 1945* (London: Routledge, 1993), pp. 175–204.

— 'Old Allies, New Neighbours: Sikhs in Britain', in G. Parsons (ed.), *The Growth of Religious Diversity* (London: Routledge, 1993), pp. 205–41.

Thoroughgood, B., *The Flag and the Cross: National Limits and the Church Universal* (London: SCM Press, 1988).

Toynbee, A., *An Historian's Approach to Religion* (London: Oxford University Press, 1956).

Troeltsch, E., *Protestantism and Progress: An Historical Study of the Relation of Protestantism to the Modern World* (Boston: Beacon Press, 1958, reprint of 1912 original).

— *The Social Teaching of the Christian Churches* (2 vols.; London: George Allen & Unwin, 1931).

UK Action Committee on Islamic Affairs, *Muslims and the Law in Multi-Faith Britain: The Need for Reform* (London: UK Action Committee on Islamic Affairs, 1993).

Underhill, E., (ed.), *Tracts on the Liberty of Conscience and Persecution, 1614–1667* (London: Hanserd Knollys Society, 1846).

Vertovec, S., 'Caught in an Ethnic Quandary: Indo-Caribbean Hindus in London', in R. Ballard (ed.), *Desh Pardesh: The South Asian Presence in Britain* (London: Hurst & Co., 1994), pp. 272–90.

Visram, R., *Ayahs, Lascars and Princes: Indians in Britain, 1700–1947* (London: Pluto Press, 1986).

Voas, D., 'Is Britain a Christian Country?', in P. Avis (ed.), *Public Faith: The State of Religious Belief and Practice in Britain* (London: SPCK, 2003), pp. 92–105.

Voas, D., and S. Bruce, 'The 2001 Census and Christian Identification in Britain', *JCR* 19/1 (2004), pp. 23–8.

Wahhab, I., *Muslims in Britain: Profile of a Community* (London: Runnymede Trust, 1989).

Walker, A., *Restoring the Kingdom: The Radical Christianity of the House Church Movement* (London: Hodder & Stoughton, 1985).

Ward, K., 'Third Introductory Paper', in Commission for Racial Equality, *Law, Blasphemy and the Multi-Faith Society, Report of a Seminar* (London: Commission for Racial Equality, 1990), pp. 30–9.

Watt, W., *Truth in the Religions: A Sociological and Psychological Approach*, (Edinburgh: Edinburgh University Press, 1963).

Webber, J. (ed.), *Jewish Identities in the New Europe* (London: Littman, 1994).

Weller, P., 'A Baptist Contribution to the Theology and Practice of Inter-Religious Dialogue' (unpublished master's dissertation, University of Manchester, 1988).

— 'The Rushdie Controversy and Inter-Faith Relations', in D. Cohn-Sherbok (ed.), *The Salman Rushdie Controversy in Inter-Religious Perspective* (Lampeter: Edwin Mellen, 1990), pp. 37–57.

— 'Freedom and Witness in a Multi-Religious Society: A Baptist Perspective. Part I', *BQ* 33/6 (1990), pp. 252–64
— 'Freedom and Witness in a Multi-Religious Society: A Baptist Perspective. Part II', *BQ* 33/7 (1990), pp. 302–15.
— 'Literature Update on the Rushdie Affair', *DCJIRE* 4/2 (1990), pp. 35–41.
— 'The Rushdie Affair, Plurality of Values and the Ideal of a Multi-Cultural Society', *National Association for Values in Education and Training Working Papers* 2 (1990), pp. 1–9.
— 'Transformed for Dialogue: Social Context and Theological Development in Britain (part I)', *MC* n.s. 32/3 (1990), pp. 51–63
— 'Transformed for Dialogue: Social Context and Theological Development (part II)', *MC* n.s. 32/4 (1991), pp. 46–54
— 'Transformed for Dialogue: Social Context and Theological Development (part III)', *MC* n.s. 32/5 (1991), pp. 42–50
— 'Transformed for Dialogue: Social Context and Theological Development (part IV)', *MC* n.s. 33/1 (1991), pp. 43–50.
— 'Inter-Faith Roots and Shoots, *World Faiths Encounter* 1 (1992), pp. 48–57.
— 'Baptist Principles as They Relate to the Four Principles of Dialogue', *DCJIRE* 5/3 (1992), pp. 53–68.
— 'The Inter Faith Network for the United Kingdom', *Indo-British Review: A Journal of History* 20/1 (1994), pp. 20–6.
— 'The Changing Patterns of Worship Space Provision in Britain', in the Inter Faith Network for the United Kingdom, *Places of Worship: The Practicalities and Politics of Sacred Space in Multi-Faith Britain* (London: Inter Faith Network for the UK 1995), pp. 4–16.
— 'The Salman Rushdie Controversy, Religious Plurality and Established Religion in England' (unpublished doctoral dissertation, University of Manchester, 1996).
— 'Equity, Inclusivity and Participation in a Plural Society: Challenging the Establishment of the Church of England', in P. Edge and G. Harvey (eds.), *Law and Religion in Contemporary Societies: Communities, Individualism and the State* (Aldershot: Ashgate, 2000), pp. 53–67.
— 'Religions in the UK: A Dialogical Enterprise', in Shap Working Party on World Religions in Education, *The Shap Working Party on World Religions in Education 2002–3. Religion: The Problem or the Answer* (London: Shap Working Party on World Religions in Education, 2002).
— 'Insiders or Outsiders?: Religions(s), State(s) and Societies: Propositions for Europe. Part I', *BQ* 39/5 (2002), pp. 211–22
— 'Insiders or Outsiders?: Religions(s), State(s) and Societies: Propositions for Europe. Part II', *BQ* 39/6 (2002), pp. 276–86.
— 'Insiders or Outsiders?: Propositions for European Religions, States and Societies', in A. Race and I. Shafer (eds.), *Religions in Dialogue: From Theocracy to Democracy* (Aldershot: Ashgate, 2002), pp. 193–208.
— 'Unfair Treatment Between Religions: Findings of a Research Project in England and Wales', *Interreligious Insight* 1/2 (2003), pp. 62–71.
— 'Religion, Ethnicity and the Development of More Inclusive Health Care',

in L. Basford and O. Slevin, (eds.), *Theory and Practice of Nursing: An Integrated Approach to Caring Practice* (Cheltenham: Nelson Thornes, 2003), pp. 376–91.

— 'The Dimensions and Dynamics of Religious Discrimination: Findings and Analysis from the UK', in N. Ghanea (ed.), *The Challenge of Religious Discrimination at the Dawn of the New Millennium* (Leiden: Martinus Nijhoff, 2003), pp. 57–81.

— 'Hindus and Sikhs: Community Development and Religious Discrimination in England and Wales', in K. Jacobsen and P. Kumar (eds.), *South Asians in the Diaspora: Histories and Religious Traditions* (Leiden: Brill, 2004), pp. 454–97.

— 'Identity, Politics and the Future(s) of Religion in the UK: The Case of the Religion Question in the 2001 Decennial Census', *JCR* 19/1 (2004), pp. 3–21.

— (ed.), *Religions in the UK: A Directory, 2001–3* (Derby: Multi-Faith Centre at the University of Derby in association with the Inter Faith Network for the United Kingdom, 2001).

Weller, P., and A. Andrews, 'How Many of Them Are There?: Religions, Statistics and the 2001 Census', *WFE* 21 (1998), pp. 23–34.

Weller, P., A. Feldman, K. Purdam *et al.*, *Religious Discrimination in England and Wales* (Home Office Research Study, 220; London: Research Development and Statistics Directorate, Home Office, 2001).

Weller, P., K. Purdam, *et al.*, *Religious Discrimination in England and Wales: An Interim Report, January 2000* (Derby: University of Derby, 2000).

Wheeler Robinson, H., *The Life and Faith of the Baptists* (London: Carey Kingsgate Press, 2nd revision, 1946).

White, B., *English Baptists of the Seventeenth Century* (London: Baptist Historical Society, 1983).

Whitley, W., 'Thomas Helwys of Grays Inn and of Broxtow Hall, Nottingham', *BQ* 7/6 (1934–5), pp. 241–55.

Whitley, W. (ed.), *The Works of John Smyth* (2 vols.; Cambridge: Cambridge University Press, 1915).

Wilkinson, J., *Church in Black and White: The Black Christian Tradition in 'Mainstream' Churches in England: A White Response and Testimony* (Edinburgh: Saint Andrew Press, 1993).

Williame, J.-P., 'Churches, Laicité, and the European Union', in *Pluralismes Religieux et Laicité dans L'Union Européen* (Brussels: Free University of Brussels, 1994).

Williams, R. (Roger), *Williams, R, The Bloudy Tenent of Persecution for Cause of Conscience: discussed in a conference between truth and peace. Who, in all tender Affection, present to the High Court of Parliament, (as the result of their Discourse) these, (among other Passages) of highest consideration* (Macon, GA: Mercer University Press, 2001).

— *A New Face of Hinduism: The Swaminarayan Religion* (Cambridge: Cambridge University Press, 1984).

Williams, R. (Rowan), *The Wound of Knowledge* (Darton, Longman & Todd, 1979).

— *Resurrection: Interpreting the Easter Gospel* (London: Darton, Longman & Todd, 1982).

— *On Christian Theology* (Oxford: Blackwell, 2000).

— *Writing in the Dust* (London: Hodder & Stoughton, 2002).

Wilson, B., *Religion in Secular Society: A Sociological Comment* (Harmondsworth: Penguin, 1969).

Wolffe, J., 'The Religions of the Silent Majority', in G. Parsons (ed.), *The Growth of Religious Diversity: Britain From 1945,* vol. 1: *Traditions* (London: Routledge, 1993), pp. 305–46.

— ' "And There's Another Country …": Religion, the State and British Identities', in G. Parsons, (ed.), *The Growth of Religious Diversity: Britain From 1945,* vol. 2: *Issues* (London: Routledge, 1994), pp. 85–121.

— (ed.) *The Growth of Religious Diversity: Britain From 1945. A Reader,* (Sevenoaks: Hodder & Stoughton, 1993).

Woodhouse, A. (ed.), *Puritanism and Liberty: Being the Army Debates from the Clarke Manuscript, with Supplementary Documents, 1647–49* (London: J. M. Dent & Sons, 1838).

Wright, N., *Power and Discipleship: Towards a Baptist Theology of the State* (The Whitley Lecture, 1996–97; Oxford: Whitley, 1996).

—*Public Truth or Private Option? Gospel and Religious Liberty in a Multi-Faith Society in the Light of the Resurrection* (Joppa Group Occasional Paper, 1999).

— *Disavowing Constantine: Mission, Church and the Social Order in the Theologies of John Howard Yoder and Jürgen Moltmann* (Carlisle: Paternoster, 2000).

— 'The Need to Disestablish', *The Guardian*, 8.10.1990.

Yorkshire and Humber Assembly, *Religious Literacy: A Practical Guide to the Region's Faith Communities* (Wakefield: Yorkshire and Humber Assembly, 2002).

ADDITIONAL SOURCES

Acts of Parliament, Orders and Regulations

Act for the Further Preventing of the Growth of Popery, 1700.
Act of Supremacy, 1534.
Act of Supremacy, 1559.
Act of Uniformity, 1662.
Breda Declaration, 1660.
Cambridge University Act, 1854.
Catholic Relief Act, 1778.
Church of Scotland Act, 1921.
Commonwealth Immigrants Act, 1962.
Conventicle Act, 1607.
Conventicle Act, 1644.
Declaration of Indulgence, 1672.
Declaration of Indulgence, 1687.
Dissenters' Relief Act, 1779.
Ecclesiastical Juridiction Measure, 1963.
Ecclesiastical Titles Act, 1851.
Employment Equality (Religion or Belief) Regulations, 2003.
Enabling Act, 1928.
Evidence Further Amendment Act, 1869.
Evidence Amendment Act, 1870.
Fair Employment and Treatment (Northern Ireland) Order, 1998.
File Mile Act, 1655.
Government of Ireland Act, 1920.
Human Rights Act, 1988.
Indemnity Act, 1727.
Irish Church Act, 1869.
Jews' Relief Act, 1858.
Liberty of Worship Act, 1855.
Nationality Act, 1981.
Northern Ireland Act, 1998.

Oaths Act, 1880.
Oxford University Act, 1854.
Places of Religion Worship Act, 1812.
Places of Worship Registration Act, 1855.
Promissory Oaths Act, 1867.
Promissory Oaths Act, 1871.
Race Relations Act, 1976.
Religious Disabilities Act, 1846.
Roman Catholic Charities Act, 1832.
Roman Catholic Relief Act, 1791.
Roman Catholic Relief Act, 1829.
Synodical Government Measure, 1969.
Test Act, 1673.
Test Abolition Act, 1867.
Toleration Act, 1689.
University Tests Act, 1877.
Welsh Church Act, 1914.
Worship and Doctrine Measure, 1974.

International Conventions

European Convention on Human Rights and Fundamental Freedoms.
Universal Declaration on Human Rights.

Biblical References

Prov. 29 v.18.
Mt. 7 v. 20.
Mt. 10 v.16.

Confessions

'1660 General Baptist Confession',
in W. McGlothin (ed.), *Baptist
Confessions of Faith* (London: The
Baptist Historical Society, 1911), p.
119.
'1677 Confession of Faith', in W.
McGlothin (ed.), *Baptist Confessions
of Faith* (London: The Baptist
Historical Society, 1911), pp. 215–89.
'An Orthodox Creed or a Protestant
Confession of Faith', W. McGlothin
(ed.), *Baptist Confessions of Faith*
(London: The Baptist Historical
Society, 1911), pp. 124–61.

Newspapers

Baptist Reporter, The, February, 1849.
Church Times, The, 24.2.1989.
Church Times, The, 4.8.1989.
Church Times, The, 11.8.1989.
Education Guardian, The, 16.3.2003
Freeman, The, 4.2.1857.
Freeman, The, 5.5.1871.
Freeman, The, 14.5.1875.
Guardian, The, 7.4.1989.
Guardian, The, 17.9.1990.
Guardian, The, 8.10.1990.
Guardian, The, 23.1.2002.
Guardian, The, 9.7.2002.
Herald, The, 3.9.1999
Independent, The, 12.4.1989.
Independent, The, 15.4.1989.
Observer, The, 'Religion and the State
 – The Observer Debate', 12.8.2001.
Scotland on Sunday, 15.02.1998.
Scotsman, The, 10.8.1999.
Sunday Times, The, 27.1.2002
Times On-Line, 3.12.2003.
Times, The, 15.2.1953.
Times, The, 8.7.1980.
Times, The, 2.3.1989.

Pamphlet Publications

*An Humble Petition and Representation
of the Suffering of Several Peaceable
and Innocent Subjects Called by the
Name of Anabaptists*, in E. Underhill
(ed.), *Tracts on the Liberty of
Conscience and Persecution, 1614–
1667*, pp. 287–308.
*An Humble Supplication to the King's
Majesty*, in E. Underhill (ed.), *Tracts
on the Liberty of Conscience and
Persecution, 1614–1667*, pp. 189–231.
*Persecution for Religion Judg'd and
Condemn'd in a Discourse Between
an AntiChristian and a Christian*,
in E. Underhill (ed.), *Tracts on
the Liberty of Conscience and
Persecution, 1614–1667* (London:
Hanserd Knollys Society, 1846),
pp. 95–188.

Other Publications

*Census of Great Britain, 1851,
Religious Worship. England and
Wales* (London: George E. Eyre
and William Spottiswoode, 1853)
reprinted in *British Parliamentary
Papers, Population 10* (Shannon,
Ireland: Irish University Press, 1970).
'Interview: Richard Cottrell, MEP',
*Update: A Quarterly Journal on New
Religious Movements*, 8, 3–4, 1984,
pp. 30–34.
'Media racism causes anti-Muslim
backlash', *Searchlight*, September
1989, p. 18; 'Blood on the streets',
Searchlight, September, 1989, p. 3.

Press Releases

Church in Wales Press Release,
27.1.2002.
Baptist Union Minutes 1833–1842.

Websites

http://www.statistics.gov.uk (National
  Statistics)
http://www.interfaith.org.uk (Inter Faith
  Network for the UK)
http://www.homeoffice.gov.uk/rds/
  (Home Office Research Development
  Statistics Directorate)
http://www.multifaithnet.org/
  (*MultiFaithNet*)

INDEX